Subversive
Horror Cinema

Subversive Horror Cinema

Countercultural Messages of Films from Frankenstein *to the Present*

JON TOWLSON

Foreword by Jeff Lieberman

McFarland & Company, Inc., Publishers
Jefferson, North Carolina

LIBRARY OF CONGRESS CATALOGUING-IN-PUBLICATION DATA

Towlson, Jon, 1967–
Subversive horror cinema : countercultural
messages of films from Frankenstein to the present /
Jon Towlson ; foreword by Jeff Lieberman.
  p. cm.
Includes bibliographical references and index.

ISBN 978-0-7864-7469-1 (softcover : acid free paper) ∞
ISBN 978-1-4766-1533-2 (ebook)

1. Horror films—History and criticism. 2. Motion picture producers and directors. 3. Motion pictures—Social aspects. I. Title.
PN1995.9.H6T69 2014   791.43'6164—dc23   2014005174

BRITISH LIBRARY CATALOGUING DATA ARE AVAILABLE

© 2014 Jon Towlson. All rights reserved

No part of this book may be reproduced or transmitted in any form or by any means, electronic or mechanical, including photocopying or recording, or by any information storage and retrieval system, without permission in writing from the publisher.

On the cover: Katharine Isabelle in the title role
of the 2012 film *American Mary* (Universal)

Manufactured in the United States of America

*McFarland & Company, Inc., Publishers
Box 611, Jefferson, North Carolina 28640
www.mcfarlandpub.com*

For Joanne,
and in memory of my parents

Table of Contents

Foreword by Jeff Lieberman   1
Preface   3
Introduction   5

1. Anti-Eugenics: *Frankenstein* (1931) and *Freaks* (1932)   21
2. Anti–1940s Home Front Propaganda: *Cat People* (1942) and *The Curse of the Cat People* (1944)   43
3. Anti–1950s Cold War Conformity: The Films of Herman Cohen   62
4. Anti-Establishment 1960s–1970s Britain: The Films of Michael Reeves and Pete Walker   80
5. Anti-Vietnam: *Night of the Living Dead* (1968), *Deathdream* (1972) and *The Crazies* (1973)   104
6. Anti-Hollywood Violence and Dark Counterculture: *Last House on the Left* (1972) and *The Texas Chain Saw Massacre* (1974)   130
7. Counterculture Revolution: *Shivers* (1975), *Blue Sunshine* (1978) and *Dawn of the Dead* (1978)   151
8. Anti-"Reaganomics": *Henry—Portrait of a Serial Killer* (1986) and *American Psycho* (2000)   163
9. Anti–1990s Materialism: Brian Yuzna and Splatstick   180
10. Anti-New Puritanism: *Teeth* (2007) and *American Mary* (2012)   197

Afterword—Subversive Horror Cinema Post–9/11   211
Chapter Notes   225
Bibliography   234
Index   239

FOREWORD BY JEFF LIEBERMAN

When I first entertained the idea of making movies, I suppose I naturally gravitated to the horror genre because it's inherently subversive, which I am by nature. The horror genre, like rock'n'roll, allows you to say and do things you can't do in any other medium. Perhaps that's why both these forms of expression appeal to essentially the same audience. Horror operates outside the boundaries of society, where neither laws nor society's accepted standards of behavior need apply. In fact, it's a place where "sick" is a good thing!

If I were to present the same satirical political and social commentary I instill in my films in any other genre format, viewers would likely be outraged, offended and, most importantly, dismissive. But position that material in the horror genre and that same audience will be open and receptive to my ideas.

In my first movie, *Squirm* (1976), I really didn't try to make any sort of social or political comment. At least not consciously. However, soon after the movie's release, critics found some very profound subtexts which I myself wasn't aware of. Nature getting revenge on man for his disrespect of ecology. The symbolism of man's mortality and his inevitable fate of becoming worm food. Even themes of suppressed sexuality in the main characters. This could all very well be true, but if it is, it was not done purposely on my part.

It was on my second movie, *Blue Sunshine* (1978), that I had enough confidence to consciously incorporate my political and social commentary on the world around me. The phenomenon of my generation, the so-called "baby boomers," making our transition from carefree hippies with our "change the world" idealism, to entry into that dreaded "real world" we always tried to tuck back into the furthest recesses of our brains, seemed ripe for social commentary. Suddenly attitudes toward the career world, the job world, the family world, all the things we spent our late teens and early twenties rebelling against, were morphing into our own reality overnight. But at what cost? Could we make this total transition unscathed? I knew we'd have to pay the piper in various ways, but I needed something symbolic to represent what the penalty for our youthful discretions might be. By tapping into the fear the government tried so pathetically to instill in us about the horrors of LSD, I used that same pre-sold fear as the basis of my story, which was set around the end of this awkward and largely hypocritical generational transition. I also saw in it the opportunity to comment on the politics and fashions of that post-hippie time, as well as the profound musical transition that was about to take place from rock'n'roll to the disco era.

This movie was followed by *Just Before Dawn* (1981) which was a complete diversion from *Blue Sunshine*. It was my homage to *Deliverance* (1972), which had a similar impact on me as *Lord of the Flies* (1963), and dealt with very similar social and political issues. I set out to make the Jon Voight character from *Deliverance* a woman, Connie, who would make the same character arc from helpless milquetoast to animalistic survivor. So my political statement, if you will, was a radically feminist one, to show that when humans are reduced to their animalistic genetic baseline, there was little difference between male and female. Connie became the ultimate "final girl," long before that term was coined.

Then came the late 1980s home video revolution (*Remote Control*, 1988). This phenomenon screamed out to me that "there's a movie here." The fact that people could now rent or purchase movies or various other types of programming and play them at home at their leisure resonated through the very fabric of Western culture. And like all cultural revolutions, it was analyzed by sociologists and psychiatrists, just about every "expert" at that time, who sought to ascertain what lasting impact this new phenomenon would have on society. To me they were all stating the obvious so I took the subversive route and stepped back and looked at the physicality of it, where another reality existed altogether, one where I could make an overall satirical statement on the entire phenomenon. I saw that people were going to these new stores which never existed before and taking home these small plastic gadgets filled with magnetic tape, then playing them on these other newly created electronic gadgets. Everything about it was new. Alien. Aliens! That's when it hit me that "the Aliens" we always heard about since childhood, who always had evil motives in sci-fi movies, were just waiting for mankind to evolve to this very point so they could impregnate these new devices with a signal that humans would voluntarily take home with them and then proceed to destroy their families and friends without the Aliens having to lift a finger. Or a paw. Or whatever monstrous appendages they had.

The 2000s ushered in a period of information overload. The Internet explosion of the '90s set the stage for iTunes, iPhones, iPads, YouTube, Netflix and video games, all converging into one constant chaotic flow of digital noise. It also coincided with me reaching a point in my creative life where I started feeling a sense of urgency to express my thoughts about modern society without holding back and taking aim at sacred cows whenever possible, the perfect mindset for subversive horror. Surveying the landscape, it struck me how difficult it must be to be a child in these times. How do you process such a bombardment of information when 99 percent of it is pure bullshit? When virtually anyone with a computer or smart phone and minimum typing skills can spout their opinions in the guise of news, or state flat-out lies in guise of facts to millions of gullible readers around the world.

If adults can't discern what's true on the Internet, what about a child? And the increasingly more realistic video games are getting harder and harder to differentiate from live action television. This was the genesis for my next movie, *Satan's Little Helper* (2004), where I re-opened the subversive gates in full attack mode. Religion, the innocence of children, the gullibility of the public, everything I could aim at that pissed me off was fashioned into the narrative in some way. To top it off, I set the movie on that most subversive holiday of the year, Halloween. And I worked the narrative in such a way that at one point one of the main characters logically concludes, "Jesus is Satan!" Try spouting that line in any other genre!

So here we are, in the second decade of the 2Ks. The time is right for a book on subversive horror. For the outsider points of view of the filmmakers examined here may very well lead to the salvation of mankind. Or at the very least make for a very interesting read!

Jeff Lieberman is an acclaimed writer and the director of the cult classic sci-fi/horror films *Squirm* (1976), *Blue Sunshine* (1978), *Just Before Dawn* (1981), *Remote Control* (1988) and *Satan's Little Helper* (2004).

Preface

This project started in many ways on July 22, 1978, when I first saw *The Crazies* (1973) as part of a late night horror film double-bill on British television. The film left an indelible mark. Shock was my reaction at the time: at the gritty realism (the muddy sound especially seemed real), the bleak despairing tone and irony of the ending, and the bloody violence. (Shock was undoubtedly the intention of the director, George A. Romero; in his work, graphic shock is intrinsically linked to ideological shock, depicting the extremity of the violence on display as absurd.) The film shows a society under threat of collapse; growing up in Britain in the 1970s I had experienced power cuts and the winter of discontent that led to the rise of the neoconservatives under Margaret Thatcher, so the film resonated on a socio-political level even if I was barely able to recognize it then.

I saw Romero's *Martin* (1977) on 16mm in a working men's social club in a place not unlike Braddock, the dying industrial town in which *Martin* is set. Although agriculture rather than steel was the industry of my English town, again the film had resonance, and by the time I saw *Dawn of the Dead* (1978) in the same working men's club, I knew (thanks to *House of Hammer* magazine) who Romero was, and a lot of other directors making horror films: Jeff Lieberman, David Cronenberg, Tobe Hooper and Wes Craven.

When VCRs were introduced into the British home around 1981 (people used their redundancy payments to set up independent video libraries in towns like mine), suddenly the films I had read about—*Last House on the Left* (1972), *The Hills Have Eyes* (1976), *Shivers* (1975), *The Texas Chain Saw Massacre* (1974), and *Squirm* (1976)—became available to see at home. I bought *Starburst Magazine* (for which I would later write) and became a fan of the genre. But by the late 1980s (an era of increasing conservatism culturally and politically) the work of these directors seemed to have become less interesting to me and I became guilty of highbrow tastes: Tarkovsky, Altman, Monte Hellman. The horror genre seemed inferior cinema.

My interest in the genre was reignited in 1999 when I started teaching film at Art College. By then I had discovered Robin Wood's essay "The American Nightmare." Up to that point, having made some short films of my own, I had largely dismissed most film criticism as "reading too much into it," but Wood's theory of the horror film struck me like a bolt of lightning. Adam Simon's documentary (also called *The American Nightmare*, in acknowledgment to Wood) took me closer to this project. Simon's intercutting of newsreel footage from the Vietnam era with clips from the key horror films of the 1970s emphasizes how directly allegorical these films are: deliberate, urgent social-political statements on the part of the filmmakers. As George Romero says in the documentary, "What's happening in the world creeps into any work—it just fits right in—because that's where it comes from, where you get the idea from in the first place."

Then 9/11 happened, followed by another war in Iraq and the worst global economic crisis since the Great Depression; and the context for subversive horror cinema's re-emergence (both culturally and in my own thinking) was suddenly there, as evidenced by recent films like *The Hamiltons* (2006), *Teeth* (2007), *Mum and Dad* (2009), *Stake Land* (2010), *The Woman* (2011) and *American Mary* (2012). The project gained focus as a result of teaching the topic "Shocking Cinema," which encouraged me to reflect on the notion of cinematic shock. More recently, writing for *Starburst Magazine* has given me access to directors such as Jeff Lieberman, Frank Henenlotter and Steven Sheil, enabling me to discuss my ideas on subversive horror cinema with the filmmakers themselves.

This book, then, is a culmination of many years spent thinking about the horror film and its place in a society that seems constantly under threat of collapse.

A number of individuals and organizations have helped me during the research and writing. I would like to thank Ronald V. Borst at Hollywood Movie Posters for sourcing images for the book from his own private collection and Margaret Borst for arranging the scans; Harvey Fenton at Fab Press, Joyce Pierpoline and Scott Limbacher at Pierpoline Films, Greg Chick at Blue Underground Inc., Nick Donnermeyer at Bleiberg Entertainment/Compound B, Luciano Chelotti at Network Distributing Ltd. and Tom Hewson at Fetch Publicity for also providing images; Joe Kane at VideoScope and library staff at the British Film Institute for their help in sourcing texts; Donato Totaro at Offscreen for his support and kind words; Wes Moynihan, Richard Gladman, Martin Unsworth and James Gracey for their support and encouragement within the "blogosphere"; Jordan Royce and Kristian Heys at *Starburst Magazine*; Andrew Parietti at *Shadowlands Magazine*; Christine Makepeace at *Paracinema*; Naila Scargill at *Exquisite Terror*; Gary Morris at *Bright Lights Film Journal*; Bernice Murphy and Elizabeth McCarthy at *Irish Journal of Gothic and Horror Studies*; and Rob Clymo at *Digital FilmMaker Magazine*. Special thanks to Jeff Lieberman for contributing the foreword to this book and to my wife Joanne Rudling who has provided support, encouragement, help and advice throughout.

http://www.subversive-horror-films.com
Twitter @systemshocks

Introduction

"The best horror films are genuinely, edifyingly subversive"[1]—Elliott Stein

The Subversive School of Horror

History (by that, I mean 20th century Western history—the history of capitalism) is cyclical: Specifically it is characterized economically by periods of "boom and bust" and militarily by times of international conflict and times of peace. The horror film, scholars have found, is also cyclical, enjoying phases of popularity particularly during the "bad times," the times of economic depression and war. Scholars have made specific links, culturally, between the major phases of the horror genre and periods of ideological conflict brought about by (inter)national crisis and threatened (or actual) social collapse. Cycles of the horror film can, in other words, be closely linked to cycles of history.

The horror films of the 1930s, for example, are said to reflect working class discontent arising from the Great Depression: Frankenstein's creation, the mummy, and the misshapen stars of *Freaks* (1932) are noticeably blue collar monsters, exploited or disenfranchised by their masters. The science fiction–horror films of the 1950s—in their fear of space invaders and giant spiders—speak of anti-communist paranoia during the Cold War and anxiety in the nuclear age. The horror films of the 1960s and 1970s, with their cannibals and psycho-killers, reflect the disillusionment of the Vietnam era; the crisis of Watergate; the struggles of the civil rights movement. And the current wave of torture-porn horror stems from homeland insecurities following 9/11 and the recent economic downturn.

Many studies of the horror film tend to treat the films themselves as cultural artifacts that simply reflect the times in which they were made. This book argues that a succession of filmmakers, from Tod Browning and James Whale onwards, have used the horror genre—and the shock value it affords—to challenge the status quo during times of ideological crisis. In other words, the often radical social commentary that can be read into their films is deliberate on the part of these filmmakers: a conscious desire to attack traditional values through the use of ideological "shock." These filmmakers, I believe, represent a strain within the horror film that can be considered the subversive school of horror; a more radical wing of the genre involving its ideological use for potentially progressive purposes. The subversive school stands apart from the mainstream, and runs counter to the majority of horror films which, by definition, can and should be considered reactionary.

Although the word "subversive" is used in this book to describe the filmmakers and their work, it should be understood that it is used in a general sense. Theirs is a broad (and often mischievous) form of subversion, targeting the predominant cultural forces within the established social order—such as patriarchy, individualism, militarism. In many cases the political outlook of the filmmakers in this book is colored by 1960s radicalism, or in the case of Browning and Whale, by first-hand experience of the First World War and the Great Depression. What all the filmmakers have in common, however, is their political engagement with the issues of the time and their use of the horror film as a form of protest against the more oppressive forces of capitalism and in particular its structures of power and authority.

In thinking about *Witchfinder General* (1968), I was struck by how that film's theme can be seen as a shared concern of all the filmmakers in this book as well as a model of history itself: breakdown in systems of authority caused by social collapse leads to regressive-degenerate forces instigating violence which is escalated by the military mind. In *Witchfinder General* the regressive-degenerate forces are personified by Matthew Hopkins (Vincent Price) who exploits the breakdown of order during the time of Cromwell for his own gain. "A lack of order in the land encourages strange ideas," as one of the characters remarks in the film. Those "strange ideas" involve Hopkins's persecution of the most vulnerable in society, a scapegoating of the weak. However, his sadism is met in equal force by the brutality of Marshall (Ian Ogilvy), a soldier in Cromwell's army. In *The Crazies* (1973) the regressive-degenerate forces (people infected by the Trixie toxin) are brought about by military error—the accidental release of a biological weapon into the water supply of a small town, and by the failure of the military to contain the outbreak. This leads to an escalation of violence by the military, resulting in total societal collapse. In James Whale's *Frankenstein* (1931) the threatened collapse of the social order lies not in the hands of the Monster but in Henry's repressed sexuality (of which the Monster is a projection—a "return of the repressed") which threatens to deprive the baron (Henry's father and overlord of the village) of a future heir. In Whale's film this repression of sexuality leads to the regressive-degenerate violence of the Monster which is escalated by the angry mob of villagers at the end of the film.

What ultimately makes these films subversive is that social collapse (literal or threatened) and its consequences are seen as a result of flaws in the system—major flaws in the capitalist system—which make social collapse inevitable. The subversive horror film "shocks the system" by revealing it as ultimately untenable in terms of providing sustained social stability on a local, national or international level.

It is in periods of crisis (the Great Depression, the build-up to World War II, Vietnam, 9/11, the 2009 economic collapse), moments of national trauma and ideological conflict when social collapse becomes a threat, that radical viewpoints are most likely to find an audience—which perhaps goes towards explaining why horror films enjoy their greatest popularity in these times. Wes Craven describes this most eloquently in the documentary *The American Nightmare* (1999), reinforcing the idea that horror films provide what governments seek to deny during times of crisis:

> What a horror film does is not frighten so much as release fright. It is a vent. And all these fears are in us all the time, from our lives, from our youths, from the world at large; everything from the most complex societal things of waging war and class struggle to very simple primal things like fear of the father and mother and fear of abandonment as a child. So these are all inherent in us and civilization tends to gloss over them, encapsulate them, deny them;

it teaches us a thousand ways to act like everything's fine but underneath this surface there is a sort of cauldron. So what a horror film does is tap in and release that tension and it does it in a way that's entertaining, amusing and safe.[2]

Times of ideological crisis are also when the tools of production are more likely, historically speaking, to be placed in the hands of radical filmmakers. The economy drive of the loss-making Universal Studios in the Depression era, for example, led to the production of modestly budgeted horror films under the direction of Browning and Whale. The rise of independent filmmaking in the 1960s and 1970s, following the demise of the studio system and aided by advances in cinema technology, opened up distribution windows for the likes of Tobe Hooper, Wes Craven, George A. Romero, David Cronenberg, and Pete Walker. More recently the emergence of digital technology (in both production and distribution), which has lowered costs considerably, has sparked an explosion of edgy low-budget horror from a new generation of subversive horror film directors whose work I consider in the final chapters of this book: Mitchell Lichtenstein, Lucky McKee, the Soskas, the Butcher Brothers, Jim Mickle and Brad Anderson in the U.S., and Simon Rumley and Steven Sheil in the UK.

This flourishing of the genre at various stages of its history is inevitably followed by a moral backlash against the horror genre in general (as can be seen in the tightening of state censorship) and certain targeted films and directors in particular. For directors labeled as difficult, this can result in periods of enforced inactivity (as was the case for Romero during most of the 1980s and 1990s) or worse, blacklisting (as in the cases of Browning and Whale). The system has ways of protecting itself when the threat to the status quo is considered too great.

Thus, co-option of the horror film's radicalism, as critic Christopher Sharrett has argued, is perhaps the greatest danger facing the genre in the era of postmodernism.[3] This can be seen in the recent spate of pastiches and remakes which purport to evoke the nihilism of the 1970s horror films, but whose postmodern veneer of self-reflexivity, as Sharrett points out, merely masks their reactionary politics. *Hostel* (2003), for example, rather than being a critique of the American arrogance over foreign policy, might, because of the tropes it shares with others in the torture porn subgenre, be placed within the reactionary strain of horror films. *Hostel* amalgamates the slasher—sexually curious teenagers are punished by brutal torture and death—and the urbanoia film—where the have-nots (in the case of *Hostel*, the East-Europeans) are exterminated with impunity by the haves (the Americans) for daring to rise up against them. In torture porn films such as *Hostel*, we are denied identification with the surviving character or final girl, thus creating an overwhelming sense of defeat that precludes any progressive reading of these films.

It is perhaps because of the prevalence of this type of film (hip, narcissistic—and, in their often outright sadism, curiously amoral and devoid of humanity) in contemporary horror that some critics disregard the significance of the subversive school in their condemnation of the genre. In *Sex and Death in the Horror Film*, Colin Odell and Michelle Le Blanc claim that "whatever champions of the genre may say, the majority of horror films are inherently reactionary and deeply conservative, however disreputable they seem."[4] While I would not entirely wish to refute this (the reactionary-conservative tradition is, for the most part, the dominant one), there clearly *is* a recognizable radical tradition within the genre, existing alongside the reactionary-conservative one, which can be traced back its very beginnings with *The Cabinet of Dr. Caligari* (1919), a film that was intended as a political allegory about the horrors of the First World War.

Dr. Caligari (Werner Krauss) uses mind control to manipulate Cesare (Conrad Veidt) to commit murder in *The Cabinet of Dr. Caligari* (1919).

The Horror Film as Political Allegory

Political allegory within the horror film, then, originates with *The Cabinet of Dr. Caligari*, made in the aftermath of World War I. The writers of *Caligari* viewed it as a conscious political statement, an attack against the authority that had brainwashed thousands into going to war and losing their lives. Hans Janowitz was a poet who served as an officer but became embittered towards the military. Carl Mayer was subject to intense examinations by a military psychiatrist that left him distrustful of authority; in *Caligari*, a mad authority figure (Dr. Caligari) uses mind control to manipulate a somnambulist into committing murder, just as the German government had done to the German people.

Subsequent filmmakers (those with a predilection for social commentary) have used allegory in similar ways. Many of the directors in this study have spoken directly of the genre affording them opportunities for social comment or even outright political "messaging." George A. Romero, for example, has described *Night of the Living Dead* (1968) as a conscious allegory of a revolutionary society overturning traditional American values. It is difficult to dispute Romero's commitment as a politically orientated filmmaker. The evidence is there in his whole body of work, as apparent in his non-horror films (*There's Always Vanilla* [1970], *Knightriders* [1981]) as it is in his *Dead* series. But what about other directors? Do they share the same commitment? Consider this quote by Tobe Hooper:

> I can't help but be a part of the times. I just think that film, for the serious filmmaker, is an osmosis of the times. That's usually what I tap for my resources: I look around at what's happening politically and economically.... I'm totally absorbed in things like CNN.[5]

Is Hooper capitalizing on what critics have read into his films over the years, or is there a genuine commitment to social commentary in his horror films? Is the allegory deliberate? One only need look at *Eggshells* (1969), Hooper's non-horror first feature, which contains many of the socio-political themes that Hooper developed five years later in *Texas Chain Saw Massacre* (in fact, *Eggshells* is illuminative of Hooper's concerns in much the same way that *There's Always Vanilla* is illuminative of Romero's), to confirm that Hooper was, at least in his early films, politically motivated, which suggests that the allegory in his films *is* for the most part conscious.

This commitment to political allegory is also evident in the horror films of the 1930s. Rather than working to uphold the bourgeois status quo, directors such as Tod Browning and James Whale repeatedly sought to challenge it (coming into conflict with the studios as a result). Radicalism in the United States is often seen as starting in the 1960s, but the aftermath of the First World War saw the rise of political movements in Europe and the States such as pacifism, the suffragettes and the philosophy of nihilism which pervades the horror films of this period. The Great Depression gave rise to social commentary in the novels of John Steinbeck, Horace McCoy and Nathanael West. It would be wrong, therefore, to suggest that radicalism in the horror film only began in the 1960s. Indeed it is possible to argue that the horror films produced in America from 1931 to 1936 are broadly comparable to those of the 1970s—a sustained subversive output—the result of a symbiosis of genre innovation, radical artists, sympathetic producers and an alienated audience; a country in the grip of economic crisis and impending war.

The Lives and Times of Subversive Horror Film Directors

The filmmakers in this book tend to have been radicalized by the times in which they lived. James Whale, for example, was a gay man of working class origin who witnessed the social effects of the Great Depression on homosexuals and working men. Although his politics were not left-wing, he developed a social conscience which compelled him to speak out in his films against the persecution of the "outsider." The work of producer Val Lewton in the 1940s challenges the moral conservatism of wartime America in terms of its gender politics. Producer Herman Cohen's films are a response to the 1950s Cold War paranoia and anti-communist hysteria which gave rise to stultifying conformism, rebellious youth, and a subsequent moral panic over juvenile delinquency. George A. Romero, Jeff Lieberman, Wes Craven, Tobe Hooper and Brian Yuzna grew up in the 1950s at the time of the nuclear threat and became politically aware during the events of the 1960s—Vietnam, the Civil Rights Movement, Watergate. They came of age at a watershed moment in American history when radical movements began to emerge in response to the conservatism of the 1950s and the insanity of authority in the nuclear age. In the words of Jeff Lieberman:

> I am a baby boomer. I was in the drug culture of the '60s and I saw everything first hand. I was at Woodstock. I did acid. Marched against the war in Vietnam. Saw *Easy Rider*. I was immersed in all that in New York. I was at the right place at the right time, at the vanguard of all that stuff. However, I have an innate cynicism so I don't ever really buy into *anything*.[6]

Just as the horrors of the First World War informed James Whale's *Frankenstein*, the specter of nuclear apocalypse is apparent in the work of all of these 1970s horror directors; their very real fear of the bomb during childhood informs their imagery and themes. It is no surprise that these directors spent their formative years (at the height of the Cold War and the "communist threat") struggling against conformism and afraid of imminent nuclear attack. Romero admits that between dodging the gangs and "the bomb about to explode in my head, I was a pretty worried kid!"[7]

In October 1962, the Cuban Missile Crisis raised serious questions about the government's credibility and their ability to protect the American people in the event of a nuclear war. For seven days the world waited with bated breath as the United States and the USSR engaged in a stand-off over Soviet plans to build missile silos in Cuba. It was the nearest mankind has ever come to all-out nuclear war, and for many people it seemed during those seven days that the end of the world had truly come. War was averted through political solutions, but arguably America was never the same again. As Alice L. George writes in *Awaiting Armageddon,* the American people emerged from the crisis "like convicted felons who receive a reprieve after being strapped into the electric chair: They sighed with relief but they could not shake the memory of near-sudden death."[8]

The crisis forced Americans to examine civil defense policy and other aspects of the Cold War after years of averting their eyes from the details—and the plans that had been put in place to protect them were found to be sadly lacking. During this era, "information" films, such as *Duck and Cover* (1952), taught children to respond to nuclear attack by hiding under their school desks, and Cold War literature routinely assured Americans that they, the government and the American way of life could survive a nuclear war. In reality, strategies to protect the civilian population were inadequate. The Gaither Report, submitted to President Eisenhower by the Security Resources Panel of the Sciences Advisory Committee in 1957, had advised the government to embark on a nationwide fallout shelter program to protect the civilian population, describing it as the "only feasible protection for millions of people who will be increasingly exposed to the hazards of radiation."[9] The president, however, elected not to follow these recommendations (although he committed billions of dollars to defense spending and building ICBMs). In 1962, President Kennedy's bid for funds to institute a shelter program was turned down by Congress. The population was instead left to build its own fall-out shelters; the few public ones that were built were not stocked with adequate food or survival supplies. The message was clear and the Cuban Missile Crisis brought it home: If war came, the vast majority of Americans would be on their own. Jeff Lieberman remembers this period vividly:

> You can't imagine how they frightened my generation with the threat of radiation. You had the governor of New York telling every resident of New York to build a bomb shelter and giving out state-approved plans. My brother and I were piling sandbags and putting in cans of food. My uncle did the same thing down in the basement. It was imminent that there was going to be this horrible atomic war. And then when you go to school the teachers in the middle of a sentence were yelling "Duck!" and you had to duck under your wooden desk, as if that was going to save you when you're vaporized into glass. But it makes you crazy, it can make a kid crazy.[10]

Confronted with this threat of Armageddon, some Americans began to recognize the faulty underpinnings of their boundless belief in the nation's power and started to see the flaws in the whole Cold War culture, of their belief in "America, the Great." The atrocities of the Vietnam War, in particular, marked an end of innocence for the American people and a revising of history by many to acknowledge the violence inflicted on indigenous peoples, drawing parallels between the slaughter of Native American tribes in the 1800s and the massacre of the Vietnamese in the 1960s and 1970s. For many, including Wes Craven, this realization came as a profound shock:

> Most of us grew up thinking that the Indian was the bad guy who mysteriously disappeared. We never thought we might have exterminated all indigenous nations in the United States to get their land. Most of us did not look very carefully at what we were doing. We didn't look at how we got Puerto Rico and most of Texas and what happened in the Bay of Pigs.[11]

Many of the issues that would create rifts in the late 1960s emerged at the time of the Cuban Missile Crisis. The government's credibility suffered during and after because it became clear that officials could not protect the population at large. In addition, the rise of the Peace Movement in the 1960s demonstrated declining faith in a foreign policy driven by an overpowering fear of Communism. The emergence of the New Left in the late 1960s and early 1970s signaled a growing rejection of patriarchal authority in all its forms, including government, which found vindication in Nixon's resignation following the Watergate Scandal in 1974.

But, in the same way that they experienced the progressive changes of the 1960s, which promised to sweep away the traditional conservative values of the previous decade and usher in a new age of greater personal freedom, greater racial and sexual equality and organized opposition to the arms race (in the forms of the Anti-War movement and CND), Romero, Craven, Hooper et al. also experienced the disillusion that followed My Lai, Altamont, Kent State and the Manson murders, which punctured the ideals of the peace and love generation. The overwhelming nihilism of the 1970s horror film arose from this disillusionment, from the feeling that the peace generation had failed.

By 1968, a landmark year in American history and for the American horror film, a mood of escalating violence gripped the United States: the assassinations of John F. Kennedy, Martin Luther King, Jr. and Robert Kennedy; the riots in Watts, Detroit and other urban areas; police violence against student protesters; the war in Vietnam and the rising crime rate. It also spread to Britain, inspiring the young director Michael Reeves to make *Witchfinder General*, a film in which violence breeds violence and is seen as inherent in the human condition. Reeves held a pessimistic view of nature which may have precluded the possibility, in his mind, of progressive change. This question of violence as inherent was taken up by Craven and others in the key American horror films of the 1970s. The horror film is considered to have entered its apocalyptic phase during this period, reflecting the ideological crisis that had beset America during the Vietnam War and which culminated in Nixon's 1974 resignation. The key horror films from 1972 to 1978, when considered as a whole, represent a sustained and developing inquiry into the causes of the breakdown in American society, locating its roots in the very "frontier spirit" that underlies the American Way. This remarkable phase of subversive horror cinema concluded with Romero's *Dawn of the Dead* (1978), which Robin Wood described as "perhaps the first horror film to suggest— albeit very tentatively—the possibility of moving beyond apocalypse."[12]

The interplay between genre and authorship can be seen in the remarkable intertextuality of key horror films both in the 1930s and 1970s. This is a direct result of the cultural interaction and exchange between filmmakers during their richest periods of achievement. An example here would be the continuity of theme from *Last House on the Left* (1972) to *The Texas Chain Saw Massacre* to *The Hills Have Eyes* (1977). This can be partly attributed to the genre savvy of the filmmakers (Tobe Hooper is said to have watched every horror film released in Texas in the year of 1972) but also to the sense of continuing shared inquiry into the heart of the American pioneer myth that these three films represent, with each film building upon theme successively. One gets the sense of a baton being passed back and forth during the 1970s horror heyday, from Romero (*Night of the Living Dead*) to Craven (*Last House on the Left*) to Hooper (*The Texas Chain Saw Massacre*) to Cronenberg (*Shivers* [1975]) to Lieberman (*Blue Sunshine* [1978]) and back to Romero (*Dawn of the Dead*)— a working-through of the issues collectively—as each delves deeper into the nature of the "apocalypse" facing the society of its time.

Thus Craven, in *Last House on the Left*, takes up the mantle of Michael Reeves in his conclusion that there is no escape from the encroaching violence in American society because the violence is in *us*. Hooper and co-writer Kim Henkel developed the savagery-civilization dichotomy in *The Texas Chain Saw Massacre* and further located the "moral schizophrenia" facing American society (as personified by Nixon) in its pioneer myths of the Old West. In *The Hills Have Eyes*, Craven staged a virtual re-enactment of the Pilgrims vs. Indians wars to implicate the former (the forefathers of American society) as the more violent of the two.

But whereas the films of Hooper and Craven seemed unwilling to move beyond the apocalyptic, the work of Cronenberg, Lieberman and Romero moved towards the possibility of a new order. *Shivers* offered an ambivalent vision of sexual revolution based on the writings of Freudian psychologist Norman O. Brown, and in its portrayal of the 1970s as a consumerist dystopia whose revolutionary ideals have been replaced by mass psychosis (zombie-ism).

Boris Karloff in *The Black Cat* (1934).

Blue Sunshine bridges the gap between *Shivers* and *Dawn of the Dead*. All three films present the consumer-capitalist impasse of the 1970s as ultimately surmountable, requiring only a fundamental shift in society, a revolution.

In the same way, the 1930s horror film, from *Frankenstein* to *Dracula's Daughter* (1936), often challenged the increasingly reactionary values seizing the country during the Great Depression and the lead-up to World War II; and reflected class conflict arising from the Hoover doctrines and anxiety following the rise of Fascism in Europe. Many of the directors of the period—including Edgar G. Ulmer, Michael Curtiz and Karl Freund—had escaped Europe before the rise of Nazism and brought with them a deeply pessimistic view of human nature that translated into the doom and nihilism of the "classic" horror film and later film noir. Recurring images of sadism and torture chambers, as featured in *The Black Cat* (1934), became increasingly prevalent in films of the era, also featuring strongly in *Mystery of the Wax Museum* (1933) and *The Raven* (1935), to name but a few. Little wonder, then, that the 1930s horror film, as theorist Andrew Tudor has noted of *The Black Cat*, leaves the overall and lasting impression of "endemic madness": a world at odds with itself.[13]

It is therefore not surprising that the innately "cynical" like Lieberman gravitate towards the horror film. "It's naturally subversive," as Lieberman claims, "and allows you to say and do things that you can't do in other forms."[14]

The Subversive Qualities of Horror

The filmmakers in this study were drawn to the horror genre because of its subversive potential, its shock value and its formulaic nature, which facilitates social commentary of a radical nature. In 1979, drawing on the writings of the New Left thinker Herbert Marcuse, critic Robin Wood described the modern horror film as depicting in its monsters a "return of the repressed": a violent eruption of those aspects of the self that each of us represses (and that are repressed by society as a whole) in order that we function as "bourgeois monogamous heterosexual capitalists."[15] The conflict, therefore, between the monster and bourgeois capitalist "normality" in a horror film, and, crucially, how this conflict is resolved, reveals its ideological orientation. Wood detected in the modern horror film a tendency towards apocalypse, an un-restorability of normality, which, by virtue, gave the modern horror film a subversive orientation. In the words of George A. Romero, the whole idea of films such as *Night of the Living Dead* is to "upset the apple cart":

> My biggest complaint about horror or fantasy is, you do it to upset the apple cart, to upset the ways of the world, and then in the end, you restore it all. Well, why did we go through all that in the first place? So I thought, I have to leave the world a mess.[16]

In depicting the world as a "mess," with normality so inherently flawed in the first place that restoring becomes no longer an option, filmmakers like Romero challenge the status quo that is traditionally reaffirmed in Hollywood narratives. Instead the modern horror film of the type Wood describes, in its tendency towards the apocalyptic, creates a profound disturbance in the mind of the viewer, a "shock to the system" which makes subsequent restoration of bourgeois normality (a sense that all is well) impossible.

The basic formula of the horror film, which Wood identifies as "normality threatened by the monster," is by virtue of its simplicity and its binary oppositions (normality is traditionally good, the monster evil) easily subverted. Thus, in the films of Whale, Browning, Lewton, Craven, Romero, Lieberman, Reeves, Walker and others, the distinction between normality and the monster is blurred: Normality becomes monstrous and the monstrous normal. The directors in this study enjoy working in the horror genre precisely because of its formulaic nature, which they can adapt to fit their own ideological viewpoints.

Lieberman's films (*Squirm* [1976] and *Blue Sunshine*), for example, can be seen as variations of the 1950s sci-fi movies that he saw as a child in their outward projection of fears instilled by governments. The atomic age fears of the 1950s, as Lieberman has commented, gave way to fears of the effects of LSD in the early 1970s and then the effects of manmade pollution: Throughout his career he has continued to employ the basic storytelling formulas of the early 1950s sci-fi "radiation movies," adapting them to the changing times.

Romero concurs:

> I think damned near anything you want to say, you can say it in genre. It's much easier because you can be a little more obvious, you don't have to be quite as eloquent. You can make anything happen that you want to happen, so you can illustrate almost any point... It's like parables, those little tales in the Bible. I think you could pick out anything, any scene that intrigued you or you felt passionate about, and figure out a way of telling it in a fantastic manner.[17]

That is not to say, however, that these directors have not found, at certain points of their careers, the formulaic nature of the genre constrictive. There are limits to how far the formula can be pushed. Cultural critic Susan Sontag has argued that science fiction–horror films, because of their generic restrictions, ultimately provide inadequate responses to major socio-political issues: While the concerns they raise might be valid, their conclusions tend to be formulaic and unsatisfactory.[18] Robin Wood identified what he thought was the essential dilemma of the horror genre which became manifest in the 1970s as the implications of the monster-normality dialectic became more and more explicit and inescapable: "Can the genre survive the recognition that the monster is its real hero? If the 'return of the repressed' is conceived in positive terms, what happens to 'horror?' And is such a positive conception logically possible?"[19]

Many of the directors in this book have attempted to work outside the horror genre, often because their ideological viewpoints have come into conflict with the restrictions of generic formula. Romero followed *Dawn of the Dead* with *Knightriders,* drawing upon the themes of the former without feeling the need to horrify. Tod Browning followed *Freaks* with *Fast Workers* (1933) in an attempt to move away from horror films to social dramas that better reflected social issues arising from the Great Depression. *Fast Workers*, a contemporary drama, examines the effects of the Depression on the psyche of the individual, particularly of "emasculated" males. In short, their social environment makes them cynical, exploitative and self-interested. Here the ideological tensions that Browning explored in *Freaks* take place not between opposing social classes of "big people" and "little people" but in the personality of the individual; in the conflict between the need to maintain interpersonal relationships and the need—during times of economic hardship—to operate in one's self-interest. *Fast Workers* confirms Browning as a keen commentator of the Depression era, above and beyond the allegory of *Freaks*. Val Lewton followed his first cycle of terror pictures at RKO with a juvenile delinquency drama, *Youth Runs Wild* (1944). Wes Craven has also shown an interest in social drama (for instance, his *Music of the Heart* [1999]).

For Craven, like Lewton, Browning and Romero, this move away from the genre signaled a need to speak more directly, without the need for allegory, about social concerns developed in, but temporarily constricted by, horror films. Interestingly, all three directors (and producer Lewton) eventually returned to the genre to produce important works, suggesting that constrictions of the genre can, to a certain extent, be overcome. Certainly this is the case for Romero, who very successfully continued to develop the social themes of *Dawn of the Dead* and *Knightriders* in *Land of the Dead* (2005) and *Survival of the Dead* (2009) without losing his radical voice.

Definitions of the Subversive Horror Film

Robin Wood formulates the horror film as "normality threatened by the monster," with the monster representing the return of the things we repress as a society in order to live within the capitalist system. The conflict between the "normal" and the "monstrous," and in particular the manner in which the film resolves this conflict, reveals its ideological orientation—either reaffirming dominant ideological values (restoring normality) or challenging them (presenting normality as un-restorable). Given the apparent simplicity of this formula, it should be straightforward to categorize any given horror film as progressive or reactionary. Are the films themselves not self-evident? The problem is, as Wood points out, "the genre carries within itself the capability of reactionary inflection and perhaps no horror film is entirely immune from its operations."[20] In other words, the potential for progressive or radical elements in the genre is never free from ambiguity or ambivalence (based partly on commercial factors, studio interference, audience expectations, etc.) Gad Horowitz (on whose book *Repression: Basic and Surplus Repression in Psychoanalytic Theory: Freud, Reich, and Marcuse* Wood based his "return of the repressed" thesis) has said that all major social phenomena are "duplicitous": simultaneously progressive and reactionary.[21] This perhaps explains why a horror film like *Freaks* for example, has variously been interpreted as both, or appears to take an ambivalent view of both normality *and* monstrosity. Wood himself made the distinction in terms of reactionary and apocalyptic, the latter type of horror film only progressive "in so far as its negativity is not recuperable into the dominant ideology, but constitutes, on the contrary, the recognition of that ideology's disintegration and its untenability."[22] The terms "subversive" and "progressive" should not, therefore, be used interchangeably; a distinction must be made between the two, and any claim to the latter must be carefully qualified. The films in this book are subversive in that they challenge the dominant values of their time, but they often contain ambiguities and contradictions that make them not entirely immune from the reactionary inflection that, according to Wood (and others) is inherent in the genre—and perhaps precludes any horror film from being truly progressive.

The subversive horror film, then, can be defined thus:

i. It is *anti-authority* in terms of its deep distrust of traditional patriarchal structures—family, military and government;
ii. By way of opposition, it is largely *sympathetic to society's outcasts and "monsters"*;
iii. Moreover, it is characterized by an *unwillingness to reaffirm normative values* within the narrative, tending instead towards the apocalyptic.
iv. It attempts to shock the audience into a higher state of socio-political consciousness by attacking their fundamental values. Graphic on-screen violence and/or emotional shock in the narrative are, therefore, *intrinsically linked to ideological shock* and the breaking of taboo.

Anti-Authority

In the subversive horror film, authority in all its forms (law enforcement, the military, medical science, government, patriarchal family) is viewed with skepticism at best, and often with outright suspicion and distrust. Many times, authority figures are shown to be "insane."

The family is often depicted in terms of its repressive effects on the individual, its part in the socialization process, of turning out docile members of society. In subversive horror films up to and including *Mum and Dad* (2009), the family is depicted as monstrous or degenerate and inevitably patriarchal. We are often taken into Freudian territory and what is described as the Oedipal Trajectory: the process by which male family members are socialized to take on patriarchal roles within the family, and by extension, wider society, thus ensuring the continuance of male power structures. Cannibalism features in many key films (*Night of the Living Dead, The Hills Have Eyes, The Texas Chain Saw Massacre, Frightmare* [1974]). Logically, cannibalism as the family "ritual" is presented as the social norm within the family–not a deviation from the social norm. Although poverty may be a contributory factor, cannibalism is seen as a monstrous extension of patriarchal family values and a way of holding the family unit together in the face of social change. The women in the family inevitably work towards perpetuating the patriarchal power structure, although they often secretly resent their exclusion from the world of male power. The subversive horror film shows that in the patriarchal family, hate masquerades as love, and the only priority is the continuance of the family.

Medical science is rarely shown as benign or beneficial. Instead, directors like Cronenberg and Romero depict a science corrupted by capitalism, harnessed by madmen or utilized for militaristic purposes. In the 1950s sci-fi radiation movies, the potentially negative portrayal of science as being destructive is inevitably balanced out by the positive light in which the military is shown: Generals are seen working with the scientists to contain the problem and destroy the monster that the scientists have inadvertently created. However, in the subversive horror film, members of the military not only fail to contain the problem but inevitably make things worse by escalating the violence. *The Crazies* (1973) depicts this escalation of violence by the military as an endemic madness extending right up to the president, who orders the release of a nuclear bomb on a small town infected by a biological toxin. It is no coincidence that during this period in history President Nixon had been roundly criticized for sending troops into Cambodia and for the Christmas 1972 bombing of North Vietnam which intensified the conflict.

Generally speaking, the Watergate scandal is considered the turning point in public trust of governments. Certainly the films produced during the Nixon era, such as *The Crazies* and *The Texas Chain Saw Massacre*, spoke of the "moral schizophrenia" encapsulated by Vietnam. Inevitably in the subversive horror film, governments are shown as being at least partly responsible for the social collapse that takes place in the course of the film. Thus, authority is shown as ultimately disclaiming responsibility for the welfare of those under their protection.

Sympathetic Monsters

The saying "Society creates its own monsters" certainly holds true in the subversive horror film. Robin Wood described the monster as a "return of the repressed," an outward projection of all that society represses. The monster is identified by society as the "other." Otherness according to Wood represents that which bourgeois ideology cannot recognize or accept but must deal with either by assimilating or rejecting and if possible annihilating. The monster cannot be assimilated, therefore it must discredited, disowned and annihilated.[23]

In subversive horror films, social evils create the monster, and the monster is cast out, disenfranchised from the society that created it and made attempts to destroy it. The pathos of the monster in Whale's *Frankenstein*, for example, arises from its bid to seek recognition from its maker and assimilation, which it is denied. Instead it is hunted down and destroyed. Subversive horror films confront us with the often uncomfortable truth that these monsters are a part of us, the part we are socialized to repress and fear.

The Monster (Boris Karloff) takes the hand of his mate (Elsa Lanchester) in James Whale's subversive masterpiece *Bride of Frankenstein* (1935).

As George A. Romero has said about *Martin*, his 1977 film about a disturbed young man who believes he is a vampire:

> *Martin* is designed to show that all those supernatural monsters that are part of our literary tradition are, in essence, expurgations of ourselves. They are beasts we've created in order to exorcise the monster from within us. Whether it's a monster made out of spare parts, one that grows out of us, or something we turn into during a full moon, monsters have traditionally been considered embodiments of our own evil. By distinguishing them from us, we could destroy them. I tried to show in *Martin* that you can't just slice off this evil part of ourselves and throw it away. It's a permanent part of ourselves and we'd better try to understand it.[24]

In cinematic terms, subversive horror films can be distinguished by their tendency to involve their monsters in "scenes of empathy." In his essay "The Scene of Empathy and the Human Face on Film," Carl Plantinga suggested that a scene of empathy in film is a prolonged closeup of a character's face that allows the spectator to empathize with the character. The pace of the narrative momentarily slows and the interior emotional experience of the character becomes the focus of attention. The power of the face in closeup not only reveals to spectators what the character is feeling but also elicits the same feeling in the viewer. We experience concern for the character (if they are protagonists—Hollywood villains are rarely afforded scenes of empathy)—what Plantinga calls "congruent feelings."[25] The mainstream cinema abounds with such scenes; indeed, the scene of empathy is crucial to the audience's emotional involvement with the film.

In the subversive horror film, these scenes of empathy are extended to the monsters. Robin Wood described these scenes as moments of "particularized vulnerability,"[26] a common intimate experience shared between character and spectator. In *The Texas Chain Saw Massacre*, for example, we are given such a scene when Leatherface is seen alone after killing Jerry and appears at a loss as to what to do next. In *Last House on the Left*, all the major characters (except perhaps the father) are allowed these moments of vulnerability; perhaps most haunting is Krug's sudden rush of shame after raping Mari. Further examples: Karloff's Monster reaching towards the sunlight in *Frankenstein*; Bub's grief at seeing his friend Dr. Frankenstein dead in *Day of the Dead* (1985).

The scenes of empathy in these films further complicate the divisions between the normal and the monstrous and make it impossible for us to view these monsters as purely "other." We are them and they are us.

Non-Restorative Endings

If the resolution of the conflict between the normal and the monstrous reveals the ideological orientation of a given horror narrative, it follows that the film's ending—whether the narrative achieves closure in the form of a restoration of normality or not—is a crucial factor in determining its political implications. We can say that a horror narrative can end in one of three ways (there are, of course, variations):

- The monster is destroyed and the status quo restored. There is a clear sense of closure and, as Rick Worland points out, the restoration of normality is often "signaled through the formation or preservation of the heterosexual couple or family group."[27] The political implication of this type of ending is clear: Normality is worth saving and dominant values should be endorsed.
- The monster is destroyed and the status quo apparently restored, but the narrative closure is ironic, as in *Night of the Living Dead*, thus undercutting any sense of resolution of wider issues or endorsement of dominant values.
- The monster is not destroyed and therefore the narrative remains open—the horror is ongoing. Normality remains under threat but its basic values are shown to be worth fighting for.

Clearly, the first type of ending denotes a reactionary horror narrative: The purpose of threatening normality is to restore it again, reaffirming traditional values in the process. This type of ending is often attributed (not entirely justifiably) to the "classic" 1930s–1940s horror film.

The second type of ending, prevalent in the 1970s (*Deathdream* [1972], *Last House on the Left*), can be seen as more subversive because the status quo is discredited; however, no alternative to the dominant ideology beyond a kind of nihilistic despair is usually offered, causing some critics to question the extent to which these films can be called in any way progressive.[28]

The third type of ending and its variation, "the monster wins—everybody dies," arguably arose from postmodernism—it is popular for franchises—and its veneer of nihilism masks its commitment to endorsing deeply reactionary values. Most slasher movies, for example, feature this kind of ending.

The filmmakers in this study are distinguished by their preference for non-restorative endings in the sense that, although the immediate threat by the monster to society may be fended off (or not, as the case may be), a wider crisis facing society remains. What concerns these filmmakers is exposing the conditions in society that created the monster in the first place. Therefore, restoring order remains impossible as long as those conditions persist. A clear example of this can be found in Larry Cohen's *It's Alive* (1974), which ends with the birth of another monstrous baby after the first one is killed. The film implies that whatever evil of society caused these monsters to be born has not been vanquished.

Shock Value

In its broadest sense, shock is concerned with subverting the traditional morality of a society in unconventional, unexpected ways. The films in this study are intentionally constructed by the filmmakers to instill shock in an audience by attacking their fundamental values. They are, in other words, deliberate shocks to the social-sexual-ideological system.

Directors have been utilizing their power to shock since the earliest days of cinema (one thinks of Edwin S. Porter's startling introduction of the closeup in *The Great Train Robbery* [1903]) and many have pushed the boundaries of acceptability to emphasize the message they are presenting. Wes Craven has spoken of the genre's potential to show "truths that are too painful for a society to admit."[29] What an audience experiences as shock reveals the conditions of a particular society at a particular point in time, its fears and taboos. The use of shock by directors of subversive horror cinema is ideologically motivated. The intention is nothing less than to address the traumas that society seeks to deny.

1

ANTI-EUGENICS
Frankenstein (1931) and *Freaks* (1932)

1932.
A microcephalic—or pinhead—stares into the camera with a goofy smile, wearing a dress with a dainty bow. Harmless enough maybe, but the pinhead's abnormality—including its lack of obvious gender—unnerves...
Meanwhile...
A scientist demonstrates to a full lecture hall how the "abnormal" brain of a criminal destines him to roam, rob and rape. Such degenerate characteristics in the brain are, the scientist pronounces, the result of defective genes and a threat to men, women and children everywhere.

These are not scenes from *Freaks* or *Frankenstein,* but descriptions of exhibits and transcripts taken from the 3rd International Eugenics Congress, held on August 22 and 23, 1932, in New York City, an event organized to further the cause of the eugenics movement during the Great Depression. The pinhead photograph was part of an exhibit called "The Letchworth Village *Freakshow*," depicting the physically deformed patients of Letchworth Village, a mental institution in New York State.[1] The pinhead in the mug shot bears an uncanny resemblance to Schlitze in *Freaks*. Indeed it is almost impossible to look at the exhibit without thinking of Tod Browning's roster of physically unusual performers. At the same conference, Major Darwin, son of Charles (founder of the modern theory of evolution), gave a keynote speech predicting the doom of civilization unless eugenic measures were implemented: namely, the so-called "elimination of the unfit."[2]

Although rarely discussed in the context of the eugenics movement,[3] the shock value of both *Frankenstein* and *Freaks* back in 1932 clearly owed something to breaking the taboos that arose from eugenics (and its related political beliefs) at the time of the Great Depression. With its scenes of real-life "freaks" rising up in revolt against normal people, *Freaks* was considered too shocking for the audience on its initial release and withdrawn from distribution. Likewise, *Frankenstein* was widely censored for its scenes of perceived blasphemy, sadism and child molestation. The power behind the shocks in *Frankenstein* becomes startlingly clear when considered in relation to the moral panics of the time: The 1930s saw war veterans, unemployed homeless men and homosexuals increasingly persecuted as a result of the "sex crimes" panics which swept America during the Depression era; *Freaks* is essentially the story of an underclass of people exploited by their perceived genetic superiors. In their willingness to break taboos arising from eugenics beliefs in the 1930s, both *Frankenstein* and *Freaks* can be read as subversive.

Tod Browning, *Freaks* and Eugenics

Any discussion of *Freaks* should take into account that the film as seen today is much changed from the original version that Browning directed. *Freaks* suffered many revisions at the hands of MGM following disastrous test screenings in 1932. The studio edited thirty minutes from the film. This involved shortening sequences of revenge, altering the ending, adding a "happy" epilogue and removing a number of scenes between secondary characters that were deemed unnecessary. One of the effects of these changes is to present an ambivalent view of the freaks that has caused consternation for many critics who claim that Browning adopts contradictory positions towards his characters. A look at the production context of the film and how Browning approached its subject matter gives a clearer view of Browning's original intentions.

Freaks, as eventually shot, was not the film that Browning had wanted to make. He'd had a less-than-happy experience on *Dracula* (1931) and was tiring of the horror genre with which he had become associated. *Dracula* had been a troubled production: Browning had gone over schedule and Universal didn't seem behind him—they didn't give him final cut. Rumor has it that Browning lost interest and Karl Freund, the film's cinematographer, had taken over some of the directorial responsibility. Moreover, Browning wanted to make *modern* films, not gothic period pieces as most horror films were in the 1930s. *Iron Man* (1931), his film after *Dracula,* was a boxing picture; and his film after *Freaks* was *Fast Workers,* about riveters building skyscrapers. These were contemporary films, with contemporary themes. They were stories "ripped from the headlines"; born of the Depression, reflecting the times.

Many books have been written about the effects of the Great Depression, both economic and social, on the American people. All agree that the poorest in the population suffered the most. While most wealthy Americans continued to live in conspicuous luxury, turning out for fashion shows and opening nights, gathering at debutante balls and banquets and vacationing at posh resorts, high unemployment in the lower classes led to many thousands of people losing their homes and to families breaking up. The jobless from rural areas flocked to the towns and cities in a fruitless search for employment, which only added to the numbers of homeless. This led to the creation of "Hoovervilles": shanty-towns built out of packing cases and junk by homeless men. They cropped up in New York's Central Park, as well as in Seattle and Brooklyn.

To make matters worse, the Depression ushered in a morally conservative era which sought to eradicate the liberalism of the 1920s. While the flapper girl had challenged traditional women's roles during the Roaring Twenties, in the Depression era women were often blamed for the threat that unemployment posed to a working man's masculinity and forced out of the workplace. Alcoholism increased, particularly in unemployed men. Some men deserted their wives and families altogether and took to the road. Homeless drifters like these became vilified—labeled as "deviants"—as were gays and lesbians.

In this atmosphere of blame and victimization, eugenics ideology reached a peak. Many states passed laws authorizing the involuntary sterilization of criminals and the mentally disabled. The propagandizing of eugenics in the Church, education system and media led to widespread discrimination against those perceived to be genetically unfit and fostered an inferiority complex in millions of Americans.

These were themes to which Browning could relate: as a working class Kentucky boy who had fled a conventional Baptist upbringing to join the circus; as an alcoholic who had suffered personal tragedy; as the "ghoul" of Hollywood, he identified with the outsider.[4] His films had often been bound to issues of injustice and social class; of the struggle between the criminal underworld and an elite upper class (*Outside The Law* [1930], *The Unholy Three* [1925]); of emasculation, jealousy and frustration (*Road to Mandalay* [1926], *The Unknown* [1927]); of deformity and mutilation (*West of Zanzibar* [1928]). In 1915 Browning had been involved in a car crash while driving under the influence of alcohol. He suffered serious injuries and his passenger, Elmer Booth, died. The trauma of the accident had serious psychological ramifications for Browning: guilt, disfigurement anxiety (it is said he suffered some form of emasculation in the accident), sexual frustration. This experience had informed his films ever since. He therefore decided that if he was to make *Freaks*, it would be as an allegory, a fusing of personal preoccupation and national trauma.

Phil Berg, an talent agent who represented most of MGM's directors in the late 1920s, claims that Browning was unique among directors of the time as he initiated his projects rather than being assigned them by the studio.[5] In the case of *Freaks*, the project had been brought to his attention by the actor Harry Earles, who no doubt saw a starring role for himself as Hans, the dwarf who enacts revenge on the "big woman" who marries him for his money and then tries to poison him. The property came as a short story called "Spurs," written by Tod Robbins. As was his bent, Browning took an active, though uncredited, hand in the scriptwriting process. It seems that, from the start, he had wanted to move away from horror film conventions so as to portray the plight of the freaks in a more sympathetic light, but was thwarted by the studio. "They wanted a macabre ending," recalled William S. Hart Jr., "but he just wanted to have a kind of sad ending." Browning originally envisaged a melancholic fadeout to the story that would underscore "the sadness of the poor people that couldn't ever be part of the other people. And they forced on him ... this wild revenge to make a macabre ending."[6]

As Browning's biographer David J. Skal comments, it is perhaps "difficult to imagine Browning shying away from what would transpire at the end of *Freaks*, given his stock-in-trade propensity for revenge stories and macabre climaxes."[7] On the other hand, Browning's proposed ending is not so hard to accept if you take into account his obvious sympathies with the freaks and his desire to move away from the horror genre in favor of social drama. Either way, despite the imposed ending, Browning transformed what Skal described as "little more than an anecdotal short story with detestable characters" into a tale of "little people vs. big people," an exaggerated reflection of the injustice, economic unbalance and widespread disenfranchisement that characterized the Great Depression.[8]

"Step right up, folks!"

Our culture has long linked physical appearance with moral worth. Christine Rosen, writing in *The New Atlantis*, points to classic children's stories as an indicator of how, throughout history, beauty has been seen as the external expression of goodness, just as ugliness has been seen as a sign of moral degeneracy.[9] The beautiful princess is imbued with inner goodness, just as her opposite, the wicked witch, is blighted by ugliness. *Freaks* itself begins with a printer roller prologue (added for the post–World War II reissue, presumably in an attempt to sugarcoat the bitter pill that audiences were about to swallow). It describes the love of beauty as "a deep-seated urge which dates back to the beginning of civilization," and then goes on to apologize that "the revulsion with which we view the abnormal, the malformed and the mutilated is the result of long conditioning by our forefathers."

A sixteenth century physiognomist, Johann Casper Lavater, claimed, "The better one is morally, the more beautiful one is; the worse one is morally, the uglier."[10] Even into the twentieth century, as Rosen notes, phrenologists, criminologists and eugenicists accepted the notion that outward physical appearance marked internal worth and used particular aesthetic standards (such as the slope of the nose and the size and the shape of the head) as justification for ranking people of different ethnic and racial groups.[11]

The equation of physical appearance with internal worth—the basis of eugenics belief—is what *Freaks* subverts. In Browning's film the outwardly beautiful are shown to be inwardly rotten and corrupt, while the outwardly freakish are revealed as blessed with inner nobility. In many ways *Freaks* is a transformation narrative, akin to the children's stories that Christine Rosen discusses: classic tales that endorse "the notion of physical transformation as the route to happiness—the Ugly Duckling, Pygmalion, and Cinderella."[12] In *Freaks* the transformation is reversed: The beautiful swan is transformed into an ugly duckling, and the notion that beauty brings happiness and therefore we should all aspire to it, is debunked.

"God looks after all his children"

Browning's first use of shock in *Freaks* occurs in the early sequences, during which the eponymous freaks are introduced to the viewer. The taboo of physical deformity—or rather the act of "gawping" at deformity—is broken by Browning's candid presentation of the freaks, creating in the audiences of 1932 a simultaneous response of fascination and horror.

"Freakshows" in exhibitions and carnivals had been a staple of popular American culture since the middle of the nineteenth century. However, the public presentation of deformity for the purposes of entertainment became increasingly restricted by law as advances in medical science explained previously mysterious "freaks of nature" as genetic mutations or diseases. Public concern on the grounds of decency eventually saw the decline of the freakshow by the mid–twentieth century. However, in the 1930s, disabled performers and curiosity acts, such as those at Coney Island, continued to draw crowds. Rachel Adams, in her book *Sideshow USA*, discusses the attractions of the circus freakshow to working class and immigrant audiences anxious to assimilate in the time of eugenics: "In theory, if not in practice, their own differences would fade into irrelevance when confronted by the spectacle of absolute alterity on the sideshow platform."[13] The extreme racial and geographical "otherness" of the freaks on display would, in other words, provide circus-goers with the reassuring confirmation of their own status as white Americans.

Tod Browning had a carnival background. At the age of 16 he had run away from home to join the circus, becoming a talker for acts such as "the Wild Man of Borneo," as well as performing his own live burial routine, "The Living Corpse." The alternative world of the circus helped to shape a disdain for normal mainstream society. As Skal has commented, "The carny ethos divided the world into rigid camps: show people and everyone else."[14] Circus life, for Browning, represented a flight from conventional lifestyles and responsibilities (not least a repressive working class Baptist upbringing), which later manifested itself in a love of liquor, gambling and fast cars; but also fostered in Browning a sense of kinship with social outsiders, such as the physically deformed performers with whom he became acquainted during his circus days.

Eugenicists, on the other hand, saw circus freaks as examples of degenerate heredity. There are accounts of field workers from the Eugenics Record Office (a center set up for eugenics and human heredity research in Cold Spring Harbor, New York) visiting Coney Island to collect data for human heredity studies from the circus and sideshow acts, often scribbling notes and pedigrees on the calling cards provided by the acts.[15]

The early sequences of *Freaks* use the structure of the circus sideshow to introduce characters like Johnny Eck, Schlitze and Prince Randian, demonstrating their talents and abilities in a series of loosely connected vignettes. These scenes evoke the sideshow's episodic feel which relies on curiosity to thrill and entertain its audiences, discouraging, as Rachel Adams writes, "any substantive interaction between viewer and performer. Curious looking enables the paying customer to see the freak as an object on display for the sole purpose of amusement or education."[16]

Browning, however, quickly begins to undercut the voyeuristic aspects of the traditional freakshow by showing the freaks engaged in the activities of everyday life, dispelling the initial shock and revulsion, and encouraging the viewer to see the freaks as individuals who have overcome their disabilities rather than as objects on display. Many of these early scenes were added to the original script as Browning became fascinated with the performers' remarkable abilities and found ways to incorporate them into the film. Prince Randian, who lacks arms and legs, is able to perform the incredible task of rolling a cigarette with his mouth. Johnny Eck, truncated from the waist, can move around on his hands with extraordinary agility. The conjoined twins, Violet and Daisy Hilton, coordinate their movements with astonishing ease.

While performing these everyday tasks, the characters are shown interacting with the able-bodied circus performers: Phroso (Wallace Ford), Roscoe (Rosco Ates) and Venus (Leila Hyams), blurring the distinctions between disabled and able-bodied performers. Indeed, it appears that the disabled and the able-bodied performers rub along just fine together. Gradually, we forget the physical deformity of the freaks and become intrigued by their domestic circumstances. *Freaks* plays like a soap opera in this respect: How will Roscoe learn to live with his sister-in-law who is literally joined to his wife's hip? How will Frieda win Hans back when he is so obviously smitten with Cleopatra? As these intrigues unfold, and with the taboo of physical deformity broken, audiences gradually forgot their initial shock and began to empathize with the freaks, whose problems—aside from the physical disabilities—were really not that different to their own. *Here, look*, Browning is saying, *they really aren't that different after all. Are we not all God's children?* In the era of eugenics, that was a subversive message, to say the least.

"The peacock of the air"

While the 1930s audience would have experienced their first sight of the freaks as an immediate, visceral shock, Browning had a subtler but arguably more powerful shock up his sleeve in his portrayal of the outwardly beautiful but inwardly ugly couple, Cleopatra (Olga Baclanova) and Hercules (Henry Victor). At the same time as dispelling the audience's initial revulsion at the freaks by inviting them to look beneath the surface of physical deformity and empathize with the person inside, he generates revulsion for Cleopatra and Hercules by gradually revealing the corruption and avarice that lies beneath their physical beauty.

Of course, matinee idol good looks and film star glamor—of which both Henry Victor and Olga Baclanova were blessed—are what drew audiences of the 1930s into the cinema in the first place. Depression era audiences in particular wanted, and needed, to identify with the beautiful people, and this is exactly what Hollywood in the golden age gave them. The Hollywood "dream factory" fed audience aspirations to physical beauty, success and happiness by providing the kind of transformation narratives that Christine Rosen refers to, in both its films and its star system. Movie magazines of the 1920s and 1930s—the heyday of Hollywood stars, Hollywood glamor and Hollywood fashion—are filled with advertisements that speak of this need for transformation; peruse these magazines and you will find advertisements that promise to fix your nose, roll your fat away and peel off your skin to leave you with beautiful new skin. "You will find the world in general judging you greatly, if not wholly, by your looks," one advertisement warns.

The 1930s, accordingly, saw a sharp rise in the demand for cosmetic surgery, as thousands of people sought to fulfill those aspirations and to cure themselves surgically of the inferiority complex that eugenics had fostered in them. But buried in the logic of cosmetic surgery are, as Rosen notes, some disturbing truths about what our culture believes:

> that it is acceptable to be satisfied by the external markers of success; that the pursuit of such markers is, in and of itself, a useful and psychologically healthy goal for people; that what used to be encouraged—a lifelong process of moral education—is less useful, in the long term, than the appearance of success, health, and beauty.[17]

Hercules and Cleopatra, by virtue of their physical beauty, should—in the eugenics way of thinking—possess moral worth, but Browning shows them interested only in the "external markers of success," and ruthless in their pursuit of them. One can only imagine how uncomfortable audiences of the eugenics era must have felt as these representatives of the beautiful people—whom the audience desperately wanted to become—are made increasingly repulsive morally.

Seen from a modern perspective, Cleopatra and Hercules are in many ways the epitome of the modern materialistic couple: obsessed with body image, narcissistic, greedy, mercenary. Browning establishes their venality early on in a pair of matching scenes: Cleo takes advantage of Hans's infatuation by borrowing a thousand francs from him, while clearly having no intention of paying him back; Hercules tries to coerce

Little Hans (Harry Earles) attempts to woo Cleopatra (Olga Baclanova) in *Freaks* (1932).

Venus into prostituting herself to earn money to keep him, prompting her to leave. Both express their "superiority" in the exploitation of others, and especially of the freaks.

As the "big people," Cleopatra and Hercules can be seen representing the elite classes who, during the height of the Depression, exploited workers by paying below subsistence wages, a situation John Steinbeck famously drew public attention to in *The Grapes of Wrath*. Steinbeck depicts whole families reduced to slave labor by bosses only too eager to exploit the unbalanced economics of the Depression. Significantly, these same wealthy industrialists were often benefactors of the eugenics movement, so-called "progressive reformers" seeking greater control of industrial labor. Eugenicists and their wealthy supporters opposed political radicalism and class struggle, and fought against the increasing strength of militant labor unions. This included passing laws against immigration which prevented migrants coming in from places that had a strong tradition of organized labor, such as Italy.

Browning himself had an ambivalent attitude towards wealth. Although he was affluent during the time of *Freaks*, he had struggled with poverty in his youth and this left him uneasy with wealth and privilege. In *Freaks*, Hercules and Cleopatra make their money through their physical attributes. Hercules is always looking for ways to display his virility; Cleopatra is a gold-digger. Browning slowly peels away the hyper-masculinity and sexual aggression to reveal a deep-seated insecurity. Both Hercules and Cleopatra fear being stripped of their status. Hercules fears the loss of his male power; Cleopatra knows that her looks will fade. Both know that without these attributes, they would be at the bottom of the pecking order, along with the freaks. In the case of this couple, beauty really is only skin deep. *Look beneath the surface of what you aspire to*, Browning is saying, *you will find it rotten and morally reprehensible.*

"We accept you! One of us!"

Audiences of 1932 must have been feeling, as *Freaks* unspooled, a growing sense of ideological shock: The glamourous couple on the screen, with whom they had expected to empathize, had been revealed as bestial. Now they were feeling their sympathies being drawn away from the normals towards the freaks. On its initial release, *Freaks* bombed in many cities including New York, Los Angeles and Chicago. Overall, it was a huge failure. However, there were places where it was popular: Boston, Cleveland, Houston. In Buffalo, the draw of *Freaks* was the talk of the town, as it grossed twice the average of the theater in which it played during its brief four-day stay.[18] Although *Freaks* famously suffered many walk-outs during its initial release, some audience members stayed, curious to see where Tod Browning was taking them. What taboos were to be broken next?

One of the most significant aspects of *Freaks* is the sense of community that Browning portrays among the physically deformed circus freaks, which is in stark contrast to the isolated, solitary lives of the normals. Solidarity between the freaks does not feature in the source material, "Spurs," but was introduced into the story by Browning, and is most famously expressed in their moral code: "Offend one and you offend them all." Through this, Browning allows us a glimpse into their alternative lifestyle, and it is one that does not conform to normative sexuality. As Rachel Adams puts it: "Here is an environment rich with polymorphously perverse sexuality, where a proliferation of erotic proclivities coexist, partners are exchanged and heterosexuality is one among many options."[19] It is this aspect of *Freaks* that is perhaps the most subversive.

The intriguing sexuality of the freaks is constantly in audience members' minds as they watch the film, and is something Browning alludes to throughout, most obviously in the central dilemma facing "Little Hans" and his "Big Woman," Cleopatra. "You should not smoke such a big cigar," Frieda (Daisy Earles) scolds Hans at one point, voicing her frustrations at the disproportion of his size in relation to that of Cleopatra. Other characters face similar sexual dilemmas. Roscoe, the able-bodied but stuttering newlywed, faces a potential *ménage-a-trois* with his wife Daisy and her sister Violet, because the sisters are conjoined twins who appear to share the same physical experiences—including sexual arousal. There are also domestic complications arising from their strange marriage, such as party girl Violet wanting to go out dancing while Roscoe wants Daisy to stay in with *him*. Browning's solution to these dilemmas is comedic but also transgressive: He turns the *ménage-a-trois* into a *ménage-a-quatre*: Violet finds her own suitor. *Such couplings are possible*, Browning is saying, *but only if you break the rules of normal society.*

In 1932, this was a direct challenge to eugenics ideology, and especially to laws against miscegenation and laws governing sterilization of the perceived unfit. The notion of freaks actually *reproducing*, as they do in Browning's film, was highly taboo. Anti-miscegenation laws, such as the Racial Integrity Act (1924), made mixed-race marriages invalid,[20] and in the *Bell vs. Buck* case of 1927, the United States Supreme Court upheld a Virginia statute calling for the eugenic sterilization of people considered genetically unfit. This provided the green light for similar laws in many states, leading to an estimated 65,000 people being sterilized without their own consent or that of a family member. The thinking behind these laws was made public by the jurist delivering the Supreme Court's decision, Oliver Wendell Holmes, Jr., who infamously declared: "three generations of imbeciles are enough."[21]

In America, film was being used to indoctrinate audiences with eugenics thinking much the same way as it was in Germany under the Third Reich. One of the earliest American eugenics propaganda films was *The Black Stork* (1917), which advocated the euthanasia of "defective" babies. And as late as 1934 a film such as *Tomorrow's Children* could assert involuntary sterilization as legal and morally acceptable. See how in *Freaks*, by contrast, Browning makes the birth of a "defective" baby a cause for celebration: The bearded lady gives birth to a girl and the freaks gather around to welcome the latest addition to the family. They congratulate the father (a human skeleton) and announce proudly that his daughter is "gonna have a beard like her mother."

Browning himself was no stranger to the stigma of what eugenicists called "degenerate heredity." As a lifelong alcoholic, he had inherited the dysgenic traits of his uncle Pete, a professional baseball player whose chronic alcoholism had resulted in his being committed to a mental institution. Browning had also practiced miscegenation. In the early 1920s his affair with actress Anna May Wong was met with disapproval in Hollywood, partly because Wong was underage and Browning already married; but also because Wong was Chinese. The Racial Integrity Act divided people into just two races: "white" and "colored." To be classed as white, you had to have "no trace whatsoever of blood other than Caucasian." Chinese people, according to eugenicists, were not Caucasian, and were, therefore, classed as colored.

In a scene deleted from *Freaks*, Frieda tries to dissuade Cleopatra from marrying Hans on the basis that their offspring might be dwarves like Hans. Cleo shudders but insists that she would marry Hans "even if he had mule's blood." It is interesting that the scene was taken out. In the end Browning shows the union between "Little Hans" and his "Big Woman" to

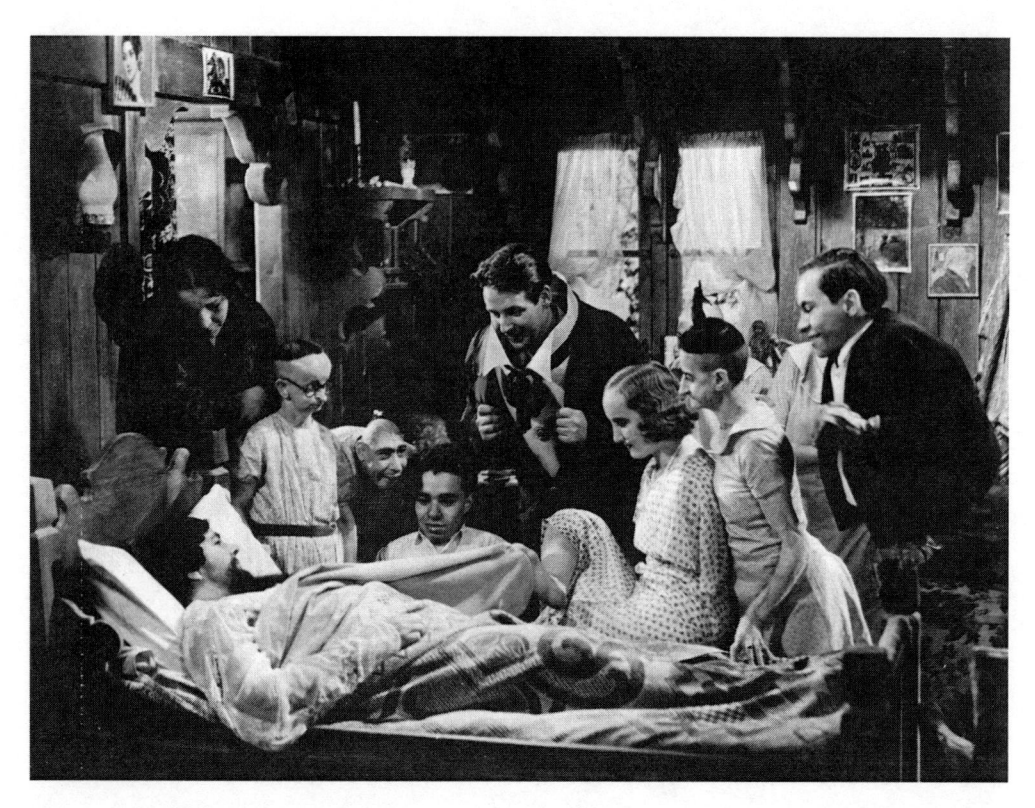

"She's gonna have a beard like her mother": Phroso (Wallace Ford, standing in center) and the cast of *Freaks* (1932) celebrate a new arrival.

be impossible; however, their most serious difference is shown not to be physical but ideological—as we see in the wedding sequence.

"Offend one and you offend them all"

Browning had drawn the audience's sympathy away from the "normal" and towards the "freakish," allowing him to break the big taboos of the time: miscegenation and reproduction of the genetically unfit. But he shocks us again as the freaks become sinister and monstrous and we are asked to empathize with their uprising. This *reversal* is perhaps more shocking to modern audiences, who become uneasy with the idea of equating physical disability to monstrosity. In 1932, the uprising of the freaks might have been understood allegorically: This was the time labor activists became militant at the height of the Depression, leading ultimately to Roosevelt's New Deal. Still, Browning was concerned with the possibility that audiences might lose sympathy for the freaks, and tried to work against the revenge plot that the studio had imposed on him by making their retribution fair and justified.

In "Spurs," Hans is portrayed as a nasty little man who takes cruel pleasure in punishing his wife for her betrayal. Browning rewrote him as a nobleman who becomes a victim of his infatuation with the beautiful Cleopatra. During the wedding feast, Cleopatra's finally reveals to all her contempt for Hans and the revulsion she feels for the freaks. She looks on, in shock

Cleopatra (Olga Baclanova, standing) rejects the loving cup offered by Angeleno (Angelo Rossitto, standing on table) much to the amusement of Hercules (Henry Victor, right), in *Freaks* **(1932).**

and outrage, as the freaks drink from the loving cup meant to symbolize their acceptance of her into their family ("one of us"). Browning dwells on the freaks as they drink; some of them drool into the cup. The thought of becoming contaminated by the DNA of the unfit is too much for Cleopatra. "Dirty, slimy freaks!" she screams. "You filth! Make me one of you, would you!" It is an extraordinary moment of truth about the era, painful to watch, voicing the ugly thinking behind eugenics.

Perhaps the freaks might already be justified in their retribution against Cleopatra based on her betrayal of Hans. Browning, however, is careful to have the freaks sit tight until they have undeniable proof that Cleopatra and Hercules intend murder. The poisoning of Hans in some ways parallels the fascism of eugenics. Underlying the argument for the sterilization of the "feeble-minded" was the desire to save tax dollars for the rich. Many of the physically and mentally disabled were housed in institutions and considered a burden on society. Sterilization, the eugenicists argued, would save the taxpayer millions of dollars a year and relieve the state of its burden of care. Of course, the Nazis took this thinking one step further in their euthanasia project. In *Freaks* the guilt of the normals becomes indisputable once it's clear that Cleopatra and Hercules plan to murder Hans, and the freaks take action to protect their own.

Part of the power of *Freaks* is the way it builds, creating ever greater visceral and ideological shock in the viewer. The storm sequence—with its images of freaks crawling through the mud to attack Cleopatra and Hercules—is certainly unparalleled in 1930s cinema in terms of its graphic impact. However, perhaps the greatest shock of all was considered too much for audiences in 1932. The final scene of *Freaks* was unacceptable to the studio and replaced with the ending that now exists and an epilogue intended to soften the overall impact of the film. It is difficult to think of another film as drastically recut as *Freaks*. What is more, footage removed from *Freaks* remains lost to this day—an indicator perhaps of how controversial it really was in 1932. Only fragments of the ending that Browning originally shot remain in the film.

In the original ending, the story jumps forward in time a year or so to reveal that Hans and Frieda are married and championing their rights to reproduce. The fate of Cleopatra is revealed as it is shown now—mutilated and almost unrecognizable, she remains in the circus but as a freak, a "chicken woman." Hercules, however, is also shown to be alive (and not killed by the freaks as the film now suggests) and still in the circus, singing the rosary. He has, in other words, been castrated. This is their fit punishment and poetic justice in action. Cleopatra and Hercules have been turned into what they feared and despised most: They have joined the underclass of the unfit. That this ending was truncated by the studio indicates a reluctance to face the implications of Browning's message.

It seems that, for Browning, the final image of *Freaks*—the emblem of the times—was always to be one of disempowerment, of "emasculation." This reflected the widespread ostracism and disenfranchisement that millions of Americans experienced in the Great Depression under eugenics laws. Eugenics ultimately used the cover of science to blame the victims of the Great Depression for their own problems.

In *Freaks*, Tod Browning metaphorically turned the tables on the eugenicists and all those who thrived at the expense of ordinary people during the Great Depression, and made *them* the ones to suffer.

James Whale, *Frankenstein* and Moral Panic in the 1930s

The critic John Russell Taylor once wrote that James Whale's "background and career were so eccentric in relation to the kind of films he was making and where he was making them that it is difficult to find anyone comparable—least of all Tod Browning, with whom he is often arbitrarily bracketed."[22] But, if one takes into account similarities in background (both were from working class families), personal pre-occupation (both were concerned with the plight of the outsider) and treatment of subject matter (both used the horror film for social commentary during the Great Depression), then comparisons between Browning and Whale become anything but arbitrary. Like Browning, Whale fused his own experience (as a gay man from a British working class family) with national trauma, creating in *Frankenstein* an allegory of social exclusion in an age of persecution and a critique of science in an era where social problems were blamed on genetic makeup. Karloff's Monster is the deviant, the criminal, the vagabond, the homeless veteran and the homosexual—an amalgam of all that society cast out and called "monstrous" or "other" in the 1930s.

"You have created a monster and it will destroy you!"

Many critics have debated whether Whale's background and sexuality had a direct influence on *Frankenstein*, particularly in terms of the plight of the Monster. Paul M. Jensen commented that it was tempting to assume that Whale identified with an individual who is an outsider in a way that perhaps the average person would not understand. "I'm sure that James Whale knew what that felt like as a youth" says Jensen, "as an artistically inclined person in a factory town, in a factory family. He knew what that was like probably well before he knew it as a homosexual, being an artist, being a sensitive person, being someone that people made fun of for whatever reason."[23]

Whale's biographer, James Curtis, takes a similar view. He argues that it was only after Whale's homosexuality became widely known in the 1970s and 1980s that revisionist readings of *Frankenstein* found a gay subtext to the isolation and scorn endured by the Monster. Curtis claims that there is no evidence to support Whale seeing himself as a misfit by being gay, and that if he perceived himself as an "antisocial figure," such feelings would "more likely have been the result of his working-class origins than anything having to do with his being gay."[24]

However, the ostracism that gay people endured during the Great Depression is unlikely to have been lost on Whale. The economic and sexual exuberance of the 1920s had seen a rejection of Victorian notions of sexuality and a greater visibility of homosexuality in large American cities, as speakeasies, cabarets and nightclubs promoted gay culture. In places like Greenwich Village and Times Square, gay men mingled with drag performers, lesbians and transvestites. However, as the Depression deepened in the 1930s, homosexuality was increasingly viewed as undermining traditional values and a threat to social and economic stability. New laws pressured owners of bars and nightclubs to ban gays, and police often raided such establishments and shut them down—including in Hollywood. The Production Code Administration came under pressure from the Catholic Church to censor references to homosexuality, and homosexuality in Hollywood films became highly coded. Typically, gays and lesbians in Hollywood films of the 1930s were shown to be tragic figures, weak and marginalized, and often associated with the criminal underworld, as can be seen in the crime films of the era. Homosexuality came to be regarded by many as a social disease, as government research studies began to link criminality, deviancy and even male unemployment with homosexuality. There is evidence that Whale's own fall from grace in Hollywood during the 1940s and 1950s was due, in part at least, to his open homosexuality.

Whale's sexuality and his class sympathies should really be viewed together in order to understand his thematic preoccupations and his desire to broach taboo subjects in his films. By breaking taboos about blasphemy and sex crimes in particular, *Frankenstein* challenged the moral panics that were sweeping America in the 1930s—fears of sexual deviancy used to mobilize political support against non-conforming individuals.

"Now I know what it feels like to be God!"

According to James Curtis, the initial preview of *Frankenstein,* held in Santa Barbara on October 29, 1931, left audiences in such a state of shock that it sent Universal executives into a panic. During the preview, says Curtis, "people got up, walked out, came back in, walked out again. It was an alarming thing."[25]

Frankenstein had been filmed twice before—in 1910 and 1915—but nothing had prepared audiences for the "tableau of death and tragedy" with which Whale presented them.[26] From the opening scenes of grave-robbing onwards, audiences had no cinematic frame of reference for the stark and morbid imagery of *Frankenstein*. This is perhaps difficult to comprehend now, given the influence of *Frankenstein* on the genre and the countless remakes and imitations we've seen; but all that an audience had by way of comparison in 1931 were the real-life battlefields and trenches of Europe, the scarred and mutilated soldiers returned from the Great War and the desolation of the economic catastrophe that had been wrought upon them. *Frankenstein* takes place in a hellish Europe-of-the-mind, a hinterland that remains curiously abstract, out of time, where the horrors of the Great War and the horrors of the Great Depression collide in a nightmarish mindscape of social collapse.

The graveyard at the beginning of the film—with its crooked headstones evoking rows of war graves and its bleakness reflecting the austere mood of the 1930s—sets the scene perfectly. The camera tracks across the faces of mourners at a funeral and there is the sense that their grief might be the grief of a nation. Bizarrely, Whale briefly focuses on a hooded skeleton behind the mourners. Death is literally among them. It is only on a second viewing that we realize that this spectral grim reaper is merely a statue in the graveyard, the symbolism is so overt.

A gravedigger begins to fill in the grave. Whale had placed a microphone inside the grave itself to accentuate the sound as the gravedigger throws in the first shovelful of dirt with a *whump*. James Curtis: "You could hear the whole audience gasp."[27] Whale swiftly follows this visceral jolt with another: as Fritz (Dwight Frye) the hunchbacked assistant cuts down a hanged man from the gallows, the body falling unceremoniously into frame. Whale does not cut away. In 1931, this was strong stuff.

Against this backdrop, Whale could broach taboo subjects allegorically, and the first to be broken was the notion of man playing God, shown in the film as Henry's desire to create life by artificial means. Henry Frankenstein (Colin Clive) represents what many in the 1930s felt about science under capitalism: that it was an instrument of potential destruction and repression harnessed by madmen. Not only had it created weaponry that had led to the greatest death toll in history (World War I), but it had mechanized the workforce, condemning millions to soul-destroying jobs in factories or put people out of work altogether (as it had farmers). And in eugenics there was the science of social engineering, the promise of creating a master race, a race of supermen, which led to the horrors of the Third Reich.

Fritz is charged with the task of procuring a human brain from the nearby medical college, but inadvertently makes off with the "abnormal" brain of a criminal instead of a normal one. The lecture given by Dr. Waldman (Edward Van Sloan) at the start of the scene could have been a key note speech given at the Eugenics Conference in 1932. Waldman compares the abnormal brain with that of a "perfect specimen," noting the "scarcity of convolutions on the frontal lobe" on the abnormal brain: degenerate characteristics which apparently "check amazingly with the case history of the dead man before us, whose life was one of brutality, of violence and murder." In the 1930s eugenicists believed that the primary cause of crime was hereditary; that the majority of criminals were "born criminals," genetically programmed for criminality regardless of their life experience, and that crime could therefore only be eliminated from society by the "extinction of the physically, mentally, and morally unfit."[28] (This, of course, is what Dr. Waldman tries to do in the film when he attempts to euthanize the Monster.)

Henry wishes to create a thing of beauty in the creature ("Where should we be if nobody tries to find out what lies beyond?") but he is doomed to failure from the start. Not because the Monster has accidentally been given the abnormal brain, but because he stops believing in his creation. At first he reasons that the Monster's imbecility is because the brain needs time to develop, but from the moment he discovers from Dr. Waldman that the brain has been taken from a criminal we see him hesitate; the seeds of doubt sown in his mind later grow into his rejection of the Monster, leading to its being cast out, demonized and finally destroyed. Henry's unquestioning acceptance of the eugenicist Dr. Waldman's ideas—that an abnormal brain (a sign of degenerate heredity or "bad genes") creates a life of brutality, violence and murder—are what ultimately seals the Monster's fate. The Monster is predestined to criminality not because of its brain but because of the expectations placed upon it by indoctrinated scientists.

Not only does Henry falter in his scientific beliefs, showing weakness and self-doubt, but his motives for wanting to create life in the first place become questionable when we learn that he has left his fiancée Elizabeth (Mae Clarke) alone in order to pursue his scientific obsession.

"The very day we announced our engagement, he told me of his experiments"

One of the most intriguing aspects of *Frankenstein* concerns Henry's sexuality in relation to his creation of the Monster. It is, as Robin Wood has commented, highly significant that Henry's decision to scientifically create a living man juxtaposes very precisely with his decision to become engaged.[29] Henry's desire to "play God" can be seen as arising from his repressed sexuality: His insane ambition to create life artificially is a sublimation of his repressed sex drive. As already mentioned, homosexuality was highly coded by Hollywood in the 1930s, and we might detect this coding in many elements of the film, including in Clive's performance which has often been described as hysterical. Given Whale's own sexuality, it is not too far-fetched to see the Monster as an outward projection of Henry's repressed homosexuality that seeks redress or recognition from its owner. Henry would rather be working in his laboratory than be with Elizabeth. But when the Monster seeks the acknowledgment of its creator, Henry disowns it. He is unable to overcome his own repression and accept his true nature. In the process of "unleashing his id," however, Henry has inadvertently created a threat to the stability of society that he must destroy; his continuance and that of the social order demands it. "There can be no wedding while this horrible creation of mine is still alive!" he proclaims in despair. "I made him with these hands, and with these hands I'll destroy him!"

There is an implied criticism of Henry in the film: that if he had not repressed his natural urges in the first place, then he would not have sought to sublimate them in the making of the Monster. Likewise, had he recognized and accepted the Monster (as a projection of his own sexuality) rather than disowned it, the Monster would not have gone on the rampage. In this unhealthy sublimation of repressed energies, Henry embodies science under capitalism in the 1930s, which was itself an instrument of societal repression, as eugenics has shown. Eugenicists "played God," but their energies were taken up in oppressing minority groups that were considered a threat to the American way of life.

Of course, Henry is himself a victim of societal repression. Henry created a monster but the social order binds him into a repressive existence as heir to his father, the baron. His continuance as Son of the House of Frankenstein—and hence that of the capitalist system under which he serves (portrayed as a feudal village in the film)—relies on his destroying

The Monster (Boris Karloff) stalks Elizabeth (Mae Clarke) on the day of her wedding in *Frankenstein* (1931).

the Monster that he created. He must repress his own id in order to go through with his marriage.

One of the most famous scenes in *Frankenstein* is also one of the most censored. At the moment Henry gives life to the Monster, his megalomania reaches a peak, verging on insanity. "In the name of God! Now I know what it feels like to be God!" he shouts gleefully. Censors cited the blasphemy laws as reasons for making a cut to this dialogue. However, the purpose of Henry's outburst is to question his right—the right of any scientist, or eugenicist—to play God. This implicit criticism of science under capitalism clearly unsettled the watchdogs of the 1930s—particularly in light of the eugenics movement—and state censorship boards were pressured to cut the scene.

"Here he comes! Turn out the lights!"

Henry disowns the Monster both on the grounds of poor eugenic hygiene (its "criminal" brain) and as a symbolic rejection of his own sexuality. This rejection creates a sense of pathos for the Monster which is timeless; from the Mary Shelley novel onwards, readers and cinema audiences have felt sorry for the Monster because it has been cast out by its maker. Karloff, taking his cue from the novel, also imbued the Monster with a noble soul which belies the hideous exterior and abnormal brain. This heightened sympathy for the Monster struck a particular chord with audiences of the time: *Frankenstein,* like *Freaks,* confronts certain prejudices that were integral to eugenics thinking in the 1930s, particularly with regards to ideas linking criminality and physical appearance.

Perhaps the greatest shock in *Frankenstein* (excluding the drowning of Maria in the lake) occurs when we are first introduced to the Monster. As Karloff shuffles through the watchtower doorway, with his back to the camera, and then slowly turns around to face us—the intention is to emphasize his ghastly face. Whale then uses a series of jump cuts that move in closer to the Monster's features, making the horror bigger and bigger on the screen. The camera thus dwells on Karloff's distinctive facial features (and Jack Pierce's iconic makeup) to create visceral shock; but also to present what eugenicists would recognize as the physiognomy of a criminal. Pierce studied criminology to help him conceptualize the look of the Monster. The Monster's protruding brow was intended to suggest evolutionary regression, as were its large stature, oddly shaped cranium and exposed forehead. Russell D. Covey, writing in *Stanford Law Review*, describes the Monster as "quintessentially Lombrosian," referring to 19th century criminologist Cesare Lombroso, whose ideas were later espoused by the eugenics movement.[30] Lombroso, like the eugenicists who followed, believed that criminality was inherited and that someone "born criminal" could be identified by careful study of their physiognomy. Specific criminals, such as thieves, rapists, and murderers, could be distinguished by specific characteristics, notably a sloping forehead, excessively long arms and asymmetry of the cranium. All of these traits were given to Karloff by Pierce to convey the "look" of a criminal.

Whale, however, immediately undercuts the effect of his introduction of the Monster, sweeping away the initial shock of its appearance with a swiftly developed sense of pathos. According to James Curtis, Whale struggled with the script for *Frankenstein,* which had gone through several drafts and several writers before being assigned to him. The emotional key to the story was given to Whale by his lover, David Lewis, after he read the original novel. "I felt sorry for the goddamn monster," Lewis remarked.[31] Up to then all the screenplay drafts had obscured the sense of pity in Shelley's novel. Whale rewrote the screenplay to inject sympathy for the Monster.

We feel sorry for the Monster almost immediately in the film as Henry orders it to sit in a chair and it meekly obeys. In this scene Whale recasts the Monster from "born criminal" to tabula rasa, a blank or erased slate, from which Henry can nurture learning from scratch. "You see!" Henry says to Waldman. "It understands." But the Monster is not merely an animal that can be conditioned. When Henry opens the shutters to expose the Monster to the light of the sun, he hopes that this will prove to the eugenicist Waldman that the Monster is not degenerate and possesses a higher form of consciousness—and indeed it does. The Monster reveals its *humanity*. He reaches up to the light, towards the Creator, trying, like Henry, to grasp its secrets ("Where should we be if nobody tries to find out what lies beyond?"); and does so with such longing that Henry, for the briefest moment, feels compelled to go to it, before Waldman calls him back.

Whale establishes this sense of humanity in the Monster using hand gestures. He drew on his own experience as an actor to direct Karloff and according to Curtis, "all the gestures the monster did were Whale's."[32] This is not to denigrate Karloff's extraordinary performance, but to illustrate Whale's sympathy with the existential plight of the Monster. Karloff's hands beg enlightenment from his creator ("What am I? why do I exist?") and also the more pointed question "Why did you make me?" To this last question, Henry seems oblivious.

Whale, then, explodes the eugenics belief in the "born criminal" both in this sequence and the one that immediately follows where the Monster's criminality is shown to be learned, not "inherited." In terms of the nature vs. nurture debate, Whale turns eugenics on its head, and he does so quickly and succinctly. In just a few minute of screen time, Karloff's Monster makes the transition from slow-thinking creature into developed criminal; the sadism of Fritz impels the Monster to resort to violence. Despite the compression of these scenes, Whale makes his point clearly and unequivocally: As Curtis remarks, "Fritz's cruelty in torturing him begat cruelty in the monster."[33] Thus Fritz becomes the Monster's first victim, establishing the pattern of justifiable homicide that Whale built into his revised screenplay. Dr. Waldman, the eugenicist, is thus killed after preparing to euthanize the Monster: "We must kill it—like any savage animal!"

The "physiognomy of a criminal": Boris Karloff as the Monster in *Bride of Frankenstein* (1935).

"He's been seen in the hills, terrorizing the countryside!"

In "Recreating the Monster: Frankenstein and Film," Martin Tropp describes Whale's Monster as "a creature from the 1930s, shaped by shadowy forces beyond its control, wandering the countryside like some disfigured veteran or hideous tramp." Tropp claims that "the special pathos of the monster, never really recaptured in most of the later films, is due in part to its affinities with the refugees from political and economic disaster cast out from a society that can find no place for them."[34]

Whale was himself a veteran of the First World War. He had been taken prisoner in 1917 and spent most of the war in a prison camp—an event that probably saved his life. In America, returning veterans suffered disfiguring wounds and psychological trauma as well as devastating flu pandemic brought over from Europe that left 675,000 Americans dead. Whale likely sympathized with the plight of many veterans who, during the Great Depression, found themselves unemployed and homeless despite having served their country. These veterans had been awarded compensation in the form of bonus certificates that they could not redeem until 1945. When the veterans demanded immediate cash payment of their certificates at the height of the Depression in 1931 and '32, they were refused. Forty-three thousand veterans and their families—dubbed the Bonus Army—gathered in Washington, D.C., in the spring and summer of 1932 and set up a camp in Anacostia Park. Their protest was met with military action. Attorney General William D. Mitchell ordered the veterans to be removed from government property. Washington police fired on the veterans, killing two. President Hoover then ordered the army to clear the veterans' campsite. The Bonus Army, along with their wives and children, were driven out and their shelters and their belongings burned. The burning-down of these "Hoovervilles" is reminiscent of the Monster being burned alive in the windmill at the end of *Frankenstein*. The Bonus Army uprising, however, began a period of labor unrest in America that continued through the Depression.

Throughout *Frankenstein*, the Monster becomes increasingly identified iconographically with all those that 1930s society sought to demonize, persecute and oppress, most notably veterans ("unionized troublemakers"), organized labor ("communists"), unemployed homeless men ("vagrants") and homosexuals ("sexual deviants"). This can surely be no accident. The physiognomy of the Monster, as already noted, was consciously based on that of the "born criminal." The creature might also represent the disfigured and persecuted war veteran, as Martin Tropp suggested. Like Pierce's makeup, Karloff's costume in the film has iconographic meaning: Robin Wood comments, "Frankenstein could have dressed his creature in top hat, white tie and tails, but in fact chose laborer's clothes."[35] The Monster's work clothes and asphalt-spreader's boots graphically represent its lower-class origins. In fact, references to class pervade the film.

The Monster's status as working class outsider is emphasized by the juxtaposition of scenes that show it wandering the countryside like a homeless drifter in the Great Depression, while Henry is welcomed back into the bosom of his upper class family. After the baron (Frederick Kerr) raises a glass to "the Son of the House of Frankenstein," Whale cuts to a shot of Henry, guilt-ridden: he has already created a "son"—and cast him out. Whale includes some wry observations about class, especially in the character of the baron, who can barely conceal his contempt for those under his rule. He orders his servants be given champagne for the wedding toast because the finest wine is "wasted on 'em." And for the villagers who gather in celebration of Henry's wedding, there is beer. "It's extraordinary how friendly you can make people on a couple of bottles of beer," the baron laughs. "And tomorrow they'll all be fighting!" Whale, the working class boy from Dudley, England, cannot resist such asides and clearly relished these scenes, which suggest both the baron's hypocritical lack of social responsibility and the easy co-option of his villager subjects. "Thank you all very much for coming. I'm very pleased to see you all," he condescends to them from his balcony, and in a gesture of *noblesse oblige* promises them plenty more beer.

The persecution of the monster is a theme that Whale went on to develop further in his sequel *Bride of Frankenstein* (1935), culminating in the infamous crucifixion scene, when the Monster's

The Monster (Boris Karloff), dressed in laborer's clothes, makes an entrance in *Frankenstein* (1931).

suffering is given Christ-like significance. The theme is, however, instigated in *Frankenstein* in the equally unforgettable (and taboo-breaking) scene where the Monster encounters and accidentally drowns a child. This action and the ensuing persecution of the Monster by the vigilante mob ties together allegorically the persecuted outsider role of the Monster with a series of moral panics in the 1930s which created in the public mind the image of the "sexual psychopath." These sex crime panics linked unemployed homeless men and homosexuals in particular to incidents of child molestation. Gay men especially suffered persecution as a result of ensuing laws which criminalized homosexuality within the broader category of violent crimes, associating homosexuality with child molestation in the public mind.

"Who are you? I'm Maria. Will you play with me?"

According to historian Estelle B. Freedman, Fritz Lang's 1931 film *M* began the public discussion of sex crimes and a growing popular interest in stories of violent, sexual murders upon which the American media seized, fueling a moral panic that soon extended into the realms of politics and law. Whether Whale saw *M*, we don't know, but the similarities between Lang's film and *Frankenstein* are marked: Both feature a pathetic, socially ostracized "monster" that preys upon children and is persecuted by a vigilante mob whose violence equals, if not exceeds, that of the monster. Freedman claims that a close look at the sex crimes panics of the 1930s reveals that these episodes were not necessarily related to any increase in the *actual* incidence of violent, sexually related crimes, but were symptomatic of a wider moral conservative backlash ushered in by the Great Depression.[36]

Concerns about sexuality had entered into discussions about migrant labor and homelessness as the Depression deepened. At the same time, criminologists became increasingly interested in sexual abnormality and male sex crime. The male deviant became the subject of particular attention, focusing on the homosexual and the psychopath. Both types of "deviant" were thought to attack children. From the origin of the concept, the psychopath had been perceived as a drifter, an unemployed man living on the boundaries of society and lacking family. Like the Peter Lorre character in *M*, the psychopath could represent the threat of anarchy, of the individual unbound by social rules. Likewise, sociological studies such as *Twenty-Thousand Homeless Men: A Study of Unemployed Men in Chicago Shelters* suggested that the underlying cause of men's unemployment was a lack of normal sexual experiences with women. These studies began finding their way into legislation, creating a whole new set of crimes on sexual deviancy: The "sexual psychopath" was born—an amalgamation of drifter, homosexual and child molester. These sex crime laws, Freedman suggests, were really aimed at curbing the non-conforming individual, by allowing the regulation of much less serious but socially disturbing behaviors such as vagrancy and homosexual practices.

The notion in horror films of the misunderstood monster may well have originated in *Frankenstein*. Certainly in the scene of Maria and the Monster, Whale blows open the taboo of the 1930s sex crimes moral panic by revealing his "sexual psychopath" monster as misjudged, improperly labeled, unfairly accused and unjustly punished. Indeed, this scene— where the Monster, through its naïveté, inadvertently drowns a child—is in many ways the crux of Whale's *Frankenstein*. Whale appears to have known this in 1931 when he made the film. When, after the disastrous preview in Santa Barbara, Universal executives wanted to trim the scene, it was the revision he fought against the most. David Lewis: "They wanted

The Monster (Boris Karloff) encounters little Maria (Marilyn Harris) by the lake in *Frankenstein* **(1931). Censor cuts to this scene grossly distorted its meaning.**

to end the scene before the drowning. Without it the audience was left to imagine what he had done to her before he drowned her. The implication with the cut was that he had raped her."[37] Whale won his argument and the scene was kept in its entirety. It is clear why Whale fought to keep it: Without it, the audience's perception of the Monster is completely reversed and the viewer loses all sympathy for its plight. A cut to the scene changes everything.

State censors in Massachusetts, New York and Pennsylvania trimmed the scene anyway, undermining Whale. Worse still, when the film was reissued in 1938, the scene was removed from the negative under the stricter dictates of the Production Code Administration and remained lost until 1985, when its partial restoration was made possible by the discovery of a trim from the original release.[38] Fortunately, this restoration includes enough of the Monster's reaction to Maria's drowning so that we understand his bewilderment, his innocent belief that she would float like the flowers. But for fifty years *Frankenstein* was a travesty of Whale's original. It is difficult to think of another film whose essential message was so grossly distorted by such a small change. As Scott MacQueen comments, "Censor cuts in Frankenstein perverted the poignant encounter with the little girl into an act of pedophilic depravity."[39]

MacQueen hits the nail on the head. By censoring *Frankenstein* in this way, the powers that be were able to reverse Whale's subversion of dominant ideology, so that *Frankenstein* appeared to uphold the status quo rather than challenge it. Those changes completely alter audiences' understanding of the Monster. A look at the trailer for the reissue shows how the audience were positioned to see the Monster differently in 1938: It depicts Karloff's creature only in the context of a rampaging beast, and the narrator's voice reinforces the "sexual psychopath" image of the creature: "It strikes terror into the hearts of men; shocks women into uncontrolled hysteria; preys on the innocence of children." The trailer begins and ends with the vigilante mob pursuing the Monster, and we are left in no doubt that it will receive its just deserts.

How did James Whale feel, knowing that the essential meaning of his film had been thus perverted? In his biography, James Curtis describes an episode near the end of Whale's life in 1956, where he was seized by despair at what he had "created" in *Frankenstein*. As recalled by Whale's friend Dlady Lacey to James Curtis:

> "I remember one day he said he'd had a good look at himself in the mirror," said Dlady Lacey, "and realized he had created Frankenstein and it had become a nightmare to him. That he had launched this horror onto the world and he couldn't stop it. He said, 'I looked at myself in the mirror and I suddenly realized what I'd done.'"[40]

That James Whale blamed himself for the fear and revulsion associated with *Frankenstein*, when he had fought to retain sympathy for the plight of the Monster, arguing for tolerance in an era of persecution, is tragic. By 1938, homosexuals were being routinely persecuted under new laws. Police round-ups of "perverts" became common. The targets of the crackdowns were often minor offenders. In Inglewood, California, not far from where Whale lived, a mob threatened lynching while the police sought the murderers of three local girls. And Whale knew not to frequent the gay bars of Hollywood as customers were routinely harassed by the police, and often beaten up and arrested.

Whale had moved on from the horror genre by then. But even in a liberal town like Hollywood, things had taken a decidedly conservative turn on moral issues in the late 1930s. Regarded by studio executives and censors as a non-conformist, his card was already marked.

* * *

It is both fitting and ironic that Tod Browning and James Whale should share in their films a common theme of the plight of the outsider. Both directors suffered later in their careers as Hollywood films became more conservative in the 1940s. Both felt increasingly ostracized by the censors, and were eventually elbowed out of the film business; forced into early retirement after falling out of favor with the studios following a series of box office flops.

Browning went from *Freaks* to *Fast Workers*. His much-cherished, never-to-be-realized ambition was to make a film adaptation of Horace McCoy's caustic 1933 novel *They Shoot Horses, Don't They?* It is clear to see the transition that Browning was trying to make—away from horror films to social dramas that reflected the despair of the Great Depression.

However, *Freaks* and *Fast Workers* were both box-office disasters (none of Browning's subsequent films managed to turn a profit) which forced Browning to remain within the horror genre with *Mark of the Vampire* (1935) and *The Devil-Doll* (1936)—neither of them bad films but both lacking the social criticism of his previous films. Browning was trying to play it safe, and for good reason: *Freaks* had been made a scapegoat by moral reformers and critics of the Hays Code, leading to Joseph Breen's strict enforcement of the Code in 1934. Even so, Browning was considered a risk following *Freaks* and soon was unable to get any further projects green lit. After *Miracles for Sale* (1939) he never made another film. He felt he had been "blackballed" by Hollywood, largely due to the controversy of *Freaks*.[41] His subsequent complete and utter rejection of cinema reflects the bitterness of a man excluded from his profession because of his political beliefs. "When I quit a thing, I quit," he is quoted as saying at the time of his "retirement" from filmmaking in the early 1940s. "I wouldn't walk across the street now to see a movie."[42]

Freaks had been taken off screens shortly after release. MGM had pulled it from a fairly successful New York engagement, deciding it was too much of a public relations problem. It would not be rediscovered until the 1960s—the era of Vietnam—where it would be seen, in the words of David J. Skal, as a countercultural text by a "profoundly alienated generation."[43]

After *Frankenstein*, James Whale made *The Old Dark House* (1932), *The Invisible Man* (1933) and *Bride of Frankenstein* (1935) before directing the highly respected musical *Showboat* (1936). When Junior Laemmle left Universal in 1936, however, Whale lost his champion at the studio. Charles Rogers' arrival, following the studio's takeover by a corporate investor, ushered in a more conservative regime. After 1936's *Dracula's Daughter*, which Whale had been attached to direct at one point, Rogers ceased production of horror films entirely.

During his time as a freelancer after his contract ended with Universal, Whale made a series of box office failures. His openly homosexual lifestyle was not appreciated by all—especially in the late 1930s. Some were discriminatory towards him (such as Columbia studio boss Harry Cohn). Big-name actors were liable, according to James Curtis, to veto him. When he returned to Universal in 1938, he was offered only "B" pictures.[44]

A new agent, Phil Berg (who also represented Tod Browning in the 1920s), got him an "A" project in *The Man in the Iron Mask* (1939) but he was eventually fired after going over budget. Curtis describes the experience for Whale as "artistically unsatisfying and professionally humiliating" and it contributed to driving him out of the industry.[45] *Green Hell* (1940) was a disaster (his seventh in a row). Finally Harry Cohn fired him from *They Dare Not Love* (1941). Whale spent the rest of his life in retirement, painting, before committing suicide following a stroke in 1957, at the age of 67.

By the late 1930s the eugenics movement had faded in popularity largely due to Hitler's rise to power in Germany. In 1939, the ERO was closed, the fate of the movement sealed by knowledge of the horrors of the Nazi application of eugenics.

It is now a part of American history that many would, perhaps, prefer to forget.

2

ANTI–1940s HOME FRONT PROPAGANDA
Cat People (1942) and *The Curse of the Cat People* (1944)

Writing in 1979, Robin Wood commented that Val Lewton's films of the 1940s were outside the mainstream development of the horror film in that they undermined the notion, prevalent in other films of the period, of horror being foreign and of the monster as being invariably male and phallic. In the Lewton film, by contrast, horror is firmly identified as American, and female sexual repression is externalized as the "other." In these ways, Lewton's films, according to Wood, "strikingly anticipate, by at least two decades, some of the features of modern horror film."[1]

The mainstream horror film of the 1940s had, in fact, entered a period of relative stagnation, brought about, partly, by an increase in censorship and a moral backlash against the genre. The Production Code Administration, through active campaigning and dissuasion, had succeeded in deterring studios from horror production by 1936. After Universal took horror films off its schedule that year, other studios followed. By the time production resumed in 1939 with *Son of Frankenstein*, the classic period was in effect over. Hollywood had changed, the production teams were different, Breen's Production Code Administration had tightened up practice: The films being produced were "safe." Ideologically, the Universal films of the 1940s reflect the moral conservatism of the war years.

By far the most popular saga of 1940s mainstream horror was that of *The Wolf Man* (1941), a franchise which spanned four films and lasted America's entire involvement with the war, from Pearl Harbor to the bombing of Hiroshima in 1945; according to David J. Skal, popular culture in the 1940s during World War II became fascinated by "the wolf"— the werewolf, the beast that must be defeated. "The wolf is an ancient symbol, deeply linked to militarism and the battlefield," writes Skal, "with special meanings in Norse and Teutonic mythology."[2] Skal comments that Hitler himself took pride in his name which meant "noble wolf," and was fascinated by lycanthropy. Moreover, in Larry Talbot (the eponymous Wolf Man of the films) and his continuing quest to put to rest his wolf-self, Skal recognizes an "unconscious parable of the war effort."[3] The winning of the war becomes equated, in other words, with the vanquishing of the beast within, the inherent violence within man. At a time when news images from the war were censored ("[T]he bestial realities of war came as a shock to untold numbers of servicemen," as Skal notes, "but a widespread recognition of the inhuman conditions of the battlefield was systematically suppressed"[4]) the Wolf Man films (along with combat films of the period) constitute the "official" depictions of the front: albeit, in the case of the Wolf Man, with the battlefield represented as the battleground of the soul, of the evil that must be defeated within.

The famous motto from *The Wolf Man* (invented by scriptwriter Curt Siodmak and passed off as a traditional folk saying)—"Even a man who is pure in heart and says his prayers by night, may become a wolf when the wolfbane blooms and the autumn moon is bright"— in many ways echoes the propaganda issued by the Office of War Information, which focused on duty, tradition and patriotism. The values of courage, optimism and patriotism are necessary to defeat the evil that lives in all men. Lewton's films, by contrast, can be seen to represent the home front rather than the battleground. Moreover, the atmosphere of grief, anxiety and often deep pessimism that pervades his films stands starkly at odds with the official line. As Martin Scorsese has said of Lewton, "He was one of the only filmmakers who looked directly at the sadness of the home front."[5]

Lewton's films are an exception to the moral conservatism of the wartime horror of *The Wolf Man*, particularly in terms of their gender politics which challenge the idealized version of the American woman as promoted by the home front propaganda of the time. Lewton's female protagonists are outcasts in a society struggling to reconcile female sexuality, femininity and changing women's roles during wartime. The patriotic values embodied by the cultural icon, Rosie the Riveter, are replaced in Lewton's films by the often suicidal grief and anxiety of his demonized-by-the-patriarchy heroines. By way of consolidating these themes, his later Karloff films, in their portrayal of male authoritarianism as being potentially homicidal, tyrannical and insane, emphasize the urgent need for the reconciliation of the feminine within the culture and the self.

In standing outside mainstream horror, Lewton's films not only anticipate the modern horror film of the late 1960s and 1970s, as Wood observes, but also provide continuity between the films of that period and those of James Whale and Tod Browning in the 1930s (as discussed in the previous chapter). The misfit-outcast theme that Edmund G. Bansak identifies in Lewton's work directly connects the RKO films to the work of Whale and Browning: Lewton makes strong use of the theme of rejection in almost all of his horror films and his misfits, as Bansak says, "often have more humanity than their persecutors, the 'well-adjusted.'"[6]

Closely linked to this sympathy with the outsider is the theme of repressed sexuality, with the emphasis being on the horror of repressing sexuality (in Lewton's films, repressing female sexuality) as opposed to the horror of sexuality itself; and the negative portrayal of authority as oppressive and paranoid (in Lewton's films, authority figures are often the greatest threats). This, of course, links back to the 1930s horror film where, as Peter Hutchings puts it, "it's often quite hard to find many straightforwardly attractive or positive authority figures"[7]; and also anticipates the overtly "anti-authority" stance of Wood's modern horror film of the late 1960s and 1970s.

Finally, Lewton's films anticipate the later period in their desire the show us the horrors perpetuated by society—horror is seen to be stemming from man himself, from man's personality. Therefore, there is an emphasis in Lewton's films on psychological horror (or perhaps more accurately "psycho-social" horror) where the supernatural element remains always ambiguous.

Val Lewton—A "Man in the Shadows"?

In hiring Lewton to head RKO's B horror unit, studio bosses, in 1942, were clearly hoping to emulate the horror success of Universal in the 1920s and 1930s under Irving Thalberg and later Carl Laemmle, Jr. Like Thalberg, Lewton was a supervising producer well-versed in all aspects of the production process, able to supervise everything from casting to set design, costumes to direction. What, perhaps, places Lewton apart from even those great producers, however, is that he was first and foremost a writer, a published novelist, and, as Joel Siegel attests, "contributed a great deal to the screenplays of his films,"[8] from the original storylines which were often his, through the various drafts and revisions; and, crucially, he always wrote the final shooting script himself. Very few producers can be called the *auteur* of their films in the way that Lewton can, not only in the sense of having control over the content of the films but also in terms of imbuing them with an artist's personal preoccupations, an artist's personality and soul. That is not to underestimate the contribution of his collaborators—in particular director Jacques Tourneur—but investigation into Lewton's background, his life and times, reveals a remarkable synergy between the man, his work and the culture in which he lived. One can argue the same for many of the *directors* in this book, but as a *producer*, Lewton is in some ways unique. He provides the unifying factor for the RKO films and it stems from his own personal traumas, his own troubled psyche and own fractured sense of identity. Understanding Lewton's psyche helps us to understand the national psyche in the war years of the 1940s.

Lewton vs. Leveton

He was born Vladimir Leveton in 1904 in Yalta in the Ukraine. His father, according to most sources, was a "dashing, but irresponsible army officer" and "a gambler."[9] His mother Nina, an educated woman, took Val and his sisters and fled the country for America when Val was five years old; they eventually settled in Hollywood. (Lewton's aunt was Alla Nazimova, a stage actress who had become one of the great stars, producers and screenwriters of the silent era; Nina would also become successful as one of the first women story editors in America.) Lewton's mother took great pains to erase his sense of origin. She Americanized his name, re-baptized him and forbade him to speak Russian. He never saw his father again, and reputedly never knew his father's correct name of Hofschneider. Val was brought up by his mother and aunt, two powerful but dominant women, without a male role model, and became something of a dreamer and a difficult child. According to Lewton's son Val E. Lewton, "There was some strange interaction going on"[10] between Lewton and his mother. When Lewton began "acting up," he was sent to military school because "he needed a man's hand."[11] One might expect such a young man to wholeheartedly embrace the military ethic but he left the academy after failing to excel, and embarked on a writing career as a reporter and novelist.

This childhood experience seems to have marked him in a number of ways: As a man he was, according to Greg Mank, "a masterpiece of contradictions: a sensitive poet with a macho Hemingway complex."[12] He also developed a lifelong anxiety neurosis: a fear of darkness and despair, and a desire for death. In Jungian terms we might see in Lewton a struggling for reconciliation with the feminine, a need to assimilate his "anima," as evidenced by his troubled relationship with his mother, his subsequent rebellion, his marrying at an early age and his fractious relationship with his daughter whom he named after his mother.

Whether Lewton was conscious of this in himself or not, it is a struggle that finds expression in his work: in the endless mirroring of characters, the light-shadow visuals that speak of the hidden self (the Jungian "Shadow") and the tormented protagonists with their divided psyches. Certainly, it is a struggle emblematic of the culture of the time, which is what made Lewton's films so insightful and resonant: masculine-feminine values were in flux during World War II, leading to a crisis of identity for men and women on an individual, collective and national level. Was Lewton aware of Jungian psychology? It seems highly likely given the presence of psychoanalysis in his films. Jacques Tourneur, in any case, had knowledge of it, passed on to him by his father, Maurice. Both *Cat People* and *The Curse of the Cat People* hinge on it.

Shock Value in *Cat People* (1942)

Val Lewton's films are celebrated for their use of atmosphere and suggestion in place of graphic horror; however, the term "shock," when used in relation to Lewton, has generally come to mean the "Lewton Bus," a technique said to have been invented by Lewton and his editor, Mark Robson, to give the viewer a jolt, a purely visceral shock. Nowadays, it is an overly familiar technique: The viewer, even on an unconscious level, is usually aware that a Lewton Bus is coming; in 1942, by all accounts, the audience was not aware and the effect was sensational. It is difficult to determine to what extent that one moment in *Cat People* where Alice is pursued through the darkened streets by Irena—with its surprising and unexpected intrusion of the bus into the frame—contributed to the success of the film with audiences; however, the notoriety of that particular scene often overshadows the quieter, more gradual emotional and "moral" shocks in Lewton's work. I am thinking particularly of Dr. Judd's planned seduction of his patient Irena in *Cat People*; of the spanking that Oliver administers to his "dreamer" daughter Amy, while Alice and the teacher Miss Callahan linger uncomfortably in the living room below in *The Curse of the Cat People*; of Jacqueline losing the will to live and committing suicide in the final scene of 1943's *The Seventh Victim* (with no optimistic coda to end the film). Perhaps the greatest shock of all in Lewton's work, however, is the overwhelming grief, anxiety and pessimism of his female protagonists—emotions that must have been mirrored to a certain extent by the audience, given the success of the films.

Lewton's films were conceived partly as women's pictures in that they are clearly designed to appeal to the women audience in the 1940s. This was, of course, a commercial decision on the part of Lewton and RKO: With a significant number of the male population leaving for war after 1941, and an increasing number of women entering the workplace to fill in for them, Hollywood targeted the burgeoning female audience with melodramas that often dramatized the guilt and confusion that many working women felt regarding their new roles. As Annette Kuhn notes: "The 1940s woman's picture, in a key moment in women's twentieth-century history, enacts and constructs a struggle between female independence on the one hand and desire for security in home and family on the other."[13]

Greg Mank defines *Cat People* as a "sex melodrama in horror movie clothing,"[14] and Lewton's own view of his films seems to substantiate this definition of his work:

> Take a sweet love story, or a story of sexual antagonisms, about people like the rest of us, not freaks, and cut in your horror here and there by suggestion, and you've got something.[15]

This perhaps lends a greater undercurrent to the stalking scene in *Cat People* than one might think. Back in 1942, Alice's fears may have become the audience's fears in a different way: as a coded expression of the feelings of guilt and confusion accompanying the shift in gender roles during the war; feelings that were often exacerbated by the home front propaganda of the time.

Betty Grable Meets Rosie the Riveter Meets the Victory Girl

Messages about femininity, female sexuality and women's roles given out by the Office of War Information in their propaganda campaigns of the 1940s were somewhat mixed. Despite the necessity to pull women into the workforce in order to take over jobs traditionally occupied by men, the war was in many ways seen as a threat to women's traditional roles; hostility to working women carried over from the days of the Great Depression. The government weighed pressures to bring women into the labor force against the need to preserve familial roles and commitments, as well as against the possibility, according to Alice Kessler-Harris, "that women workers would develop self-images independent of the family."[16] The propaganda of the early 1940s shows the government, therefore, attempting both to attract women to the war service while insisting their identities remain rooted in home and motherhood. Women war workers were depicted in magazines and films as working only for the duration of the war effort—they would return full time to the home afterwards. The motive for women to go to work was promoted in terms of "bringing your men back earlier." Home front war propaganda thus stressed that the shift in gender roles was temporary and necessary only in as much as it would help things return to normal sooner.

The patriotic woman worker, doing her bit for the war effort, was iconized in pop culture by the character of Rosie the Riveter, with her sleeves-rolled-up, muscles-flexed message: "We Can Do It!"[17] However, in reality, Rosie's courage, optimism and patriotism would have been countered by the strain of trying to combine motherhood with full-time war work, by hardship and rationing, and by the psychological pressure of having sons, husbands and brothers drafted overseas and not knowing whether they would return. Expressing the grief, anxiety and sense of loss that arose from this was considered unpatriotic. Instead women were encouraged to put on a happy face, make sacrifices and bravely endure the hardships of war, much as Claudette Colbert does in David O. Selznick's *Since You Went Away* (1944). In that film, Colbert goes from being a lost housewife to a woman with inner strength able to inspire similar courage in others. (In many ways, Lewton's *The Curse of the Cat People* can be seen as a riposte to Selznick's film, especially to its Christmas scene that brings joy and hope to Colbert as she receives a gift from her husband who had been previously thought missing in action; her patriotic duty thus rewarded, she can now go back to being a normal housewife on her husband's return. Things can go back to how they were before the war. In Lewton's vision, only a fundamental shift in the family dynamic offers hope.)

Music of the war period dwelled on themes of love, loneliness and separation: Women were told to "keep the home fires burning" because *they* were what men were fighting for. Betty Grable, the beautiful girl-next-door, became the poster girl of the armed forces; women were pressured to stay beautiful and glamorous for their men. An idealized version of the American woman began to emerge, one that emphasized her relative freedom, affluence and glamor, but also her courage and devotion to family and country. This became the constructed national identity in terms of womanhood in the 1940s, and what women were expected to be.

At the same time, universal fears of losing control of female sexuality led to a double standard, particularly in the armed services. The public had never accepted women in the military, and women who joined up in patriotic fervor risked their reputations, and in some cases suffered sexual harassment. Many women in the military became the victims of slander and gossip campaigns, were accused of being "camp followers" and prostitutes, or faced charges of lesbianism. Wartime also saw the rise of the "victory girl" (a woman who sought the company of soldiers), which led to concerns of the spread of venereal disease among troops. It was seen as a form of misguided patriotism; 1940s literature portrayed the victory girl as a single young woman and part of the problem of female "sex delinquency" (see Chapter 3), although studies suggest, conversely, that many victory girls were young married women "testing the perimeters of social freedom" afforded by the shifting gender roles.[18]

All in all, the home front propaganda of the 1940s belies a society struggling to reconcile femininity, female sexuality and female independence. The conflicting, sometime contradictory and hypocritical messages given by the media in terms of gender ideology contributed to a correspondingly conflicted sense of identity for women in wartime. In Lewton's films, we can see this in the "divided selves" of the women characters. Alice (played by Jane Randolph) in *Cat People* is in many ways the quintessential American woman of 1940s propaganda myth: hard-working, perky, patriotic (she is doing her bit for the war effort by working as a naval draftsman), a modern career woman (but willing to give up her career for family life). However, Irena (Simone Simon) is her doppelganger, her Jungian "Shadow" whom she vainly tries to repress, and who returns seeking assimilation. Irena is hidden within the darkness of Alice's psyche, waiting to pounce.

Hidden Selves and Divided Selves in *Cat People* and *The Curse of the Cat People*

There is the sense that Lewton moved beyond the horror genre with the *Cat People* films because of his identification with the "monster." Irena is a symbol of repressed sexuality and oppressed womanhood, an outcast from a hypocritical society.

In his book on Lewton, J.P. Telotte makes the point that Lewton's films lack a clearly externalized "other" in the usual sense ("[W]e find none of the zombies or leopard men the titles promise, and nothing as visually satisfying or iconic as Universal's Frankenstein's monster"[19]). By vacating that otherness, though, Lewton's films, as Telotte explains, are able to reveal that in essence we are "they": "that the otherness we fear actually resides within, although it goes denied or unperceived in the welter of daily life."[20] Our real fears, consequently, are shown to be of this hidden portion of the self that threatens the "normal" being which we show to the world in our efforts "to remain in harmony with its formidable appearance of normalcy."[21] According to Telotte, this "hidden portion of the self" is symbolized in the recurrent shadow imagery of Lewton's films which renders a sense of absence, an absence that is "lodged at the center of the self."[22]

In *Cat People* and *The Curse of the Cat People*, that "hidden portion of the self" is closely tied into issues of repressed female sexuality and repressed femininity. This applies not only to the female protagonists Irena, Alice and Amy (Ann Carter), but also to the principal male, Oliver (Kent Smith), who—like Lewton and the rest of the American nation in the 1940s—struggles to reconcile the feminine (the "anima") within his own psyche. Not only is this portion of Oliver's self "hidden," but his psyche is divided, his anima projected on to Irena as "other." Consequently, for Oliver, female sexuality—and therefore femininity itself— is a taboo subject, as it was for most of America at the time.

"You're Irena, you're here in America, you're so normal you're even in love with me, Oliver Reed, a good plain Americano!"

We can see in his comments about *Cat People* that Lewton wanted the film to work as a psychological drama. "Just substitute either insanity or a social disease for Irena's mad beliefs and you'll see that the story still stands up," he wrote.[23] Irena's "mad beliefs," in fact, are closely bound up with sexual repression, stemming from her Old World upbringing: Her family's superstitious bid to control her sexuality. Lewton had originally intended the story to begin with the arrival of German Panzer tanks at Irena's Serbian village, causing an exodus and thus explaining that Irena fled to America and freedom. She therefore arrives in New York still believing herself suffering from the family curse, but sensing the possibility of escaping it, as she escaped the village, and becoming "normal." Assimilation becomes the possible means of escape from the curse. At first her foreign-ness, her strangeness, proves to be an obstacle to that assimilation, until she meets Oliver, the "Americano," who is attracted to her feminine mystique which represents the hidden part of him. Jung might have been speaking of Irena, in 1925, when he wrote in his essay "Marriage as a Psychological Relationship" that "there are certain types of women who seem by nature to attract anima projections."[24]

Oliver can be seen, in the words of psychotherapists Lyn Davis Genelli and Tom Genelli, as an "undeveloped male" who eventually becomes oppressive because he cannot respond to, or recognize within himself, "the animal, the erotic, the feminine,"[25] and therefore he is

Oliver Reed (Kent Smith) finds himself irresistibly drawn to the enigmatic Irena Dubrovna (Simone Simon) in *Cat People* (1942) (photograph courtesy Ronald V. Borst/Hollywood Movie Posters).

driven to repudiate it and stamp it out. Oliver is a masculine male, decent, patriotic (he too is a naval draftsman); like Alice, he is an emblem of wartime gender ideology, an epitome of American manhood. Therefore, Oliver will become torn between his desire to remain "normal" and his need to reconcile with his hidden self that he has denied up until meeting Irena. When he explains his fascination with Irena to Alice, he might be talking of his own anima: "I'm drawn to her. There's a warmth from her that pulls at me. I have to watch her when she's in the room. I have to touch her when she's near. But I don't really know her. In many ways, we're strangers." Oliver and his anima are strangers too but she pulls at him in much the same way as Irena does. Essentially, *Cat People* and *The Curse of the Cat People* are about Oliver's journey towards reconciliation with the "spirit" of Irena and what she represents. By showing the social pressures on Oliver and Alice to remain their normal divided selves, however, Lewton maintains our sympathy for them, despite Oliver's growing authoritarianism and their eventual demonizing of Irena on the basis of her difference.

"Moia sestra?"

There are, of course, other ways to interpret Irena's "curse." Some critics have detected undertones of lesbianism in the film, and have taken the cause of Irena's madness as her repression of her own bisexuality. This was, in fact, a common reading of the film back in 1942, and Greg Mank tells the story of how Lewton received a letter "congratulating him on the lesbian subtext"[26] in the scene where the mysterious Elizabeth Russell character greets Irena as "sister" in the Serbian restaurant. From Lewton's reported reaction, it seems the subtext was not intended, at least not by him (the screenwriter DeWitt Bodeen maintains that *he* wrote it in deliberately), but it is a valid interpretation in the sense that sisterhood is a motif in *Cat People* (and in Lewton's later work) that makes its appearance at this stage in the film. The Russell character is a kindred spirit: something developed in *The Curse of the Cat People* where Lewton again cast Russell as a fellow outcast to Irena. In *Cat People,* the sisterhood of Irena and Russell's mysterious Serbian "cat woman" is further symbolized by dubbing Simone Simon's voice over Russell's part.

From this point in the film, a wider "double" motif is developed. In the restaurant scene, after shunning the fellow Serbian, Irena turns to Alice for acceptance. It is clear that Irena wants to be "akin" to Alice, the American woman, and not the mysterious Serbian. She seeks assimilation into the American culture. However the tragedy that follows—Irena's eventual rejection by Oliver and Alice on the basis of her difference—is foreshadowed by the whispered comments of Oliver's workmates about Irena being pretty and nice but "a bit odd." Alice and Irena are, in essence, two parts of a divided self—Alice is the embodiment of the American womanhood that Irena pursues (literally in the stalking sequences) but cannot assimilate into; and Irena is the hidden self that Alice, in turn, cannot reconcile. Alice recognizes in Irena the "absence" lodged at the center of her own self, her own unexpressed grief and anxiety, her own suppressed insecurity.

Alexander Nemerov has written of Lewton's films as "icons of grief" crystallizing the sorrow and worry of the home front experience, expressing emotions that were at odds with the official insistence on courage, optimism and patriotism.[27] In the Alice-Irena dichotomy, we can see the woman's conflicted home front experience crystallized and this gives extra resonance to the stalking scenes in *Cat People*: Alice, the working woman, guilt-ridden and suppressing her anxiety as she makes her way home—how many women must have felt that

Alice Moore (Jane Randolph, right, with Mary Halsey) discovers her towel shredded in the famous swimming pool scene of *Cat People* (1942) (photograph courtesy Ronald V. Borst/Hollywood Movie Posters).

way, in 1942, as they struggled during the war effort, feeling torn between home and workplace, so that even public transport came to symbolize dread?

The "dark sister" motif, later developed in *The Seventh Victim*, is expressed in the guilt and fear of reprisal that Alice feels after encouraging Oliver to spurn Irena because she is different. Alice understands that Irena can never assimilate into American culture and feels sorry for her because of this, but she also wants Oliver for herself. Alice's growing belief that she is being stalked by Irena as a panther is itself a sign of neurosis.

"These things are very simple to psychiatrists"

> Even as fog continues to lie in the valleys, so does ancient sin cling to the low places, the depressions in the world consciousness.

Cat People's opening quote, attributed to Dr. Judd (Tom Conway) in the film, in fact came from Freud, according to Greg Mank.[28] It is typical that the good doctor should try to pass the quote off as his own! Psychoanalysis became a popular staple of 1940s cinema in the film noir and the women's picture, as wartime neurosis was high in the public consciousness. Guilt and neurosis are typically Freudian concepts and it is fitting that Lewton should portray psychiatry, in the time of war, with suspicion. In *Cat People*, Dr. Judd becomes a figure of distrustful authority. In his dealings with Irena, he shows himself increasingly arrogant, vain and predatory. He manipulates Oliver into placing Irena in his care, so that he can seduce her, and in so doing, abuses his position of trust. (We can see Dr. Judd as Oliver's shadow, a projection of Oliver's suppressed predatory urges. Oliver, for his part, seems unaware of his own aggression towards Irena in triggering her jealousy.)

Judd sees his own bestial nature in Irena, and interprets her metamorphosis-neurosis in purely aggressive terms. He doesn't understand that she would be willing to sacrifice her own life for the sake of Oliver and Alice's safety. When he describes the panther that Irena visits in the zoo as an "instrument of death," he means it as a weapon that Irena would use against others with aggression, rather than as a weapon she would use against herself in desperation. Moreover, he seeks to control her sexuality, as her family had. He is oppressively patriarchal and, therefore, Irena is compelled to repudiate his authority as a psychiatrist. He cannot help her, she tells him, because her problems lie in her soul, not in her mind.

In portraying Dr. Judd this way, Lewton shows psychoanalysis as being used to perpetuate repression, rather than to liberate it. Ultimately, it is Dr. Judd who prompts Oliver and Alice to reject Irena, to cast her out as "other," by playing to their need for normalcy. Why did Lewton choose to show psychoanalysis in such a negative light? Was he trying to warn us of the dangers of psychiatry as it was in the 1940s? Or was it the representation of psychoanalysis in cinema that he took issue with? It is difficult to say for sure; however, in *The Desire to Desire*, her study of the woman's film of the 1940s, Mary Ann Doane concludes that in many films of the era, "psychoanalysis is used very explicitly to reinforce a status quo of sexual difference."[29] Clearly not what Lewton had in mind in *Cat People*.

"I know it was Irena who called. She could call from downstairs. She may be on her way up now!"

As *Cat People* unspools, Irena's position becomes increasingly hopeless: Her attempts to find a psychiatric cure fail, and, meanwhile, she becomes estranged from her husband who rejects her in favor of a "normal" American woman. It suddenly becomes clear to her that her true curse is to be excluded from the society she longs to be part of: a society that inevitably demonizes her as the "other." The sequence in which Irena follows Oliver and Alice to an all–American diner visually reinforces her exclusion from their normalcy. During the scene, Irena is shown to be excluded spatially: She is outside in the cold looking in; Oliver and Alice sit inside enjoying hot coffee. Lewton's use of the black waitress, Minnie (Theresa Harris), in the scene is interesting: Her inclusion seems to make implicit criticism of Oliver's (self-)restricted sense of identity. Minnie asks Oliver if he wants the Jamaican chicken gumbo, but he orders apple pie instead. "Doesn't anybody want the chicken gumbo?" Minnie complains (herself another Lewton outsider).

In his book *Horror and the Horror Film*, Bruce Kawin discusses the ambiguity that he feels is lost in *Cat People* when we glimpse Irena in panther form as she stalks Alice and Oliver in the office. According to Kawin, including the shots of the panther (which RKO insisted Lewton do in the scene) makes it definite that Irena turns into a panther.[30] There is, however, another way to interpret the scene: By this late stage in the film, both Oliver and Alice have come to believe in Irena's curse; they have rejected her difference to the point that she "becomes" the panther in their eyes. In the hysteria of the moment, the manifestation of Irena in panther form is what they believe they see; such is the severity of their repression. It has been impossible to assimilate Irena's difference into their way of thinking so it becomes projected outwards in an extreme form as a literal embodiment of evil.

From that point, Irena is forced into her role as a "cat person," in much the same way that Martin (John Amplas) is forced into his role as vampire in George Romero's *Martin* (1977): They are simply enacting the roles that society has imposed upon them in a self-fulfilling prophesy. Therefore, when Dr. Judd forces his attentions on her, Irena attacks him as a "panther." Lewton and Tourneur show this attack in shadow form on the apartment wall, inviting us to see Irena's transformation as symbolic.[31]

In a state of abjection, there is nowhere else for Irena to go except to the zoo's panther cage; her only option becomes death-suicide. There is the sense that she has foreseen this moment in the very opening scene of the film, in her drawing which depicts the panther pierced by the lance of King John of Serbia (she is later wounded by the blade of Dr. Judd's sword stick), as though she has understood from the first that her assimilation is impossible in such a repressive society as wartime America. In this final sequence, Irena becomes one of Lewton's many "lost souls"; harboring despair, desiring death.

"She never lied to us"

The ending of *Cat People* is essentially ambiguous: what does Oliver mean by this comment? Has Irena returned to her true panther form? Or is Oliver acknowledging his rejection of her as the cause of her tragic death? It is this last that lends itself to a sequel, *The Curse of the Cat People*, which explores Oliver's divided self in greater detail and looks at circumstances that might effect a possible change in him, leading to his reconciliation with Irena's "spirit" and what she represents.

Lewton's RKO films were all made within a four-year period (he produced eleven films in total between 1942 and 1946). The intensity of producing so many in such a short time no doubt contributed to their remarkable continuity of theme, style and approach: the sense of overlap between them; the impression we get of Lewton working through his preoccupations with each successive film. *The Curse of the Cat People*, made in 1944, is, in many ways, the culmination of Lewton's first cycle of RKO films that included *I Walked with a Zombie* (1943), *The Leopard Man* (1943) and *The Seventh Victim* (1943). Before moving on to *The Curse of the Cat People,* let us look briefly, then, at how Lewton developed his themes in those intervening films.

"Lost souls"

I Walked with a Zombie, like *Cat People,* is concerned predominantly with horror and insanity caused by repressed female sexuality in the family: Jessica (Christine Gordon), the wife of Haitian plantation owner Paul Holland (Tom Conway), falls into a zombie-like catatonic trance after entering into a love affair with her brother-in-law Wesley (James Ellison). As with *Cat People*, there is an essential ambiguity in the film: Has Jessica been driven mad by her husband's oppressive love or have voodoo priests really turned her into a zombie? Betsy (Frances Dee), the nurse employed to take care of Jessica, becomes an observer of the situation and sees that all members have become afflicted: Wesley is turning into an alcoholic, and Paul no longer sees beauty in the world, only death and decay. In short they are becoming, in Paul's words, "empty and dead," like the zombies that the superstitious natives fear. Eventually, Wesley, in a bid to free Jessica from her living death, drowns both Jessica and himself.

In the original script there is a coda in which Paul and Betsy (who have fallen in love) are seen starting a new life together. Lewton chose to excise this scene, perhaps because he felt it undermined what for him was the point of the story: repression in the family as an impasse that only death can break. Instead, we are left very much in doubt that Paul can be liberated from his own turmoil, his own oppressive tendencies. The abrupt, downbeat ending would become a characteristic of Lewton's films up to *The Curse of the Cat People*, as if Lewton himself could not at this stage see any answer to human misery except death; and the surviving characters in *I Walked with a Zombie*, *The Leopard Man* and *The Seventh Victim* are very much left dangling like lost souls in a meaningless world.

The Leopard Man, consequently, is set apart by the arbitrary nature of its plot, which follows the victims of a murderer almost at random. Set in New Mexico, the film begins with a leopard accidently let loose on the population and seemingly killing some women. Lewton uses the shock tactic (anticipating *Psycho* [1960]) of elaborately setting up characters only to kill them off suddenly and seemingly without reason. This theme of capricious fate is underscored in a speech by museum curator Dr. Galbraith (James Bell), who points to a ball floating atop a restaurant fountain and claims: "We know as little about the forces that move us and move the world around us as that empty ball." The terrible irony is that the psychotic Galbraith *is* the killer and furthermore does not know why he kills—spinning us still further into a world where chaos and disaster reign and existence is meaningless.

This theme of bleak fatalism is continued in *The Seventh Victim*. The plot involves a naïve young woman, Mary Gibson (Kim Hunter), and her search for her missing sister, Jacqueline (Jean Brooks). Mary traces Jacqueline to Manhattan, only to find her tangled up in Satanism. Lewton consciously borrows from Dante in this modern take on the Inferno, depicting New York as an underworld of lost souls engaged in a fruitless search for meaning. Again, there is mirroring of the characters and the sense that everyone in the film has a divided psyche (including each of the Palladists). The reappearance of a somewhat chastened Dr. Judd in the story reinforces the film's continuity with *Cat People*. Overwhelming despair leads to the "dark sister," Jacqueline, committing suicide at the end (the most nihilistic conclusion Lewton ever committed to film). Steve Haberman, in his *Seventh Victim* DVD commentary, claims that Jacqueline is the key to the philosophy of the film: "Her life is the very nightmare version of life that Val Lewton portrays in many of his movies: a meaningless existence, trying to find meaning, always failing and in the end seeking a sort of peace through death."[32]

Some critics have called *The Seventh Victim* Lewton's masterpiece, quintessential Lewton. *The Seventh Victim* is, however, only one side of Lewton, and in its disturbing fixation on the darkness of the human soul it goes beyond even wartime grief and anxiety. After *The Seventh Victim*'s relative failure at the box office, Lewton must have sensed the need to pull himself—and his audience—back from the abyss into which he was staring; to stop dwelling on the symptoms of malaise and start looking for a cure.

"She could almost be Irena's child"

The Curse of the Cat People marks the end of Lewton's first phase of horror films for RKO, and his intended swan song in the genre. He had wanted, like Tod Browning, to move into social drama. He was unhappy with the marketing of his films and the way they were represented as Universal-type horror films with "monsters"; he felt a certain disdain for those types of conventional horror films, and perhaps for the formulaic nature of the genre as a whole. By the time of *The Seventh Victim*, he even seemed to be tiring of his own formula which he had reduced thus: "A love story, three scenes of suggested horror and one of actual violence. Fadeout. It's all over in less than seventy minutes."[33] Broader themes of femininity and authority carried over into his non-horror pictures *Mademoiselle Fifi* (1944) and *Youth Runs Wild* (1944); in *The Curse of the Cat People*, however, there are indications that Lewton felt the need to reconcile the divided self—in Oliver's case, in his own case and in the nation's case too.

We can see, therefore, *The Curse of the Cat People* as perhaps the most personal of Lewton's films (Greg Mank claims that it is both "an exorcism of his childhood and a love letter to his thirteen-year-old daughter"[34] with whom, it seems, he had a love-hate relationship). In *Curse,* Oliver fears that his dead wife Irena has "cursed" his daughter, Amy, with being like her; he worries that her child's sense of fantasy may develop into delusion the way it did in Irena. Deep down, he is again threatened by his fear of women, female sexuality and femininity. He is, as Mank puts it, "still haunted by Irena's ghost and the reason for her suicide."[35]

Oliver does not know how to deal with Amy because he cannot reconcile his own feminine side: His journey towards doing so therefore becomes the film's focus. For Oliver, for Lewton, and for the nation at war, failing to do this means continuing darkness and hopelessness. Although Lewton's films rarely reference the war directly, Lewton had strong feelings about it, not only in terms of the home front experience and its effects on society and the individual, but also about the conflict itself which he saw as cataclysmic: "I'm convinced it's the return to barbarianism," he once wrote, "the savage wars that mark the end of a cycle of civilization."[36] The reconciliation of the divided self thus becomes a necessity, in Lewton's mind, for mankind's continuance.

Curse is set in Tarrytown,

Oliver (Kent Smith) and Alice (Jane Randolph) find themselves haunted by the "ghost" of Irena (Simone Simon) in *The Curse of the Cat People* (1944) (photograph courtesy Ronald V. Borst/Hollywood Movie Posters).

New York (where Lewton grew up amid tales of Sleepy Hollow and the Headless Horseman), and this provides a suburban normalcy that becomes increasingly oppressive and false to Amy as the film progresses. Alice has now become a full-time wife, mother and housekeeper (women workers were expected to return to the home full-time after the war). She and Oliver have, no doubt, moved to the suburbs because they view it as a more suitable place to bring up their daughter than in the city (which they still associate with Irena's memory).

In the script, Amy is described as possessing a childishness that still keeps her in touch with the memory of another world, "a memory which fades with each passing day, and whose fading leaves a sense of emptiness and loss." At the same time, Amy is introduced as a misfit, on the verge of being persecuted by her friends and, of course, her father, who wants her to be "normal." Amy's essential dilemma is that she must let go of that magical part of herself in order to fit in socially and to secure her father's love and approbation. Eventually, Amy turns to an imaginary friend, Irena, whose photograph Amy has found hidden in a drawer. Amy senses that Irena is, like herself, a misfit, an outcast, and therefore feels a sense of kinship with her. Irena, in turn, offers Amy the acceptance that her father denies her.

In *Curse*, Lewton celebrates Amy's difference, and by doing so, he also celebrates Irena's. This is nowhere more apparent than in the Christmas scene; here, the false bonhomie displayed by the "socially accepted" is contrasted with the truly magical friendship between "outcasts." In the scene, Oliver opens his home to some passing carol singers, providing them with a drink while Alice plays the piano. The carol singers are portrayed as boorish and ostentatious (even Oliver thinks so) and their message of good cheer hypocritical. Amy is put off by them and drifts over to the window when she hears, over the carol singers inside,

Lonely child Alice Reed (Ann Carter) summons the spirit of Irena (Simone Simon) in *The Curse of the Cat People* (1944) (photograph courtesy Ronald V. Borst/Hollywood Movie Posters).

a lilting voice: Irena is singing a French carol, "Il est né le divin enfant" ("He is born, the divine child"). Outside in the snow, Irena stands alone, but she is luminescent, no longer excluded as she was outside the All-American diner in *Cat People*. The garden is her home, her place of wonder, which she willingly shares with Amy in the true spirit of Christmas.

Amy's friendship with Irena inevitably results in Oliver becoming oppressive and authoritarian towards his daughter. Lewton does not shy away from showing this or the hypocrisy of it, and yet we understand that Oliver is not doing it because of any ill will towards his daughter—or Irena—but simply because his masculinity feels threatened. Lewton is left, then, with the problem of making Oliver's journey towards acceptance believable. Amy's teacher, Miss Callahan (Eve March), who understands the situation, is able to articulate it for the benefit of Oliver and the audience using a Robert Louis Stevenson poem as a reference: Once Amy feels safe in her love with her parents, then "the unseen playmate," Irena, will go away. In the script, Miss Callahan makes it plain that Amy desperately needs Oliver's understanding and Oliver seems to accept this immediately. In the film, however, his acceptance is delayed until the very last scene, after Amy's flight to the Farren house and Oliver's subsequent reunion with her. This change reinforces Oliver's journey towards enlightenment, and it is this journey that *Cat People* and *The Curse of the Cat People* are structured around.

"Yes, darling, I can see her"

Seven weeks after *The Curse of the Cat People* finished principal photography, Lewton put it back into production. This was a significant decision on the part of Lewton, who had a record of bringing his films in on schedule and on budget; but *Curse* had become too personal for him. He had, according to Mank, "become haunted by his own film and couldn't let it go."[37] The problem for Lewton was the ending, which remained dark.

In the script, Barbara Farren (Elizabeth Russell) lapses into madness caused by the sudden death of her mother, Julia (Julia Dean), to whom Amy has fled for shelter. Oliver and the police arrive in time to save Amy from the deranged Barbara, who is taken into custody. Oliver is reunited with Amy and he tells her he can now "see" Irena. In the film, Lewton changed the ending to effect an additional reconciliation of sorts between Amy and Barbara (who has been jealous of her mother's affections towards the little girl). As Mank notes in his DVD commentary, Lewton wanted to give compassion to Barbara, the darkest character in the film, with whom he identified too.[38] Barbara has been deprived of maternal love since the age of six, and has been driven to drink and madness by it. As Barbara's situation clearly mirrors that of Amy (who, at the age of six, is also in danger of losing the love of her parents), there is also the sense, then, that Lewton would not allow Amy, as an adult, to "become" Barbara and that made reconciliation between the two characters a necessity.

However, something more happens in the final film: Before hugging Barbara, Amy "projects" Irena's face onto her—Lewton superimposes Simone Simon over Elizabeth Russell photographically—in a visual representation of the "sister" motif in *Cat People*, which leaves us with a sense of reconciliation between Irena and Barbara as well; a coming together of the divided self. The film's final section—as rewritten by Lewton—thus becomes concerned with reconciliation, and Oliver's subsequent reunion with Amy and his professing to "see" Irena carries more weight than it did in the original script because the motif of bringing together the divided self is already in our mind. We are more ready to accept that Oliver is on his way to assimilating his "anima." Certainly, the film makes it clear that Irena has saved

"Yes, darling, I can see her": Oliver (Kent Smith) and Amy (Ann Carter) reconciled at the end of *The Curse of the Cat People* (1944) (photograph courtesy Ronald V. Borst/Hollywood Movie Posters).

the relationship between Oliver and his daughter and has caused Oliver to reconcile with Irena's memory too (hence, Irena fades away in the film's final shot, suggesting that she has finally been assimilated into the family and no longer stands outside of them as a secret and as a curse). That Oliver is not looking in Irena's direction when he affirms that he sees her, has been taken by some critics to suggest that he doesn't really see her at all, that he is lying (which is what Lewton might have feared when he decided to revise the ending); however, Oliver is looking at Amy when he says those words, implying that he sees Irena in *her*.

According to Lyn Genelli and Tom Genelli, Jungian analysts might interpret the "curse of the cat people" as the fury of the repressed anima, the inner knowledge of the feminine inside a man. When the anima in a man's psyche is not acknowledged and respected, it creates a schism within him. The man then becomes both fatally attracted and profoundly repelled by feminine sexual power, as Oliver did with Irena. Their encounter, ruled as it was by the dark power of sexual mystery, ends in violence and death. Oliver is, however, given a second chance in *The Curse of the Cat People*:

> Again the anima returns to his awareness, this time sexless and innocent, in the form of his daughter Amy. He is given another chance to "see" Irena, now in the innocent guise of a fairy tale princess, no longer a "cat woman." Amy and Irena are both still fascinating and mysterious, but they no longer carry the threat of dark, animal sexuality. When Oliver can confront

the feminine without its pantherlike aspect, he can at least begin to acknowledge "her" by telling Amy, "I see her too."[39]

The vulnerability of the female perspective in wartime showed signs of a similar assimilation into the national identity after 1944, as Americans wanted more realism from the media on the grounds that they could handle bad news. This was acknowledged by the government allowing photographs of dead soldiers to be printed in newspapers—the grief and anxiety of the home front began integration into the national psyche.

* * *

The Curse of the Cat People depicts in painful detail the process of inculcating one's values into one's children through the use of coercion and oppression, stifling in them that which society considers unacceptable. It is fitting, then, that Lewton chose juvenile delinquency as the subject for his next film, *Youth Runs Wild* (1944), which sought to dramatize a crisis in parenting in wartime, a theme closely aligned to that which runs through his subsequent "Karloff" series of horror films. By way of a conclusion to this chapter, let us briefly consider how these films might fit into Lewton's body of work, in particular his growing interest, at that point, in repudiating patriarchal authority within his films.

The Ghost Ship (1943), *Youth Runs Wild* (1944), *The Body Snatcher* (1945), *Isle of the Dead* (1945) and *Bedlam* (1946)

Lewton reconciled the divided self in *The Curse of the Cat People*, thus concluding the thematic development of his first phase of his RKO horror films, what one might term his "women's pictures" by virtue of their female protagonists. Lewton's second phase (which really starts with 1943's *The Ghost Ship*) with their predominantly male central characters are no less subversive in their depiction of authority as paranoid and homicidal and can therefore be read as a consolidation of Lewton's preoccupation with reconciling the feminine within the culture and the self.

In *The Ghost Ship*, Tom Merriam (Russell Wade), a young merchant navy officer, signs on as third officer under the apparently benign Captain Stone (Richard Dix). However, after the deaths of two crew members, Tom begins to see his mentor as a psychopathic madman who is prepared to eliminate anyone who threatens his authority. Tom tries to start a rebellion among the crew but he finds himself isolated; none of the others are prepared to "rock the boat." Eventually, Tom manages to convince his friend Jacob (Edmund Glover), the radio operator, to help him but Stone kills Jacob too. Finally, a mute crew member, Finn (Skelton Knaggs), comes to Tom's aid and together they manage to topple Stone. In Finn, the silent witness finally compelled to act when all others are afraid for their positions, we can see a precursor to Chief Bromden in *One Flew Over the Cuckoo's Nest*, and Lewton's film is comparable to Ken Kesey's novel as an allegory about authority's coercion and control of the individual. Indeed, *The Ghost Ship* still stands as a bold statement about the need for the "silent minority" to speak out against oppressive and paranoid forms of authority. *The Ghost Ship* shares themes of masculinity and mentorship with *The Body Snatcher* (1945)—the best of the Lewton-Karloff films—and the overtly didactic *Youth Runs Wild*.

Inspired by wartime moral panic over juvenile delinquency, *Youth Runs Wild* opens with spinning news headlines alerting us to the spreading problem. We cut to a street sign: "Drive Safely—We Love Our Children." The sign is backed into by a careless truck driver. A moment later, a child playing on the same street is almost hit by a passing motorist. *Youth Runs Wild* sees Lewton at his most heavy-handed, as though being freed from the horror genre and from the need to make his points allegorically has made him overeager to ram his message home.

The plot involves fifteen-year-old Frankie Hauser's (Glenn Vernon) descent from school truancy to delinquency and the attempts of his brother-in-law Danny (Kent Smith), a war veteran, to keep Frankie on the straight and narrow by acting as a role model. Lewton very quickly levels blame partly on "latchkey-ism"; the adults are either off to war or busy with the war effort and cannot mind their children. Teenagers like Frankie and his friends lack parental guidance. However, Lewton doesn't only blame the war: other parents, such as those of Frankie's girlfriend Sarah (Tess Brind), are portrayed as selfish and neglectful; and some of the adults, like Larry the garage owner (Lawrence Tierney), who sends the impressionable youths to steal tires for him, are shown as criminal. Frankie is portrayed sympathetically: Social pressures, as well as a lack of guidance, are what ultimately get him into trouble. At the end of the film he is sent to forestry camp for rehabilitation. In its final scene advocating youth camps as the answer to juvenile delinquency, *Youth Runs Wild* resembles the kind of mental hygiene film discussed in the following chapter.

Youth Runs Wild's dramatic inertia and muddled messages are not all Lewton's fault, however. According to Bansak, the film was diluted and made tepid by studio reworking. Many controversial scenes were cut (including a patricide subplot) and the simplistic ending tacked on. The changes made by the studio were extensive enough for Lewton to want to have his name removed from the film. Bansak claims that the film Lewton had wanted to make had a much harder edge. The aforementioned patricide subplot—in which an abused teenage boy kills his sadistic father—is an example of the kind of brutal honesty Lewton had intended.[40]

In *The Body Snatcher*, Lewton reprises the themes of *The Ghost Ship* and develops the theme of patriarchal authority gone bad that RKO studio chiefs had objected to so much in *Youth Runs Wild*. Russell Wade again plays a young apprentice, in this case a medical student, Donald Fettes, who comes to understand—and

War veteran Danny (Kent Smith) plays role model to troubled teenager Frankie Hauser (Glenn Vernon) in *Youth Runs Wild* (1944).

reject—the corruption and insanity of his mentor, Dr. McFarlane (Henry Daniell), whom he discovers is procuring cadavers from the body snatcher, John Gray (played by Boris Karloff). Lewton's portrayal of McFarlane's insanity is humane and sympathetic (as indeed was his portrayal of Captain Stone's in *The Ghost Ship*: Lewton never encourages us to see his antagonists as inhuman—these are men who have been turned rotten by the establishments to which they belong). Gray is, in essence, McFarlane's homicidal alter ego—the dark side of the male-dominated medical establishment. The film's finale sees McFarlane haunted by the "spirit" of Gray (whom he has been forced to murder in order to protect his own reputation) returning to him in the form of a hallucination: McFarlane subsequently loses control of a carriage and he dies in the crash.

Authority again becomes paranoid and homicidal in *Isle of the Dead*. On a Greek island during the 1912 war, several people are trapped by quarantine for the plague. Karloff plays General Pherides, who takes it upon himself to keep order. A superstitious old woman suspects that Thea (Ellen Drew) is a vampiric spirit called a Varvoloka. Karloff eventually goes insane and tries to kill the girl. *Isle of the Dead* is a nuanced study of how a man's sense of duty, when taken to zealous extreme, can lead him to act irrationally and unreasonably. Karloff's General Pherides is portrayed as an essentially decent officer whose downfall comes from his paranoia and susceptibility to superstition, which leads him to demonize his quarry whom he feverishly tries to hunt down and kill. *Isle of the Dead* shows us how easily those in authority can become tyrannical when forces conspire against them.

The demonization of woman (and by extension femininity) by male authority forms the basis of Lewton's final RKO horror film, *Bedlam* (1946). Karloff plays Master George Sims, the apothecary general of the eponymous asylum who contrives to have the reformist Nell Bowen (Anna Lee) committed after she threatens to expose his grievous mistreatment of the patients. Lewton based the headstrong Nell on historical accounts of eighteenth century women who were incarcerated in asylums by their wealthy husbands. *Bedlam* thus sets out to expose the ruthlessness and hypocrisy of such a patriarchal society.

Bedlam is also marked by Lewton's desire to resolve the themes that he has developed through the Karloff series, as *The Curse of the Cat People* had done for his first cycle of horror films. Nell's growing kindness and charity towards the patients in the asylum, encouraged by her Quaker confidante, thus "defies" Sims's authoritarianism; however, Sims almost leads Nell to despair her own humanity, as Captain Stone does to the gentle Tom Merriam in *The Ghost Ship*, through his deep contempt for those under his authority. "This is to show you that all those mawkish theories you learned from the Quaker were lies," Sims tells Nell. "Men are not brothers; men are not born good and kind. Even the mindless ones must be ruled with force." To prove him wrong, Nell accepts Sims's challenge to enter the cage of a chained, seemingly savage inmate, to "conquer him with kindness." We fear for her, and not just for her safety: but that the darkness of Sims's philosophy—that men are savage animals—might be true. However, the inmate is calmed by Nell's gentle and calm acceptance. Lewton's belief in the feminine wins out once and for all. The tyrant Sims is then toppled by a rebellion of lunatics and bricked up alive in the walls of his own asylum.

Bedlam was being shot as World War II was coming to an end. As Tom Weaver has commented, "*Bedlam*'s a movie about bringing about reforms, about the end of a dark age, about a country starting to put a terrible time behind it and moving ahead into a new and more hopeful era."[41]

Bedlam is also a film which vindicates its woman protagonist. It is, as Weaver suggests, perhaps the first horror film to feature a feminist heroine.[42]

3

ANTI–1950s COLD WAR CONFORMITY
The Films of Herman Cohen

Most critics agree that the science fiction–horror films of the early 1950s reflect the Cold War paranoia and anti-communist feeling of the time. A film like *Invaders from Mars* (1953) clearly plays to the fear of communist infiltration ushered in by McCarthyism at the start of the decade; with its slogan "Reds under the bed" literalizing the child's fear of the monster lurking under the mattress (or landing outside the child's bedroom window, as the Martians do in the film). The right wing sentiment of the film, equating Martian invaders with communist spies, is unavoidable.

Other science fiction films of that decade admittedly took a more liberal outlook: There were films that dealt with fears arising from the arms race and the threat of nuclear annihilation (*The Day the Earth Stood Still* [1951]) and films that addressed the alienation of the Cold War era (*Invasion of the Body Snatchers* [1956]). However, despite the sort of liberal platitudes typified by *The Day the Earth Stood Still* ("We must all learn to live in peace or be destroyed"), the conservative tendencies of 1950s science fiction–horror films on the whole remained strong.

Invasion of the Body Snatchers, for example, criticizes conformism of any sort—McCarthy-ist or Communist—instead favoring rugged individualism, and meanwhile expresses a nagging fear of female sexuality and of women's independence in the postwar era. Likewise, *Tarantula*, directed in 1955 by Jack Arnold (who, like Don Siegel, had a penchant for social commentary), while expressing atomic age fears of radiation and its potentially catastrophic threat to society (as embodied by the giant tarantula which menaces a small desert town), also—very pointedly—questions the wisdom of upsetting the "natural order" of things in terms of changing gender roles. While Maria Corday as the film's female scientist is initially portrayed as a strong, intelligent woman, she is subsequently imperiled by her involvement with the experiment and has to be rescued by the men. The film thus implies that the woman's place remains in the home and that to go against "nature" in that way risks catastrophe akin to that posed by atomic mutation.

Herman Cohen's series of low-budget shockers for AIP, by contrast, took the decisive step of locating the "horror" of that era in the life of the American teenager, caused by stultifying conformity and the threat of imminent nuclear annihilation; and leveled the blame directly on authority gone insane—the same authority, in fact, that could create the hydrogen bomb and take the world seemingly to the brink of destruction. Starting with *I Was a Teenage Werewolf* (1957), Cohen went on to write and produce a number of horror films in which patriarchal authority is shown to willfully create monsters out of teenagers, a deeply subversive message for the time (and one which would be taken up again in the radicalized sixties by the director Michael Reeves). Indeed, the message of *I Was a Teenage Werewolf* was such a resonant one with alienated youth in the 1950s that it ushered in a whole new horror subgenre—that of teen horror—which remains with us today. Moreover, by utilizing the tropes of exploitation cinema in order to spread this message, Cohen helped pave the way for the likes of *Night of the Living Dead* (1968) and the modern horror film of the 1970s, which thrived on its own disrespectability and disregard for the mainstream; on its very "trashiness." By virtue of their positioning as shock-exploitation, *I Was a Teenage Werewolf* (and the films that followed) enabled Cohen to sidestep many of the constrictions facing Hollywood teenage melodramas like *Rebel Without a Cause* (1955). In *Teen Movies: American Youth on Screen*, Timothy Shary describes Hollywood's dilemma in the 1950s when it came to portraying teenagers on film: "Teen life is filled with sexual urges," Shary writes, "drug and alcohol temptations and challenges to authority—issues that the studios could not very well address under the Production Code"[1]; issues, nonetheless, that films like *I Was a Teenage Werewolf* could address *allegorically,* with the added exploitation possibilities and shock (or rather, "schlock") value traditionally afforded by the horror genre.

Shary speculates on the particular appeal that horror has for teenagers as "so many issues with bodily changes, alienation and anger arise during the teen years."[2] It is not surprising, therefore, that the teen horror subgenre would become one of the most popular within teen cinema, although, as Shary acknowledges, teen horror was slow to develop during the 1950s. This can partly be attributed to 1950s science fiction–horror up until *I Was a Teenage Werewolf* not readily lending itself to teenage experience; "aliens and monsters," as Shary observes, "had to have a reason to target teens, or to 'be' teens themselves."[3] This required a fundamental shift in the ideology of 1950s science fiction–horror narrative in order to speak to a teenage audience—exactly what Cohen provided in *I Was a Teenage Werewolf.*

"I have always felt that teenagers think that adults—their parents, or their teachers, anyone that was older and that had authority—were the culprits in their lives," Herman Cohen told Tom Weaver in 1994. "I know I felt that way as a teenager, and in talking to many teenagers, I found out that that was how they felt."[4] Cohen was to develop a simple formula in *I Was a Teenage Werewolf* that he would repeat in all of his subsequent teen horror films: Teenagers are manipulated or transformed into monsters by an evil adult. The typical Cohen storyline runs thus: A teenager with behavioral problems is placed in the care of a scientist who promises to cure them of their problem. Instead, following their own agenda, the scientist uses the teenager as a guinea pig in an experiment that degenerates the teenager's social disease, regressing the teenager into a primitive monster state. Using hypnosis or some other form of mind control, the scientist unleashes the teenage monster on an unsuspecting community. However, the teenage monster eventually returns to its maker and destroys him/her before itself being destroyed. Meanwhile, the authorities try to keep the killings hushed up while the police investigate.

This basic story, with only slight variation, is also used in *I Was a Teenage Frankenstein, Blood of Dracula* (both 1957), *How to Make a Monster* (1958), *Horrors of the Black Museum* (1959) and *Black Zoo* (1963). It must be said that there is little development of the basic theme through the series (and the films themselves become increasingly nonsensical with each permutation); however, it is somewhat significant that in each successive film a trustworthy adult becomes noticeably harder to find, and that relationships between the teenagers and authority figures become increasingly fraught as a result, while the scientists become more ruthless, irrational and unethical in their ambitions. By virtue of their exploitation tropes, Cohen's films address social issues often crudely, but there is little doubt whose side Cohen is on.

Herman Cohen, American International Pictures and *I Was a Teenage Werewolf*

Herman Cohen came into the movie business as an exhibitor, managing cinemas in Detroit, and then—following his tour of duty as a Marine—as a sales manager for Columbia before becoming a producer of B pictures. He was also a screenwriter of his films under the pseudonym of Ralph Thornton or Kenneth Langtry. He must take the credit for writing (with his co-screenwriter Aben Kandel) and producing *I Was a Teenage Werewolf*, the first horror film made for a teenage audience (and, according to Samuel Z. Arkoff, the first horror film with "teenage" in the title); however, it is important to acknowledge that Cohen was working within an already burgeoning teen-movie genre (pioneered by Cohen's distributor and backer, AIP), itself part of a growing youth culture in the 1950s.

In a Guardian Film Interview which took place at London's National Film Theatre in August 1991, Arkoff recalled how post-war economic prosperity, along with mass suburbanization and the proliferation of television, led to the rise of teenage movie-going in the 1950s:

> The young marrieds and the middle-aged and the old people sat at home, particularly in the United States, in the new homes being built, and watched TV. The only audiences who went to theaters were the young people. Why? First of all, because they had to get out of the house and in second place their parents *wanted* to get them out of the house. By this time the Depression was over, the parents had money, gave it to the kids, the kids were out getting jobs in fast food restaurants or wherever. So this was the audience.[5]

At this stage in the early 1950s, the major studios, according to Arkoff, did not yet realize that teenagers were the main cinema audience and were still making films with stars that did not hold meaning for the new teenage audience. James Nicholson, president of AIP, and his vice-president Arkoff saw this gap in the market and formed a company in 1954, American Releasing Corporation (which became American International Pictures in 1956), to produce films made for teenagers and using teenagers. Tapping into the teen trends of the time, AIP promoted films in a number of subgenres: hot rod movies, rock movies, beach movies, teen melodramas and, of course, teen horror films. (AIP would go on to capitalize on the youth protest movement of the 1960s with a number of biker and counterculture films produced and/or directed by Roger Corman, such as *The Wild Angels* [1966] and *The Trip* [1967].)

AIP's critics have suggested that the company's formulaic appeal to the male youth market contributed to postwar era American cinema becoming juvenile, as we see to this day (the so-called "Peter Pan Syndrome").[6] However, it must also be said that AIP was one of the first companies to use focus groups to poll American teenagers in the 1950s about what they wanted to see, using their responses to determine titles, stars, and storylines. Typically, Nicholson and Arkoff would come up with a title and accompanying artwork and then take these out to high schools and colleges. If the title and storyline met with a good response from teenagers, a script would be written from which the film would be made. So it was with *I Was a Teenage Werewolf*, a title which Arkoff has often described as a "million dollar title on a hundred thousand dollar picture" (the film did, in fact, earn more than $2 million in box office receipts).

Cohen became involved with AIP through Nicholson who had approached him to make a movie for the youth market. It was Cohen's idea to combine genres to make a teen-horror. *The Wild One* (1954) had started a massive wave of JD (juvenile delinquent) films which AIP was keen to exploit. Therefore Cohen proposed the title *Teenage Werewolf*, to which Nicholson added *I Was a*.

I Was a Teenage Werewolf may have been the first horror film to feature "teenage" in the title but the basic plot was similar to "classic" Universal monster movies, only with teenagers as the protagonists. Contemporary reviewers tend to emphasize the simplicity of the concept ("adults are so bewildered by teenage behavior that they refer to adolescents as monsters ... so what if they actually were?"[7]) but the ramifications, in 1957, of a film entitled *I Was a Teenage Werewolf* should not be overlooked. This was the first time a teenager had been a "monster" in popular culture and back then it was taboo to discuss youth rebellion in such a way. The implication of such a metamorphosis from teenager to monster, as Gary Morris has written, was a "transformation clearly symbolic of their violent rejection of assimilation/socialization"[8] and fed into the "ephebiphobia" (fear of youth) that was rapidly spreading throughout the United States in the 1950s as the result of moral panics over juvenile delinquency.

Although *I Was a Teenage Werewolf* broke little new ground in terms of a movie monster's crimes against society (violence, murder and suggested rape featured in Whale's *Frankenstein*, as we have seen), the film's explicit link between teenage lycanthropy and juvenile delinquency was too near the knuckle for many social commentators. Dr. Frederick Wertham (who wrote 1954's infamous *Seduction of the Innocent*, implicating comic books among the causes of juvenile delinquency) spoke in his testimony to the 1954 Senate Subcommittee hearings into Juvenile Delinquency of his concerns about the types of delinquent behavior seen in youth offenders, listing them as vandalism, violence against others, drug addiction, childhood prostitution, fire-setting and sex offenses. Some of this behavior is exhibited by Tony Rivers (Michael Landon) in the film, during his periods of werewolf transformation, representing a troubled youth's deeply antisocial instincts.

However, the film's refusal to

High school delinquent Tony Rivers (Michael Landon) is turned into a drooling beast in *I Was a Teenage Werewolf* (1957).

level the blame for this behavior at Tony himself sets *I Was a Teenage Werewolf* apart from the JD films being made by the major studios at the time. JD movies of the 1950s (unlike the delinquency tales of the 1930s which primarily placed the blame on poverty), as Shary notes, "began examining delinquency as a manifold systemic condition, with culpability placed not only on poverty, but on schools, parents, courts, urbanization, suburbanization, and increasingly on the teens themselves."[9] *I Was a Teenage Werewolf* levels the blame on none of these things, instead placing culpability on Cold War authority.

Film historian Thomas Doherty has commented that *I Was a Teenage Werewolf* owes most of its success to its title, timing and perfectly executed exploitation campaign. Not to be discounted, however, is a narrative that takes teenage subculture on its own terms:

> Most teenpics are products of adult minds racing madly to interpret adolescent tastes. By contrast, AIP teenpics seem to be the kind of motion pictures a group of high schoolers let loose with 35mm equipment might come up with, an impression due in equal parts to market savvy, youthful talents and bargain-basement budgets. With the audience that mattered, the company's unpretentious product generally fared better than the transparently calculating teen attractions of the established studios.[10]

This obvious sympathy on the part of Cohen and AIP with teenage rebellion inevitably drew criticism from the authorities and pressure groups like the PTA and the FBI, which said that the company glorified criminality. In 1958, producer Jerry Wald denounced AIP's films, saying such pictures "may make a few dollars today [but] they will destroy us tomorrow." To which Arkoff famously replied: "AIP's monsters do not smoke, drink or lust."[11] Although AIP did make a move towards respectability in the early 1960s with its *Beach Party* films featuring "clean teens" (only to return to renegade form with the biker movies of the late 1960s), their teen films of the 1950s, including those made by Cohen, are characterized by their very refusal to conform.

"Adjust to what?"

In *I Was a Teenage Werewolf*, Tony (like AIP in the 1950s) is pressured by the adults around him to conform, or to "adjust." "Adjust to what?" he answers back. "What's this adjust kick?" It is a line akin to one of Marlon Brando's in *The Wild One*: When asked what it is he's rebelling against, Brando replies, "What have you got?" Like many teenagers in the 1950s, Tony appears at first to be kicking against a homogenized suburban existence. Rockdale, the fictional setting of *Teenage Werewolf*, exists in a cookie cutter world of tract housing, all–American high schools and main streets with soda fountains. Tony's father (Malcolm Atterbury) is an automotive factory worker, but there are signs of *embourgeoisement*: Tony has his own car, for example, and they appear to live relatively well. Tony's father, however, has had to kowtow to others in the process, and is portrayed as somewhat emasculated as a result. ("Sometimes you just have to do it the other fellow's way," he advises his son.) Tony, by contrast, doesn't like to be pushed around. Their predicament seems typical of the era in which giant corporations (such as the auto industry), suburbanization, television, a consumer culture (Tony with his car and his father with his kitchen full of white goods) and a rabid fear of communism bred homogeneity and conformity, making youth rebellion such as Tony's all the more troubling to adult society.

According to Gail McGregor, the early 1950s saw the number of juveniles charged with crimes of delinquency increase by 45 percent.[12] This gave rise to a major moral panic started by the press and fueled by the wider popular media (which included book publishers and the film industry). By 1954, public anxiety about growing youth crime was such that the government felt the need to respond: A state subcommittee was set up to investigate juvenile delinquency and the role played by the entertainment industries, particularly comic books, in "corrupting" the nation's youth. This can be seen as an attempt by the government to deflect attention from those doctors and educators who saw poor social conditions as the most likely cause of juvenile delinquency.

Some modern commentators claim that, in actual fact, the rise in statistics for crimes of juvenile delinquency in the 1950s can largely be attributed to the fiat laws: the declaration by the juvenile court system that a juvenile is delinquent without any trial and finding only probable cause (the reasonable belief that a person has committed a crime). Many states have laws that confer more lenient treatment on juvenile delinquents than on adult offenders. In return, the juvenile gives up certain constitutional rights, such as a right to trial by jury. Very few juvenile delinquents, in other words, actually broke any law. Most were simply rounded up by the police after an event that possibly involved criminal action (such as the youth "riots" that followed the film *Rock Around the Clock* [1955]). They were brought before a juvenile court judge who found them delinquent only because the police action established probable cause.

In truth, most teenagers in the 1950s were themselves part of the consumer culture, targeted as they were by record companies, television networks, the fashion industry and, of course, the movies. The moral panic over juvenile delinquency in the 1950s can be seen as arising from what sociologists call deviance amplification (in much the same way that the 1930s saw the incidence of male psychopathology exaggerated by similar media hype). The result of all this, however, was to give the authorities a reason to exert greater social control over teenagers. One of the ways in which they did this was through mental hygiene movies.

What About Juvenile Delinquency? (1955)

Although the representation of juvenile delinquency in both Hollywood mainstream movies and exploitation films has attracted much attention from film scholars over the years, the portrayal of juvenile delinquency in classroom films of the 1950s is no less fascinating and telling of the era. The mental hygiene film is social coercion at its bluntest. Generally less than fifteen minutes long, these films offered teenagers guidance in good behavior and preached conservative moral values. Subjects ran the gamut: substance abuse (*The Terrible Truth* [1951]); sex before marriage (*How Much Affection?* [1951]); personal grooming (*How to Be Well Groomed* [1949]); reckless driving (*What Made Sammy Speed* [1957]); mealtime manners (*Good Eating Habits* [1951]); social conduct at parties (*What Makes a Good Party?* [1950]). Taking their cues from the training and propaganda films of World War II, mental hygiene films would often use scare tactics to enforce their message, presenting both an idealized vision of American youth and a potentially apocalyptic one: Conforming to social mores would guarantee success, happiness and popularity. However, transgression or rebellion would bring dire consequences, not just for the individual but for society as a whole.

According to Ken Smith, who wrote the book *Mental Hygiene: Classroom Films 1945–1970*, thousands of mental hygiene films were produced during the period of 1945 to 1970. Over the three decades, millions of schoolchildren saw these films that had the blessing of contemporary social scientists. "The movies thrived in a climate of confusion and nervousness in America," Smith writes, "when moral codes and social norms were being increasingly challenged and disobeyed."[13]

The mental hygiene film *What About Juvenile Delinquency?* gives us some idea of what teenagers in the 1950s had to face. It offers a ludicrous but depressing "official" representation of youth, with the underlying assumption that there is something fundamentally wrong with young people, that they are a threat to society. It shows the police under pressure to clamp down on youth crime and teenagers pressured by the authorities into conformity for fear of curfew and other punishment. In many ways it is the flipside to *I Was a Teenage Werewolf* and is, therefore, worth looking at in more detail.

What About Juvenile Delinquency? tells the story of Jamie, a teenager whose father, by unhappy coincidence, is beaten up by a gang of boys—the same gang that Jamie has recently joined. This attack is the latest in a wave of youth crimes sweeping through town. When the city council holds a special meeting to discuss sanctions against the town's youth, Jamie is pressured to speak out against his gang and join the fight against juvenile delinquency instead. The film ends with the council's decision resting on Jamie's shoulders, and the viewer is asked what they would do if they were Jamie.

Smith describes the mental hygiene genre as "ham-fisted, dogmatic and frequently brutal,"[14] and so it is with *What About Juvenile Delinquency?* The film opens in the living room of a typical suburban middle-class 1950s home. We see a closeup of the father's portrait being lovingly dusted by Jamie's mother. Jaunty music plays on the radio. Father, in the picture, is respectably dressed in suit and tie. The camera pans down to Jamie lying on the couch lazily. His mother asks him if he has any homework to which Jamie replies that he is going out as soon as "the guys" come to pick him up. We can tell by Jamie's disrespectful attitude towards his mother and his general impudence that he is already on the road to delinquency. "I don't know why you can't stay home for one evening," the mother sighs. Like most mental hygiene films, the script is generally inept and often implausible. We see Jamie with his gang, who are dressed in the same high school jackets, in a diner. The gang leader has a retractable pencil which he has stolen from the guy they have "bumped" prior to picking up Jamie. "Hey, those are great!" Jamie exclaims of the pencil. "My dad has one just like it." It is at that point that Jamie recognizes the gang's victim as his father.

If such contrivance fails to convince, no matter: The rest of the film plays relentlessly on guilt to manipulate its youth audience. Jamie returns home to find his beaten father on the couch being tended by his mother and is immediately struck with remorse, compounded by his father's pathetic helplessness. This film and others like it positioned adults as innocent victims of their children's crimes, guilt-tripping the teenage viewer in the process. The camera lingers on Jamie as he retreats to his room, conscience-stricken. The script and music inflate the melodramatics, serving to emphasize Jamie's feelings of shame—disproportionate though they may be (he has already disowned the gang, after all). The classroom audience was not supposed to watch and be enthralled by the direction, cinematography, acting or editing, but they were supposed to adopt the film's point of view (and the point of view of *What About Juvenile Delinquency?*, despite its bluntness—or perhaps because of it—is nothing if not clear). "Education theory," as Smith points out, "held that young people were social mimics who would imitate whatever behavior they saw acted out on screen."[15] In this respect, the social coercion of *What About Juvenile Delinquency?* becomes somewhat more insidious when one considers the emotional blackmail inherent in its message: Failing to conform is nothing less than a betrayal of your parents.

What About Juvenile Delinquency? ups the ante for Jamie and the audience when the high school students hear of the city council's proposed plans for a curfew and other possible actions to stop the spread of youth crime. "It won't be funny if the city council does what they're talking about," one of the students warns to camera. (Sanctions include the somewhat punitive measures of upping the age of driving licenses as well as cancelling football games and dances.) "Most of the high school students haven't had anything to do with the things that have been happening," another student opines, "but we are all going to suffer for it." The urgency with which the students speak of the wave of youth crime is reminiscent of the hysteria following *Rock Around the Clock*: Authorities held similar meetings to determine how to handle the young when the film came out. However, the relatively minor nature of the crimes that the students are talking about here (a statue broken, theater seats slashed) hardly constitutes a serious juvenile delinquency problem, and seems to have given way to a mounting hysteria escalated by the authorities themselves.

"We're not just talking about a few pranks," intones a member of the town council at the special meeting, "we're talking about criminal acts of violence! If these kids want to go around beating people up to prove how tough they are, it's time we proved how tough we are!" However, as well as showing the get-tough face of authority, the film also presents an alternative to the students: offering them, in effect, a choice of the carrot or the stick. "We don't want to punish all teenagers for the trouble a few are causing," says the mayor, "but something has to be done." A group of clean-cut students and Jamie are then invited to put forward suggestions to help the authorities stamp out the problem. The film concludes with Jamie turning his back on the gang and coming forward to testify against them. "What would you do if you were Jamie?" a narrator asks. "What can we do about juvenile delinquency? What would you say?" Like at the end of *The Blob* (1958), a large question mark appears on the screen.

You wonder why teenagers should have the answers (the film implies that teenagers are themselves to blame for juvenile delinquency). Of course, what *What About Juvenile Delinquency?* is *really* demanding of the audience is that they respect patriarchal authority, reminding them, in the process, of the "big stick" that can be used on all if the minority are not brought into line. At the end, Jamie is presented with a more suitable peer group than the gang of juvenile delinquents. These are, of course, all respectable kids, who already hold office within the high school as head of student council and captain of the football team; they are already co-opted by the high school system. Adhering to society's rules, which includes obeying one's parents (particularly one's father), is thus a moral obligation, as Jamie learns. Ultimately, *What About Juvenile Delinquency?* (like so many of the 1950s mental hygiene films) speaks to Cold War paranoia on the part of the authorities, who feared that teenagers not properly controlled by family, school and community might rebel against the capitalist system and turn to communism.

What About Juvenile Delinquency? is the antithesis of *I Was a Teenage Werewolf*; it illustrates by stark contrast just how radical Cohen's film really is—how completely Cohen subverts the official line on juvenile delinquency, its causes and its social significance. Needless to say, Cohen's representation of juvenile delinquency is far more sympathetic and far less socially coercive. We might also compare *I Was a Teenage Werewolf* to mainstream Hollywood JD films of the era, such as *Rebel Without a Cause* (1955) and *Blackboard Jungle* (1955) and draw much the same conclusions. Although, in *Rebel Without a Cause,* director Nicholas Ray creates a sympathetic portrayal of juvenile delinquency in the mixed-up-and-misunderstood Jim (played by James Dean), the cure to Jim's problem is hopelessly conventional. By the end of the film, Jim has discovered his own paternal instincts, found a girl whom he might marry, and become closer to his mother and father. He is, in other words, ready to follow social norms.

Likewise, in *Blackboard Jungle,* director Richard Brooks advocates a similar solution to dealing with juvenile delinquents as that taken by the authorities in *What About Juvenile Delinquency?* (and his film is clearly an influence on *What About Juvenile Delinquency?* in terms of its basic plot); namely, run 'em out of our schools. Shary says that *Blackboard Jungle*'s "otherwise positive closure is betrayed as just another Hollywood happy ending, and its presentation of the moral group defeating immoral anarchy is dubious. The goal of the film is not to educate but to influence adolescent behaviour."[16] Cohen, on the other hand, is not interested in either educating youth or influencing their behavior (beyond enticing them into the drive-in). His films are therapy for teenagers, and he presents no easy answer to juvenile delinquency; instead he redefines the problem in startling and subversive ways.

"I say things, I do things, I don't know why"

What causes Tony's inexplicable anger in *I Was a Teenage Werewolf*? In the film, Tony is portrayed as isolated in his alienation: He belongs to no gang of criminal misfits. As such, Tony's delinquency is not presented as symptomatic of a social disease spreading through suburbia—a blanket response to the tedious uniformity of suburban life—so much as a deeper psychological problem affecting him and other individuals like him.

Some films in the 1950s, such as *Crime in the Streets* (1957), showed juvenile delinquency as a result of parental abuse (one thinks of the excised patricide subplot in Val Lewton's *Youth Runs Wild*), but *I Was a Teenage Werewolf* portrays its adults as generally supportive of Tony. Both his father and Donovan (Barney Phillips), the kind-hearted cop, are sympathetic to Tony's problem, as is the school principal Miss Ferguson (Louise Lewis). They think he is a good boy at heart who needs to learn to adjust to society's expectations. Indeed, the scene early in the film which establishes the relationship between Tony and his father, Charles, is a tender one: Charles is concerned about Tony's behavior, and forever trying to compensate for the absence of a mother in Tony's life (we learn that she died when Tony was small). Therefore, Cohen rules out the possibility that adult abuse or neglect is behind Tony's delinquency.

Neither are Tony's peers nor his social network to blame. At the party in the haunted house, Tony's friends are shown to be docile and fun-loving, which makes Tony's violent knee-jerk response to the harmless prank that Vic (Ken Miller) plays on him all the more alarming. The mental hygiene film *Control Your Emotions* (1950) suggests that such a lack of temper control was seen as a problem in teens of the day. The film presents a Pavlovian view of human behavior based on stimulus-response theory. A youth is shown to become progressively angry over a period of a few hours as a result of growing frustration: A trick to try and impress his friends goes wrong; he stumbles over a hedge in a hurry to get home; finally his anger boils over when he can't get his car started. The film warns hot-headed teenagers that repeated temper tantrums such as this may lead to a "warped personality." Feeling thwarted is what leads to such angry outbursts, the doctor in the film tells us; therefore the advice is "rather than get angry, try to see the humor in the situation."

Although Tony claims that people "bug" him, *I Was a Teenage Werewolf* shows no obvious source of great frustration in Tony's life that might cause his anger (he is popular among his friends despite his fiery temper; he is intelligent and achieves high grades; he is economically secure) except, perhaps, the "four years of waiting—college and all" that lies ahead of him before he and his girl Arlene (Yvonne Lime) can become engaged to marry. Arlene reminds Tony of this in a scene reminiscent of similar scenes in many teen movies and mental hygiene films: The young couple discusses the need to "wait." The Coronet-produced instructional film *Are You Ready for Marriage?* (1950), for example, spoke to growing concerns that couples were rushing into marriage (for the same reasons that they were often drifting into going steady) and advocates a long engagement where the couple can get to know each other platonically at first, ensuring a lasting and stable marriage later. Sexual abstinence, therefore, as the social norm, is likely to create some frustration for Tony (as is suggested later when Tony, in his werewolf form, attacks the leotard-clad gymnast, Theresa, played by Dawn Richard). But we get no tense scenes between Tony and Arlene signaling his frustrations, and sexual frustration in itself does not appear to be the root cause of his uncontrolled violent outbursts.

"You've got to bow to authority"

The social guidance film *Are You Popular?* (1947) features a scene similar to that in *I Was a Teenage Werewolf* where Arlene invites Tony in to meet her parents when he arrives to take her on a date. In *Are You Popular?* the parents approve of the boy because he is polite and shows respect ("Home, parents and personality all help boys and girls to be popular," the film informs us). The outcome is reversed for Tony. Arlene's father thinks Tony is a "smart aleck" and tells him he has to bow to authority. Tony, however, is mistrustful of authority—and for good reason: Cohen's film is a cautionary tale to teenagers, playing on their fears of being abused and exploited by the authority figures in whom they have placed their trust. Tony does not want to surrender his power to Dr. Brandon for this reason. He fears (correctly) that Brandon will not cure him, but somehow make him worse.

Brandon, played by Whit Bissell, initially appears to be another well-meaning authority figure, like Donovan and Miss Ferguson. The fact that he is a respected doctor makes his subsequent unethical behavior (like Dr. Judd's in *Cat People*) all the more shocking. Bissell often played doctors and other benevolent authority figures—his casting here as an insane scientist is all the more subversive for that reason. Scenes showing the police trying to hush the murders up suggest the hypocrisy of a society that would place such a man as Dr. Brandon in a position of authority.

Brandon is a social scientist straight out of the 1950s (*I Was a Teenage Werewolf*, as Cyndy Hendershot observes, "displays the horror genre's deep-seated suspicions regarding the medical establishment"[17]). Like Frankenstein and the many other mad scientists that followed, Dr. Brandon is driven by an insane ambition to control and change the world, but that drive is a sublimation of repressed sexual energies which are projected outwards in degenerate form in the monster he creates.

Social science came into its own in this era of rigid social control and one cannot help but see Dr. Brandon as a caricature of the educational collaborators involved in the mental hygiene films: men like Reuben Hill, Ph.D. (*Appreciating Our Parents*; *How Do You Know It's Love?*; *Are You Ready for Marriage?* [all 1950]), a social psychologist specializing in family relationships who started out as Mormon missionary. The conservative sexual morality of a Reuben Hill is satirized in Brandon's puritanical belief that man's bestial instincts are to blame for social malaise and must be controlled. For Brandon, man is essentially a savage whose primitive instincts have taken the world to the brink of nuclear destruction.

A transformed Tony Rivers (Michael Landon) stalks the woods in *I Was a Teenage Werewolf* (1957).

Tony's "werewolf," then, is born primarily of 1950s sexual repression, but his delinquent aggression is fueled by atomic age fears of impending annihilation, with insane authority to blame. Hence, the film's most famous scene is also its most powerful: Tony transforms into a werewolf while watching Theresa, dressed in her gym-slip, practicing on the parallel bars. His subsequently attacking her is a rape metaphor that suggests Tony's return of sexual repression in degenerate form. But—significantly—the transformation itself is activated (like his previous hair-trigger temper) by a loud noise—in this case the school recess bell—that startles Tony.

"Mankind is on the verge of destroying itself"

In her book *I Was a Cold War Monster*, Cyndy Hendershot claims that "studies have made connections between the angst of 1950s' teens and the potential doom of nuclear war that hung over their heads."[18] If authority figures not only failed to provide teenagers with adequate role models, she argues, but had insanely created a weapon capable of destroying the world, then who could be surprised that teenage culture in the 1950s was in degeneration? Hendershot quotes Lewis Mumford's *In the Name of Sanity* (1954), a rumination on the nuclear age, in positing the reactions of teenagers to the threat of nuclear destruction: These reactions include a sense of purposeless, sexual promiscuity, escape into fantasy—a degenerated psychological state.[19] Accordingly, Cohen locates the cause of Tony's delinquency ultimately in his unconscious awareness of impending nuclear doom. Tony—as all teenagers were told to be in the 1950s—is on constant alert against potential nuclear attack. The ever-present threat of nuclear war places him in a constant state of anxiety—his "flight or fight" response to this threat causes him to become aggressive when even slightly provoked. "Fear is the response to loud noises," intones the doctor in *Control Your Emotions*. In *I Was a Teenage Werewolf*, Tony's aggression is stimulated by such noises or sudden shocks: the friendly tap on the shoulder that starts the fight in the opening scene; the horn that Vic blows in Tony's ear, causing him to lash out; the recess bell that prompts his fateful transformation. (In *Control Your Emotions* the doctor diagnoses the youth's angry outbursts as "an accumulation of stimuli that brought about an abnormal response.")

Control Your Emotions advises the audience to "eliminate the stimulus, modify the stimulus, or modify the response" as a way of controlling their anger and aggression. In Tony's case, and in the case of millions of teenagers growing up with the threat of nuclear war in the 1950s, this proved impossible, not least because propaganda films of the time sought to imprint the impending peril so firmly in their minds that they were *unable* to forget it.

"Always remember: The flash of an atomic bomb can come at any time, no matter where you may be!"

The famous instructional film *Duck and Cover* (1951) told teenagers about the horror of nuclear war while preparing them for the inevitability of an atomic attack on America. The purpose of the film is ostensibly to inform children how they might protect themselves from the blast of an atom bomb; however, many commentators now see the film as Red Scare propaganda intended to make children frightened of the Soviet Union and of the communist threat. Either way, the film's overt message (repeated insistently throughout) is that the bomb could drop at any moment. "You will know when it comes," the narrator of *Duck and Cover* announces ominously. "We hope it never comes but we must get ready." The consequence of not being ready, the film reminds us, is that the bomb "could hurt you in different ways." Therefore, children were urged to learn to "duck and cover"—take shelter under a desk or against a wall and cover one's face and neck to protect against the effects of the bomb.

Duck and Cover was produced partly in response to fears that the Soviets might launch a pre-emptive surprise attack on America during the time before an effective early-warning system was put in place. Therefore, it speaks of two types of possible attack: with warning and without warning. As if the first isn't frightening enough, the film posits the second as the more likely: "If there is a warning you will hear it before the bomb explodes, but sometimes—and this is very, very important—sometimes the bomb might explode without any warning!"

"You may be in your schoolyard playing when the signal comes," intones the narrator. We see a group of boys playing baseball when they hear the air raid siren: They stop their game and make their way inside the school in an orderly manner. "You might be out playing at home when the warning comes," advises the narrator. "Then be sure to get into the house fast where your parents have fixed a safe place for you to go." Accordingly, we see children abandon a game of catch as the siren sounds and calmly retreat inside their house.

Like the mental hygiene films, *Duck and Cover* uses audience identification figures such as "Paul and Patty," whose behavior the audience might imitate: They are shown to be in a constant state of alert. "Here they are on their way to school on a beautiful spring day," the narrator chirps, "but no matter where they are or what they do, they always try to remember what to do if the atom bomb explodes right then!" In another sequence we see a boy (coincidentally named Tony) on his bicycle: "Here's Tony going to his Cub Scout meeting. Tony knows the bomb can explode any time of the year—day or night. He is ready for it." Lest we begin to forget the film's message: "Sundays, holidays, vacation time—we must be ready every day, all the time."

The intended psychological effect of information films such as *Duck and Cover* was to keep the threat of nuclear war high in the public mind, but the deeper psychological effects on the Cold War teenagers living in the shadow of the bomb, knowing they could die at any moment, is still open to conjecture. Writing in 1953, Albert E. Kahn described Cold War propaganda as creating a climate of horror for America's children and teenagers, citing instances of acute sleep disturbance, hysteria, depression, eating disorders and truancy as evidence of psychological trauma caused by constant exposure to such films and literature. He sharply criticized *Duck and Cover* for that reason, claiming that it stressed "the constant likelihood of disaster" without offering any positive solution; that the emphasis on the possibility of a bomb falling when children were alone would produce "intense feelings of insecurity"; and that the main effect of the film would undoubtedly be "to promote anxiety and tension in children."[20]

One thing is certain: The fear of attack among children was pervasive, and nuclear war was seen by many teenagers as inevitable, a matter of not "if" but "when." This state of psychological high alert was reinforced by the authorities in other ways beside propaganda films: in regular school drills during which children practiced getting under their desks quickly to shield themselves against the blast; in regular tests of the Emergency Broadcast System which often took place during children's television, interrupting cartoon shows with a loud continuous beep accompanied by ominous instructions; and, of course, in the civil defense air raid warning siren that would sound in most towns and cities on a regular basis, often during the school lunch break.

Few studies of juvenile delinquency in the 1950s associated the problem with teenagers having to live with the threat of the bomb and the psychological trauma that entailed. *I Was a Teenage Werewolf* does, albeit allegorically. The bells and horns and other loud noises that stimulate an abnormal response in Tony are clearly symbolic of the air raid sirens and warning bells that created involuntary fear in the film's teenage audience. As such, its conclusion that there is little hope for a cure to juvenile delinquency when authority is, itself, so degenerate as to threaten the world with nuclear destruction, is entirely logical. Conformity in the face of such an authority, as the film suggests, is impossible. "Ultimately," writes Cyndy Hendershot, "*I Was a Teenage Werewolf* presents a very harsh view of the problem of authority and juvenile delinquency."[21] Tony and Brandon destroy each other, and all Detective Donovan can do to help Tony at the end of the film is to kill him.

The ending is nihilistic when considered in those terms; however, it is not entirely hopeless. Tony, in death, returns to normal, suggesting—somewhat tentatively—that he has finally expelled his anger by killing Brandon. Donovan's final line of dialogue ("After the newspapers have had their field day, one thing will be clear. It's not for man to interfere in the ways of God...") also offers hope. Donovan has finally seen through Dr. Brandon and his desire to play God: By 1957, anti-nuclear groups had begun to emerge in America and Britain (where the Campaign for Nuclear Disarmament was formed that year); the following year the scientist and peace activist Linus Pauling presented the United Nations with a petition signed by more than 11,000 scientists calling for an end to nuclear weapon testing.

"Teenager or Terrifying Beast?": *Blood of Dracula*

I Was a Teenage Werewolf was a resounding success. Cohen and AIP rushed out a series of follow-ups: *I Was a Teenage Frankenstein*, *Blood of Dracula* and *How to Make a Monster;* produced quickly and cheaply as cash-ins. This partly accounts for the lack of thematic development in the films: All three rehash the basic formula *of I Was a Teenage Werewolf* without exploring its themes in any greater depth.

It is significant that Cohen seems to take a dimmer view of authority with each film. The most interesting of the three is *Blood of Dracula*, almost a scene-by-scene remake of *I Was a Teenage Werewolf*, but here Cohen makes the delinquent teenager a troubled young woman called Nancy (played by Sandra Harrison), sent to a strict boarding school by her callous father. Ostracized by the other girls, Nancy falls into the clutches of a ruthless science teacher, Miss Branding (Louise Lewis, Tony's principal in *Teenage Werewolf*), who transforms her into a vampire as part of her experiment to release the "terrible power" in mankind.

Adults by now in Cohen's films are almost all cast as bad: We find this out in the first scene in which Nancy is being driven to the school by her father and stepmother. Nancy tries to run the car off the road in a desperate attempt to persuade her father not to make her go. His response—shockingly—is to administer a back-handed slap to his daughter's face—immediately establishing parental abuse and neglect. "I warned you at home that I don't want to go there," she protests tearfully. "Well, you have to!" he bullies, grabbing her arm roughly. Nancy's new stepmother is no more compassionate, proclaiming that Nancy has "lost her marbles" and that she's "glad they're getting rid of her." It is apparent straight away that we are entering a harsher world than that of *Teenage Werewolf*—a world where, as Wheeler Winston Dixon notes, "only money and power matter."[22] Nancy's father is portrayed as selfish and hypocritical, and the stepmother—dressed in pearls and furs—materialistic and sarcastic. This becomes all the more apparent when we learn that Nancy's mother has only recently died and Nancy is, in effect, being dumped in the school at the behest of her new stepmother, making Nancy's rebellious behavior wholly understandable.

In taking female juvenile delinquency as its subject and setting the story in a boarding school, Cohen combines the teen horror film with the reformatory schoolgirl film, itself a hybrid of the women-in-prison and JD genres, which was popular in the 1950s. Oren Shai writes of the women-in-prison film:

> [T]he male prison picture often dealt with escape from repression; the female prison was inherently tied to ideas of reform, often through the acceptance of patriarchy. Rather than being set free, the incarcerated woman passes from one form of oppression to another.[23]

Shai also notes that the women-in-prison films of the 1950s are characterized by "existential despair and the failure of reform."[24] Hence, in *Blood of Dracula*, Nancy passes from one form of oppression—a neglectful and abusive father—to another—a manipulative teacher. Her reform entails giving up her rebellious attitude and accepting patriarchy. Reform fails because authority, of course, turns her into a monster.

Caged (1950) established the conventions of the women-in-prison film: A young woman arrives at the institution, where the benevolent head warder attempts to reform her, but is thwarted by the vicious head guard who brutalizes the inmate. Cohen follows the formula set by *Caged* fairly closely in terms of stereotypes and their functions. Thus, in *Blood of Dracula*, the principal, Miss Thorndyke (Mary Adams), shows compassion towards Nancy's plight and emerges as the film's only sympathetic authority figure. Nancy's fellow students are portrayed in equally formulaic terms: "If you want to get in on things and have some fun around here, you have to be one of us," they inform Nancy. The girls, who are all assistants to the teachers, have adopted the authoritarian ways of their mentors. Therefore they require Nancy to bow to their authority. Nancy, however, claims that she never wants "any medals for obedience."

Miss Branding is ultimately a more complex and contradictory authority figure than her male equivalents played by Whit Bissell and Michael Gough in Cohen's other films—and is in fact reminiscent of Val Lewton's conflicted authoritarians. Her motivation for using Nancy in the experiment is the desire to compete in a world governed by male authority. "We live in a world ruled by men for men," she tells her assistant. "They won't even consider my thesis." But despite her quasi-feminist proclamations, Branding ultimately adopts patriarchal methods to pursue her ambition: oppressing Nancy to get what she wants. Branding intends to release Nancy's inner power, believing that by doing so, "nations will stop looking for new artificial weapons because the natural ones, we, the human race, will be too terrible to arouse." The implication is that releasing female sexuality can change the world. However, any progressive potential of the experiment is again undermined by Branding's methodology: Nancy is tricked into becoming aggressive and it is this aggression that becomes the basis of her transformation—the "power" that Branding brings out of Nancy is negative. Miss Branding may be well-meaning in her ambitions but her oppression and manipulation of Nancy—her willingness to act unethically—proves her undoing, as she creates yet another Cohen monster.

Commentators have detected homophobia in Cohen's basic scenario of an older male "corrupting" the younger male (or older woman corrupting a younger woman in *Blood of Dracula*), claiming that it reflects the stereotype of the predatory homosexual-lesbian luring boys-girls into performing homosexual acts.[25] However, horror arises in Cohen's films from the repression of sexuality, not from sexuality itself (Cohen himself claimed that the teen protagonist's status of outsider was really the cause of their misfortunes). In *Blood of Dracula*, unfortunately, the repression of female sexuality is not a theme that is fully explored. Early in the film, there are hints that Nancy's relationship with her boyfriend might constitute sexual delinquency in the eyes of her father and the boarding school authorities: As Shai comments, "[B]oys generally committed more violent crimes; girls were detained for moral crimes."[26] Her sexuality is therefore seen by authority as a dangerous force; and her becoming a vampire is the release of that pent-up sexuality. However, Nancy's vampire is not a particularly sexualized one either in appearance or behavior (in comparison with Michael Landon's werewolf, who stalks his victims—most notably the teenage gymnast—in lust). Possibly this would have posed a challenge to censorship of the time, and one might also argue that Nancy's vampire represents repressed sexuality in its degenerate form (hence her monstrous appearance), but nonetheless, Nancy's vampire is a disappointment. Like *I Was a Teenage Werewolf*, *Blood of Dracula* lacks development in theme and plot past the first killing. It is a shame that Cohen was not able to offer a more challenging commentary on the hypocrisy of the female sexual delinquency moral panics of the 1940s and '50s.

After Nancy (as the degenerate vampire) almost kills her boyfriend, she pleads with Branding to set her free. "Free to do what?" Branding asks. "Free to be myself," Nancy replies.

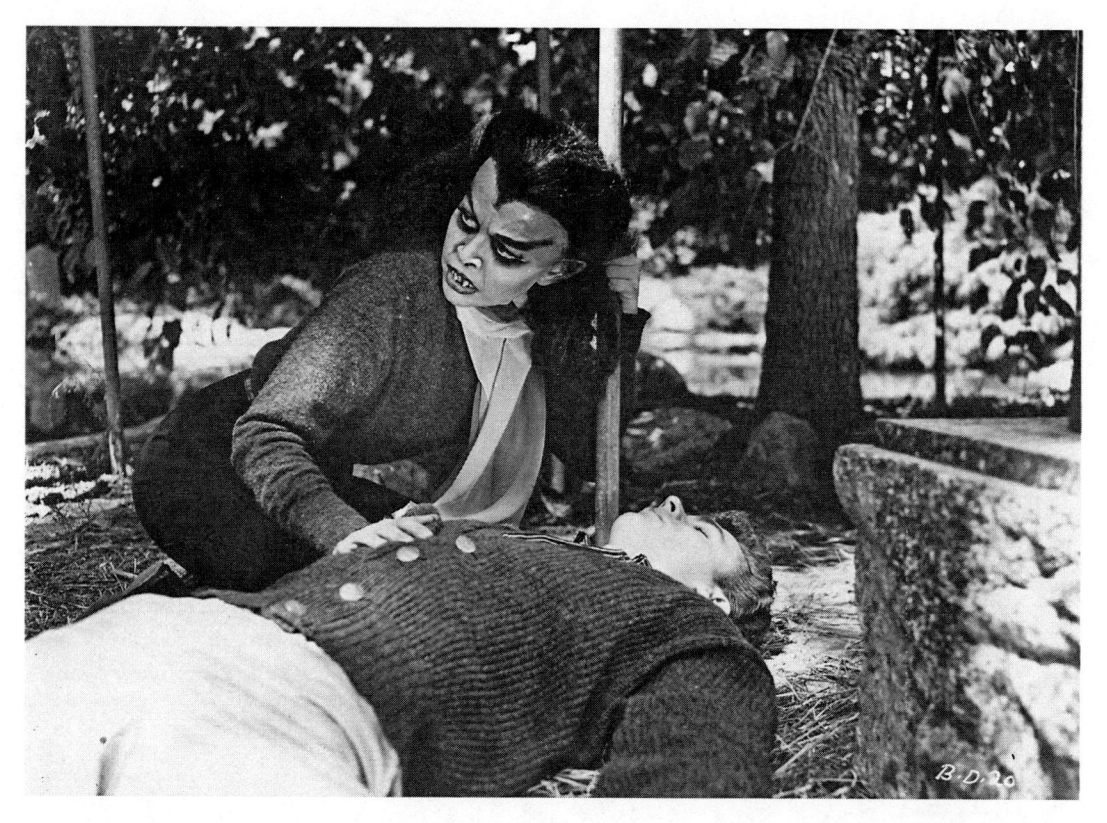

Teenage vampire Nancy Perkins (Sandra Harrison) prepares to feed on Tab (Jerry Blaine) in *Blood of Dracula* (1957).

Unlike Tony in *Teenage Werewolf*, Nancy at least comes to understand her problem. Tony never realized that insane authority (in the guise of Dr. Brandon) was the culprit; Nancy does. "I know who you are and I know what you've done to me," she tells Branding. "It's horrible—what I do, what I've become." Nancy stands up to Branding, smacking the glass from her hand when Branding tries to erase her memory with a potion. "You'll do what I say," commands Branding. At this point she grips Nancy's arm like Nancy's father did at the start and the film comes full circle: Nancy has moved from one form of oppression (her father) to another (Branding). Fittingly Nancy destroys the monster maker, but is herself destroyed. Although rushed, the ending is more satisfying than that of *I Was a Teenage Werewolf* because Nancy achieves some self-knowledge: an understanding of her delinquency and of the role of authority in turning her into a monster.

"Speak! You've got a civil tongue in your head, I know you have because I sewed it there myself!"

In Herman Cohen's filmography, authority figures become increasingly degenerate: Each film presents its mad scientist as more homicidal than the film before it, and the reasons for the murderousness become more perverse. Dr. Brandon in *Teenage Werewolf* may not be complicit in the werewolf's killings, but he covers up his part in creating a monster; by contrast Whit Bissell's mad doctor in *I Was a Teenage Frankenstein* deliberately manipulates his monster to kill, and does so in order to cover his tracks, to keep his experiments a secret so that he can continue his work. This is, of course, a more damning indictment of male authority, and a provocative statement about the nature of juvenile delinquency: that it is directly caused or created by authority itself (in *Teenage Frankenstein* the teenage monster is literally assembled by Bissell from body parts and automated—Caligari-like—through hypnosis). Hypnosis is again used by the makeup artist Pete Dumond (Robert H. Harris) on his monsters in *How to Make a Monster*; here, however, he makes them kill for revenge. By contrast, Edmund Bancroft (Michael Gough) in *Horrors of the Black Museum* programs his teenage protégé, Rick (Graham Curnow), to kill in order to satisfy his own sadistic urges. In Cohen's films, as Wheeler Winston Dixon observes, the adults truly are the real monsters, using teenagers as their tools of murder and mayhem.[27]

By the time of *Horrors of the Black Museum*, Cohen's films were beginning to lose their appeal to youth audiences. "The rising optimism of the 1960s," writes Dixon, "didn't dovetail with Cohen and Kandel's unremittingly bleak vision of adolescence."[28] Towards the end of the 1950s, changes had challenged old beliefs about conformity, and the younger generation began to feel empowered by these changes. Youth culture, the Beat movement and the civil rights movement all fought against social alienation and sought ways to overcome it. Meanwhile, the anti-nuclear movement grew in popularity as more Americans grew fearful about the escalation of the arms race and its potential consequences. At the same time, many young

The hypnotized Rick (Graham Curnow, center) runs amok in a fairground in *Horrors of the Black Museum* (1959).

Americans began to reject consumer culture: TV quiz shows turned out to be rigged; disc jockeys such as Alan Freed confessed to accepting bribes from record companies to play their records; consumer debt rocketed to an all-time high by 1960. The cracks in Cold War America began to show and conformity gradually gave way in the 1960s to radicalism, led by the youth.

After *Horrors of the Black Museum*, Cohen's output deteriorated in quality and originality: *Konga* (1961) was followed by *Black Zoo* (1963) (again featuring Michael Gough as a sadistic authoritarian); *Berserk!* (1967) (set in a circus with Joan Crawford as the ringmaster); the critically abhorred *Trog* (1970); and finally *Craze* (1974), starring Jack Palance.

It is fitting that Herman Cohen should, after 1959, pursue much of his career in Britain: His films trace a line of development to two important British directors who would share many of his themes and concerns. His use of lurid and deliberately shocking exploitation tropes; his appeal to youth audiences via American International Pictures and the drive-in circuit; his depiction of a world of cruelty and brutality; and—crucially—his portrayal of a degenerate older generation preying on "permissive" youth—all were later to be found in the work of Michael Reeves and Pete Walker.

4

ANTI-ESTABLISHMENT 1960S–1970S BRITAIN
The Films of Michael Reeves and Pete Walker

In March 1968, police clashed with anti-war demonstrators in London during protests against the Vietnam War. Present at the "Battle of Grosvenor Square" was the young director Michael Reeves, whose film *Witchfinder General* was to break new ground in its depiction of graphic and shocking screen violence. Reeves had just completed post-production on the film, on which he had feared censorship, and joined the protestors outside the American embassy—most likely just to observe. But as mounted officers charged on protestors who retaliated by throwing smoke bombs, stones and bottles, Reeves must have felt strangely vindicated in his defense of his film to the censor and become even more determined to keep the film intact. "Watching the chaos unfold around him, the police beatings and intimidation," writes Benjamin Halligan, "Mike would have understood the context for his study of violence and society and that, more importantly, this context would be understood by those who would soon see the film."[1]

By 1968, a mood of escalating violence was rapidly gripping America—and now threatened to spread to other countries, including Britain. Social upheaval in the United States, primarily the struggle for civil rights and mass protest against the war in Vietnam, had culminated in some of the most destructive riots in American history, such as Watts, Los Angeles (in 1965), the 12th Street riots in Detroit and the Newark, New Jersey riots (both in 1967). Violence also erupted at a mass student protest at the 1968 Democratic National Convention in Chicago, where police brutality was televised live to the nation and even journalists and reporters were caught up in the violence. Added to this were the assassinations of John F. Kennedy, Martin Luther King and Robert Kennedy; rising crime rates; reports of atrocities in Vietnam—it seemed that violence was endemic in American society. And many began to question the role of the state in all of this, particularly after the shooting of student protestors at Kent State University in 1970. Was the Establishment to blame for this mounting violence?

Witchfinder General and *The Sorcerers* (which Reeves made in 1967) explore the notion that violence breeds violence within the patriarchal society (and "to that end," as Reeves himself wrote, "violence in itself is insanity"[2]). Like the violent protestors and police in Grosvenor Square, Reeves's protagonists exhibit what Erich Fromm, a social psychologist and prominent New Left thinker, described in the 1960s in relation to the escalating violence as "lustful destructiveness" arising from feelings of uncertainty, impotence and powerlessness in the face of a repressive, hypocritical and often brutal Establishment.[3] In Reeves' films, the "good" person is driven to these acts of violence by society's old guard, who are themselves vindictive and ruthless in their suppression of the rising generation. Accordingly, the films of Michael Reeves have been described by Leon Hunt as examples of British generation gap horror, "a narrative in which the old, metaphorically cannibalistic generation preys on the 'youth' at what should be the moment of its 'liberation.'"[4]

It is a phrase that has also been used to describe the work of Pete Walker, a director who—perhaps more than any other—took up the mantle of Reeves after Reeves' early death in 1969. In his "terror pictures" of the 1970s, Walker deliberately courted controversy by attacking the Establishment and its sacred institutions (family, the penal system and the Church) as instruments of repression and generational violence. His films written with David McGillivray (*House of Whipcord* [1974], *Frightmare* and *House of Mortal Sin* [1976]) are remarkable in their condemnation of a reactionary older generation brutally suppressing "permissive" youth.

Michael Reeves, Generation Gap Horror and *The Sorcerers* (1967)

Hunt calls *The Sorcerers* the first British generation gap horror film, but it is possible to see Herman Cohen's *Horrors of the Black Museum* as having an influence on the films of Reeves (and later Walker). *Horrors of the Black Museum*, like *The Sorcerers*, features disaffected youth, mind control, sadistic thrill-kills and a degenerate older generation playing out its repressions through the youth they prey upon. Cohen's film, like those of Walker, also has a peculiarly British sense of perversity (which marks it as different to his American teenage horror films, despite its repeating the same basic plot), "a frothing mix of prurience with fascination with all the horrible details" as author and critic Kim Newman described the characteristic, "and then this mealy-mouthed disapproval."[5] *Horrors of the Black Museum* was, at the time, one of several films (which included Michael Powell's *Peeping Tom* [1960]) to take sadistic entertainment as its subject (as would *The Sorcerers*), operating both as an exercise in sadism and a criticism of the vicarious enjoyment of it. Interestingly, the British press (which traditionally has been nothing if not prurient and mealy-mouthed) excoriated these films when they were first released, perhaps because they were too close to home.

Prurience can be linked to the "British desire to challenge institutions in authority, be they the Royal family, governments or the Church"[6] (and this can certainly be seen in the films of Reeves and Walker, which delight in the ghoulish details of flogging, torture, murder, sexual violence—even cannibalism [in *Frightmare*] perpetrated by the malicious elders); the British press has traditionally fed on this while simultaneously condemning it. *Horrors of the Black Museum* criticizes yellow journalism of this sort, depicting the journalist played by Michael Gough as crippled, impotent and twisted with hatred and jealousy. In the same way, Reeves, in *The Sorcerers* and *Witchfinder General,* criticizes the vicarious enjoyment of screen violence by using it to slap the audience in the face.

This dichotomy of prurient fascination and hypocritical condemnation, a very British trait, reflects a society caught between repression and liberation as Britain arguably was in the early 1960s. The Profumo Affair, in 1963, marked the turning point from a pre-pill, pre-promiscuity age, and a time of deference to those in government, to a more permissive era—one in which the established order was being challenged. The scandal of the affair between Conservative MP John Profumo, Secretary of State for War, and call girl Christine Keeler, who was also sleeping with a Soviet naval attaché, and the press coverage of it, ultimately toppled the Conservative government. The Profumo affair exposed the hypocrisy of the Establishment and ushered in a time of sexual revolution known as the "swinging sixties." *The Sorcerers*, in fact, offers a critique of the swinging sixties, showing it as commodification and commercialization of sexual revolution (what pre-eminent New Left theorist Herbert Marcuse termed "repressive desublimation"—the co-option of sexual liberation to serve the repressive social order)—as is symbolized by the London district of Soho, the area associated historically with Britain's sex trade.

Indeed the Profumo scandal had exposed the relationship between the British Establishment and the sex trade, which until then had remained hush-hush. According to Halligan, "the Establishment's mistresses more often than not graduated from the Soho school, sometimes leaving damaging 8mm films, or persistent rumors of such films behind them."[7] Soho's Wardour Street, in the 1960s and the 1970s, was also the heart of the mainstream British film industry, where many film companies kept their offices. Tigon, which produced *The Sorcerers* and *Witchfinder General,* had a background in soft-core pornography and Reeves himself, according to Halligan, had hung out with Soho pornographers at the start of his film career "making cutting suggestions as he watched hacks slap 16mm porn together."[8] *The Sorcerers* was therefore conceived as a comment on film as voyeurism, as well as a critique of "Swinging London" and its hypocrisy.

"From now on we are going to control your mind. From time to time we'll put thoughts into your head and you will obey those thoughts"

In his book *Lights Out for the Territory*, Iain Sinclair discusses the films of Michael Reeves (whom he had known and worked with at the time of *The Sorcerers*) in terms of what he calls "the stock Reevesian preoccupation": "the apparently 'normal' citizen pushed to locate the evil within himself, to absorb and reciprocate all the venom of his oppressor".[9] In *The Sorcerers* the apparently normal citizen is a wealthy but bored young Chelsea-ite, Mike Roscoe (Ian Ogilvy), who holds a nominal job in an antiques shop disconcertingly called The Glory Hole, and spends his nights either languishing in a South Kensington club, Blaises (a real-life club described as "a swinging spot of the era"[10]), or listlessly walking the London streets alone. He is curiously detached from his environment unlike his friends who seem to relish the newfound freedom of 1960s Swinging London. (Sinclair has described Reeves's films as "almost existential in their deadness and alienation at the soul of them."[11])

During one of his late night sojourns to a burger joint, he is approached by a disgraced hypnotherapist, Marcus Monserrat (Boris Karloff), who offers "extraordinary experiences." Intrigued, Mike accompanies Marcus to his drab flat which he shares with his bitter wife, Estelle (Catherine Lacey), who is complicit in her husband's experiments, using them to release her own pent-up urges. There they strap Mike to Marcus' mind control machine, which (like a psychic broadband router) forges a three-way connection between Mike, Marcus and Estelle. Marcus and Estelle discover that not only are they able to control Mike's behavior, but they can experience vicariously all he does and feels. Mike is thus pushed, in Sinclair's words, "from ennui towards unmotivated acts of violence"[12] for the voyeuristic pleasure of the two elderly "sorcerers."

An intriguing aspect of *The Sorcerers* is its ambiguity: While Mike is shown as being at the mercy of the old couple who control his mind, it is also suggested that he himself may

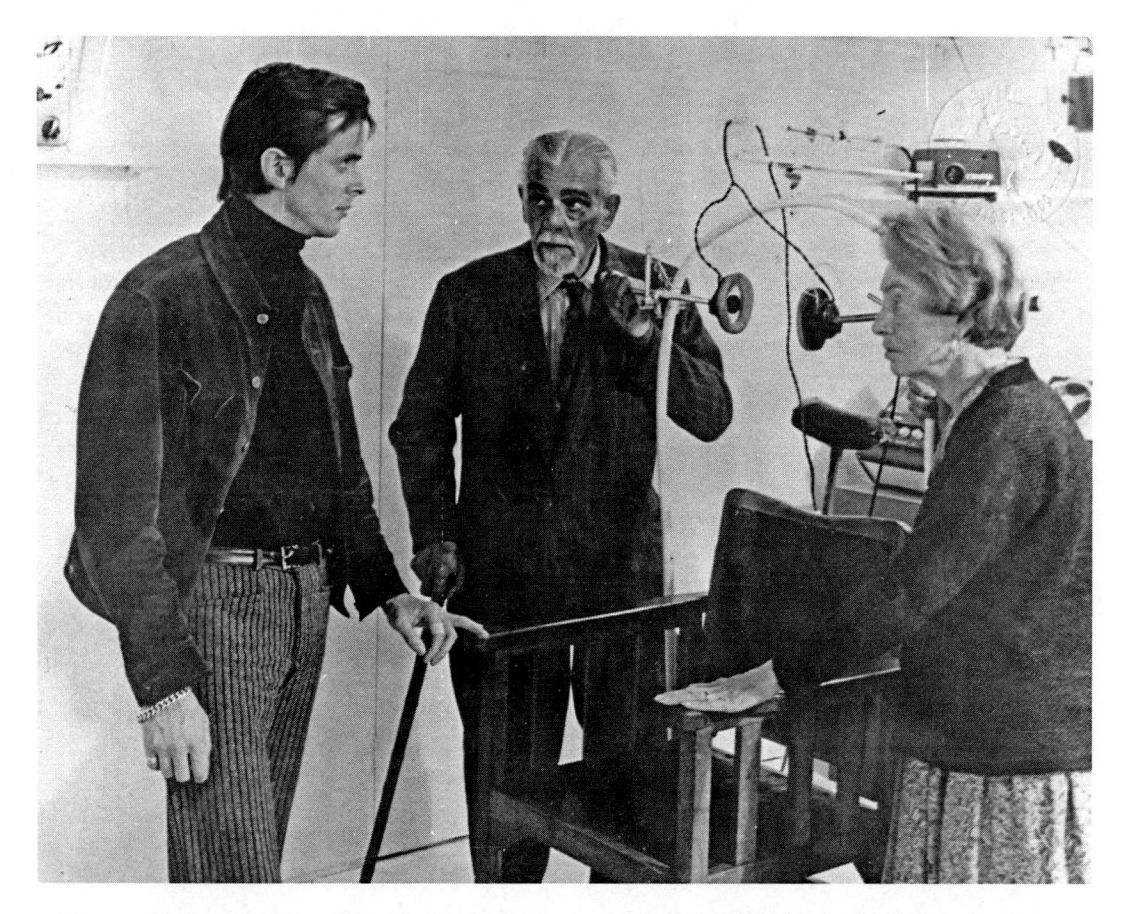

Marcus (Boris Karloff) and Estelle (Catherine Lacey) persuade Mike Roscoe (Ian Ogilvy) to try their mind machine in *The Sorcerers* (1967).

be enjoying the thrill of killing—that the perverted desires being fulfilled are not only Estelle's but also Mike's. As Kim Newman has written, "[I]t's a despairing vision, of generations not so much in conflict as collaboration, soullessly feeding each other's worst instincts."[13] As the film progresses, Mike increasingly falls mercy to violent forces that have been released both in Estelle and in himself. These forces are beyond his understanding and his control, and make him both the "destroyer and the destroyed."[14]

The question of whether violence is inherent in human nature is one that preoccupied social commentators during the turbulent 1960s and early 1970s—as violent protests, urban guerrilla warfare, My Lai, Altamont and the Manson murders blighted the rise of the New Left and tarnished the idealism of the peace movement and the love generation. The right wing cited damage to property by groups like the Weather Underground (who bombed buildings) and violence incidental to anti-war demonstrations as evidence of the need for greater "law and order." Arguments of the school of evolutionary biology became popular in the late 1960s through the writings of zoologist Desmond Morris (*The Naked Ape* [1967]) and others. Their arguments were an implicit denial that human beings could organize a fairer society because of their "innate" competitiveness and aggressiveness.

New Left thinkers, like Erich Fromm, opposed these points of view, putting forward the argument that stricter punishment and enforcement of law and order would increase violence rather than decrease it; and that aggression in the modern age arose primarily in response to social discontent. In an essay entitled "The Nature of Violence," written in 1968 for *Colliers Year Book*, Fromm argued that continued anxiety about the possibility of nuclear war, racial antagonism between black and white, and middle-class fears about slipping on the ladder of success, combined with the passivity of the consumer age, had created a climate of violence and destructiveness in the West. Fromm predicted that in the long term fear, uncertainty and boredom would likely increase violence in the whole population: "[T]he minority will rebel more, and the majority will take increasingly violent countermeasures against attempts at rebellion."[15] Fromm described the nature of this violence as a "lustful destructiveness" stemming from feelings of impotence brought about by the mechanization of life, the passivity of consumerism (and the "unaliveness" that results from it), the lack of aim and vision for Western society beyond more production and consumption. Lustful destructiveness, according to Fromm, is characterized by sadism and a desire for complete control over other people. These, of course, are the traits of the lustful destructiveness that overcome Mike and Estelle in *The Sorcerers*.

"Do you really think it will work, Marcus?"

The Sorcerers opens with a sequence that shows the Monserrats as relics of a bygone age: Theirs is the generation of austerity, of genteel poverty as evidenced by the décor of their apartment, with its brown floral wallpaper, its butler sink in the kitchen, its quietly ticking clock on the mantelpiece. They are, like their surroundings, caught in time; but also in their apartment, behind a locked door, is the mind control machine that promises a release from their repression—a chance to partake of the material and fleshly delights of the new age. Estelle is eager for them to test the machine. Despite playing the supportive wife, she resents a lifetime of deprivation and self-denial caused by her husband's ruined reputation at the hands of the press. "Don't we deserve something for all those years of no money, no reputation?" she asks when the experiment proves to be a success and her husband immediately wants to turn the machine over to medical science for the benefit of others. Estelle's impotence, born of the grayness of her daily life, leads to her craving complete control over Mike that goes beyond mere sexual excitement; it is a need for omnipotence, a desire to transcend the limitations of her existence through the complete control of Mike.

This feeling of impotence is something that Mike shares. His boredom and passivity is established with typical Reevesian economy. We first encounter him in the "den of iniquity," as he describes the nightclub which he frequents four nights a week solely, he claims, for the purposes of giving his nominal girlfriend Nicole (Elizabeth Ercy) a good time. He appears to be telling the truth: As the girlfriend goes to dance with another man, Mike surveys the club and its "dolly birds" with the boredom of an uninterested shopper pushing his cart down the aisle of Walmart. The commodification of the sexual revolution, as presented in the 1960s club—emblematic of Swinging London—with its mechanized dancers, instills not lust but languor; Reeves based Roscoe partly on himself, and gave him his own mercurial traits, including the habit of leaving his friends on a whim in order to walk the streets whenever the "scene" started to pall.

"The restlessness," according to Sinclair (who presumably experienced it first hand), "the non-job, the apparent means to do whatever he wants to do is a sympathetic caricature of Reeves' own dilemma. Ogilvy is a smoother Reeves with terminal angst, other directed, driven to contact the violent, risk-taking aspects of himself."[16] Mike's impotence is both sexual and existential: After the Monserrats seize control of his mind, they direct him to take Nicole to a swimming pool; the thrill of sneaking past the porter for a late night dip, of doing something spontaneous and exciting, arouses Mike sexually and he wants to make love to Nicole. According to Ingrid Cranfield, sexual impotence was something Reeves himself experienced, caused by depression.[17] Like the "castration" that Tod Browning suffered, and which personified his characters, Reeves links his personal feelings of emasculation to powerlessness felt by *his* screen characters.

"You can't hold me back now!"

Sadism, according to Fromm, is the blending of the desire to control and sexual excitement, and is another form of lustful destructiveness. It manifests itself in the desire to inflict pain on another person since there is no better way to experience absolute control over another person more completely than by "forcing him to endure pain."[18] Thus Estelle, in her craving for complete control over Mike, and her desire to experience omnipotence, compels him to commit sadistic murders. These murders are sexual in nature, and constitute perhaps the most lurid aspects of *The Sorcerers*, but they are never gratuitous: The shock value is ideologically driven, and in keeping with the film's thesis, which reflects Fromm's ideas on the nature of violence, lending the film social and psychological value.

Because of the sexualized violence, the scenes remain shocking. Mike visits an old girlfriend, Audrey. The casting of Susan George, then a "sex kitten," and clothing her in a slip, emphasizes the sexual nature of the killing. There is still tenderness between her and Mike, a sense that things may not have worked out between them because of Mike's malaise. The specter of Mike's impotence (past and present) hangs over the scene. She wonders why he has come to visit; we assume it is because he needs a confidant but, again, there is intriguing ambiguity. Has Mike come because of some unconscious desire to exert control over Audrey through sadism? The killing, using scissors, represents a sublimation of the sexual act, a symbolic penetration. It is significant that Mike does not rape his victims—the control that Estelle exerts over him ultimately renders him once again sexually impotent. Depravity is born of repression, and it is interesting in connection to this, to note that the décor of Audrey's bedsit is the same as that of the Monserrat apartment: It is Estelle's psychogeographical space we are in. The murder of Laura the night club singer is equally sexual in nature. Mike takes her in a cab to a darkened alley—again, the possibility of rape is suggested—but strangles her instead. Rape is another form of lustful destructiveness in that it symbolizes the absolute control of a person. Therefore, strangulation, once more, becomes an indication of Mike's impotence, and of Estelle's sadism.

Reeves includes a rather perfunctory subplot involving a somewhat caricatured police detective investigating the crimes. Mike's girlfriend Nicole and his mechanic friend, Alan (Victor Henry), also make a bid to stop Mike before it is too late.

The Sorcerers addresses issues of class in interesting ways. The mingling of the social classes became fashionable in 1960s London: musicians, photographers, models and actors rose from the working classes and shared the same social circles as members of the so-called gentry. Being working-class was seen as "cool" among the Chelsea Set, "a hard-partying, socially eclectic mix of largely idle 'toffs' and talented working-class movers and shakers."[19] Mike, despite being a man of means, affects a similar classlessness.

But at the same time, the 1960s was a period of labor strife in Britain as union militancy increased and strikes became common. This, and the end of deference, brought about class tensions, reflected in several notable films including *The Servant* (1963), directed by Joseph Losey, and *The Collector* (1965) starring Terence Stamp (himself an icon of "mod London"). *The Sorcerers* opens with Marcus having to endure a lack of deference from a lowly news agent who has removed his advertisement from the shop window. When the news agent refuses to acknowledge Marcus's presence ("You'll have to wait a minute"), Marcus thumps his cane imperiously on the counter. The insolent news agent calls Marcus "grandpa" and makes a lewd joke about him doing some "spade work on a little dolly he's got lined up."

Similar sparring takes place between Mike and Alan in the nightclub. Although references to each other's class at first takes the form of apparently good-natured banter ("The man's learning respect"; "It's all those years pulling coal-carts down the mine, sir"), antagonism between the two increases throughout the film and results in several vicious fistfights. Growing class tensions eventually erupt in Reeves's film, just as they would in Paris in May 1968 as a rebellion spread among the working class, leading to unrest in other countries.

Considering *The Sorcerers* in terms of Fromm's ideas about lustful destructiveness goes some way towards justifying the portrayal of Estelle as "monstrous" and partly dispelling accusations of misogyny that some critics have leveled at the film. It is logical to cast Estelle as the most sadistic character, as she has been the one most repressed, the one most excluded from living a life. Her function as wife and cook has left her with no vent for her frustrated energies.

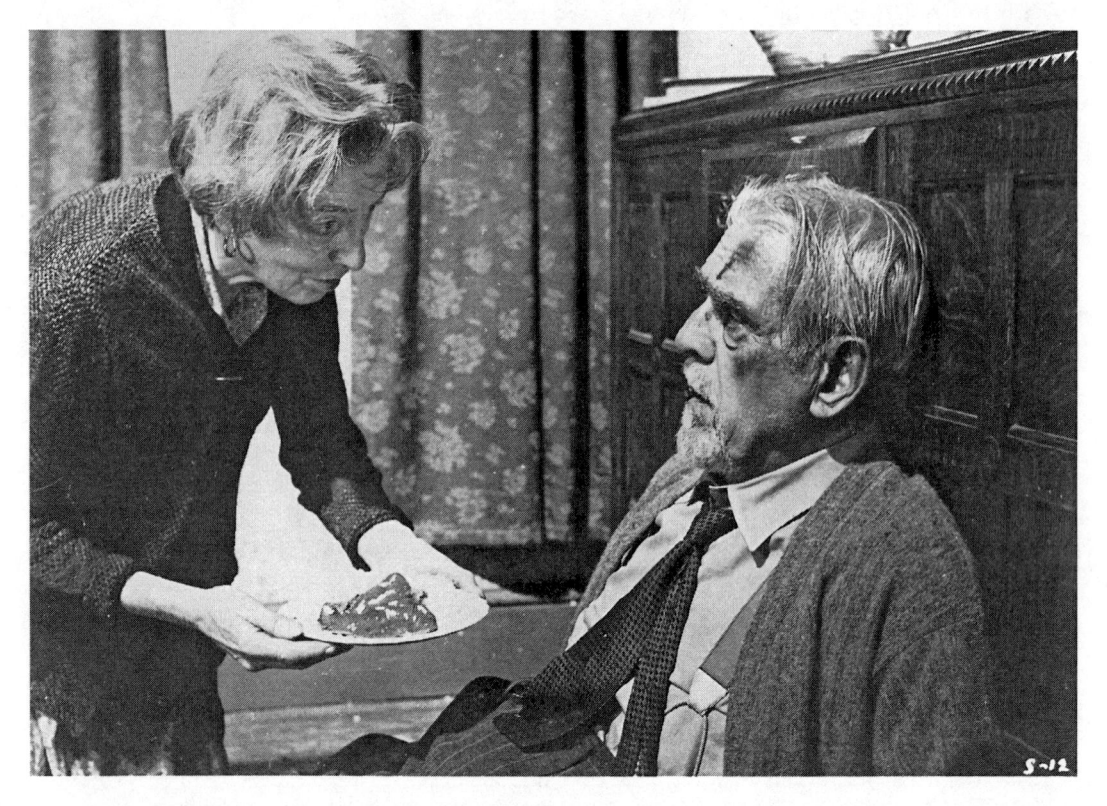

Estelle Monserrat (Catherine Lacey) offers her husband Marcus (Boris Karloff) dinner after tying him to the floor in *The Sorcerers* (1967) (photograph courtesy Ronald V. Borst/Hollywood Movie Posters).

She dotes on Marcus but secretly despises him because he has effectively imprisoned her. The film's central idea of vicarious pleasure in spectatorship, hinges on Estelle's sadism. If *The Sorcerers* is an allegory about cinema and our enjoyment of violence in cinema—as many critics argue—then it is Estelle's character that forces us to question why such a vent is necessary. Her sadism becomes ours, and we are thus forced not only to ask why we might feel lustful destructiveness, but equally importantly why violent entertainment is provided to us as catharsis for such antisocial feelings. Questioning the function of cinema in this way is in itself subversive, as it threatens to draw attention to cinema as an Ideological State Apparatus by which dominant values are inculcated. Reeves comes perilously close to doing this in *The Sorcerers* and perhaps closer still in *Witchfinder General*, in which he desired to overcome the "once-removed sadism"[20]—the violence without consequence—traditionally afforded by cinema, by making the violence in his tale of 17th century witch burning shocking, graphic and brutally realistic.

"A lack of order in the land encourages strange ideas": *Witchfinder General*

In *Witchfinder General* the breakdown in systems of authority caused by a collapse of the social order leads to a regressive morality that instigates violence and cruelty which is

Matthew Hopkins (Vincent Price, right) prepares to torture Sara Lowes (Hilary Dwyer) as the jailer (David Webb) looks on in *Witchfinder General* (1968) (photograph courtesy Ronald V. Borst/Hollywood Movie Posters).

escalated by the military mind. Although set in 1645 at the time of Cromwell, "Civil War England is equated," as Quentin Turnour points out, "with the culture wars of the 1960s. *Witchfinder General*'s themes are related to the tensions that led to May '68."[21] Turnour briefly mentions My Lai in his analysis of the film, and indeed *Witchfinder General* speaks with chilling prescience of the "ecstatic hate" (to use another phrase coined by Erich Fromm) that led to the atrocities of My Lai on March 16, 1968 (the day before the Battle of Grosvenor Square), when American troops raped, mutilated and massacred up to five hundred Vietnamese civilians in the hamlets of the Son My village. In Ian Ogilvy's Roundhead soldier, Marshall, and his alter ego John Stearne (Robert Russell), we see the potential for this type of lustful destructiveness that comes in times of war, when the taboo of killing is broken and sadistic impulses can take over. In *Witchfinder General*, Matthew Hopkins (Vincent Price) and his assistant Stearne may represent the regressive morality that arises, according to the narrator who opens the story, in "an atmosphere where law and order have collapsed," but Marshall, the hero, is the military mind who pledges his vengeance and thereby escalates the violence instigated by Hopkins.

"The army has taught you rough manners"

We first glimpse Marshall's potential for brutality when he comes home on leave after he has shot the Royalist soldier—an act which marks not only his first kill, but has also been the occasion for his promotion to coronet. There is also another "prize" waiting for him at home: his fiancée Sara (Hilary Dwyer), whom he beds for the first time on his return. Thus the film raises the notion that soldiers fight for their women back home; and that by implication, the reward for battle is sex—women are the spoils of war. When Marshall embraces Sara he is initially animalistic, making her recoil from him. This, it seems, is a part of him that has been released by killing, which he must make an effort to control.

In "The Nature of Violence," Fromm writes of war as a trigger mechanism that can lead to outbursts of lustful destructiveness; the soldier is given permission to kill, and in some soldiers this first breaking of the taboo on killing will lead to the emergence of sadistic impulses; and these soldiers will be prone to engage in "lustful, cruel acts to the degree that they can get away with it."[22] Fromm is careful to emphasize that only a small percentage commit such acts, but also makes it clear that what happened in My Lai would not have taken place had the first step not been eased for the soldiers who took part in the rape and murder by lifting the taboo on killing. In this way we can see Marshall's killing of the Royalist soldier in *Witchfinder General* as unleashing his potential for the lustful destructiveness that he engages in later when he brutally murders Stearne and Hopkins.

Marshall becomes completely absorbed in his hate and destructiveness, beyond all reason. He vows several times that he will kill Hopkins, and when, during a confrontation, Hopkins reminds Marshall, "The law is with me, remember," it seems as though it has never crossed Marshall's mind that Hopkins should be tried and punished by the magistrate with due respect to whatever law and order remains. This is an example of Fromm's "ecstatic hate," the form of lustful destructiveness by which a person channels their full energies into their hatred towards another person. In this state, according to Fromm, a person becomes completely absorbed by his hate and destructiveness; he is completely seized by fury and the wish to kill and control. In this absoluteness of hate he is thoroughly resolute, but at the same time he loses contact with the world outside him and also with his own self. "This sacred fury leads close to the border of madness,"[23] writes Fromm. From the moment Marshall

"Ecstatic hate": Richard Marshall (Ian Ogilvy) gleefully axes Hopkins (Vincent Price) to death in *Witchfinder General* (1968).

makes his vow to God, and raises his sword in offering to him, so that he might deliver Hopkins for divine judgment, Marshall feels as though he is on a God-given mission to kill Hopkins and is completely driven in pursuing this goal. However, in giving in to his hatred and destructiveness he does indeed lose contact with himself, and his savage killing of Hopkins represents a descent into madness and the loss of his love, Sara.

In this way, we can see Marshall's mirror image not in Hopkins, but in John Stearne, the sadistic torturer employed by Hopkins to elicit "confessions" from the persecuted. Stearne's lustful destructiveness arises from his desire for complete control over others, a desire given free rein and with the full blessing, via Hopkins, of what little law remains. As in *The Sorcerers*, there is class tension between Stearne and Hopkins, but the pair are curiously interdependent, and Stearne is ultimately given the opportunity to exercise unlimited power by his master; lowly as Stearne is, without Hopkins, such power would be impossible. Fromm describes what he calls the "rape-robbery-destruction" syndrome observed in the behavior of victorious soldiers if, for a limited time, they have permission to take absolute control over a conquered population. "The indiscriminate raping of women," writes Fromm, "is not so much an expression of sexual desire as of absolute control."[24] Thus after torturing a female victim in the dungeon, Stearne pursues his desire to achieve omnipotence by seeking out

Sara in order to rape her. His raping and pillaging is born ultimately of class oppression creating lustful destructiveness within him.

Hopkins, by contrast, was conceived by Reeves as "part ridiculous authority figure, part Frankenstein's monster"[25]: It is an apt description, as Hopkins embodies the tyranny that arises when democracy is allowed to fail. He rides on the coat tails of Cromwell, who represents the possibility of progressive change, but for his own gain he preys upon the superstitions of country folk, the regressive beliefs that the people have fallen back on as a defense mechanism in a time of social collapse. One might question the parliamentarian Cromwell's culpability in the film: Why has Hopkins not been brought to trial but instead been promoted to the primary witchfinder in England? (This indicates, as Halligan notes, "that witchfinding, by the close of the film, is now not so much a facet, but a possible model of the society to come."[26]) Cromwell is portrayed as somewhat self-serving, clearly enjoying the spoils of war, extolling the delights of good food and "valor"; a pompous wart-hog surrounded by sycophants. This depiction of authority as ultimately corrupt has led critics like Halligan to describe the film as an "exposé of the Establishment interconnectedness of high moral righteousness, political power, slaughter in God's name and corruption."[27] *Witchfinder General* may indicate social breakdown as allowing the ascendency of a Hopkins, but the notion of society and what is "good," in Halligan's words, "comes to be seen as little more than a sham to begin with."[28]

"You took him from me!"

Where does this leave us with regard to Reeves's beliefs concerning the nature of violence? In the introduction to this book I described *Witchfinder General* as a film in which violence is seen as inherent in the human condition. This is based on the evidence of the film itself which offers no alternative to an inevitability of violence. It is a view shared by several critics. Halligan sees society in the film as "a device to keep in check, or channel man's capacity for violence."[29] Sinclair speaks of "the ordinary man ... capable of absolute evil. By his actions he was revealed to himself."[30] Wood mentions "the morally outraged seeking a revenge that ultimately degrades them to the level of their quarry."[31]

Having said that, Reeves's personal beliefs about the nature of violence, whether man is inherently violent or *potentially* violent, and therefore whether or not it is in man's capacity to build a world largely free of violence, remain unclear. In his passionate defense of the violence in *Witchfinder General* in a letter to John Trevelyan, the censor of the day, Reeves wrote of violence as "insanity," and there is no doubt that *Witchfinder General* is as "anti-violence as it can be."[32] Certainly Reeves was appalled by violence both in real life and in the cinema. His friend and star Ian Ogilvy has commented on Reeves's views of screen violence during an interview with Chris O'Loughlin for *We Belong Dead* magazine:

> He always professed to be appalled by it, citing the John Wayne saloon punch-ups, in which nobody ever seemed to get hurt. He said he thought that was the height of hypocritical immorality. He said he wanted to point out that when you hit a man on the jaw with your fist, one of two things happen—you break your knuckles and/or break his face and, if you show that graphically, perhaps somebody might take a lesson from that and refrain from violence in the future.[33]

When critics condemned *Witchfinder General*'s sadism, Reeves passionately defended the film's violence as being moral. "Surely the most immoral thing in any form of entertainment," Reeves wrote in a letter to *The Listener*, "is the conditioning of the audience to accept and enjoy violence? Is this not exactly the attitude that could lead to more and more *casual* indulgence in violence, spiraling nauseatingly upwards to a crescendo of international bloodletting?"[34] It is interesting that Reeves contextualizes his film in terms of "international bloodletting," indicating, as Halligan notes, a "sensibility of 1968 internationalism"[35] and a sentiment of pacifism on Reeves's part. This gentler side of Reeves's artistic personality is not often commented on by critics, partly, no doubt, because of *Witchfinder General*'s overwhelming brutality. Halligan, however, does pick up on the film's continual contrasts between the idyllic and the brutal, with the film's brutality constantly "offset by the pervasive beauty of the world"[36] as shown in the film's depiction of nature. Robin Wood went further in his evaluation of Reeves's sensitivity as an artist, noting that whereas *The Sorcerers* was almost entirely dominated by destructive evil, *Witchfinder General* by contrast shows a "strong feeling for positive potentialities, with emotions like love and tenderness becoming real presences in the tone of the film, so that through their destruction, it moves closer to true tragic feeling.... The use of landscape is felt as an extension of this awareness of human positives."[37]

But as Wood also notes, Reeves's work has a neurotic quality. In a letter to Ingrid Cranfield, written after her son's death, Reeves's mother Betty wrote, "All [Michael's] life he had had a deep vein of pessimism".[38] That pessimism perhaps precluded Reeves from being able to foresee the likelihood, in 1968, of progressive change, despite him somewhat uncharacteristically, according to Halligan, flirting with "hippiedom" near the end of his life.[39]

The censorship of *Witchfinder General* and its condemnation by certain critics speaks to an Establishment striking back at Reeves, who felt misunderstood and that he was being punished for staying true to his principles. According to Cranfield, the deep depression which led up to his death by accidental overdose of prescription drugs was triggered by this backlash against him. *Witchfinder General*, Cranfield asserts, represented Reeves's deepest-held principles: "[I]t was his manifesto, championing peace against violence, justice against persecution, morality against sin, good against evil. It was an exposé of his soul. And nobody understood."[40]

In the words of Wes Craven, perhaps "some truths are too painful for a society to admit."[41] Nonetheless, the moral backlash that Reeves experienced following *Witchfinder General* felt like a personal smear. "It was," Cranfield writes, "as though his entire good character had been annihilated. The raves and plaudits could do nothing to redress the balance. A once fragile personality had been mortally wound at its most vulnerable point."[42]

It is sadly fitting, then, that shortly before his death Reeves was working on an adaptation of Walker Hamilton's novel *All the Little Animals*, a parable about virtue corrupted and destroyed by adult society.

Pete Walker: *House of Whipcord* (1974), *Frightmare* (1974) and *House of Mortal Sin* (aka *The Confessional* and *The Confessional Murders*) (1975)

A discussion of Michael Reeves inevitably leads to conjecture in terms of what the director might have gone on to achieve had he not died so young. Like other directors in the horror field, Reeves showed a penchant for social drama, and it is likely that he would eventually have pursued a career away from the horror genre. After his death, he was, as they say, "a hard act to follow," despite there being a few talented contenders (such as Stephen Weeks, Piers Haggard and Michael Armstrong). The director who best filled his shoes, however, was arguably Pete Walker, for a number of reasons: Walker, like Reeves, had a background in the British exploitation cinema of the 1960s: He cut his directorial teeth, according to Steve Chibnall (who has written an in-depth study of Walker), on 8mm glamor shorts at the time of the Profumo affair, before going on to make "nudie cuties" and later, violent thrillers.[43] His films, like those of Reeves, thus rely on sensationalism, but are better made than most, stemming from a commitment to cinematic craft arising from and reflected in the close study of a "master": in Reeves's case, Don Siegel; in Walker's, Alfred Hitchcock. (The specific influence of Hitchcock is apparent in Walker's films in their creation of suspense by purely filmic means and in their set piece murder sequences.)

Walker can be seen as the preeminent proponent of generation gap horror in the 1970s, carrying the baton that Reeves had taken from Herman Cohen the previous decade; Walker's themes are similar to those of Reeves in that respect, referring, as they do, to (in Chibnall's words) "the threat posed to new permissive lifestyles by a vindictive and morally bankrupt older order and its repressive institutions."[44] They are, however, more unambiguously progressive than other films of this period in their largely sympathetic views of the plight of the young. Walker subverts the gothic tradition in order to strip it of its mythologizing. In Walker's films, girls do not ultimately succumb to the power of the (good or evil) patriarch and boys do not inevitably inherit the sins of their fathers. Walker's villains are instead the puritans and moral guardians of the Establishment: perpetrators of institutional violence against the dangerously liberated young.

Walker's "terror films" provide a radical commentary on the conservative forces at play in Britain during the time which followed the suspension of capital punishment, the legalization of abortion, decriminalization of homosexuality and the relaxation of divorce laws.

Three-Day Weeks, Power Cuts and the Nationwide Festival of Light

Social reforms of the Harold Wilson government had led, by 1970, to a newfound sexual freedom for the young as well as a relaxation in censorship in the arts, film and theater. The incoming Conservative government, fronted by Edward Heath, precipitated a moral backlash against this so-called "permissive" society by campaigners such as Mary Whitehouse and Lord Longford who sought a return to traditional moral values. The response by horror filmmakers of the period has thus been called generation gap horror, and is characterized by depictions of an Establishment "perverted by power and the repression of their sexual natures"[45]; a hypocritical older guard who turn vindictively on a new generation which challenges their orthodoxies and rejects the suppression of desire. Chibnall terms this the "monstrous anachronism": "puritan discourses of social order and responsibility transmuted into psychopathic preoccupations with violent repression."[46]

Arguably, the reactionary moral backlash represented by the National Festival of Light—a Christian-led protest against a perceived moral and social breakdown in British society—stemmed from deeper cultural anxieties following the growing class tensions and trade union militancy of the late 1960s. Britain's working classes had enjoyed a period of consumer credit towards the end of that decade, bringing an increase in the standard of living for many families; however, this caused, by 1973, high rates of inflation and rising prices. When the Heath government sought to cap public sector pay, the unions flexed their muscles; the National Union of Miners, in particular, staged a number of national strikes which (coinciding with the OPEC Oil Crisis) effectively brought the country to its knees, leading to Heath's ruling of the "three-day week" to reduce commercial electricity consumption. Heath took on the unions, called a general election and lost; and this brought with it deep consternation among Establishment types like Longford and Whitehouse, as they surveyed what they perceived to be the unruly classes running riot.

It is an era which people remember as being both literally and metaphorically grubby. Public sector strikes meant that garbage was often left uncollected for weeks at a time, accumulating in the streets, causing problems with rats and other vermin. Hospital workers and even mortuary staff went on strike; cadavers went uncollected, bodies unburied. Walker's films have been described as similarly "grubby,"[47] "revoltingly gruesome and ugly"[48] and "reflecting how Britain was at that time"[49] (Walker himself agrees: "That's us—grimy!"[50]). Visually, Walker's films capture this era by virtue of their low-budget, shot-on-location aesthetic. The metaphorical grubbiness of Walker's films arises from the hypocrisy of the moral crusaders who are themselves made dirty because of it.

"We wanted to create a bit of mischief"[51]—Pete Walker

No discussion of these films should go without acknowledging the contribution of David McGillivray, the screenwriter who worked with Walker on several projects including those that are the subject of this chapter. McGillivray was first approached by Walker in 1973 to write what became *House of Whipcord*; McGillivray had already admired Walker's soft-core sex film *Cool It Carol* (1970) because of its rejection of orthodox morality. McGillivray went on to write the screenplay for several sex comedies, including *I'm Not Feeling Myself Tonight* (1976) starring Mary Millington. Walker contends that McGillivray was politically much more left-wing than he was; McGillivray, for example, opposed censorship, whereas Walker agreed with it. What united them, despite political differences, was a hatred of the Establishment's hypocrisy and its abuse of authority. Walker's non-judgmental message in *Cool It Carol* came about because of Christine Keeler and Mandy Rice-Davies, whom Walker knew, and whom he claims were both "branded for life" by the Profumo Affair.[52] McGillivray would similarly defend Millington after her suicide following harassment by the authorities and repeated police threats.

Together, McGillivray and Walker delighted in causing "mischief"—to agitate the moral reformers of the day and maintain "the disreputable status crucial to commercial viability"[53] within the exploitation market. McGillivray describes his films with Walker as "a harmless outlet for overgrown school boys who were really doing little more than trying to see how much they could get away with before they were sent to bed."[54] Walker contends that they deliberately "rubbed people up the wrong way"[55] and set themselves up as "the *enfants terribles*"[56] of the day in order to gain an audience. Walker was, and still is, an astute businessman, who financed his movies himself, filmed them quickly for the drive-in market and moved swiftly from project to project so he could make his money back. Paradoxically, this only serves to lend the films what Tim Rayner calls a "bizarre integrity,"[57] which finds a common ground for commercialization and subversion. The causticity of the films lies in their outrageousness and the transgression of their ideas, used, as Chibnall notes, not simply to shock and challenge but to question the moral universe which audiences of the 1970s inhabited.[58] Arguably, Walker and McGillivray pushed the opportunity for shock and transgression afforded by low-budget exploitation further than any other British productions since *The Sorcerers* and *Witchfinder General*.

"You are detained at Her Majesty's pleasure"

House of Whipcord, according to Harvey Fenton, started as a conversation between Walker and McGillivray about the audience for exploitation films. "What turns them on?" they pondered. "Sadism and flagellation" was the conclusion. Agreeing that the only way in which a sado-masochistic fantasy could get past the censor was in the context of an institutionalized regime of punishment and retribution—in this case a correctional facility for wayward women—McGillivray wrote a script in which a young model, Ann-Marie (Penny Irving) is humiliated, flogged and eventually hanged for her moral shortcomings, by the "utterly insane geriatric proprietor of a private prison."[59]

Although conceived primarily, then, as a "fladge" fantasy, *House of Whipcord* captures the allegorical moment with extraordinary precision. According to Chibnall, the film deals with the "secret rites at the heart of British imperialism,"[60] namely, sado-masochism in the form of corporal punishment, which provides an outlet for repressed sexual drives and political instincts: "the twin thrills of power and submission fixed in the iconic image of the ritual flogging."[61] David Pirie, in his book *A Heritage of Horror,* recognized this quality of English sadism as "Selwynisn," named after 18th Century aristocratic parliamentarian George Selwyn, who was fascinated with sexual sadism, flagellation and executions.[62] *House of Whipcord* became one of the few films, alongside Lindsay Anderson's *If...* to register the link between Establishment-sanctioned corporal punishment and sadism. However, despite the sensational S&M selling point, *House of Whipcord*'s real power arises from its connection of sadism to necrophilia under the guise of capital punishment. Indeed, Walker's concept of the film first came to him in the form of the poster image of "a girl's face screaming through a noose"[63] and he then built his concept around that image. It is the image that remains most iconic to the film, and forms the basis of its suspense: the horrible inevitability of Ann-Marie's hanging by the prison proprietor. At the time of *House of Whipcord*'s production in 1973, the restoration of hanging was being debated in Parliament, primarily as a response to the IRA's bombing campaign in London; and the reintroduction of the death penalty is something that some conservative politicians have continued to campaign for.

House of Whipcord utilizes a spiraling structure that emphasizes this constant sense of punitive threat. It is like a recurring nightmare "in which you keep going back to the same dreadful place."[64] According to Walker, he was inspired by Jacques Tourneur's *Out of the Past* (1947), and we can see the structural similarities to that film, which, like *House of Whipcord*, begins with a character who believes themself to have escaped a bad situation, only to be drawn inexorably back into it. In *House of Whipcord*, all the main characters are inevitably lured to the prison, and the structure of the film also resembles *Psycho* in this respect. Ann-Marie's friend Julia (Ann-Michelle), in an attempt to find her, arrives too late to prevent the execution and is herself captured by the prison staff, and in turn has to be rescued by her boyfriend Tony (Ray Brooks). Walker's manipulation of these suspense elements are indeed Hitchcockian, as we are made well aware in advance what fate will befall these characters should they fail to escape or not be rescued. Rehabilitation and release is, of course, out of the question, making *House of Whipcord*, in Fenton's words, "a compelling descent into the depths of despair."[65]

House of Whipcord also uses the conventions and stereotypes of the women-in-prison film. Ann-Marie is the "new fish," the audience-identification character who has to learn the politics of the institution in order to survive; Walker (Sheila Keith) is the dyke guard whose repressed desire for Ann-Marie makes her single out the new prisoner for especially sadistic

Walker (Sheila Keith, left) and Bates (Dorothy Gordon) contemplate the hangman's noose in *House of Whipcord* (1974) (photograph courtesy Ronald V. Borst/Hollywood Movie Posters).

treatment and special attention; Wakehurst (Barbara Markham) is the corrupt and paranoid governor who sees the new prisoner as a threat to her authority; Justice Bailey (Patrick Barr) is the ineffectual judge who believes in rehabilitation but is powerless to enforce it and thus becomes an object of ridicule; Bates (Dorothy Gordon) is the initially sympathetic wardress whose obedience to the system prevents her from helping the persecuted women.

Oren Shai describes the historical development of the women-in-prison film in terms of its ideological values: Ideas of reform dominate the early cycle (1920s-1940s), existential despair and the failure of reform in the mid cycle (1950s), and community-based revolution in the late cycle (1970s).[66] In *House of Whipcord*, values of reform barely figure. Ann-Marie is not expected to reform, merely to accept punishment for her supposed sins. The rank injustice of her situation is highlighted by the ludicrous nature of her so-called crime: She posed naked for a photography shoot in a public park. Her job as a model is equated in the puritanical mind with the "sin" of prostitution (the truck driver who comes to her rescue early in the film also assumes that she is a prostitute but is sympathetic to her plight). The early cycle of women-in-prison films sought to reform their hedonistic female convicts: *House of Whipcord* clearly belongs to the late cycle, and although revolution is not on the cards in Walker's world, *House of Whipcord* subverts the women-in-prison genre's conventional attitude toward sex, which is shown as power to the woman's advantage rather than the source of her condemnation.

"I'm going to make you ashamed of your body"

In Walker's critiques of patriarchal authority, the males are paradoxically shown as weak and corrupt, dominated by monstrous matriarchs who uphold the repressive institutions and ensure their continuance. Younger, potentially liberated women are persecuted by these older, puritanical women. Those most susceptible to malevolent and violent impulses in Walker's films are not the young but, as Chibnall points out, "their fathers and mothers, who have had more time to be corrupted by a misguided and repressive system."[67] Like the murderous authoritarians in Val Lewton's Karloff films, Walker's monstrous matriarchs are complex and tormented characters.

In *House of Whipcord*, Sheila Keith plays Walker, her lesbian warder character, as sadistic and puritanical, but prone to temptation and inner conflict. Her character, like John Stearne in *Witchfinder General*, seeks total control over her prisoners, and this takes the form of sadism that culminates in the flogging she administers to Ann-Marie in punishment for attempting to help a condemned inmate escape. Like Stearne, Walker is a subordinate who is given a limited opportunity to exercise power. When such opportunities arise, such as whipping a prisoner, she derives sadistic pleasure from it. However, her feelings of sexual excitement are tempered by her self-loathing: She is herself the victim of a repressive system. After she has flagellated Ann-Marie, she visits the girl in her cell and surveys her whip-marked back with fascination and desire. She tentatively reaches out to touch the girl's skin, but draws back, and instead goes to fetch Ann-Marie a glass of water, a momentary act of kindness to atone for giving in briefly to temptations of the flesh. In Keith's Walker we can again see Fromm's "lustful destructiveness": Her sadism is the manifestation of her desire for complete control over another and a sublimation of her repressed sexuality.

Wakehurst, the prison proprietor, also has the need to control. She is a character akin to Richard Dix's paranoid sea captain in *The Ghost Ship*. Like Captain Stone, she becomes ruthless whenever her authority is threatened, and her need to retain power and authority, whatever the cost, eventually sends her spiraling into madness. Pete Walker claims that he always liked the "theme of the past coming back to haunt you"[68]: Wakehurst sees in Ann-Marie the ghost of the French girl whose suicide led to her dismissal from the prison service thirty years before and she becomes unhinged by her own neurotic fears of history repeating itself. She harbors resentment that mistakes were made by her prison officers which caused her downfall and that Justice Bailey did not do enough to secure her reinstatement.

Judge Bailey (Patrick Barr) is portrayed as weak and hypocritical. According to McGillivray, it was the censor of the time, Stephen Murphy, who read *House of Whipcord* as a satire of the moral reformers, Whitehouse and Longford. This was not intentional on Walker's part (although he seized the opportunity to court controversy by subsequently adding a dedication to the film "to those who are disturbed by today's lax moral codes"), and he maintains that the film's social commentary was primarily a response to politicians such as Cyril Black who campaigned for the reintroduction of corporal punishment. It is difficult, however, *not* to see Justice Bailey as a lampoon of Longford, the eccentric peer who campaigned against pornography, while touring the sex establishments of Denmark with former prison doctor Christine Temple-Saville as part of his "research" into the sex industry. Chibnall describes Justice Bailey as "the spiritual center of the disintegrating British Empire and State, undermined by a personal history of adultery, unmarried co-habitations and fathering of a child out of wedlock."[69] Similarly, Longford's sex club sojourns undermined his credibility and exposed him to ridicule in the British press.

"Beyond redemption"

House of Whipcord begins as what seems like a persecutory fantasy but is made chillingly believable by McGillivray and Walker's insightful characterizations. The film gradually exposes the fine line between tyranny and insanity, so that the basic premise, which initially appears outlandish, becomes increasingly plausible: Wakehurst and Bailey setting up their own private prison in order to continue exerting power and control over others rings disturbingly true. It is impossible, now, to watch *House of Whipcord* without thinking of the Magdalene asylums, slave labor laundries which operated well into the twentieth century throughout Europe. They housed "fallen women" and subjected them to corporal punishment, enforced silence and sexual abuse. Many of these asylums were church-run, particularly in Ireland, where the last Magdalene laundry closed in 1996. However in February 2013 a report commissioned by the Irish government found significant state collusion in the admission of thousands of women into these institutions. Evidence exists that Irish courts routinely sent women convicted of petty crimes to the laundries, the government awarded lucrative contracts to laundries without ever insisting on fair treatment for the workers or inspecting conditions inside, and state employees like the Irish police force and social workers brought women to the laundries and returned those who had escaped.[70] In *House of Whipcord*, a banner in the prison refectory where the floggings take place reads "The World for Christ," capturing perfectly the collusion of the church and state in administrating oppressive penal institutions: Walker was not prescient, so much as he was daring, in effect exposing in 1973 what both the state and church had denied for decades and would continue to deny until forty years later. In February 2013 the Irish prime minster, Enda Kenny, issued an official state apology to the victims of the Magdalene laundries.

Christian morality in *House of Whipcord* is, however, a veneer for imperial and class domination by the old guard. Although Walker denies an interest in class struggle, the very classlessness of the younger generation in his films is, in itself, a threat to the older generation. As Chibnall notes, in Walker's films, "class is a 'hang-up' which the young do not need."[71] *House of Whipcord*, like *The Sorcerers*, portrays in its young people a merging of the classes, but in Walker's film, friends from different classes do not appear to experience the same underlying tensions as they do in *The Sorcerers*. For example, Julia (Ann Michelle), the well-spoken, apparently middle-class flat-mate of Ann-Marie, is having an affair with a married man, Tony (Ray Brooks), who is of a lower social class. It's transgression in terms of morality and class allegiance, but no class antagonism appears to exist between them, no cultural differences.

Interestingly, only the young aristocrat among them, Mark Dessart (Robert Tayman), is revealed as duplicitous: No one in Ann-Marie's circle knows him, and we discover later that he has infiltrated the crowd in order to secure a victim for his mother, Mrs. Wakehurst. His duplicity is again emphasized when he offers to help Ann-Marie escape, but this turns out to be further deception. We are left, up until then, unsure which side he is really on: that of liberated youth or that of the puritanical old order. He therefore becomes the film's only truly evil character, as his cruelty is without motivation. This theme of the passing-down of evil from the older to the younger generation is one that would become more central to Walker's next film, *Frightmare*, and that film's conclusion is consequently bleaker than *House of Whipcord*'s.

Mark is a traitor to his generation, and ultimately receives his just deserts: He is accidently stabbed to death by Wakehurst, who subsequently hangs herself. At the end of *House *of Whipcord*, then (poetic) justice prevails. Even in a world seemingly dominated by the corrupt older generation, Walker gives us hope that basic human kindness still exists (as established at the start of the film by the middle-aged truck driver who attempts to help Ann-Marie) and that tyranny can thus be overcome. In *Frightmare* and *House of Mortal Sin*, however, all possibility of redemption is removed.

"Some people are day people, but we like being night people, don't we?"

If *House of Whipcord* attempted to stir up controversy by breaking taboos of sadism and "Le Vice Anglaise," as embodied in its scenes of flagellation and hanging, then *Frightmare* was a conscious attempts to shock audiences by breaking taboos related to cannibalism and family madness (crystalized memorably in a single image of a deranged old mother brandishing a power drill in order to tripan the brains from her victims). While *House of Whipcord* uses shock to question the morality of a ruling class administering "correction," *Frightmare* arguably goes further in its use of shock to challenge that most sacred and fundamental of social institutions: the family. Specifically, *Frightmare* makes the case for the nuclear family as an instrument of repression, and does so with remarkable insight and astonishing clarity of purpose. Walker calls *Frightmare* his most fully realized film in terms of its ideas: "It actually did have the moral tale that I wanted it to have, and it told it in no uncertain terms. I believed at the end that I had made the point."[72] It is a supreme example of what critics have termed the "family horror film," and within that, one of the first and best of a subgroup of family horror films concerning cannibal families.

Robin Wood first made the point that horror cinema has, since *Psycho*, implicitly recognized Horror as familial; that the threat posed by the monster to society, far from being an external one, is created by repression within the family.[73] Wood cites *I Walked with a Zombie* as a quintessential family horror film in this respect, as it "explicitly locates horror at the heart of the family, identifying it with sexual repressiveness in the cause of preserving family unity."[74] Unity within the family is also the driving force of *Frightmare*'s social criticism, and that of several notable cannibal family horror films since, including *The Texas Chain Saw Massacre*, *The Hills Have Eyes*, and more recently *Mum and Dad* (2008).

In the introduction to this book I briefly described the main characteristics of the cannibal family horror film: Most significantly, cannibalism in these films is presented as the social norm within the family, not a deviation from the social norm. In other words, cannibalism is seen as a monstrous extension of patriarchal family values and a way of holding the family unit together in the face of social change. The cannibal women in these films inevitably work towards perpetuating the patriarchal power structure, although they often secretly resent their exclusion from the world of male power; therefore hate masquerades as love, and the overriding priority within the family is its continuance: The family must stay together at all costs. The family horror film and within that, the cannibal family horror film externalize as "horror" the tensions that exist within the modern nuclear family.

Frightmare, in identifying the family as the incubator of psychosis and schizophrenia, links not only to other horror films of the period but to the anti-psychiatry stance of R.D. Laing and David Cooper that was influential in the early 1970s. Laing and Cooper argued that mental illness within the family arose not from biological factors, but as a result of a child's restrictive upbringing, which worked against liberation and self-knowledge, leading instead to a fractured sense of identity. Walker ridicules conventional psychiatry in *Frightmare*, showing it to be inadequate in the same way that Laing and Cooper rejected the psychiatric orthodoxy of the day which viewed mental illness as symptomatic of underlying medical disorder. Thus detention and drug treatment are seen, in *Frightmare*, as ludicrous treatment for the "pathological cannibalism" of which Dorothy (Sheila Keith) is diagnosed.

Walker has been subject to criticism for his portrayal of mental illness. "The real obscenity of this seedy movie," Fergus Cashin wrote in 1974, "is the message that the mentally sick breed insane children, and should be locked up for life if found guilty of a criminal act."[75] Chibnall adds, "[T]here is some justification for these criticisms in McGillivray's flippant attitude towards the mentally ill and Walker's conservative views on their incarceration."[76] Walker maintains that he "wasn't saying that they should be locked away and throw away the key,"[77] but that he wanted to discuss in the film how people were being released before they were properly cured. The film retains an element of ambiguity: The reactionary inflection exists alongside the radical one. As Chibnall concedes, "Walker and McGillivray were never committed Laingians, but they did share their skeptical anti-psychiatry stance."[78] As to the message that "the mentally sick breed insane children," even though Walker confirms that this was indeed the film's conclusion, *Frightmare* itself remains ambiguous as to whether daughter Debbie's (Kim Butcher) psychopathology is hereditary or inculcated by her mother. Although Debbie supposedly has never met her mother, we learn during the course of the film that Debbie is in fact in touch with Dorothy, and it is implied that she has been assisting in her murders at the farmhouse (and may have been for a period of time). In other words, Debbie's need for identity may have led her to reunite with her mother earlier in the story and take part in the family "ritual." The passing-down of the rite of cannibalism as the family's means of nourishing and sustaining itself from one generation to the next is, indeed, a staple of the cannibal horror film, dramatizing the continuance of repressive family traditions.

Frightmare's use of cannibalism is therefore allegorical: a symbol, as we have seen, of family repression. Criticisms of *Frightmare* as a study of mental illness are, in any case, somewhat irrelevant. The cause of Dorothy's pathological cannibalism (or "caribanthropy" as McGillivray calls it) is a McGuffin (she was traumatized as a child when made to eat her pet rabbit). More telling is the context of this trauma: It occurred at the height of the Depression when meat was scarce. This links cannibalism, allegorically, with consumer-capitalism, of which it is a logical extension. "Cannibalism," according to Wood, "represents the ultimate in possessiveness, hence the logical end of human relations under capitalism."[79] The basic although unstated tenet of capitalism, as Wood observes, is that people have the right to live off other people: The cannibal family in *Frightmare* simply takes this to its logical conclusion.

Dorothy manipulates family members to this end. Her stepdaughter, Jackie (Deborah Fairfax), secretly provides her with food parcels which, it is revealed, contain animal brains. Jackie does this in the hope that a substitute for the real thing will keep Dorothy's cannibalism at bay; however, Jackie is haunted by nightmares of her stepmother returning to her previous self. (A similar dream sequence in Bunuel's *Los Olvidados* [1950] comes to mind. In both films a child watches her mother approach holding a dripping hunk of dead flesh.) This image—with its evocation of the child's fear of the mother—resonates throughout *Frightmare*. Edmund, Dorothy's husband (Rupert Davies), is guiltily complicit in her cannibalism, and is loyal to the end. Having already feigned insanity so that he could remain with her during incarceration, he is even willing to sacrifice his daughter Jackie when she proves a threat to family unity. Underlying this complicity of Edmund and Jackie is a sense of inevitability: Dorothy slipping back into her old ways, they feel, is simply a matter of time—after all, this is what families "do." This theme of inescapable fate is symbolized by Dorothy's reading of the tarot (her method of drawing victims to the house); the sense of lives predetermined, controlled by a greater force. However, the secret that binds the family together also threatens to tear it apart, resulting in tension and dishonesty. Chibnall describes Dorothy as "all the things a mother should not be—controlling, self-obsessed and ultimately, psychopathic."[80] (Walker has said that his own mother "had the habit of being very nice—and then sticking the knife in."[81]) Dorothy is compelled, despite her own moments of quiet despair, to use the people around her, including her own children, as commodities to aid her "consumption." Her family, in their bid to maintain unity, feel obligated to go along with her compulsion. Dorothy eventually favors the one most willing to follow, and the family ritual is thus passed down to Debbie.

Those like Jackie who reject this ideology are annihilated or forcibly assimilated—eaten. It is significant that the victims who are drawn to the cottage for Dorothy's tarot readings are young and single, free from family ties. Jackie is herself portrayed as independent, unmarried, and enjoying city life. She has little desire to spend any more time with her father and stepmother than is necessary, and shows no particular inclination to start a family of her own. Her liberated lifestyle is therefore seen as a threat to the family, who must perpetuate repression at all cost. Jackie, then, becomes the final victim of her psychotic family. As Robin Wood points out, it is no accident that the most intense horror films of the 1970s at exploitation level are all centered on cannibalism, and on the specific notion of present and future (the younger generation) being devoured by the past. "The implication," writes Wood, "is that 'liberation' and 'permissiveness' as defined within our culture, are at once inadequate and too late—too feeble, too unaware, and too undirected to withstand the legacy of long repression."[82]

"I was put on this earth to combat sin, and I shall use every available means to do so"

In their third film together, McGillivray and Walker took on one of the bedrocks of the Establishment: the Catholic Church, whose legacy of repression (and abuse) is indeed long and, until recently, shrouded in secrecy. In *House of Mortal Sin*, individuals repress their feelings so that institutions can carry on, but the by-product of that repression is insanity and murder. Anthony Sharp plays Father Meldrum, whose vow of celibacy has pushed him over the edge: He routinely harasses the young women whom he takes for confession, driving them to suicide. Jenny Welch (Susan Penhaligon) reveals to him that she has had an abortion, and Meldrum blackmails her. When she attempts to expose him, Meldrum embarks on a string of murders to cover up his crimes.

In *House of Mortal Sin*, Walker laments the abuse of authority that he experienced as a child in a Catholic boarding school, linking the abuse at the hands of priests to sexual repression; he portrays the Catholic Church as a closed system from which there is no way out. For its victims there is, as Chibnall observes, an "inevitable fate which is sealed by the complacency and hypocrisy within the system"[83]—a collusion of Establishment and Church in the perpetuation of repression. Because of Walker's personal experiences, the idea of a killer Catholic priest made sense to him. "I was brought up in Catholic schools, so I know what I'm talking about in *Mortal Sin*," he said in 1976. "I have strong feelings about celibacy in the church. I know about the frustrations, what they turn priests into, the monsters they become."[84]

As he did with *House of Whipcord*, Walker showed considerable daring in exposing corruption at the heart of such a powerful patriarchal institution. Child sex abuse in the Roman Catholic Church became a public issue in the late 1970s and 1980s but not until the Church clergy abuse crisis in 2002 (with four percent of Catholic priests in the United States accused of sexual abuse) did the Roman Catholic Church publicly acknowledge cases of abuse leveled at it. Up until then, a worldwide scandal had been covered up, with the Vatican refusing to cooperate with civil authorities in the investigations of claims of abuse, and priests accused of abuse merely being shifted to new parishes. With the abdication of Pope Benedict XVI in 2013 following the Vatican's twenty years of publicly battling this scandal, *House of Mortal Sin* has particular contemporary resonance.

House of Mortal Sin utilizes exploitation tropes in tackling its themes (sometimes to its detriment) but it remains a remarkably powerful work, and may be considered Walker's most mature (if you can use that word in conjunction with shock-exploitation) film. For one thing, Walker's use of the camera became increasingly sophisticated throughout his career until with *House of Mortal Sin* he achieved the controlled yet unobtrusive style of Bunuel (whose influence can also be seen in the film's savage anti–Catholic satire): His refined dolly shots carefully reframe and follow the actors in a skillful staging of *mise-en-scene*. The moving camera shots in *House of Mortal Sin* also reference the gothic tradition of Whale and Terence Fisher, with the camera constantly gliding through the architecture to rest upon some object of terror—a fluttering Bible or the confessional itself.

Jenny's encounter with Meldrum in the confessional arouses his prurient interest in her sex life, which he then turns into puritanical oppression, locking her into his obsession (she reminds him of the woman he loved but gave up in order to join the priesthood). He is unable to accept his own sexual interest in Jenny, and instead tracks her down with the intention of punishing the "sinner"—her boyfriend Terry (Stewart Bevan), who, in Meldrum's mind, forced Jenny to have the abortion. Once again, Walker and McGillivray contrast the permissive lifestyles of the liberated younger generation with the repressive ones of their elders. Jenny and her sister Vanessa (Stephanie Beacham) occupy an apartment above a craft shop in Richmond, a salubrious outer London borough. When Terry moves out, they let the spare room to Bernard Cutler (Norman Eshley), Vanessa's ex-boyfriend, who is now himself a Catholic priest in Meldrum's parish. Early in the film, Walker and McGillivray introduce the debate of celibacy in the context of a conversation on the subject between Bernard and Meldrum. Bernard is revealed, in stark contrast to Meldrum, as a progressive (and, as such, is viewed

A psychotic priest, Father Xavier Meldrum (Anthony Sharp), prays for strength in *House of Mortal Sin* (1976) (photograph courtesy Ronald V. Borst/Hollywood Movie Posters).

sympathetically by Walker and McGillivray) who believes that celibacy should not remain a condition of Roman Catholic priesthood. Meldrum's response is to accuse Bernard of wanting to "rip away the fabric of the Catholic church." Meldrum's viewpoint becomes clear: Despite his own sexual feelings, repression must remain in place, and sin must be punished. When Bernard suggests that the Church must change with the times, Meldrum demands indignantly, "By whose orders?"

"The old temptations, they've returned. They've been growing for some time"

Visually, Meldrum's domestic environment is used to symbolize him as stuck in the past in contrast with the liberated younger generation. His presbytery, which he shares with his senile mother (Hilda Barry) and the housekeeper Miss Brabazon (Sheila Keith), is as archaic as his views on the Catholic Church: All are in a state of degeneration. Once again the class issue rears its head: Meldrum has a social standing as befits his upper middle class background and position. We assume at first that his contempt for his subordinates, Miss Brabazon and Bernard, arises from this class superiority (Anthony Sharp's suitably patrician casting works wonderfully in this respect). His status becomes a weapon against his victims later in the film: Society automatically affords him the respect that his victims—who are invariably women or working class young males—are denied. Hitchcock's influence is apparent not only in the serial murders perpetrated by Meldrum, but in Meldrum's devotion to Mother, which, like that of Norman Bates, is itself born of repression: It was Mother who demanded that Meldrum choose the priesthood over love and marriage, thus sealing his fate. Intriguingly, Mother emerges as one of the film's more sympathetic characters. She is victimized by Miss Brabazon (whom it transpires is the woman Meldrum rejected in order to become a priest, and who has followed him into the Church in order to be near him). In a startling reversal late in the film, Mother turns out, despite her degenerative state, not to be senile after all and indeed is fully compos mentis with regard to her son: "Help me—my son is mad," she writes in a note to Vanessa, who stumbles into her room to find the old woman in terror of the monster she has helped to create.

As Chibnall comments, *House of Mortal Sin* is "bizarrely decorated with gratuitously offensive and sacrilegious Guignol, obscured by sensation-seeking and softened by camp."[85] Meldrum resorts to violence too early in the film: He immediately follows Jenny home after her confession and assaults her ex-boyfriend by throwing boiling water in his face. It is a scene straight out of a giallo and casts Meldrum straight away as a psychopath when a more gradual reveal of his capacity for violence would have been thematically more effective. Walker's reasons for the "sacrilegious Guignol" were, of course, to stir up controversy through a generous helping of blasphemy. Hence Meldrum dispatches his victims by suitably sacrilegious means: death by poisoned host, strangulation with rosary beads. On the one hand this works in terms of institutional ritual, recasting the Roman Catholic rites as monstrous (in the same way that *House of Whipcord* uses the ritual of corporal punishment and recasts it as monstrously unjust, and *Frightmare* recasts the family meal ritual as cannibalism). On the other hand, *House of Mortal Sin* lacks the perverse sexualized use of religious iconography that made *The Devils* (1971) and *The Exorcist* (1973) genuinely shocking. Nothing in *House of Mortal Sin* compares to the rape of Christ sequence in Ken Russell's film or the crucifix masturbation scene in *The Exorcist*.

However, as *House of Mortal Sin* progresses and Meldrum's motivation becomes clear, the character does turn out to be truly and chillingly monstrous: an ultimate evil nemesis in terms of his ruthlessness and his ability to remain one step ahead of those who threaten to expose him for what he really is. His power as a villain arises because he is aided and abetted by the Establishment: No one believes Jenny's accusations that a priest would do such things. At one point, Meldrum sermonizes on the failure of parents to prevent their children's promiscuity and berates the congregation for their hypocrisy in blaming society instead of themselves. The scene speaks to the Church's own alleged abuse of authority and its lack of accountability at the time of filming in 1975.

"The Lord will forgive us for preserving the honor of His Church"

When Walker made *House of Mortal Sin*, he was incensed by the lies of the Church and its lack of culpability for child abuse, which served only to perpetuate the cycle of abuse. In *House of Mortal Sin*, Bernard decides to give up the priesthood in order to be with Vanessa, whom he loves. He seeks the guidance of an enlightened elder, Father Duggan (Mervyn Johns), who advises him to follow his heart without shame. "I've never been able to understand why the Catholic Church looks upon itself as a kind of prison," the old priest laments. "If you stayed on, you'd be a hypocrite and we've enough of those as it is." Thus Duggan gives Bernard his blessing to leave the Church. But Meldrum, the antithesis of Duggan, murders Vanessa after she stumbles across his secret, and he persuades Bernard to stay. Thus Bernard is destined to follow in the footsteps of Meldrum and lead a life of hypocrisy and repression: This, following the murders of all who threatened his exposure (including his own mother and the woman he once loved, Miss Brabazon), is Meldrum's final victory. In this way, Walker and McGillivray portray the Catholic Church as ruthless in its self-preservation and its single-minded bid for continuance. Lying to Bernard, claiming that the murders were committed by the housekeeper who was "jealously obsessed" with him, Meldrum solicits Bernard's silence and compliance: "We must cover up our involvement for the minimum of scandal."

The film's final image is of Meldrum donning his cape and black gloves as he prepares to go out to kill Jenny—the last remaining witness to his villainy. As he pulls the presbytery door shut behind him, the circle closes. The cycle of repression and abuse is complete, and set to remain firmly in place, in perpetuity. It is a remarkable ending to a remarkable film, and snaps shut on the mind like the trap that imprisons its characters.

5

ANTI-VIETNAM
Night of the Living Dead (1968),
Deathdream (1972) and *The Crazies* (1973)

Pete Walker made films primarily for the American drive-in market. His career nose-dived in the late 1970s–early 1980s, mainly due to the decline of the drive-in. The importance of the 1960s–1970s drive-in to horror cinema—particularly subversive horror cinema—should not be underestimated.

Although the drive-in reached its peak of popularity in the 1950s as American teenagers found themselves mobile with money to spend, the exigencies of maintaining an audience in the decades that followed led many drive-ins, during the 1960s and 1970s, to program exploitation, thus opening up a market for a number of directors in this book such as Walker, George Romero, Wes Craven, Tobe Hooper and numerous other regional filmmakers working in the horror genre. *Night of the Living Dead* first became a hit at the drive-in before finding its way into inner city theaters whose managers, noting the success of exploitation in drive-ins, began to program exploitation. This, of course, coincided with the rise of American youth counterculture in the wake of the Vietnam war.

In the 1960s and 1970s, youth sought alternative cinema and this was provided not only by the drive-in, but also by the repertory theater, college cinemas and the aforementioned inner-city theaters showing exploitation double-bills and midnight movies. To these audiences, independent cinema—and particularly cult cinema—equated with countercultural alternatives. Romero himself commented on the emergence of a 1960s cult audience in his preface to John Russo's novelization of *Night of the Living Dead*, describing the phenomenon as evidence of "the clutching search of the public mass towards something new or as yet unexperienced."[1]

The opening-up of exhibition to a counterculture audience, which started at the drive-in, led not only to a glut of independently made product, but also to what most critics believe was a fundamental shift in the horror film paradigm, from the classical to the modern, as filmmakers sought to appeal to the revolutionary youth of the 1960s and 1970s:

The "Classic" Horror Film (1930s–1940s)	The Modern American Horror Film (1960s–1970s)
Production Context	*Production Context*
Stars (Lugosi, Karloff, Chaney)	Unknown actors
Studio-produced (Universal, RKO, et al.)	Independent productions, filmed on location
Medium budgets	Low budgets

Genre Conventions
Foreign monster
Monster is a supernatural being
Equilibrium is restored—good triumphs
Society (i.e., religion, science, family) is "good"

Formal Signifiers
The horror is suggested off-screen
Expressionist lighting style, hard shadows
Classical mise-en-scène and continuity editing

Genre Conventions
Indigenous monster
Monster is psychopath and/or cannibal
The horror never ends—nihilism pervades
Society is to blame—family is seen as instrument of repression

Formal Signifiers
Graphic on-screen horror
Documentary realism, location sound
Post–French New Wave camerawork and editing

This paradigm shift was partly due to changes in industry practices as well as changes in audience expectations. The 1930s and 1940s horror films were studio-produced. Universal was, at the time, already a major Hollywood studio with its own sound stages and production personnel. Although modestly budgeted, their horror films were fairly lavish productions filmed in the studio with, for their time, elaborate sets and special effects (the latter sometimes Oscar-nominated). The horror films of the 1970s, by comparison, were typically produced independently, often outside of Hollywood (such as the Pittsburgh-made *Night of the Living Dead*) for very low budgets, shot on location with unknown actors. Whereas the directors of the 1930s and 1940s were predominantly inspired by expressionism, from the 1960s onwards directors adopted the stylistic conventions of documentary realism: Hand-held camerawork, naturalistic lighting, location shooting, direct location sound and the use of 16mm film stock became customary. This was partly due to low budgets; however, many of the directors including Romero, Hooper and Craven had backgrounds in documentaries. In the 1930s and 1940s shadows and suggestion predominated the horror film whereas from the 1960s onwards, in the time of Vietnam, cinema generally, and the horror film in particular, became increasingly graphic—and deliberately shocking—in its depiction of violence and bloodshed.

This is, of course, a "broad strokes" comparison: It is possible to argue against the ideological distinction of the "classic" horror film of the 1930s being inherently conservative perhaps (certainly in the cases of *Freaks* and *Frankenstein*, as discussed in Chapter 1); but the significance of this comparison, as made by Wood and others, is to emphasize the revolutionary aspects of the modern horror film from 1968 onwards, with its radicalism a reflection of the changing political viewpoints of the audience. In short, the arrival of the modern horror film with *Night of the Living Dead*, *Targets* and *Rosemary's Baby* (all 1968) marked the juncture where—in the wake of Vietnam—traditional social values became, at least to the youth audience who watched horror films, largely obsolete.

In 1967, cultural rebellion by the younger generation culminated in the San Francisco "Summer of Love" which brought the hippie alternative into the public consciousness. Nineteen sixty-seven also saw mass demonstrations against the Vietnam War and race riots in Detroit and New Jersey as a result of the divisive civil rights struggles. Filmed during this time, *Night of the Living Dead* depicts an America where repressive 1950s conservative values have become defunct and dysfunctional, leaving it under threat by a revolutionary new order. The film's deliberate attack on traditional American beliefs in the shadow of Vietnam is a smorgasbord of taboo-breaking, ranging from patricide to cannibalism, and continues to shock—as does its nihilistic conclusion.

The Canadian-produced *Deathdream* (1972), written by Alan Ormsby and directed by Bob Clark, and Romero's *The Crazies* (1973) are both derived from *Night of the Living*

Dead. They depict a literal bringing-home of the Vietnam War in different ways but arguably with the same conclusions. *Deathdream* portrays its returning soldier not as a hero but shockingly as a monster seeking revenge on the society that sent him to war in the first place. Made in the year that the My Lai massacre came to public attention leading to a huge swing in public opinion against the war, *Deathdream* levels blame on the American patriarchal family for espousing the "macho John Wayne–ism" that had now come back to haunt the nation. *The Crazies* depicts the escalating violence of Vietnam as a madness espoused by all patriarchal authority, including the military—even extending to the president himself!

In addressing the Vietnam War in these terms, suggesting as they do that violence is the inevitable outcome of socially conditioned repression, all three films show a radicalism that is largely missing from most Hollywood-produced films about Vietnam. They also precede the best-known "serious" dramas about the Vietnam War—*Heroes* (1977), *The Boys in Company C* (1978) and *Coming Home* (1978)—by several years.

"From Watts, from 'Nam": *Night of the Living Dead*

The cover of *Time* magazine from August 4, 1967, could be the poster of a George A. Romero film. It depicts the 12th Street Riots that had taken place in Detroit the previous week.[2] Lasting five days, the 12th Street Riots were among the most destructive in American history: a culmination of a summer of rioting that began in Buffalo, New York, on June 22. Race rioting would continue in the aftermath of Detroit and Milwaukee, and spread to Washington. As the rioting proliferated, "the nation's black ghettos," according to *Time*, "shuddered in paroxysms of rock-throwing, fire-bombing and looting."[3] *Night of the Living Dead*'s poster evokes the *Time* cover to a remarkable degree, depicting a society under siege by a literal "return of the repressed."

According to Romero, *Night of the Living Dead* was written as an allegory "to draw a parallel between what people are becoming and the idea that people are operating on many levels of insanity that are only clear to themselves."[4] *Night of the Living Dead* does not make direct references to Vietnam in the way that *The Crazies* does, but Vietnam haunts the film nonetheless, just as, in real life, Vietnam was the linchpin for the race riots, the student protests and the youth rebellion that took place in the 1960s.

Romero follows through the allegory of *Night of the Living Dead* in his iconography, most famously in his use of black and white, at times almost newsreel-like photography, which gives some scenes the look of a TV news report. The notion of representing current events in an allegorical manner by evoking them iconographically was not new in 1967; as discussed in Chapter 1, James Whale referenced news photographs of Hoovervilles being burned to the ground in his images of the Monster burned alive in the windmill at the end of *Frankenstein*. However, *Night of the Living Dead* also comments self-reflexively on the influence of television images in the social-political upheaval of the 1960s. "The final scenes in the film, which were all hand-held," Romero remarked in 2010, "I was trying intentionally to make that look like the news that we were seeing, from Watts, from 'Nam."[5]

According to Sean O'Hagen, two technological innovations had transformed the nightly news by 1968: the use of videotape and the same-day broadcast, which meant that images of protests, rioting and warfare were disseminated across the country almost as they

Opposite: **Poster for** *Night of the Living Dead* **(1968).**

5. Anti-Vietnam

happened. "Vietnam," writes O'Hagen, "became the first war beamed into the living rooms of America, and the images were as raw and visceral as today's are diluted and controlled."[6] The immediacy of television news reporting in the 1960s is mirrored by the documentary techniques that Romero utilizes in *Night of the Living Dead*, techniques derived from cinéma vérité and direct cinema.

Direct cinema was a movement begun in the United States in the late 1950s and early 1960s by documentary makers such as Albert Mayles and D.A. Pennebaker, to present social and political issues in a direct, unmediated way, recording events as they happened with the minimal involvement of the filmmaker. Similarly, cinéma vérité, a minimalist style of filmmaking originated in France, conveys the sense that the viewer is given direct view of what is happening in front of the camera without the artifice usually incorporated in the filmmaking process. By 1967, cinéma vérité and direct cinema techniques were being used in feature films, most notably those of Ken Loach in Britain and Milos Forman in Czechoslovakia. Romero's decision to use these techniques thus speaks both to the allegorical nature of *Night of the Living Dead* and his commitment to oppositional cinema which does away with the usual paraphernalia associated with Hollywood production.

This commitment to subversion and political allegory in *Night of the Living Dead* is crystallized in a single image early in the film. As Johnny (Russell Steiner) and Barbra (Judith O'Dea) pull into the cemetery on the way to visit their father's grave, the camera frames the United States flag in the foreground. Romero's credit as director is superimposed on the screen. It is a visual reference akin to the beginning of Polanski's 1965 *Repulsion*, a film Romero admired, in which Polanski superimposes his director credit over an extreme closeup of an eye, acknowledging the cinema of Bunuel and Hitchcock. However, in Romero's case the symbolism is overtly political. He's saying: America has become a graveyard, and I will sign my name to this statement.

"They're coming to get you, Barbra"

Night of the Living Dead is often spoken of as a manifesto for the modern horror film. In their 2004 retrospective of the horror film, the British Film Institute, for example, described *Night* as "a forerunner of the angry thrills of *Last House on the Left* and *The Texas Chain Saw Massacre*," going on to assert that it takes its inspiration "from the racial and political strife of late–60s America to create an anarchic vérité nightmare which overturned the conventions of fantastical horror."[7] *Night*'s vérité aspects are often highlighted by critics, in conjunction with its iconoclastic nature, its breaking of generic conventions. Without wishing to undermine the pioneering qualities of the film, it is worth reiterating that part of *Night*'s subversive power derives from its continuity with "classic" horror as well as its departure from it. The zombie is traditionally a "blue collar" monster, often used as a symbol of slavery. Romero has cited director Victor Halperin's *White Zombie* (1932) and *Revolt of the Zombies* (1936) as influences.

> I remember being frightened by the old zombie films but it was always the guy out doing the work while Lugosi was up in the castle. What always intrigued me was—you're not going to be able to control them, you're not going to be able to get them to take out the garbage for you. What scared me was the idea of somebody dead walking around.[8]

Despite his take on the zombie as rebellious and uncontrollable (in contrast to those in Halperin's films), Romero was not even the first to depict zombies as modern age symbols of a lumpenproletariat rising up against its masters. The notion of zombies as exploited workers was developed in Hammer's *The Plague of the Zombies* (1966); and much has also been made of the influence, visually and thematically, of *The Last Man on Earth* (1963), an adaptation of Richard Matheson's *I Am Legend*, the novel upon which Romero consciously drew for the story of *Night of the Living Dead*. Indeed, modern-day zombies resurrected en masse by science gone wrong or by the will of an alien force were the subject of several 1950s B pictures made by director Edward L. Cahn. *Invisible Invaders* (1959), for example, pioneered the classic Romero zombie shuffle ten years prior to *Night of the Living Dead*; while *Creature with the Atom Brain* (1955) has its zombies revived by radiation, *a la Night*. *Zombies of Mora Tau* (1957) presents images of revived corpses advancing slowly against the living, again reminiscent of *Night*. Intriguingly, both *Zombies of Mora Tau* and *The Last Man on Earth* showed on Channel 11's *Chiller Theatre* in Pittsburgh in the summer of 1967, when Romero was filming *Night of the Living Dead*. One wonders if he saw these films (the host of *Chiller Theatre*, Bill Cardille, was a friend of Romero's and appeared in *Night of the Living Dead* as a news reporter) and consciously or unconsciously utilized their imagery.

Crucially, then, *Night of the Living Dead* might be understood as transitioning the horror film from the "classic" to the modern. This transition can be seen in the structure of the film itself: The early graveyard sequence utilizes standard 1950s science fiction–horror tropes (particularly in Romero's use of library music), while slyly undermining them. Barbra's subsequent flight to the farmhouse feels like a journey not just to another place but to another *film*: She runs out of a "classic" horror film and into a modern one. Her arrival at the farmhouse evokes the madness of *Repulsion*, thus banishing the lampooning tone of the earlier sequence (as exemplified by Johnny's impersonating Vincent Price), in favor of the starkness of Polanski's film. The transition is furthered with the arrival of Ben (Duane Jones), when it becomes clear that the characters are besieged in the house. (Interestingly, Romero's lighting change after Ben manages to turn on the electricity emphasizes the apocalyptic scenario, as Ben attempts to fortify the house against attack, turning it into a kind of white-walled nuclear bunker in the process.) *The Birds* (1963) is often quoted as an influence on the survival horror of *Night of the Living Dead*, but Romero's depiction of a dying world whose last survivors are contained in an enclosed space also evokes such post-apocalyptic dramas as *On the Beach* (1959) and the BBC television play *Underground* (1958) and racial antagonism between survivors featured in *The World, the Flesh and the Devil* (1959) with Harry Belafonte. Indeed, Romero references these earlier films thematically as well as iconically, in the portrayal of characters unable to give up society's doctrines, even after an apocalypse has destroyed society and rendered those doctrines obsolete. However, it is the nature of Romero's zombie threat that finally completes the transition from "classic" horror to modern apocalyptic horror: Making the monsters flesh eaters resonates with the blue collar nature of the zombie and the apocalyptic scenario, to complete the allegory of a society "devouring" itself from within, a metaphor which underlies the modern horror film of the 1960s and 1970s. As Barry Keith Grant commented in 2004:

> It is perhaps instructive that the apocalyptic vision of the horror film's stellar period is now accepted as commonplace by many of the most intelligent and interesting international filmmakers, who see horror as the only sensible response to the murderous conditions of patriarchal, late-capitalist society.[9]

Night of the Living Dead takes us into this stellar period almost in real time. The story is compressed into a single night, as the title suggests. Within that, the bulk of the apocalypse, or at least our growing realization (along with that of the characters) that apocalypse is taking place, happens in ninety minutes of almost continuous time. The effect on the viewer is to create very powerfully a sense of a definitive point of change: We see the precise moment of apocalypse, the end of history. Watching *Night of the Living Dead* is like watching the big bang in reverse: Life as we know it diminishes at a rapidly accelerating rate until suddenly there is nothing left on the screen of the world we once knew. The film evokes this beautifully through its characters' response to it. (Significantly, the apocalypse takes place on the first day of seasonal change: The clocks have gone forward, denoting the shift.) During a quiet moment, Ben and Barbra tell each other their stories, of the events directly leading to them seeking refuge in the farmhouse. Ben's monologue fulfills the normal functions of exposition: We learn, for example, that he escaped from a diner that was attacked by the living dead. Barbra's monologue, however, fulfills no such story function: We already know what has happened to her. Her speech merely repeats what we have already seen, but somehow this increases the poignancy of the moment, the point at which we, along with the characters, realize that apocalypse is upon us and that nothing will ever be the same again. No other film of the 1960s (perhaps of any era) captured the allegorical moment so completely. At the time of *Night of the Living Dead*'s release, it seemed to many that America was, itself, at the point of social collapse.

"It's not just like a wind that's passing through"

Charles Derry, in his book *Dark Dreams*, identified within films depicting "horror of Armageddon" (a subgenre that begins with *The Birds*) a certain structure that *Night of the Living Dead*, among others, follows. The structure consists of three parts: proliferation, besiegement and annihilation.[10] The first part of *Night*'s narrative is concerned primarily with the increasing number of living dead gathering outside the farmhouse. This motif is crystallized in one shocking moment that takes place early in the film when Ben drives an attacking zombie out of the house: As the zombie staggers backwards through the door, Romero reveals more zombies in the background advancing towards the camera in a diagonal formation. Suddenly there is no longer one zombie but many.

As the zombie numbers increase, and Harry and the other characters emerge from the cellar, *Night* then emphasizes the besiegement motif. They are now trapped inside the house by the zombie masses and must fight their way out. Finally, after a failed escape attempt, the film moves inexorably into its final stages, that of annihilation. (R.H.W. Dillard, in a perceptive early analysis of *Night of the Living Dead*, concluded that much of the film's horror arose from its total surrender to the fear of death. "The plot is one of simple negation," he wrote, "an orchestrated descent into death in which all efforts toward life fail."[11]) Derry compares the "horror of apocalypse" film with the plays of Ionesco, particularly *The Killing Game* (1974), which shares the same structure, the same absurdist view of human folly and miscommunication, and arguably the same essential message as *Night of the Living Dead*: Wherever one finds social functions, one finds alienation.

The motif of proliferation in *Night of the Living Dead* finds its real-life correlation in the spread of protesting and rioting taking place in America in the 1960s, an uprising of the masses in the wake of Vietnam. Although Romero referred in interviews to the Los Angeles Watts riots of 1965, his consciousness was no doubt raised further by increasing racial tensions closer to home, such as the ongoing interracial violence, vigilante action and police brutality

A revolutionary "new order": The ghouls lay siege to the farmhouse in *Night of the Living Dead* (1968).

in York, Pennsylvania (two hundred miles from Pittsburgh), which escalated in the mid–1960s, leading to riots. There were student protests in nearby colleges, such as Cheyney College, Pennsylvania, where in May 1967 four hundred African American students seized control of the administration building in protest at Vietnam and in the fight for civil rights. Although much of the early proliferation sequence in *Night* consists of shadows revealing or concealing action within the house, evoking the "classic" horror film, rioting imagery also features, particularly in the fire-setting against the ravaging hordes. The *Time* magazine cover of the 12th Street Riots depicts looting and firebombing, with black rioters making off with stolen goods from a burning shop, like the *Night* zombies who ransack the burned-out truck for pieces of the charred remains of Tom (Keith Wayne) and Judy (Judith Ridley). It is perhaps no coincidence that Romero has Ben wield a blazing torch in the film.

Romero's conjoining of Watts and Vietnam suggests that the race riots and the Vietnam War protests were inextricably linked, part of a wider revolutionary force of hitherto oppressed social groups. Mass movement against Vietnam and resistance to the draft ultimately led to the tragedy at Kent State University when, in 1970, armed police shot and killed student protesters. Blacks challenged segregation in the South, stimulating the youth movement which peaked in riots at the 1968 Democratic National Convention in Chicago. The following year saw the Stonewall riots and the birth of the gay rights movement. The early 1960s saw the first wave of feminism culminating in the protest against Miss America in 1968. The New Left began to rise in the early 1960s with the Students for a Democratic Society at its core: the younger generation rebelling against the conservative social norms of the Cold War; hippies advocating sexual revolution, questioning authority and government, rejecting traditional social structures such as marriage and family, and demanding rights for women, gays and minorities. The underground press served as a unifier and a means of dissemination. Psychedelic drugs and music were used to raise consciousness.

Meanwhile, an increasing number of Americans turned against the Vietnam War, especially in protest against the use of chemical weapons such as napalm and Agent Orange. The decision to introduce conscription further fueled protest, especially among young black men. As Tony Williams comments of *Night of the Living Dead*'s casting of a black man as its lead: "[I]t recalls a Vietnam situation of non-white ethnic groups bearing an overly proportionate share of combat during the conflict."[12] Civil rights leaders protested against the fact that middle class students had their draft deferred whereas the poor and ethnic minorities were being sent to fight. By 1968, the war was costing a staggering $66 million a day, paid for largely by cuts to public spending. Martin Luther King argued that the war was becoming a "demonic, destructive suction tube" drawing men, skills and money, and that America would never invest the necessary funds to rehabilitate the poor as long as the war continued.[13] The inner cities had been abandoned by industry and the middle classes who fled to the suburbs, leaving the poor and the ethnic minorities behind; they became like tinderboxes ready to ignite. Subsequently (the mid–1960s), the black ghettoes exploded in violent rioting.

Ben (Duane Jones, left) wields a blazing torch in *Night of the Living Dead* (1968). Soundman Gary Steiner (in the doorway) is caught in the shot.

Much has been made of the fact that *Night of the Living Dead* places no particular emphasis on Ben's ethnic origins; however, Romero feels in retrospect that he made a mistake in not doing so. Ben is written as an angry character, and casting a black man, Duane Jones, in the role gave that anger, Romero now feels, a much greater context than he realized at the time: "That character makes mistakes and it's out of anger.... I think sometimes a person from a minority sees certain things very clearly but then is blinded to certain other things because of this anger that arises from not feeling included."[14] Romero is himself a second generation American, of Cuban-Lithuanian descent, and like many of his generation denied his ethnic origin for the sake of assimilation, only referring explicitly to his background recently. In 2009, he revealed to Lee Karr:

> I'm half–Latino ... my Dad is Cuban, my mom is Lithuanian. My dad says, "I'm not Cuban!"—but you were born in Cuba? "I am Castilian, from Spain!"... Okay, well, let's say you're a Cuban, you're a Spanish guy? "Yes, but I am not Puerto Rican!" I grew up in New York ... in the days of *West Side Story*... I have a Latino Dad who's telling me Puerto Ricans are shit. I mean, this is a very confusing situation.[15]

It is telling, then, that racism in Romero's films is often portrayed disturbingly as a form of insanity (one thinks particularly of Wooley, the National Guardsman who goes on a kill-crazy rampage during the tenement raid in *Dawn of the Dead*). In *Night of the Living Dead*, the animosity between Ben and Harry Cooper (Karl Hardman) culminates in Ben shooting Harry, an act that is hardly justifiable, and is, as Williams points out, symptomatic of "more irrational aspects of destructive masculinity."[16]

Racism and destructive masculinity are, however, but two issues in *Night of the Living Dead* that prevent the characters from working together to find a solution to the problem of survival. The theme of non-communication is a recurring one in Romero's films as he himself has pointed out: "I have characters who are not communicating, going along with an ideal, which speaks to the fanaticism or patriotism or whatever that causes war."[17] In *Night* as well as *The Crazies*, the theme of non-communication is visually reinforced by mismatching eye lines—characters in conversation repeatedly look in the wrong direction, not at each other. This is unintentional on Romero's part: He was as yet unaware of the 180-degree rule that filmmakers use to avoid "crossing the line" of action in order to preserve continuity. The jarring nature of the mistake, however, serves only to heighten the sense of miscommunication between people. Romero's films depict an atomized society of isolated individuals, unwilling and unable to communicate, instead following the ideologies promulgated by media, church and government. For Romero the possibility of progressive change lies within the individual. "It's very easy to blame government or corporations or anything else," he told Robin Wood in 1979, "but it's really our own responsibility. We must make decisions ourselves."[18]

In Romero's films, characters unwilling or unable to take this responsibility because they are stuck in the old ways, inevitably perish in a graphic and gruesome manner. As Tony Williams has observed, *Night of the Living Dead* "explicitly presented the image of an America in which the old values were now harmful and obsolete, leading to a chaos very few would survive unless some drastic personal, political and social change would follow."[19] Romero's attack on the "old values" that led to Vietnam is what gives *Night of the Living Dead* its shock factor: He subverts generic conventions and also invokes social taboo in terms of the film's graphic scenes, not merely to challenge dominant values but to negate them entirely. Robin Wood has commented: "[*Night*'s] transgressions are not just against generic conventions: Those conventions constitute an embodiment, in skeletal and schematic form, of the dominant norms of our culture."[20] Thus *Night* explicitly breaks taboos of death and decay, incest, cannibalism, matricide and child sexuality.

The film represents a breakdown of the repressive mechanisms of society in several ways. Familial ties, for example, are portrayed as a form of "living death"; firstly in the scenes with Johnny and Barbra. Their responsibility for remembering their dead father ties them to the past, to tradition, and prevents them from moving forward. Both are presented as regressing: Johnny still plays the same tricks on Barbra as he did when he was a boy—an expression of sadism that seems to arise from repressed desire for his sister. As Williams observes, Johnny's "orally aggressive incestuous desires" culminate in his returning as a zombie to reclaim Barbra at the end of the film.[21] Barbra's catatonia throughout, while partly caused by shock, can also be seen as hysteria born of Catholic repression. "I haven't seen you in church for a while," she chastises Johnny in the early scenes. Both Johnny and Barbra embody repressive Christian values of family and chastity before marriage (it is assumed that neither are married as they are unaccompanied by spouses); but these values are overturned by the dead coming back to life, and the Christian sanctity of death (like the sanctity of marriage and family) is irrevocably violated ("The bereaved will have to do without the dubious comforts that a funeral service provides. They're just dead flesh!") by the film's graphic focus on bodily wounding and physical decay. In *Creepshow* (1982), Romero depicts a dead man literally rising from the grave to claim a grieving relative; one wonders if this is a trick he missed in *Night of the Living Dead*: Johnny might equally have been killed by his father's rotting corpse returning to devour him.

It follows that patriarchy in its various forms is repudiated in the film. Harry, the father, is discredited throughout, and the collapse of his authority is seen as part of a wider cultural disintegration. Specifically, the discredited authority of the patriarchal family is counterpointed by the collapse of authority on a national level. The zombie outbreak is exacerbated by patriarchal institutions such as the military and government science, which struggle to deal with the developing crisis. Washington officials are seen retreating from reporters who are seeking clarification, aid and information on the public's behalf. When advice *is* given by the authorities on how to survive the attacks, it is confusing and sporadic and it changes by the hour. At first people are told to stay put in their homes, and then later they are told to travel to rescue centers. This speaks to a woeful lack of civil defense planning on the part of the authorities that had echoes of the Cuban Missile Crisis and also anticipated future events like Hurricane Katrina (an event which is strongly echoed in Romero's 2005 sequel *Land of the Dead*).

The authorities are in effect too disorganized to save the population in *Night of the Living Dead* and it is left to local sheriffs and vigilante groups to enforce order. Meanwhile, would-be patriarchal heroes like Ben and Harry are too busy engaged in a "pissing contest" to lead the other survivors to safety. Each man's inability defer to the other's plan of action (both of which are shown to be mistaken) prevents the rest of the group from accepting the authority of either, leaving the voice of reason to the eldest woman (Harry's wife Helen [Marilyn Eastman]) and the youngest male (Tom), both of whom are ignored because of their place in the group hierarchy.

Romero expanded on these themes in *The Crazies* and *Dawn of the Dead*. There we witness those in authority within law enforcement and the emergency services deserting their posts as the disaster strikes. Those who remain act irresponsibly towards the public, like the TV station manager in *Dawn of the Dead* who knowingly broadcasts erroneous civil defense information, risking the lives of many. In that film, the government is conspicuous by their absence (presumably all have flown off to their private islands), again leaving law and order in the hands of beer-swilling rednecks who are, as one of the characters comments, "probably enjoying the whole thing."

In *Night of the Living Dead*, although there are an equal number of men and women in the group of survivors, the women's opinions are not valued, and their presence barely acknowledged by the men. Even Tom discounts his girlfriend Judy from the group effort. Women are there to be protected and take orders. Only Helen queries the men's actions but makes a point of backing down when Harry shows his annoyance at having his authority questioned. "We may not enjoy living together, but dying together isn't going to solve anything," she tells Harry. Salving her husband's fragile ego is the price Helen has been willing to pay for the sake of family unity. Staying together "for the sake of the children" ironically results in the child-monster turning on her parents later: punishment for her father's dominance and her mother's submission.

We see parallels between Harry and Helen's marriage in Tom and Judy's relationship. Although the younger couple are "in love" now, Tom seeks dominance within the relationship, and Judy is passive. As the future nuclear family, they are destined to become like Harry and Helen, and that is why they must perish. Their deaths also preclude the continuation of normality as traditionally symbolized by the heterosexual couple in horror films. That they are consumed in a cannibalistic "orgy" by the zombies symbolically undermines the myth

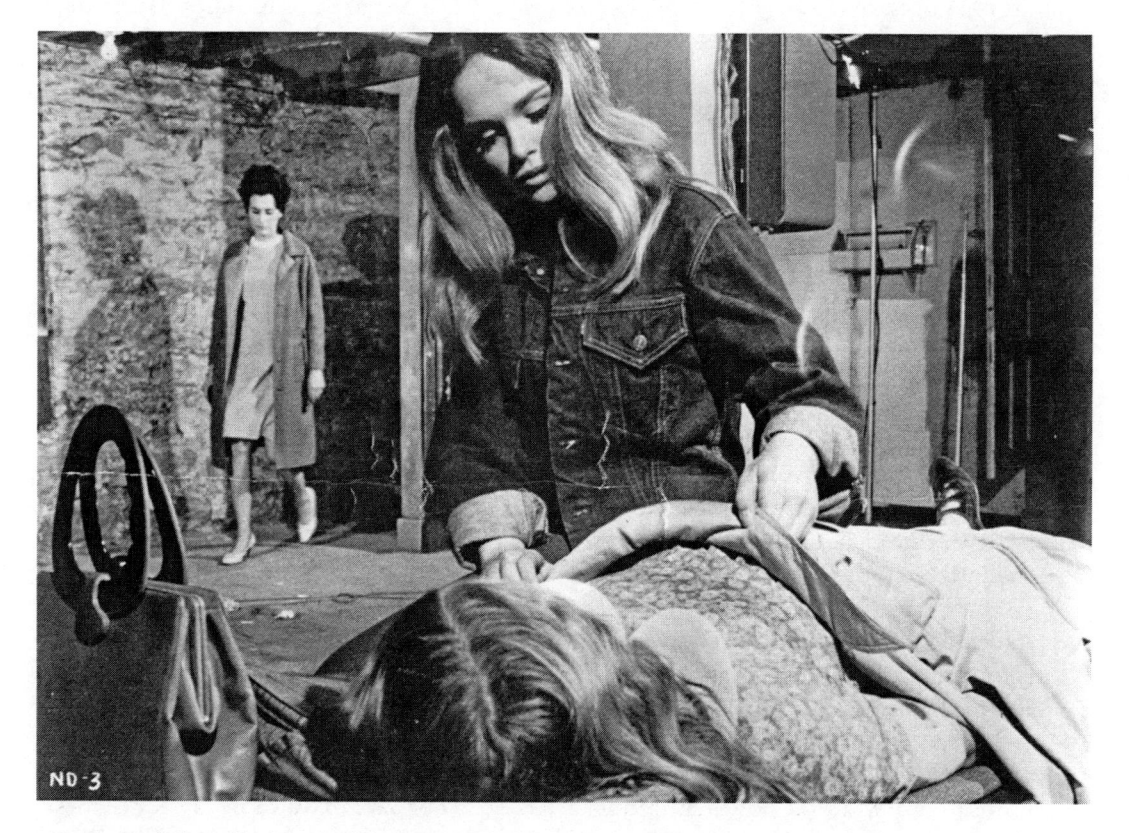

Judy (Judith Ridley) cares for the wounded Karen Cooper (Kyra Schon) while Karen's mom (Marilyn Eastman) stands in the background in *Night of the Living Dead* (1968).

of romantic love, with its ideals of monogamy and exclusivity so important to dominant ideology. Their bodies, which they have pledged only to each other, are messily ripped open and their organs shared indiscriminately among the group of living dead for consumption, a violation of the sanctity of Christian marriage which confers exclusive rights to each other's body to husband and wife. We metaphorically see the very "guts" of society being eaten (many 1960s teenagers joyfully cited this moment as the most delightfully shocking in the film).

Finally, *Night* challenges the idea of the un-contamination of childhood, that children are somehow unaffected by the values of our society and remain "pure." When Karen rises from the dead and proceeds to eat her father and murder her mother (and subsequently attack Ben and try to bite him), these actions take on a disturbingly sexualized element that remains taboo. In particular Helen's stabbing has sexualized overtones (in the penetration imagery and in Marilyn Eastman's "orgasmic" performance). We can see Karen's zombie as a "return of the repressed" in monstrous, perverse, even incestuous form; a cannibalistic-sexual attack on the repressive mechanisms of family. The resonance of this attack is intensified by Romero's cross-cutting of Johnny's incestuous devouring of Barbra (Barbra is the sullen, inhibited woman Karen might have become had she lived).

As Ben descends into the cellar to take refuge from the final zombie attack, Romero moves to the heart of his metaphor. One of the most potent aspects of Romero's zombie films is the transformation from human to zombie, the allegorical statement of "what people are becoming"; hence Harry and Helen become zombies because they are unable to relinquish the old values. In *Dawn of the Dead*, Romero gives this motif perhaps its fullest expression in the character of Roger, whose metamorphosis is given greater emphasis than the transformations of Harry and Helen, a result of his inability to let go of the old values. However, in *Night*, the metaphor is still powerfully conveyed: We see Harry's eyes open, symbolizing his resurrection; Ben shoots him; the same action is repeated with Helen, reinforcing the motif of metamorphosis in our minds. *Invasion of the Body Snatchers* was one of the pioneers of the invasion-metamorphosis narrative, but Romero with *Night of the Living Dead* was the first to use it to make the statement definitive: that "they" are "us."

"Another one for the fire"

Night's final scene takes us back to the main focus of the film, relocating it in the context of Vietnam and the Civil Rights struggles. The old values might be dead and gone but even worse and more regressive values threaten to take their place: Middle America, as represented by Harry, Helen et al., is perhaps no more, but the vigilantes gain control—a right wing backlash that makes victims of the innocent and those in minority. So it was in the 1960s and into the early 1970s, when Kent State, white supremacy groups in the South, and the Bloody Friday riots in New York signaled a reactionary counter-revolution mounted against students and peace protesters by police, vigilantes and the right-wing press playing to the patriotism and bigotry of blue collar workers. Thus, news footage of the posse in *Night of the Living Dead* evokes real news footage of civil rights protesters brutalized by police in the Southern states, as well as the news reports from Vietnam; Ben's body is seen being thrown onto the fire in a series of still frames that evoke the lynchings and burnings of blacks by vigilante groups; while the posse's using hooks so they do not have to touch Ben's body echoes news images from the Vietnam war in which American soldiers used wire when disposing of dead Viet Cong for the same reason.

As many critics have observed, *Night of the Living Dead* restores equilibrium at the end of the narrative: The zombie outbreak is contained and social authority is reinstated. However, this is accompanied by a sense not of optimism but of despair. The wider "human" crisis remains and, if anything, has gotten worse. For Romero, 1968 marked the start of decline in American culture:

> We were '60s guys, we really thought we'd had an honest chance at having changed the world. And then you turn around and not only has it not changed for the better but to some extent for the worse. Things were actually starting to get worse back then: That was the beginning of things going downhill.[22]

Bringing the War Home: *Deathdream* (1972)

Nineteen sixty-eight saw the assassinations of Martin Luther King and Robert Kennedy, the Paris uprisings, and riots at the Democratic National Convention in Chicago. As Romero has suggested, it was the year that did indeed seem to mark the beginning of things going downhill. It was also the year of the Tet Offensive and My Lai, two events that finally turned the American public against the Vietnam War. In January, the Viet Cong and North Vietnam launched a surprise attack on U.S. troops and South Vietnam during a two-day ceasefire for the Tet Lunar New Year celebrations. The Tet Offensive shattered the public's illusions that the U.S. had the situation in Vietnam under control, and public opinion on the war began to shift. However, it was the My Lai Massacre that ultimately lost American hearts and minds in Vietnam. The event was covered up by the Pentagon for eighteen months, but in March 1971 platoon leader William Calley was found guilty of twenty-two murders. Five hundred thousand Americans marched in protest in Washington that April and a Harris poll taken the following month found that 60 percent of Americans opposed the war. Thus, My Lai brought the true horror of the Vietnam War home to America with a vengeance. "Ideologic codes were thrown into crisis," as Tony Williams states. "The average American farm boy soldier was no longer Audie Murphy but a cold-blooded killer."[23]

Not surprisingly, the My Lai atrocities were difficult for the public to face, especially as it came to light that the massacre was not a one-off event but symptomatic of a wider military strategy of attrition which placed heavy emphasis on "kill ratios" and "body counts." In January and February 1971, Vietnam Veterans Against the War invited veterans from all branches of the U.S. military to bear witness to the atrocities they had seen and taken part in during their time in Vietnam. The purpose of the investigation, according to VVAW, was to "preclude the further scapegoating of individual officers for what is in fact Official United States Military Policy."[24] The testimonies of veterans revealed how incidents akin to the massacre at My Lai were not only commonplace, but were "committed on a day-to-day basis with the full awareness of officers at all levels of command."[25] As Ellie Lachman puts it in her notes to the documentary *Winter Soldier* (1972), "the atrocities seemed to the veterans to be an epidemic problem—one that stemmed from the very essence of American military training and procedure."[26] Training involved the systematic dehumanization of soldiers at boot camp, which played on an already troubled masculinity based on inculcated feelings of aggression towards those who were different. One of the young soldiers in the film says of the Vietnamese civilians he murdered, "It wasn't like they were human. We were conditioned to believe this was for the good of the nation, the good of the country."[27]

Deathdream depicts allegorically this "coming home" of Vietnam. Andy Brooks

(Richard Backus), the dead soldier who returns to his family as a zombie, represents the awful truth that My Lai forced America to confront: that home-bred racism and tribalism had made monsters out of many soldiers. As Robin Wood has remarked: "My Lai was not an unfortunate occurrence *out there*; it was created within the American home."[28]

"They said my son was dead." "I was"

Alan Ormsby's script for *Deathdream* started as a play in the late 1960s, inspired by Irwin Shaw's expressionist anti-war play *Bury the Dead* (1936) about dead soldiers who refused to go into their graves and came back to haunt those who sent them to war. Brecht's poem "Ballad of a Dead Soldier" was also an influence, as was "The Monkey's Paw," W.W. Jacobs' horror tale of a woman who wishes her dead son back from the grave. Ormsby saw in the horror genre the possibility to create a metaphor for the psychology that had caused the Vietnam War and the "anger of the guys getting killed over there."[29] Several high school friends of Ormsby's had been killed in Vietnam by friendly fire; like many of his generation, Ormsby felt he was being lied to by the government about Vietnam, and wanted to address the conservative dynamic that had brought about the war in the first place. "There was a macho thing going on," according to Ormsby, "which came back to haunt us."[30] Ormsby saw this "John Wayne–ism" as starting in the family.

The opening scenes of *Deathdream* establish with extraordinary economy and insight the family dynamic, which according to Ormsby "reflects the conservative dynamic in the country"[31] during the time of Vietnam. Critics have praised *Deathdream* for these insights into family repression and its role in patriarchal conditioning, with the logical outcome of such repression creating in Andy a murderous zombie-soldier—the metaphorical face of My Lai. Following a pre-credits sequence in Vietnam, in which Andy is shown to be killed by sniper fire, an establishing shot of a middle–American family home is accompanied by the sound of crickets, the same as were heard in the Vietnam scenes; immediately the link is made between the American home and events in Vietnam. It is dinner time. Andy's family—his mother Christine (Lynn Carlin), father Charlie (John Marley) and sister Cathy (Anya Ormsby)—say Grace. Christine's private prayer, however, is to Andy, who "promised that you'd come home." Charlie and Cathy are disturbed by Christine's evident obsession with her son. All her conversation is centered on him. We learn that part of the reason for Christine's incipient madness is because they have received no word on Andy. Suddenly there is a knock on the door and Charlie goes to answer it. Outside stands a senior soldier with "sad news." The meaning of the scene is heavily signified by director Bob Clark, in the use of closeups, looks and gestures. The meaning, however, would not need to have been spelled out to the audience in 1972—this would have been a familiar scenario for many. Only Cathy's response is healthy. She looks to her father for strength but he does not have it—he cannot comfort her. Christine's instinct on receiving the news is also to back away from her daughter, and she goes into complete denial, becoming angry and accusatory towards the soldier bearing the bad tidings.

In this first scene, then, we glimpse in microcosm the power relationship between mother, father, daughter and (absent) son. The women inevitably work towards perpetuating the patriarchal power structure, although they secretly resent their exclusion from the world of male power. As discussed in the introduction to this book, the subversive horror film shows that in the patriarchal family, hate masquerades as love, and the only priority is the continuance of the family values. *Deathdream* is no different. As in *Frightmare* (discussed in the previous chapter), mother rules the roost, and it through her dominance that patriarchal values are pursued. Christine, as Robin Wood has pointed out, "devotes her frustrated energies entirely to the perpetuation of patriarchy in the shape of her obsessively adored son."[32] Cathy, on the other hand, is relegated to unconsidered subordination by her mother and an "impotent and furtive complicity with the ineffectual father."[33] As the future patriarch, everything is to be sacrificed for Andy. During dinner, Christine delivers a speech about it being "traditional that the head of the family carve," an honor that has already been bestowed upon Andy, as Charlie has taught him to carve meat. Cathy tries to change the subject by mentioning that her friend has a recipe for vegetarian cutlets, an attempt to draw attention to herself and away from traditionalism. But Christine quickly turns the subject back to Andy. Cathy and her father exchange a weary glance—acknowledgment that both of them are lower down in the pecking order than the son.

Ormsby apparently based the family on his in-laws, whom he described as a "traditional family" in contrast to his own family which was unconventional (Ormsby grew up in a "Tennessee Williams environment with strange Southern gothic women"[34]). His mother-in-law was controlling, and the father took this as an affront to his position. Indeed, Ormsby saw the father in *Deathdream* as being younger and more macho (playing sports with Andy, taking him fishing and calling him "buddy"). He is afraid that Andy is a "momma's boy," which is a threat to his own masculinity, his sense of self and his control in the family.[35] The power struggle between father and mother for the control of Andy is implied to be one of the reasons for Andy's enlisting for Vietnam: to escape his mother's suffocating influence and his father's constant criticisms. These tensions within the family can be seen as a byproduct of the repressive mechanisms that facilitate values of patriotism and imperialism to be inculcated.

Ormsby has also cited the play *Sticks and Bones* (1971) by David Rabe as having influenced the *Deathdream* screenplay; indeed the basic story is very similar. In *Sticks and Bones*, a soldier's return from Vietnam threatens the value system of his parents. David, the soldier (who is blind and, like Andy in the later scenes of *Deathdream*, wears dark glasses to hide his eyes), has a Vietnamese lover, which poses a challenge to his parents' racism and patriotism: He has taken a "yellow whore." Rabe was himself a Vietnamese veteran, and in the play, David speaks of the war atrocities he has seen (and, it is implied, taken part in). This truth, like Andy's secret (that he is a killer zombie) in *Deathdream*, threatens to blow the quintessential American family apart.

In *Deathdream*, like in *Sticks and Bones*, the parents' response to their son's alienation is, at least initially, to deny that anything is wrong or that he is strange or different. Andy returns to the family home late at night; at first they think he is an intruder. Charlie's reaction, tellingly, is to get his gun from the drawer. A suspense sequence leads to the shock revelation of Andy, in full military uniform, standing by the front door. Fear turns to delight at his return. The family convenes at the kitchen table. There is an expressive shot through the darkened hallway showing the family gathered in the background; on a mantelpiece in the foreground are framed photographs of the family—darkness has symbolically fallen on them. It is immediately clear that something is not right about Andy. He is cold and distant. "They said you were dead," Charlie probes. "I was," Andy replies emotionlessly. The family members treat this last comment as a joke. Their laughter borders on hysteria. At this point, Clark pulls the camera back from the window of the house, once again to frame the home as he did at the start of the sequence. The film returns to the same establishing shot of the house throughout, reinforcing the idea that what has come back from Vietnam to haunt the family originated there in the home.

"I died for you, Doc. Why shouldn't you return the favor?"

In his DVD commentary, Bob Clark says of this particular shot that he would have moved the camera back from the heart of the home to show the whole town if he could have.[36] It is an insightful observation about the nature of patriotism and is telling of what, to a certain extent, is missing from *Deathdream*.

Preston Sturges' *Hail the Conquering Hero* (1944) is another work that bears remarkable similarities to *Deathdream*. Sturges' returning World War II veteran is celebrated as a local hero by the patriotic townsfolk and made a candidate for mayor; meanwhile, his ex-girlfriend is persuaded to break off her current engagement in order to marry the hero. However, things are not as they seem. The "hero" has taken part in a deception that has gotten out of hand: He has not even been to war, but spent his time working in a shipyard while pretending to be fighting overseas. He is a false hero. *Hail the Conquering Hero* is a satire of small-town patriotism; the values of patriotism and imperialism espoused in the family are fed upon and reinforced by the wider community and used by politicians for their own gain. *Deathdream* only partially explores the ways family and community interact in this way to perpetuate dominant ideologies; what is missing, largely, are the political figures of *Hail the Conquering Hero*, who stood to gain in popularity from their support of military imperialism.

In this way, *Deathdream* perhaps represents the beginning of America's unease with returning Vietnam veterans, a suspicion of soldiers in the wake of My Lai. Police detectives question a diner owner following Andy's murder of a truck driver and pinpoint the suspect as a soldier. One of the characters conjectures that the soldier might not be a local, "might just be passing through," a scenario reminiscent of David Morrell's novel *First Blood* (1972) which dealt with a vagabond soldier taking revenge on a community that shuns him on his return from Vietnam. In *Deathdream*, Dr. Allman (Henderson Forsythe) embodies the troubled authority who continued to draft young men abroad in the furtherance of imperialism, while privately holding concerns about the effects of the war on the individual. Allman, therefore, immediately suspects Andy to be the killer of the truck driver; he alone seems to understand that Vietnam might have turned Andy into a murderer.

In some ways, however, *Deathdream* does attempt to depict the perpetuation of patriotic and imperialist values through Andy's standing as a returning hero within the community. Most notably, Ben (Arthur Anderson), the postman and World War II veteran, is invited to join the family's celebration of Andy's return. Although cornball characterization, Ben, the Okinawa veteran, represents a form of World War II nostalgia. He is insensitive to Andy's trauma; Andy grows increasingly angry and eventually walks away—a reflection of Vietnam being a different, "unjust" war compared to World War II. Later, Andy is visited by a group of young boys who hero-worship him and try to impress him with their own macho karate demonstration. Andy's response is to kill the family dog in front of them—bringing home to them the true horror of killing, debunking their glorification of war. Thus, throughout the film, Andy (like David in *Sticks and Bones*) systematically dismantles patriotic and macho ideals.

The film's final destruction of patriarchal values (and perhaps *Deathdream*'s most shocking and subversive sequence) takes place when Andy meets with his girlfriend Joanne (Jane Daly). It has been established that Joanne has dutifully waited for Andy, "staying home and watching the late show," so that they can pick up where they left off on his return. As in *Hail the Conquering Hero*, the returning hero is expected to marry his girlfriend and take his place within the patriarchy, as an endorsement of family values and the imperative of ensuring the family's continuance as an institution. Joanne is also a symbol of the good times they used to have before Andy had gone off to war. The film therefore plays with our expectations— might Andy somehow be saved by Joanne's love for him? Might he be redeemed? When Joanne confesses to Andy that she still has feelings for him, we wonder if she might, against the odds, uncover some shred of humanity left within him (which, in fact, the film leads us to believe might still exist). Earlier in the film Andy visited Joanne's house at night and watched her through the window from afar, as though lamenting the loss of the life he once knew. *Deathdream* at that moment reveals its roots as a melodrama about the traumatizing effects of war on individual and community. (In Ormsby's script, Andy's night walk held greater significance—showing Andy looking at more places in the town, like his school—that he knew from before he went to Vietnam.) Andy, however, turns against the institution that produced him, as Williams observes, by vampirizing Joanne—the figure whose role, as future wife, is ideologically approved for him.[37] As she claws away his darkened glasses, his full monstrosity is revealed thus; and Andy proceeds to feed noisily on the flesh and blood of the woman who waited for him to come home from the war.

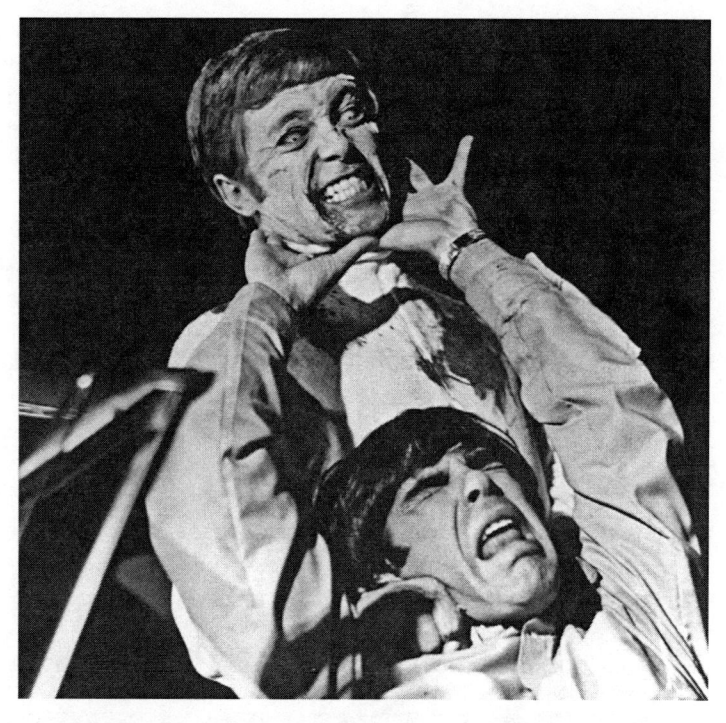

The living dead Andy (Richard Backus) attacks his sister's boyfriend Bob (Michael Mazes) in *Deathdream* (1972) (photograph courtesy Blue Underground, Inc.).

"Stand up, Andy, and face me"

Andy returns home to confront his parents with the truth of what they have turned him into. Throughout the film, we have witnessed the family's gradual realization that Andy is not the son that they thought he was, that Vietnam has made him a monster. However, both Christine and Charlie must accept that it was their will that sent him to Vietnam— they are complicit in making him into a dehumanized killer. Confronting the family with their own values and the "corruption" that lies beneath those beliefs (metaphorically expressed in Andy's physical deterioration as a zombie) causes the family unit to collapse internally. While the mother accepts Andy in all his monstrousness (he is still her son and her instinct is to protect him no matter what), the father cannot. Leveling his gun at Andy, Charlie orders his son to stand up and face him, needing to see the full horror that is of his own creation. The film plays this scene beautifully: We see from Charlie's point of view as Andy turns to allow his father to see the shocking truth. Andy's rotting zombie is the true "face" of Vietnam, of the atrocities that took place there, of My Lai. But Charlie cannot bring himself to shoot his son. Instead, in admission of his own culpability, he turns the gun on himself.

Deathdream's conclusion differs significantly from that of *Sticks and Bones*. In Rabe's play, the parents are unable to admit that their beliefs are in any way wrong. They need to preserve the internalized image of the "happy family" that their son David's return has disrupted. Luckily, they have a second son, Rick, who is no such threat to their beliefs, so David can be sacrificed, and patriarchy can still continue, with the younger son taking the place of the older one. The family members are happy to remain in a state of denial about Vietnam. *Sticks and Bones* was written in 1968, before the horrors of My Lai came fully to light, before mothers and fathers were forced to confront the fact that their sons had possibly committed atrocities.

By 1972, however, the Vietnam narrative could not be expelled from the family the

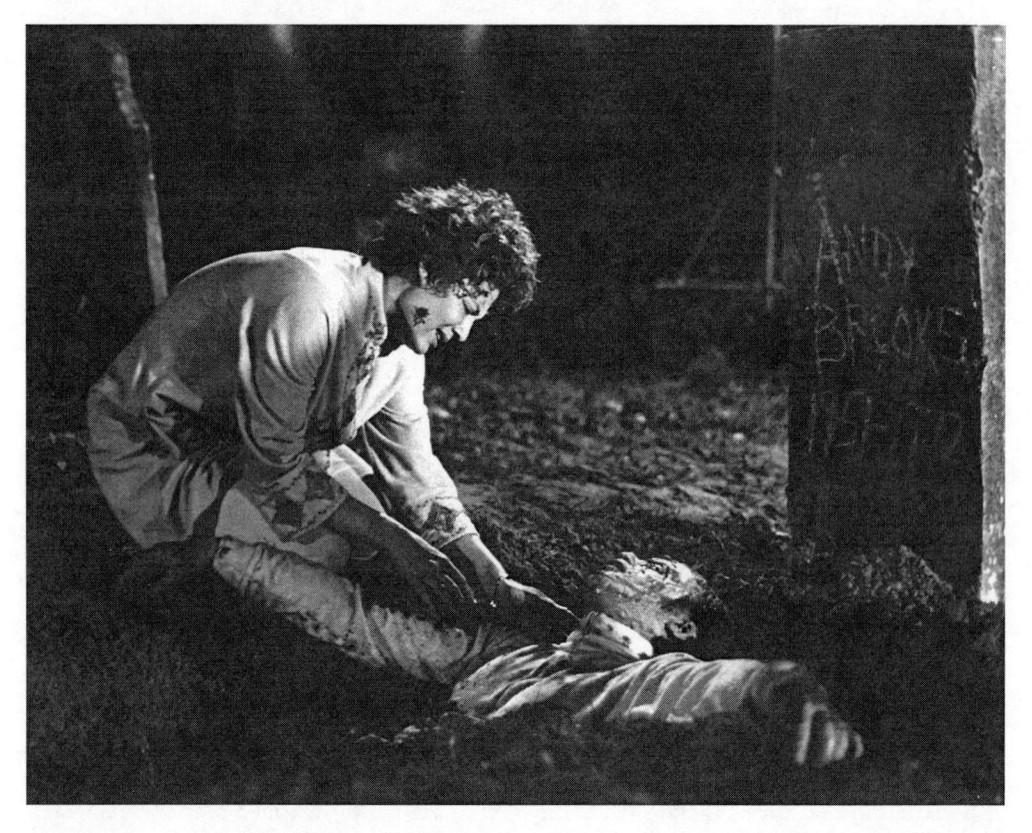

Christine Brooks (Lynn Carlin) buries her undead son, Andy (Richard Backus), in the final scene of *Deathdream* (1972) (Blue Underground, Inc.).

way it is in *Sticks and Bones*. By virtue of *Deathdream*'s positioning as apocalyptic horror, Christine and Charlie's admittance of Vietnam and its atrocities causes the disintegration of the family and its values. Andy is not recuperable into the dominant ideology and there is no other son to replace him. All Christine has left at the end of *Deathdream* is the opportunity to finally bury her son, and with him her old patriotic values. Acting on his will, Christine thus drives Andy to the cemetery where it is revealed he has already prepared his own grave, which he duly climbs into. Christine finally accepts that Andy died in Vietnam and it is only at this point, as Christine brings herself to let go of Andy, that he is able to pass away: He has, in fact, been doing her will all along. *Deathdream* therefore ends with Christine at her son's grave, recognizing that it was her doing that turned Andy into a monster. "Some boys," she tells the police, "never come home."

The Madness of War: *The Crazies* (1973)

While My Lai brought the horror of what was going on *out there* into the American home via television, Kent State represented a direct encroachment of the Vietnam War on home soil. The violence in Vietnam could no longer be ignored as something taking place miles from home in South Asia; the shooting of students by Ohio National Guardsmen on May 4, 1970, seemed to be an extension of the killing taking place overseas, inextricably linked to aggressive government policy. A week after Kent State, two students were killed and twelve injured by police fire during a protest at Jackson State University in Mississippi. The police action was later found to be unjustified. To many, America seemed to have gone mad.

George A. Romero's *The Crazies*, which depicts the madness of Vietnam re-enacted on home territory, was a failure when first released, something Romero largely attributes to poor marketing but also to the film's inescapable associations with Kent State and what it represented. "I think maybe it was a little ahead of its time," he reflected in 1977. "At the time I made it, we were still in Vietnam and it was a very heartfelt problem, a part of the national consciousness, and I don't think anyone was ready to see that situation—even though it's not a Vietnam film, it's an anti-military film."[38] In 1981 he added, "Ultimately, I think, the film deals with the politics a little too lightly. It has sort of an outrageous bawdy style, and some people may have thought we were making fun of politics, exploiting Vietnam and the Kent State tragedy. We weren't at all. In fact, *The Crazies* was a very angry and radical film, if one sees through the comic surface."[39]

Despite its perceived shortcomings by its director, *The Crazies* now looks like a definitive statement on the insanity born of Vietnam. It presents the violence espoused by patriarchal authority—family, military, government—as a form of madness contaminating America. *The Crazies* builds on the themes of *Night of the Living Dead*, depicting how easily the victim becomes the monster: "What I'm trying to show is how the monster, the evil, is not something lurking in the distance, but something actually inside us all."[40] Romero, however, does not consider human beings as innately violent or evil. "*Potentially* evil is a better way of putting it," he told Tom Seligson in 1981. "I don't think there's an intrinsically evil side to man. But I think all of us at certain times in our lives do things that are compromising, things that go against our conscience."[41] For Romero, then, violence is largely inculcated in us by social and political structures; and the only way to immunize oneself from such "infection" is to recognize the insanity of patriarchal violence and consciously reject it, as David, the ex–Green Beret, does in *The Crazies*.

"The whole thing's insane! How can you tell who's infected and who isn't?"

The opening scene of *The Crazies*, in which a young boy tries to scare his sister, reprises the opening of *Night of the Living Dead* with Johnny and Barbara, as many critics have noted; however, it also makes intrinsic connections between patriarchy, power, violence and madness. The power play between brother and sister in the scene is an aggressive assertion of the boy's male dominance; Romero immediately parallels this action with their father's smashing up of the house after having killed his wife, introducing the theme of madness as an extension of normality. Military drums play on the soundtrack as the credits roll over shots of the house in flames, set alight by the crazy father, linking the male aggression in the house with the military mind-set as forms of patriarchal violence; the burning house evokes images of burning Vietnamese villages and napalm attacks. One might read the sequence as a statement that man's inherent aggression is what leads to militarism; however, the trick of *The Crazies* as it unspools is to show social breakdown as the prime cause of the violence in the film, a situation exacerbated—indeed brought about in the first place—by military and government: Trixie, a bacteriological weapon that army scientists have been developing (for use, it is implied, in Vietnam) has been accidentally released into the town's water supply; the effect of the toxin is to leave you dead or incurably mad.

At first we are told that Trixie is a virus that the Army is trying to contain; the military is a peacekeeping force brought in to protect the town's inhabitants from themselves. However, the campaign seems disorganized (supplies of antibiotic are insufficient) from the get-go. "You put martial law on a town and you're just polarizing the situation," protests Hawks (Robert J. McCully), one of the bureaucrats making the political decisions behind the scenes. "That army becomes an invasionary force, those people are going to resist." As Hawks predicts, the army meets immediate opposition from farmers with guns, and it becomes apparent that military authority is not capable of rational decision-making in moments of national crisis. Soldiers raid the homes of civilians with orders to round them up and take them to the high school, which has been designated as a holding area. Romero shows soldiers abusing their authority: looting (one steals a man's fishing rod) and forcibly removing people from their houses. As Linnie Blake observes, Romero "offers a coruscating indictment of America's ongoing love affair with the gun."[42] The gun is, of course, associated with the white-suited, gas-masked soldiers, but within the ostensibly peaceful family homes they invade are gun cabinets, toy machine guns for the kids, framed prints of sons away fighting in Vietnam and plastic toy soldiers that are ironically stepped on and crushed by the home invaders (dispelling any romantic ideas about the army that we may hold). "The martial law that is imposed upon Evans City from without," Blake comments, "is thus echoed from within by the townspeople themselves, whose home-made weapons and personal fire-power affirm their own intrinsic adherence to the culture of the gun."[43]

The tendency of the military mind to escalate violence is reflected by the order to confiscate every civilian weapon. Tempers flare when the Constitutional right to bear arms is rescinded. When a police officer refuses, he is killed in the ensuing scuffle. At this point madness takes hold of the hitherto ordinary, peace-loving townsfolk; however, the spreading insanity of violence is a response to authoritarian rule. Tellingly, Romero shows the military and politicians preparing to raise the ante even further: The president is asked to sanction the use of a nuclear weapon on the town should the perimeter be broken. This invocation of the chain of command emphasizes the spread of madness through the ranks, but again the boundaries between normality and insanity are constantly blurred. Colonel Peckham (Lloyd Hollar), brought in to contain the outbreak, does not think of the moral implications of the orders he issues to his men, orders that might make sense to him or his superiors, but when carried out unquestioningly by the soldiers under him, in a situation of chaos and fear, lead to atrocities. Thus bodies are ordered to be burned, and wounded civilians are incinerated by flame-thrower while still alive. Romero emphasizes the human factor in the scenario: Miscommunication between the army and the government scientists is rife, an understandable human failing. The soldiers, scientists and doctors attempting to deal with the situation, such as Peckham, Dr. Watts and Major Ryder, are doing their best considering the circumstances—they are given scant information by their superiors, and they have little choice but to obey orders in the interests of national security. These soldiers are mere cogs in the military machine, as they are well aware. "I'm a combat man, I shouldn't even be here," Peckham laments. "I just happened to be available—even expendable."

On the other hand, the high-level military and politicians are shown to become increasingly delirious as the film progresses: "The radiation scenario covers us," remarks one, as they discuss ways to cover up the increasingly likely bombing of the town. They look tired and unkempt, and their conversation sounds more than a little crazy. The president, meanwhile, is depicted as a mysterious figure on a television screen; only the back of his head is shown, and he is willing to commit the insane act of detonating a nuclear weapon above an American town. *The Crazies* is, as Blake puts it, "very much a product of Nixon's first term of office,"[44] but anticipates the shocking discomposure of Nixon during the Watergate scandal in his second term. Nixon's invasion of Cambodia and Kent State sent him on a downward spiral in the opinion polls; he won the presidency in November 1972 with the lowest voter turn-out since 1948. However, his bombing of North Vietnam on Christmas Day 1972, after having declared through Henry Kissinger that "peace is at hand," drew widespread criticism and a feeling that the president was suffering from a moral schizophrenia. Matters seemed to reach a peak during the Arab-Israeli War in October 1973, when he increased the Def-Con status, placing nuclear weapons on stand-by, and thus astonishing the Soviets. The president, who seemed to have his mind on other things, made decisions that were rash and potentially disastrous for the nation, as do the delirious politicians in *The Crazies*.

The Watergate scandal, and Nixon's actions during the Arab-Israeli War (which arguably led to the OPEC Oil Crisis and ensuing economic crisis), are emblematic of authority losing control and bringing about social collapse. Similarly, *The Crazies*, as Williams observes, "reveals disintegration of all levels of civilized society—family, law, science, medical, military, and government. All are interdependent structures and collapse like a fragile house of cards."[45] What makes these structures interdependent are that they each represent forms of patriarchy. Thus *The Crazies* constantly draws parallels between these various disintegrating structures, with the madness of patriarchal violence as the common factor; Romero intercuts between military, government and family as each become increasingly irrational. The insanity caused by Trixie, as William rightly points out, "releases socially repressed tensions that erupt both violently and sexually."[46]

Hence, in the film, fathers make incestuous advances to their daughters, who respond in kind; an old woman stabs a soldier to death with a knitting needle; and a father bludgeons his wife to death before trying to burn his children. But at the same time Romero blurs the boundaries of insanity, so that we cannot always tell who is infected and who is not, as in the case of the priest who immolates himself because his church was invaded by soldiers (a direct reference to the Buddhist monk Thich Quan Duc who, in 1963, immolated himself in a busy Saigon street to protest South Vietnam's treatment of Buddhists). Is he infected by the toxin or making a violent protest? In the end, of course, it makes no difference. Violence resulting from the release of repression (as can be seen in the actions of insane people, who effectively lose their socially conditioned inhibitions), violence resulting as a response to oppression (such as the priest's suicide), and violence perpetuated by patriarchal institutions (family, military and government) are inextricably linked. They are, in effect the same thing, a "madness" that is infectious. It follows, then, that those traditionally excluded from the patriarchy—children and young women—are also affected in a predictable way, regressing to a near-powerless state of retardation and submissiveness, such as the girl who listlessly sweeps up in a field filled with the dead and wounded after rednecks fight back against the soldiers. She attempts to brush away the madness and the violence with her broom, but Vietnam has come home—and it can't be swept under the carpet.

"Action, adventure! Evans City's only Green Beret! Christ, I can't believe that was me!"

In his *New York Times* review of *The Crazies*, Vincent Canby says the film's real subject "is not bacteriological weaponry or the idiocies of the military but the collapse of a community presented as a spectacle."[47] Romero's insight is that any society based on aggressive values is bound to collapse. In a recent interview with the BBC, the psychologist Steven Pinker, discussing his book *The Better Angels of Our Nature*, argued that modern history has seen a decline of violence, closely aligned to the rise of education, the pursuit of human rights and the empowerment of women. He made the point that marriage has a civilizing effect on young males. "Men are learning to exert greater self-control and not give in to macho displays of violence and sexism."[48]

In *The Crazies*, David (W.G. McMillan), the ex-soldier, rejects his past as a Green Beret and with it the violence that he has perpetrated. His time in Vietnam has taught him about the madness of male violence, and its associated machismo. He has, as Williams notes, "unthinkingly followed the masculine pursuits of his culture and showed no awareness of a woman's real personality."[49] His relationship with a caring and compassionate nurse, Judy (Lane Carroll), has enabled him to connect with his anima. As Lewton did in the 1940s, Romero, during the time of Vietnam, sees urgent need for this reconciliation of the feminine within the culture and the self. Romero has championed women in his films since *Jack's Wife* (1972): Fran in *Dawn of the Dead* and Sarah in *Day of the Dead* (1985) particularly represent a feminist perspective that goes beyond the demand for gender equality to constitute a complete rejection of patriarchal consumer-capitalist values in favor of a new social order entirely. The working towards this new state of being in Romero's films is led by the women characters; and the strong sensitive males (like David in *The Crazies* and Peter in *Dawn of the Dead*) follow their lead.

The Crazies, then, as Williams points out, "reveals the conscious development of a male hero who learns from his past mistakes, rejects the macho values of his culture, and wishes to pursue a new direction for his life. It signifies Romero's deepest concerns in articulating the necessary personal trajectory of breaking away from deeply ingrained ideologically induced cultural habits and trying to move towards a new form of society."[50] Romero repeat-

Judy (Lane Carroll) tells David (W.G. McMillan) that she thinks he may be immune to the Trixie toxin in *The Crazies* (1973).

edly contrasts David with Clank (Harold Wayne Jones), the man that David might have become had he not consciously rejected the macho values of his culture, based as they are on male insecurity. Clank, unlike David, still abides by the way of the gun, and is destined, therefore, to die by it (symbolically shot in the head—a fate foreshadowed by his complaining earlier that "my head feels strange"). David's rejection of the gun is further symbolized by Romero in a shot taking David's point of view as he angrily grabs his rifle. Although he has rejected the violence of his past, and is therefore now symbolically immune to the madness-inducing effects of Trixie, David's tragedy is that he is being drawn back into a war situation against his will. He wishes to reject the weapon but knows he must retain it to survive. *The Crazies*, then, depicts a progression from *Night of the Living Dead*, and bridges *Dawn of the Dead* in terms of its characters moving towards the self-awareness necessary to re-structure society; but they still have a ways to go in order to achieve active enlightenment. Judy, for example, is portrayed in an early scene as emotionally needy and slightly insecure in her relationship with David: She needs him to marry her. She is pregnant and worries that if something happens to the baby, he will back out of the marriage. Her vulnerability appears to be based not so much on a lack of trust, as a need to make her relationship official through the institution of marriage (perhaps this is why, later in the film, she regresses to childlike behavior as she succumbs to the toxin). David's tragic flaw, the film shows, is his rugged individualism. He abandons his post as a voluntary fireman (a symbol of collective action and community spirit) in a bid to survive alone, but rugged individualism, as Linnie Blake points out, is revealed in the end to be "a sorry substitute for cooperative social endeavour."[51]

Clank (Harold Wayne Jones, left), Judy (Lane Carroll) and David (W.G. McMillan) hide in the woods to escape the military in *The Crazies* (1973).

"Brookmyre told Judy to keep isolated. That's good enough for me"

David naturally has little trust in the army, who in his own experience "can turn a campus protest into a shooting war"—an obvious reference to Kent State. He also recognizes the dangers of the situation getting out of control with the townspeople bearing arms against the military invasion. His decision is to reject quarantine in favor of going it alone with the small band of survivors he leads. This course of action, flying in the face of authority, although understandable in the circumstances, only leads to Judy's death and David's eventual recapture by the soldiers. In his bid to survive alone rather than cooperate with the authorities, David fails. His tragedy is that, given the choice between his cooperative ideals and the individualism that, as Linnie Blake says, "imprinted the figure of the lone frontiersman, the gunslinger and the bike outlaw upon the national consciousness,"[52] he picks the latter. Bitter irony has it that he loses his best friend and his wife because of this decision, and therefore does indeed end up alone. Merely rejecting patriarchal violence is not enough to save society: Romero is saying that we must learn to communicate, to work together to bring about change.

As he did in *Night of the Living Dead*, Romero increases the shocks in *The Crazies,* so that the final act becomes a similar catalogue of atrocities: Artie's (Richard Liberty) incestuous rape of his daughter Cathy (Lynn Lowry) is quickly followed by Artie's hanging himself in shame; Cathy subsequently dies, like a sacrificial lamb, or flower child, at the hands of soldiers; Clank is shot in the head in a graphic manner (which recalls the execution in 1968 of a Viet Cong soldier, Nguyen Van Lem, by South Vietnamese General Nguyen Ngoc Loan, which was filmed by an NBC cameraman and transmitted around the world—its bloodspurting reality helped to galvanize the anti-war movement). As I stated in my preface: In Romero's work, graphic shock is intrinsically linked to ideological shock, depicting the extremity of the violence on display as absurd. Thus the savagery of the violence in *The Crazies*, in breaking screen taboos, is linked to the insanity of it—the bright red blood is almost comical in effect, emphasizing its absurdity.

"Sooner or later they'll find a human who is immune"

In January 1973, Nixon suspended offensive action in Vietnam, and he took the troops out of the country by March; as Linnie Blake says of *The Crazies*, "Romero evokes the futility of the already lost but yet to be concluded Vietnam War."[53] The bleak irony and tragedy of Romero's film sums up America's involvement with the war and its divisive effect on the American people. Yet, at the film's end, the military congratulate themselves on having successfully contained the Evans City situation. Nothing has been learned, it seems, and Peckham is transferred to another town in Kentucky where symptoms of the Trixie virus are present in the population. Romero's final irony is to have David brought into quarantine where the soldiers decide against giving him an immunity check. David smirks in response: It is one final misjudgment by the authorities. Only David—and we the audience—are party to the irony, and David keeps his knowledge of his immunity to himself, still unwilling, it seems, to enter into any cooperative endeavor for the sake of the greater good. By making us privy to the irony, however, Romero leaves open the door for hope, despite the apparent pessimism: If more men like David show "immunity" to the madness of patriarchal violence, we have a chance. As the elderly priest says in *Dawn of the Dead*, "We must stop the killing or lose the war."

6

ANTI-HOLLYWOOD VIOLENCE AND DARK COUNTERCULTURE

Last House on the Left (1972) and
The Texas Chain Saw Massacre (1974)

Night of the Living Dead represented a transition from "classic" horror to modern apocalyptic horror, but the modern horror cycle in America, as Peter Hutchings notes, actually took several years to gain momentum. Romero's film did not lead directly and immediately to sustained horror production of the type that would later be labeled modern. There exists a four-year gap between *Night of the Living Dead* and—arguably the next key modern American horror film—*Last House on the Left*; and as Hutchings says, "a regular flow of American horror does not develop until the mid–1970s."[1] The changes occurring in the American horror genre in the late 1960s and early 1970s, he argues, were "more gradual than sometimes supposed."[2]

Not often remarked upon by critics is the influence of the revisionist western on the emerging modern American horror film during the years between *Night* and *Last House on the Left*. The revisionist western coincides historically with the apocalyptic horror film; both grew out of the late 1960s, and the revisionist western enjoyed its heyday on the cusp of the 1970s—in the gap between *Night* and *Last House*. *Soldier Blue* (1970) in particular seems to have paved the way for the likes of *Last House on the Left*, *The Texas Chain Saw Massacre*, *The Hills Have Eyes* (1977) and even *Dawn of the Dead*: not only in terms of its graphic violence which caused huge controversy (and was seen, like *Last House on the Left*, as "un–American") but also in its implicit linking of its brutal on-screen massacres to atrocities in Vietnam and its revising of pioneer myths relating to the Indian wars and American expansionism. Ralph Nelson, the director of *Soldier Blue*, is said to have become enraged by America's historic mistreatment of its Indians during his research for the film, and decided to make *Soldier Blue* as an anti-war statement. According to Angela Aleiss' book *Making the White Man's Indian*, the filmmaker had served honorably in the Air Force during World War II but America's recent atrocities in Southeast Asia had "shattered his illusions of military glory and national patriotism"[3]: "We like to think of our soldiers as epitomes of grown-up Boy Scouts incapable of evil," said Nelson, "[but] in *Soldier Blue* I have tried to show the true face of war ... how it changes normally peaceful men into savage beasts."[4]

In *Soldier Blue*, Peter Strauss plays a naïve soldier whose illusions of military glory and patriotism are shattered when he witnesses the massacre of the population of an Indian village by marauding soldiers who, in their bloodlust, commit atrocities similar to those that were reported in Vietnam: Women are raped and their breasts cut off, children are shot point blank and dismembered, warriors are disemboweled. Nelson based the film on the 1864 Sand Creek Massacre in Colorado and the 1890 Massacre of Wounded Knee, but the references to My Lai are unmistakable: a case of, in Nelson's words, "history repeating itself."[5] In the lead-up to the brutal massacre, *Soldier Blue* explores the relationship between Strauss's character (who is positioned as the audience's identification figure) and the white former wife of a Cheyenne chief (played by Candice Bergen) who admits that she would rather be a Cheyenne than a "bloodthirsty soldier of any army you can name." In her dress and attitudes Bergen's character is coded anachronistically as a woman of late 1960s counterculture: feminist, anti-war, more sympathetic, it seems, to the enemy than to her own countrymen. She is both mentor and antagonist to the Strauss character, who is simultaneously attracted and repelled by her unpatriotic beliefs, until the bloody massacre of the Indians finally opens his eyes to the truth. "In 5,000 years of recorded civilization," *Soldier Blue* begins, "mankind has written history in blood."

This theme of violence as intrinsic to American history—and thereby intrinsic to the American psyche—as postulated by the revisionist western, is also central to the apocalyptic horror film—perhaps even more so. As Christopher Sharrett has noted, films like *The Texas Chain Saw Massacre* and *The Hills Have Eyes* might be even more revisionist than westerns like *Soldier Blue*, as they portray the overall ideology underpinning frontier development as socially and psychologically, as well as politically, unstable, equating it with psychosis.[6] Sharrett also points out that the apocalyptic horror film insists upon a "criticism of despair."[7] Society is shown, because of the psychotic violence inherent in man, to be always on the verge of calamity, and a way out of calamity is never in evidence.

The abject pessimism that is an abiding characteristic of the apocalyptic horror film does not allow for suggestions of revolutionary programs of change; at least, not in the early 1970s when America was still reeling from My Lai, Altamont and the Manson murders. Both *Last House on the Left* and *The Texas Chain Saw Massacre* view American counterculture during this period as extremely dark: a reflection of the popular view, at the time, that even peace-loving hippies harbored antisocial, violent impulses. It was only later in the decade that films like *Shivers*, *Blue Sunshine* and *Dawn of the Dead* were able to consider counterculture more positively again, assimilating its darker elements so as to find a way out of apocalypse and begin to follow through with ideas of social change.

The Road Leads to Nowhere: Wes Craven and *Last House on the Left*

On March 29, 1971, William Calley was found guilty of 22 murders in My Lai. That night, on NBC News, correspondent Frank McGee's report of the My Lai story included eyewitnesses to the massacre—soldiers in Company C—who claimed they had been ordered by their commander, Captain Ernest Medina, "that when we leave out the village there shouldn't be anything standing. That's villages, women, children, babies, pigs, chickens, anything."[8] Calley supporters claim he was a scapegoat for an even more sinister involvement to the U.S. military view of the Vietnam War; Calley's plea, that he was merely following orders, was rejected by the jury of army officers at his court martial. The general feeling in the country was that—if My Lai had been covered up—what other atrocities were taking place in the Vietnam War that the public was not being told about?

Six months after the news stories made the full shocking details of My Lai public, Wes

Craven wrote the script for *Last House on the Left*. Speaking in the documentary *The American Nightmare*, Craven recalled the impact that news reports from Vietnam had on him at the time: "Those kids running down the road screaming naked after the napalm attack—that was my coming of age into realizing that American weren't always the good guys and that things that we could do could be horrendous or evil or dark or impossible to explain—My Lai for instance."[9]

The incident Craven refers to—a napalm attack on the small South Vietnamese village of Trang Bang—took place on June 8, 1972, while Craven was editing *Last House on the Left*. Photographer Nick Ut subsequently won the Pulitzer Prize for his shot of the naked child Kim Phuc, whose body was severely burned by the napalm. The famous photograph of the child's violated body that so disturbed Wes Craven is evoked in *Last House on the Left* in the forced stripping and rape of the woman-child Mari (Sandra Cassell). Another famous image from Vietnam that haunted Craven—the 1968 execution of Viet Cong soldier Nguyen Van Lem (mentioned in the previous chapter), taken by photographer Eddie Adams—was directly quoted by Craven in the film. "That methodical execution style," Craven reveals "was translated right to the shooting of Mari at the lake."[10]

Much news footage of the Vietnam War was suppressed by broadcasters and the government, but the napalm attack on Trang Bang was allowed to be shown, reflecting the shift of public opinion against the war. *Last House on the Left* arose partly from the desire, on Craven's part, to capture the same kind of raw reality as the documentary footage coming out of Vietnam that Craven suspected was being censored: "It was a time when all the rules were out the window, when everybody was trying to break the hold of censorship," Craven told David A. Szulkin. "The Vietnam war was going on, and the most powerful footage that we saw was in the actual documentary films of the war. There was a great amount of feeling that 'the worst of it is being censored, so let's try to get our hands on what's really going on over there.'"[11] Recent studies of the media's coverage of Vietnam, such as *The "Uncensored War"* by Daniel C. Hallin, corroborate this, with claims that only a small percentage of news reports showed actual combat, and that civilian casualties in North Vietnam were barely reported at all.[12] Craven wanted to break the hold of censorship and get to the truth about Vietnam and, beyond that, the truth about the nature of interpersonal violence.

Although the Vietnam footage was censored, Craven felt that it was candid about violence in a way that Hollywood cinema was not. Craven, like Michael Reeves, objected on moral grounds to the sanitization of violence by Hollywood, and saw it as part of the ideological apparatus that enabled the State to condition soldiers for warfare. "The more you can know about violence, the more you can walk away from it and not be attracted to it," Craven stated in 1999. "The more it is glamorized and shown to be a glib solution to things and people walking away heroically—the one-shot western hero—the more the people up there—government—can say 'Go and do that—be a hero' and you come back shattered."[13] In *Last House on the Left* Craven thus set out to show violence "the way we thought it really was, and to show the dark underbelly of the Hollywood genre film."[14] One of Craven's strategies was to blur the distinction between violence that is morally justifiable and violence that is sadistic, "where the people who did violence were always bad and if a good guy did it to the bad guy, it was very clean and quick."[15] The atrocities committed by American soldiers at My Lai showed that distinctions are not clear-cut. "That was the sort of attitude that America had gone into Vietnam with ... that they were the bad guys and we'd go in like *Gunsmoke*, face 'em down, and bang, they'd be dead. The fact of the matter was that the war involved horrendous killings piled upon killings."[16]

Part of the film's power is to create empathy between the audience and the villains, which makes it impossible for us to view them—despite their sadism—as inhuman. Conversely, the film shows the process by which normally empathetic people, such as the Collingwoods, can demonize others in order to justify acts of vengeance. The film examines the way in which a nation casts its enemies as "other" in order to vindicate warfare; and at the same time, in creating empathy between the audience and the villains (in a way that 1974's *Death Wish*, for example, does not), *Last House on the Left* reflects what Adam Lowenstein describes as the tendency of 1970s counterculture to identify with the demonized other. According to Lowenstein, the American Indian was "fetishized as a revolutionary figure" by many, including students who participated at the Kent State demonstrations dressed as Daniel Boone and Davy Crockett, "historical figures famous for their mythic adoption of Native American ways."[17] Sympathy to the plight of American Indians can be seen in the documentary *The Winter Soldier*, and the film draws parallels between the atrocities in Vietnam that the soldiers in the film bear witness to and the Native American massacres one hundred years before.

The plight of the American Indian was brought to public attention partly by the civil rights campaigns of the late 1960s and early 1970s which revealed the American government's failure to fulfill treaties with Indian peoples. In 1973, Oglala activists seized and for three months occupied the town of Wounded Knee in South Dakota, the site of the 1890 massacre, fighting the FBI who cut off the electricity and tried to prevent food supplies from entering the town. The protracted siege reopened history for many, including Craven, who commented on the 1890 Wounded Knee massacre in a 1980 interview with Tony Williams, likening it to Lee Harvey Oswald, Manson, Vietnam and the Bay of Pigs as a historical example of America externalizing the violent part of its psyche as "other" in order to disown it; a place "we could have orgasms of violence and then deny what was happening."[18]

Americans in the 1960s and 1970s were becoming more aware of their history and of the role violence played in the forging of a nation. This led to the growing perception, among progressive thinkers like Craven, that their national identity was tainted with bloodshed. Certainly violence plays an ambiguous role in United States culture and history. From the War of Independence, through the great westward drive in pursuit of Manifest Destiny, and the civil and Indian wars, to the dubious honor of being the only power so far to use nuclear weapons in anger, violence has been closely intertwined with the USA as a state. In other forms it is woven into the fabric of American society, where various kinds of violence have at times been culturally institutionalized: the Southern racial lynching; the violence of industrial relations; violence against women; the use of guns by private citizens. Violence is threaded through American identities, constituting and threatening them all at once. It is not surprising, therefore, that in considering the intersection between cultural and personal identity in *Last House on the Left*, Craven was prompted to raise the question: Is violence an inherent part of us as individuals?

"All that blood and violence—I thought that you were supposed to be the love generation"

In 2003, Craven commented, "I haven't over a long career been able to totally differentiate where one's own inner self ends and one's reflection on the outer world begins."[19] It's a telling comment from Craven, whose own upbringing in a Baptist fundamentalist family caused him to see parallels between things that were not talked about at home and suppression of truth and the denial of history as a nation. Violence, for Craven, is easy to fall into—no one is immune from it. It is part of the soul, an inescapable part of us. In the 1980 interview with Williams, Craven commented that Mari in *Last House on the Left*, despite being part of the peace and love generation, is attracted to Bloodlust, the symbolically named rock band whose stage act in the film includes biting the heads off live chickens. Craven goes on to state that it was always ironic to him that the peace movement (of which he professes to have been a part) was "also very violent." "When I lived on the lower East Side of New York in the sixties," he claims, "the street culture was very violent, as was Haight-Ashbury."[20] Craven's thinking (despite his own experience "on the street") appears to have been influenced by the popular view, promoted by the media following Altamont and Manson, that the peace movement was ultimately foiled by violent impulses that are an "inherent" part of human nature. In his 2003 book *Violent London*, historian Clive Bloom's assessment of the 1960s protest movement illustrates how the same ideological view point persists today:

> The great tide of 1960s anti–Americanism, anti-imperialism, anti-sexism, anti-capitalism and anti-"oldism" was driven by a new youthful and hopeful utopianism yet left a backwash of the disaffected and the disdaining. In the commune and squatter community that had grown up on the fringes of protest society which finally became the heart of counterculture, a new and more aggressive "hippiedom" born of disillusion and marginality had crystallized amongst hard-line radicals.[21]

The legacy of 1960s–1970s counterculture, according to this point of view, can be seen in the rise of violent revolutionary groups that commentators like Bloom claim grew out of the ashes of the New Left: Yippies, the Black Panther movement, the Weather Underground, the Baader-Meinhof gang in West Germany. These violent factions, and Charles Manson (not to mention the Hells Angels, whose members were responsible for the fatal stabbing of Meredith Hunter at Altamont), have sullied the ideals of the 1960s (as embodied by the peace-loving hippie) within the collective memory. However, as early as December 1969, *Time* magazine published the piece "Hippies and Violence" by Dr. Lewis Yablonsky, which put forward the view that Haight-Ashbury (the hippie "Mecca") was a violent place, and that hippies themselves were inherently violent: "They have had so few love models," Yablonsky opined, "that even when they act as if they love, they can be totally devoid of true compassion. That is the reason why they can kill so matter-of-factly."[22] As Christopher Sharrett writes in reference to the nihilism of *Last House on the Left* and *The Texas Chain Saw Massacre*, "[T]he constraints of dominant culture allow for abject pessimism but not for suggestions of revolutionary programs of change."[23]

In *The Winter Soldier,* we see that American soldiers who, having witnessed and in many cases taken part in atrocities in Vietnam, have subsequently embraced hippie ideals of peace and love. Haight-Ashbury itself, however, after 1969, became as much associated in the public's mind with Manson (who lived there in the 1960s) and the Hells Angels (whose headquarters were on the same street—Ashbury—as countercultural heroes Janis Joplin and the Grateful Dead) as it was with the Summer of Love. Curt Rowlett comments on how the media-constructed image of the drug-crazed, murderous hippie became prevalent following the Manson murders. Other lesser-known horror stories about so-called "LSD murders" also began to take their toll on the image of the hippie movement. Writes Rowlett: "Tales of alleged LSD-fueled violence were sensationalized in virtually every newspaper and television screen in America, both directly and indirectly blaming psychedelic drugs and the hippie lifestyle for violence."[24] Soon Hollywood would join in with the release of several films exploiting the Manson case such as *The Other Side of Madness* (1970), featuring Manson's songs and filmed on actual locations where the Manson family had resided, and the documentary *Manson* (1973).

Rowlett suggests that much of the public's hysteria about the hippie movement had to do with the explosion of hippie youth communes, constituting a threat to bourgeois norms of social behavior. Consequently the media sought to foster the belief in the public that such communes were invariably dirty dens of rampant drug use and free love. Rowlett makes the point that the history shows a far more diverse picture than what the stereotype suggests. "Many communes were founded on a religious basis or with an emphasis on spirituality and very disciplined lifestyles," Rowlett writes. "Others were simply created in the search for a Utopian society."[25] The Back to the Land Movement that grew out of the Flower Children of Haight-Ashbury led to the setting-up of many communes, such as the Black Bear Ranch in Siskiyou County, California, revitalizing the organic farming and environmental movements that continue to flourish today. As for Haight-Ashbury being violent, as Craven suggests; according to residents there during the late 1960s, the media circus that descended on the "Haight" during the Summer of Love attracted heroin dealers, which caused violence to escalate, while the hippies moved out after 1967 to form communes in the countryside.[26]

In *Last House on the Left*, Krug (David A. Hess) and his "family" can be seen as a corruption of 1960s ideals. Like the Manson family they represent a dark counterculture in which rape, murder and sadism have replaced peace and love as the alternative to bourgeois social norms (and therefore represent no real alternative at all). Craven references the Manson murders throughout the film, in the brutal, frenzied stabbings of the girls, the mind control that cultish leader Krug exerts on his company (including his own son, whom he controls through heroin addiction), and in the inclusion among the killers of a woman named Sadie—a reference to one of Manson's crew. (Sadie is played by Jeramie Rain, who, prior to *Last House on the Left*, portrayed the Manson family's Susan "Sadie" Atkins on stage.)

The film changes every icon of potential social or sexual liberation that grew out of the political awareness of the 1960s into a symbol of oppression, in much the same way that the Manson murders debased the hippie image. Sadie, for example, demonstrates a nascent understanding of women's liberation and Freud, but for her, equal representation constitutes more women for the men to victimize and use as sex objects; whereas Freud's theories of sexual repression are perverted into the gang planning the "sex crime of the century." Early in the film, Mari is presented with a peace symbol necklace by her parents—the cultural emblem of the Flower Children. By the film's end, our hopes for love and peace die with Mari in the river, while the peace symbol necklace is transferred to Junior (Marc Sheffler), the burned-out junkie. "I'm sorry!" Junior cries out in his sleep after Mari is killed; like the drug dealers who moved into Haight-Ashbury, he has betrayed his generation and is doomed to self-destruction. In another bitter irony, the discovery of the peace symbol necklace hanging around Junior's neck becomes the catalyst for Mari's parents exacting revenge on the gang. Finally, Krug's blue collar right-wing antagonism towards the middle-class hippie girls reflects the reactionary spirit of construction workers beating up anti-war protesters ("Bloody Friday," May 1970), precluding the possibility of the working class joining forces with the hippies and the students in the fight for liberation, and instead choosing to remain complicit in their own oppression.

"You gotta change your head around—become someone else altogether"

Several characters in *Last House on the Left* talk of change: Sadie tells Junior that he has to try to get on better with his father; with Krug out of prison, she sees the opportunity for a new start for them all. Likewise, Mari remarks that, like the changing seasons, she is blossoming. Change is a subject close to Craven's heart. In interview he has spoken of changing oneself as being the key to changing society.[27] He does, however, acknowledge that such change happens at great cost and very rarely. Craven himself rejected his fundamentalist upbringing in order to find his own truth as a writer and filmmaker; his personal journey mirrors the cultural changes of his nation in the 1960s more closely than any other filmmaker in this book—and was equally as traumatic.

He grew up in a working class Baptist family in Cleveland (in a "milieu of hatred and prejudice"[28]), brought up by a repressive mother after his father died when Craven was a child. Following a Baptist education he became a humanities professor, married young, but found himself increasingly drawn to the peace movement and a bohemian lifestyle at the time of Vietnam. Disillusioned with academia, he left teaching in the late 1960s and moved into the lower echelons of film production. By the early 1970s he was divorced and penniless, having abandoned "everything everyone was pleased that I was doing."[29] Such a course of action—in effect he was "dropping out"—must have struck everyone around him at the time, and Craven himself perhaps, as dumb and irresponsible, self-destructive even. In his book *Shock Value*, Jason Zinoman vividly captures this difficult period in Craven's life:

> Craven moved out, sleeping on couches in the Lower East Side while the bills piled up. His credit cards and driver's license expired. He fell off the grid. Slowly, he even fell out of touch with his mother. "She didn't understand me. She never tried to," he says. "I think something about the way my mother looked at me, behind her eyes was the sense that her son was crazy. The word 'crazy' came up all the time."[30]

Craven cites Junior in *Last House on the Left* and Ruby (Janus Blythe) in *The Hills Have Eyes* as examples of characters in his films who, like him, tried to break from the hatred and prejudice of their upbringing.[31] But this note of optimism is, as Sharrett has commented, "ambiguous at best."[32] Junior succeeds in breaking away from the savagery of his family group but this costs him his life. What he should have done, as Craven has commented, is shoot his father instead of himself as he does at the end of *Last House on the Left*.[33] Ruby's rejection of her family in *The Hills Have Eyes* results in an uneasy complicity with the Carter family, who have become as barbaric as the cannibal family who attacked them. Craven shot an alternative finale for the film which showed Ruby joining the surviving Carter family but this "happy ending" rings false, coming as it does after the Carters' descent into savagery, and was rejected in favor of the harsher, nihilistic ending echoing that of *Last House on the Left*. More truthful to the pessimistic spirit of these films is Craven's observation that attempts to change are often doomed to failure, as in the case of the Stillos, who set out to escape but keep getting sucked back into their old violent patterns of behavior.[34] Perhaps the sense of positive change never being fulfilled in *Last House on the Left* and *The Hills Have Eyes* stemmed from Craven's own feelings of guilt after he rejected his family; or from apocalyptic sentiment that stems from the remnants of his fundamentalist background; or simply from the feeling, shared by many in the early 1970s, that peace and love had failed.

Sharrett makes the point that the self-destruction of Craven's characters can be viewed as part of the psyche's attempt to provoke guilt and punishment when disturbing truths are revealed or when the alleviation of repression is attempted.[35] The psyche is so conditioned into accepting repression as the norm that when liberation or revelation occurs, it is often accompanied by feelings of guilt and a withdrawal back into the repressed state. Certainly the nihilism of *Last House on the Left* and *The Hills Have Eyes* is something Craven was unable to move beyond in subsequent films. Instead his oeuvre suggests violence is a never-ending circle: The victim inevitably becomes the aggressor, so violence becomes an inescapable fact of life; a violation of the self that is, nevertheless, unavoidable.

"What's new in the outside world?" "Same old stuff. Murder and mayhem"

In *Last House on the Left*, Mari's parents, the Collingwoods, have set up home in the Connecticut countryside to escape the spreading urban violence of the late 1960s. However, as the film makes clear, there is no escaping the encroaching violence because it is already in *us*. The ludicrous crimes for which Krug and Weasel (Fred Lincoln) have been imprisoned are indicative of a cycle of violence: Krug murdered a priest and two nuns; Weasel is a child molester and peeping Tom. It seems likely that both men have been brutalized or abused in their early lives and are merely continuing this cycle, as soldiers in Vietnam and later as violent criminals. Although they have served their country in the war, they are disenfranchised by the state and patriarchy. They are in many ways "the cream of American manhood" as Krug ironically claims. Weasel's fear of emasculation (he has a nightmare in which his teeth are extracted with a hammer and chisel) and his attraction to Mari's mother, Estelle (Cynthia Carr), speak of an Oedipal conflict. The emasculation becomes literal when Estelle later bites off his penis.

Last House on the Left presents its violence as acts of degradation and extreme bodily violation, with the rape and murder of Mari as its culmination; presented as a violation of the self, of the human spirit. Closely aligned to this theme of violation is the idea of boundaries (geographical and interpersonal) that are invaded or violated. Thus the film starts with Mari's body as the most intimate, most proximate boundary, and opens out to ever wider geographical boundaries, only later to close back inwards from the wider world to the home again. In the opening scene we glimpse Mari taking a shower; viewing her through the frosted glass of the shower screen, we are kept at a respectful distance—Craven making us aware of the sanctity of the body.

From there the film opens out geographically and interpersonally to introduce the house, home and family, where Mari's parents discuss the problem of the telephone not working, our first indication of social breakdown taking place in the wider world. "What's new in the outside world?" Estelle asks her husband John (Gaylord St. James), who reads the newspaper. "Same old stuff," he replies. "Murder and mayhem." Then the film takes us outside the house and family, to the nearby woods and the river where Mari meets her friend Phyllis (Lucy Grantham); the woods will become the scene of Mari and Phyllis's rape and murder. From there we follow the girls further into the outside world, to the city and wider society, where they encounter Krug and his gang. There is a further geographical boundary, unseen but strongly felt—Vietnam—from which Krug and Weasel have returned as killers. Traditionally, land boundaries are marked by water, hence the significance of the river which Craven emphasizes throughout the film that separates the house and the woods from the

Phyllis Stone (Lucy Grantham, right) and Mari Collingwood (Sandra Cassel) share a bottle of wine by a waterfall in *Last House on the Left* (1972).

city. (Mari renames Junior "Willow"; a willow is a tree found in desolate places by water.) The film doubles back on itself as Krug and his gang kidnap the girls, transport them back to the woods and then, after murdering them, stumble unknowingly into the house of Mari's parents while seeking shelter, where they are themselves killed. The film's violence thus stems from the home and from Vietnam simultaneously, like concentric circles that have their centers at the same point. The film makes the connection between the micro (violation of body and self) and the macro (the violence of Vietnam), and posits these as really one and the same.

"Piss your pants": Shock and Taboo in *Last House on the Left*

The controversy caused by the violence in *Last House on the Left* has been huge, resulting in the film being banned in a number of countries, including Britain, where it was only granted release on DVD in an uncut version in 2007. There are many possible reasons why it has been so problematic for the censor: It is a film that belongs to the exploitation genre which is traditionally seen as disreputable; the violence is graphic and explicit; but more significantly, Craven uses cinematic shock to challenge and subvert the ideological values typically espoused by the codes and conventions of Hollywood product:

> We consciously took all the B movie conventions and stood them on their heads... so that just when you thought the shot would cut away, it didn't. Someone gets stabbed, but then they get back up and start crawling.... [D]eath becomes more protracted and sexual. That was all breaking of convention.[36]

The sense of shock that the film creates in the viewer stems largely from the breaking of convention that Craven describes. In his depiction of violence, he instead emphasizes the sense of violation that acts of violence constitute to body and self.

From the film's first graphic sequence, in which Phyllis is forced to urinate on herself while Krug and the gang watch, Craven emphasizes a very clear mood change from the playfulness that marks earlier scenes. The camera is hand-held, evoking the documentary realism that Craven wanted to appropriate from news footage of the Vietnam War. There is no traditional "mood" music score: The feel of the scene is cold and degrading. At this point *Last House* begins to take us inside the ugly truth of the act of humiliation. Phyllis's disbelieving reaction to the gang's obvious pleasure as she is made to soil herself evokes in the viewer unpleasant memories of childhood, of wetting oneself in public and feeling ashamed. The tight closeup of Krug as he issues the order to Phyllis emphasizes his power as the group's patriarch. Phyllis stands before him like a disgraced child. When Junior intervenes, we think the humiliation is over, but his suggestion to "make them make it with each other" draws Mari into the action, worsening the growing sense of violation that the film evokes within us from this moment on.

The ironic counterpointing of David Hess's plaintive love song "Now You're All Alone" (aka "Junior's Theme") which Craven introduces into the film as Phyllis and Mari are forced to strip, emphasizes the sense of isolation that humiliation creates in the individual. The overall effect becomes one of a monstrous travesty of the tenderness between human beings. Craven hired Hess not just to act in *Last House* but also to compose the music. In interviews and commentaries about the film, Hess emerges as the collaborator who comes closest, with Craven, to understanding the film's moral complexities. This is evident not just in his extraordinary portrayal of Krug ("a character just like anybody else ... who just happens to kill people sometimes"[37]), but also in his approach to creating the soundtrack.

The soundtrack to *Last House on the Left* is in itself lyrical, memorable and beautifully composed, but it is in conjunction with the film that the full power and meaning of the music comes across. The same can be said about the film: The soundtrack and film are symbiotic. What Hess detected in the screenplay was its sense of moral contradiction, its absurd violence. He is, for example, one of the few who understands the film's ironic counterpoint of violence and buffoonish comedy ("absurd violence—absurd comedy"[38]) and his music counterpoints the on-screen action in the same way, at first confusing the viewer's responses but ultimately leading to a deeper engagement with the moral complexities of the film.

One of the most powerful *Last House* scenes is Krug's moment of self-revelation after raping Mari by the riverbank. It is both profoundly disturbing and strangely moving because, while Krug has committed the vilest of acts (the violation and humiliation of another human being), we cannot entirely distance ourselves from him. His reaction to what he has done—at his own depravity—elicits sympathy, however fleeting, because we suddenly see his vulnerability and it forces us to recognize the aggressor in ourselves. It is a strikingly edited scene made up of gazes averted, fingers picking dirt from hands, clothes being straightened—but the moment is given its full disturbing power by Hess's ballad which counterpoints the scene. The song—deeply ironic—is tender, and speaks of loneliness and the search for comfort in a loveless environment. But its counterpointing with the scene brings out the full horror and sorrow of what has just taken place (the feeling of alienation, powerlessness and isolation that violence creates in both the victim and the aggressor, and also in the observer).

The film's violence is, as Craven has noted, sexualized. Craven has spoken of violence within society as an eruption of repression in a sexualized form.[39] In *Last House*, the stabbing

Death of the hippie: Phyllis (Lucy Grantham) is stabbed by Weasel Padowsky (Fred Lincoln) in *Last House on the Left* (1972).

of Phyllis is highly sexualized, partly because of its phallic nature but also in the orgiastic way it is conducted by Krug, Weasel and Sadie. Phyllis's trousers are pulled down and blood trickles down her naked thighs. Finally she is disemboweled. Craven was influenced by the Sharon Tate murders in his depiction of the frenzied, protracted stabbings, but similar sadistic acts were reported in Vietnam. Disemboweling the enemy seems to have been a ritual perpetrated on the enemy. Likewise, Krug's carving his name on Mari's chest with his knife is also perhaps a reference to the atrocities of Vietnam, where soldiers carved their names on the bodies of "gooks."

Last House's sexualized violence is an eruption of repression in the form of sadism. The act of torture is thus something that Craven believes human beings take pleasure from, and this truth should not be denied, according to Craven, because the repression of it leads to greater atrocities.[40] Craven seems to have "discovered" much of the film's effect on the viewer—the complex process of identification with *both* victim and aggressor that the film invites—during post-production:

> Especially in the editing room I began to become aware of how strong it was for me just to work with it. I felt "I don't like what's happening to these people, but at the same time, I do like it." I had to be not only the victim but the murderer, to be the person who could get into somebody being tortured enough to make it sound like she was really suffering. At the same time part of me felt "I've been tortured like that. I've felt like that, totally isolated from everybody else. I've seen people take pleasure in my own personal discomfort." All sides of me were coming in at the same time but there were sides of me that I never knew existed, did not recognize or ever want to see revealed. I think that was the key to it.[41]

The complexity of interpersonal violence as Craven describes it is further amplified in the film by the rapists seeing themselves—albeit momentarily—in their victims (as Krug does in his moment of self-disgust after raping Mari) and then themselves becoming victims at the hands of the parents. Although the rape and murder of Mari is presented as the most morally repressible violation of personal boundaries in the film, the Collingwoods' revenge on the gang is shown to be a continuance of bodily violation, albeit in ever less plausible, ever more extreme and sensationalist forms. Hence, Weasel's castration, the slitting of Sadie's throat, and the decapitation of Krug by chainsaw take on a sense of the absurd that ultimately shifts *Last House*'s viewpoint into the nihilistic. This sense of absurdity has, in fact, been increasingly developed throughout the film in the counterpointing of the absurd antics of the buffoonish policemen with the horror of the rape and torture sequences and the parodic treatment of the domestic scenes featuring Mari's parents. Indeed, the cutting-away from horror to "comic relief," only then to pull the audience back into horror when they thought they had escaped the worst, combined with the film's ludicrous representation of the police, serves to create an experience for the viewer that Jonathan L. Crane describes as not only intolerably suspenseful but "maddening."[42]

Last House on the Left, on final analysis, is what Gad Horowitz describes as "duplicitous"[43]: In terms of its presentation of violence, the film is simultaneously progressive and reactionary. On the one hand, violence is shown truthfully as a violation of the self that solves nothing; on the other, it is portrayed as inherent to the human condition and thus inescapable. Christopher Sharrett has criticized the apocalyptic horror film for the way in which it "momentarily inoculates the spectator with criticisms of a failing dominant order, but then reneges on this criticism by denying that there is any worth in carrying through this critical process through to a conclusion."[44] Instead there is only despair. The apocalypticism of *Last House on the Left*, which is confirmed by *The Hills Have Eyes*, precludes the possibility of progressive change, as Sharrett suggests, and ultimately serves to strengthen pre-existing attitudes and beliefs. Unfortunately, this critical assessment of Craven's work seems to be confirmed by his co-option into Hollywood, with the 2009, Craven-produced remake of *Last House on the Left* standing as a negation of any progressive aspects the original work might have had. Indeed the remake recasts the original within a torture porn context. Craven's original intentions are reversed: We are encouraged to enjoy the *Death Wish*–like rape and revenge scenario without moral compunction. Krug, in the remake, is resolutely "other." The remake seems to be saying that violent retribution is not only justifiable but *necessary* when there are such bad people in the world.

"My family's always been in meat": *The Texas Chain Saw Massacre*

The title of Tobe Hooper's 1974 film is an example of exploitation marketing at its sensational best. One doubts if *Head Cheese* or *Leatherface* (the film's early working titles) would have sold the movie to a horror-counterculture audience quite as successfully. Horror film history has shown repeatedly how a title can capture the attention of an audience by evoking the zeitgeist. The title *Last House on the Left*, for example, is not only less generic than Craven's original title *Night of Vengeance*, but also conjures, politically, the final death throes of the New Left in the early 1970s. *The Texas Chain Saw Massacre*, in a similar manner, evokes atrocities associated with contemporary events in Vietnam and the Manson murders, as well as historical Indian War massacres and the Battle of the Alamo. Moreover, the inclusion of *Chain Saw* in the title (and in the film itself) indicates a certain generic cross-over between *Texas Chain Saw Massacre* and *Last House on the Left*.

Although Hooper claims not to have seen Craven's film, *The Texas Chain Saw Massacre* builds on *Last House*'s themes. If the encroaching violence taking over our society is inescapable because it is inherent in the American psyche, as Craven suggests, Hooper and co-writer Kim Henkel go on to trace the roots of this to the pioneer myths of the Old West. The western, as mentioned before, entered its revisionist phase in the late 1960s, coinciding with the emergence of the apocalyptic horror film, but the civilization-savagery dichotomy that lies at the heart of the revisionist western, and which informs the apocalyptic horror film, particularly *Last House on the Left*, *The Texas Chain Saw Massacre* and *The Hills Have Eyes*, was being explored earlier in the films of Anthony Mann and John Ford (with Ford's *The Searchers* [1956] a primary work in this respect). *Texas Chain Saw* takes up the civilization-savagery motif of *Last House on the Left* and the revisionist western, and recasts it as a form of psychosis afflicting its characters. In Hooper's film, modern capitalist society has become degenerate, and the apocalypse can be traced back to the pioneers themselves. The frontier spirit—the drive that propelled American civilization forward—has led to moral schizophrenia in the Watergate era.

Watergate, No Gas

Legend has it that Hooper came up with the idea for *Texas Chain Saw* while doing his Christmas shopping in Montgomery Ward in December 1972.[45] Finding himself stuck in the hardware department, unable to move because of the crowds, his eye caught a chain saw hanging on the wall of the store and a method of cutting his way through the throngs of shoppers came to him. The truth is probably more complex than that. *Texas Chain Saw* seems to have been born of a variety of cultural forces harnessed by Hooper and his co-writer Kim Henkel.

Many accounts of the making of *Texas Chain Saw* cite the true case of Wisconsin farmer Ed Gein as its main inspiration. In the 1950s, Gein murdered women and used their skins to fashion lampshades and items of clothing for himself. Another part of the legend has it that Hooper had been fascinated by the Gein case as a small child, when Wisconsin relatives would regale him with tales of Gein's macabre deeds. However, this seems to have been played up by Hooper himself, who, born as he was in 1943, would have been fourteen years old at the time of the Gein trial.

More of a direct influence on Hooper and Henkel during filming was the discovery of another serial killer, Dean Corll, in Houston, Texas, who, with his associate Elmer Wayne Henley had, during the early 1970s, kidnapped and murdered a number of teenage boys. What struck Henkel in particular about Corll and Henley's behavior, when he saw them on TV, was that they seemed to display a set of values completely at odds with their earlier psychotic behavior. Henkel thought of this disparity as "moral schizophrenia" and saw it as a national malaise sweeping the country and even affecting then president Richard Nixon.[46] This was the time when the Vietnam War was at its height in late 1972. Upon election Nixon had stated his intention to end the war but had instead escalated it by bombing Cambodia, an action that many found inexplicable. Moral schizophrenia in *Texas Chain Saw* is characterized most memorably in the role taken by Jim Siedow as the older brother who claims that he "can't take no pleasure in killing" while, in fact, seems to be taking a lot of pleasure in watching Sally (Marilyn Burns) suffering at the hands of Leatherface (Gunnar Hansen) and the Hitchhiker (Ed Neal). Interestingly, Siedow's wolfish features resemble those of Richard Nixon.

Another theme in the film that many critics have picked up on is that of intergenerational conflict—generation gap horror—the idea of the old traditional but degenerate family preying on the progressive youth. Hooper preceded *Texas Chain Saw* with *Eggshells* (1969), a psychedelic "head" movie that encapsulates the end of the peace and love decade. Set mainly in a Southern gothic Texan house, very much like the one inhabited by Leatherface and his clan, *Eggshells* follows the lives of a commune of hippies (including Allen Danziger, who plays Jerry in *Texas Chain Saw*) as they become aware of a strange alien force that inhabits the basement. If the characterization of the youths in *Texas Chain Saw* seems rather sketchy, it may be because Hooper had already created a detailed portrait of hippie youth in *Eggshells*. Intriguingly, *Eggshells* opens with a shot of a girl riding in the back of a pick-up truck, foreshadowing *Texas Chain Saw*'s famous ending of Sally escaping in the back of a pick-up truck, and further evoking the sense of a narrative structure in *Texas Chain Saw* that folds back in on itself.

It was partly the poor financial performance of *Eggshells* that prompted Hooper and Henkel (who had also acted in Hooper's debut) to write a horror film. Hooper, a self-confessed horror freak, had grown up reading EC Comics and watching the Universal horror movies of the 1930s and 1940s. He and Henkel set themselves the task of combining the most disturbing images of all the best horror films that they had seen, including *Frankenstein*

Tobe Hooper directs the cast and crew of *The Texas Chain Saw Massacre* (1974). From left to right, Hooper, Marilyn Burns, director of photography Daniel Pearl and Jim Siedow.

and *Night of the Living Dead*. Indeed, the trailer to *Texas Chain Saw* is almost a textbook example of horror iconography. It abounds with symbols of death, masked killers, screaming victims, terrible houses and phallic weapons. Henkel has since referred to the way he and Hooper pieced the story together as "nightmare syntax."[47] Hooper drew on his own phobias: his fear of family get-togethers, developed during an unhappy childhood caught between fighting parents. In *Texas Chain Saw*, perhaps the most traumatic scene involves a family meal; Sally, an unwilling guest, is forced to witness the madness between the cannibal brothers. It is perhaps how Hooper felt as he shared the dinner table with parents who hated each other.

As well as personal trauma, Hooper and Henkel consciously fused national trauma into the script. One of the film's key plot points is that the youths are stranded in the countryside because the gas station that they pull into has itself run out of fuel. This was at the height of the OPEC oil crisis in 1973, when the Arab nations placed an embargo on oil which created fuel shortages across the States. As Hooper recalled, it seemed for a while as though the whole of the Western world might collapse due to a lack of fuel, an apocalypse in the making.[48] The film is infused with this sense of impending social collapse as though civilization itself has run its course and is imploding on itself.

Texas Chain Saw has been variously interpreted by academics as an inverted fairy tale, an example of apocalyptic art, an allegory of Vietnam and a metaphor for rampant consumerism and economic meltdown in late-capitalist society.[49] That the film yields to such a variety of interpretations (which are by no means contradictory readings) speaks to the density of its text. Critics have, in fact, been merely peeling away the multiple layers of meaning lent to the film by Hooper and Henkel during a lengthy screenwriting process. Henkel's first approach to the story was a modern-day version of Hansel and Gretel, "only instead of being lured to a gingerbread cottage with gumdrops, it was a little more sinister."[50] Jason Zinoman says this was an inspired choice for a horror film: "[A]fter all, the Brothers Grimm fairy tale begins with abandonment and moves on to kidnapping, imprisonment, suggestions of cannibalism."[51] Hooper, who had been impressed by *Night of the Living Dead*, and perhaps thinking of the house in *Eggshells*, suggested setting the main action in a remote house, evoking also the apocalypse of *The Birds*. Hooper had become fascinated by sunspots and solar flares, how they might reflect behaviors. In August 1972, U.S. cable lines were knocked out by a huge solar flare, one of the largest ever recorded. This was followed by six days of high levels of solar activity. The *Texas Chain Saw* script opens on a huge shot of the sun, "a liquid rope of molten gases arcs into space and then slowly, heavily falls back into the sun."[52] Hooper saw this cosmic activity as influencing the events in the story, "the structural puzzle pieces, the way it folds continuously back in on itself, and no matter where you're going it's the wrong place."[53] The apocalyptic dimensions of the film were therefore already in Hooper's mind during the scriptwriting.

Henkel, was, however, reluctant to play up the supernatural aspects of the story, believing that "the underlying social motivations get stripped out, if it moves in that direction."[54] Instead he and Hooper started to draw on their own experiences of Texas, asking themselves: What would turn someone into a killer? According to Zinoman:

> They came up with the idea of a family or redneck Luddites who saw their way of life under threat. Like many people they knew, these uneducated locals had been laid off, made expendable by changes in industry. Their quiet Southern town was falling apart, and they blamed it on the modern world and took it out on the poor teenagers visiting from out of town. To be sure, Henkel was talking about crazy people, but not so crazy that they weren't recognisable.[55]

It is at this point that Hooper most likely had his chain saw "epiphany": the final piece in the metaphorical puzzle that locked together the allegory of present-day social-political-economic apocalypse having cosmic and historical dimensions. The Texas setting evokes the history of the pioneers—the Alamo, Davy Crockett, cattle drives, frontier justice, the Indian wars—but *Texas Chain Saw* inverts this iconography, in the same way it inverts the fairy tale. Leatherface's mask is thus made of human skin instead of buckskin, "rekindling," as Sharrett puts it, "the savage origins of history,"[56] and "debunking the myth of utopia beneath the civilizing process."[57] In *Texas Chain Saw* the civilizing spirit has run its course and become degenerate; moreover, as Sharrett points out, the American civilizing process itself "is revealed to have had from the beginning the seed of barbarism."[58]

"A bad day for everyone"

In 2002, Hooper reflected on the synthesis of themes in *Texas Chain Saw*:

> *The Texas Chain Saw Massacre* was a play about morality, in a strange way, and family values. It was all bubbling up at once out of the times and out of Watergate. Once again, I underline, that we found out as naïve students that they don't always tell you the truth. So it's a film about a bad day for everyone, Leatherface, everyone.[59]

The bad day in question is August 18, 1973, as the opening crawl tells us. This documentary aspect to the film has led some to believe that *Texas Chain Saw* is a fictionalized account of real events (*Last House on the Left* opens with a similar claim that the film is based on a true story). This myth was perpetuated by the marketing publicity of the film ("It Happened!"). As Gunnar Hansen has joked, Hooper, the cast and crew were actually filming that day.[60] It may in fact have been the day the notorious dinner scene was shot. But as Sharrett notes, Hooper presents the notion of an "apocalypse in microcosm that is gradually revealed to have universal significance."[61] That date *is* significant in some respects: Ten days earlier, on August, 8, 1973, Elmer Wayne Henley led police to the bodies of several murder victims, leading to the discovery of the Houston Mass Murders that Henkel has cited as an influence on the film. During filming, the Watergate scandal was breaking and cast and crew watched live TV coverage of the hearings in between takes. The film thus invites us to make connections between these things: moral schizophrenia on a local and national level finally imploding during a "bad day for everyone."

In the script, the youths have been to Colorado and New Mexico, and are returning to their home in Houston, when they decide to check on the grave of Sally's grandfather after learning that "somebody broke into some graves ... they stole some bodies." As well as doing a little skiing on their holiday, they have been "looking for land too," presumably to set up as a commune. As in *Eggshells*, the hippie family consists of two couples and a social misfit. *Eggshells* was Hooper's attempt to make "a real movie about 1969, kind of vérité but with a little push, improvisation mixed with magic. It was about the beginning and end of the subculture."[62] The film begins, like *Texas Chain Saw* ends, with a girl called Mahlon (Mahlon Forman) traveling in the back of a pick-up truck. Mahlon arrives in Austin and goes to stay in a commune house where she forms a relationship with the equally free-spirited Toz (Kim Henkel). Set against the backdrop of the peace movement, *Eggshells* intersperses this growing relationship with documentary footage shot at the University of Texas by Hooper of a mass student demonstration against Vietnam. Hooper's idea was to "show the end of the Vietnam war, with the troops coming home, but tell it through the eyes of the commune."[63] Although Hooper considered himself a "non-political hippie,"[64] this sequence highlights the oppressive presence of armed police with emphatic closeups of police weaponry and riot gear.

Like the youths in *Texas Chain Saw*, the hippies in *Eggshells* form an alternative family in order to escape from the brutal patriarchal system, but find themselves constrained by the gothic commune house in which also resides a strange entity, a "crypto-embryonic hyper-electric presence"[65] that influences the house and the people in it, but whose existence is only apparent to the misfit boy. Much of the film is improvised—there are long, rambling dialogue sequences in which the characters discuss politics and communism. Hooper attempts to dramatize the overturning of hippie idealism in 1969—symbolized by the changing season as the Summer of Love turns to Autumn—in a striking opening sequence during which a paper plane explodes, symbolizing the loss of freedom. Hooper was highly influenced by Fellini and Antonioni at this point and *Eggshells* seems to look towards Antonioni's *Zabriskie Point* (1970) as an ode to the death of counterculture in both detail and tone. The two couples in *Eggshells* eventually part ways: Amy and David move towards convention, marriage and a family inheritance, while Toz and Mahlon join the psychedelic machine and a darker counterculture. Both couples seem to operate under the possibly malign influence of the presence in the basement of the house.

In *Texas Chain Saw*, the dark counterculture figure is Franklyn (Paul Partain). While ostensibly one of the hippies, he is the only one who understands the degeneracy of the cannibal family, and fears it, recognizing his kinship with the Hitchhiker, seeing his own sadistic streak and barbaric drive mirrored in the "other." When the youths visit the Franklyn house, it dawns on the viewer, on repeated viewings, how close geographically their ancestral home is to the cannibal house. Sally and Franklyn spent their childhood in this ancestral home, so we wonder if Franklyn crossed paths with the Hitchhiker and Leatherface as a child. Sally and Franklyn's parents now live in Houston, leading typical middle-class lives ("Mother's probably half-drunk on martinis and Father's probably playing golf," Sally comments rather cynically in the script), but at some time in the past, the Franklyns and the Sawyers (as the cannibal family became known in the sequels) have co-existed within close proximity, in worlds that might have appeared parallel but were in fact overlapping. That the film presents two "haunted houses" (and confounds our expectations as to which is the malign one) further blurs the distinction between the "normal" Franklyns and the "degenerate" Sawyers.

Texas Chain Saw's structure, in particular its use of symmetry, suggests that this hidden face of America—as embodied by the Sawyers—that had hitherto been kept secret, in the dark, slowly degenerating, is gradually revealing itself. The associations with Gein is clear: Here was a real man whose drives became necrophilic, whose Oedipal trajectory had failed, resulting in a morbid transvestism that extended beyond dressing in his mother's clothes to dressing in the skin of female corpses. Leatherface shares those same impulses, as does Norman Bates in Robert Bloch's novel *Psycho* (which was also based on the Gein case). They are all victims of the Western socialization process gone wrong. It is, however, the same socialization process from which most of us emerge relatively unscathed. Therefore, in *Psycho*, as in *Texas Chain Saw*, there is continuity between normal and abnormal, between the normal neurosis of Marion Crane, which manifests itself in guilt and compulsive-obsessive behavior, and the abnormal psychosis of Norman Bates, which drives him to murder.

Of course, the Sawyers, like Norman Bates, represent the dark side of the American way: They are a grotesque parody of the traditional capitalist family. In the face of economic collapse, they have set up shop slaughtering human beings, instead of animals, and selling the meat as barbecue in the local gas station. Hooper has described *Texas Chain Saw* as being "a film about meat, about people who are gone beyond dealing with animal meat ... crazy, retarded people going beyond the line between animal and human."[66] Indeed, the film's shock sequences revolve around the breaking of taboo involving the slaughter of animals for mass consumption. Cinema has explored this taboo before and since *Texas Chain Saw*: One thinks of the slaughterhouse sequences in George Franju's *Les Sang des Betes* (1949) which contrasts the dispassionate butchery of animals with the seemingly oblivious bourgeois normalcy of the surrounding Parisian suburbs where reside consumers of the meat; also, the shocking butchery of a horse at the start of Gaspar Noe's short film *Carné* (1991), made all the more "real" for having been filmed in color.

It may be that the key to the power of the slaughter sequences in *Texas Chain Saw* is that we are painfully reminded of the very processes of the food industry that most of us choose not to think about, to ignore. When Kirk (William Vail) is smashed on the head by a sledgehammer and dismembered by chain saw; when Pam (Terri McMinn) is hung on a meat hook to "drain"; or Sally made to suffer the killing blow of a lump hammer, her head hanging over a tin bath to catch the spilled blood, we can't help but substitute in our minds the relatively inexplicit on-screen human "carnage" of *Texas Chain Saw* for the blood-spurting, still-twitching reality of the meat industry, of slaughtering live animals for their meat. The taboo of death as a physical reality is broken in *Texas Chain Saw* not because of what it shows but because of what it implies. And in the same way that *Le Sang des bêtes* implicitly links the mass slaughter of animals—so unflinchingly and graphically presented in the film—to the demands of bourgeois consumption, making it appear depraved in the process, *Texas Chain Saw* presents its cannibalistic butchery as merely symptomatic of the excesses of capitalism. As Naomi Merritt says of Hooper's film: "The family who kill to 'make a living,' the home which doubles as the slaughterhouse, the blurring of the boundaries between animals and humans, the consumers who become the consumed, and the cannibals who are cannibalized, represent America 'devouring' itself."[67]

"Franklyn, you're crazier than he was"

Symmetry in *The Texas Chain Saw Massacre* is emphasized in the original script by the opening and closing sequences. The first shot of the sun, with its molten mass, slowly dissolves into a glazed eye, which is revealed to be the eye of a dead dog (changed to an armadillo in the final film) whose putrid carcass lies at the side of the highway; in the background, the hippies' van becomes distinct. The final scene mirrors the opening one: After Sally has escaped in the pick-up, receding into the background of the last shot, the camera re-focuses on the dead Hitchhiker, who, like the dead dog in the opening scene, lies in the foreground with his lower jaw

Paul Partain as the deranged Franklyn displays injuries sustained during filming in this publicity still from *The Texas Chain Saw Massacre* (1974).

nearly ripped from his head after the collision with the truck. Meanwhile, "The full red morning sun rests just above the rim of the earth."

At the heart of *Texas Chain Saw*, central to its symmetry, is the mirroring of Franklyn and Leatherface. Franklyn, as the pioneer-stock figure, carries the seed of degeneracy, but Leatherface represents the potential triumph of savagery over the civilizing forces, the same degenerate pioneer spirit in its full malevolent, barbaric glory. It is no accident that Paul Partain (who plays Franklyn) and Gunnar Hansen (who plays Leatherface) physically resemble each other. Like Franklyn, Leatherface is the invalid of the family. Hansen played Leatherface as retarded, drawing on his own experience of working in mental institutions to create the character. Franklyn is crippled, wheelchair-bound—Hooper and Henkel deliberately played against expectation by making him an obnoxious and unattractive whiner. (Partain, for his part, exaggerates the grotesque aspects of his character.) Accordingly, only Leatherface and Franklyn are given scenes of empathy where we share a moment with the character alone. In Franklyn's case this occurs at his own decaying ancestral home, emphasizing his isolation from the family group. Hansen remarked of his own scene of empathy as Leatherface:

> You can see the family as the protagonist and the kids as the antagonist. It's the kids who are invading the family. Because up to this point nobody had done anything against the kids except when the kids have come into the house. The first three people who Leatherface kills all trespass in the house. So his reaction is "Where are these people coming from? Why are these people invading us?" They're just trying to live their lives in the woods.[68]

Henkel confirms that this sense of ambivalence towards the "good" characters was intentional:

> *Chain Saw* is not unlike most urban myths—what they all involve is a certain kind of transgression and then there's a response to that transgression, and these characters who are purportedly the good ones, they transgress: they trespass and then they endure the consequences.[69]

In keeping with its symmetrical structure, *Texas Chain Saw* gradually shifts perspective from the new age family to the degenerate cannibal one, with Franklyn as the point of intersection between the two. Significantly, he is the only character actually killed by the chain saw, slaughtered, in effect, by his "twin." (Again, it is worth noting that the film emphasizes a sense of continuity between the supposedly normal family and the abnormal one—cannibalism as the logical extension of capitalism.) Franklyn, by being so similar to Leatherface, eases this transition. Franklyn's death marks a pivot in the story, the point at which, in Sharrett's words, "the civilizing spirit has run its course, its energies depleted, its myths not only dead but inverted and forced to show the consequences of their motivating force."[70] Barbarism, in the form of the cannibal family, takes over. Sally represents the final civilizing force left, fighting for survival.

"Now you just hush. It won't hurt none. Ol' Grandpa's the best killer there ever was"

Sally, as played by Marilyn Burns, is coded in *Texas Chain Saw* as the remaining civilizing force (certainly she is a civilizing influence on Franklyn, curbing his excesses throughout). Interestingly, she would go on to play Linda Kasabian in the 1976 adaptation of *Helter Skelter*, Vincent Bugliosi's book on Charles Manson. Kasabian had been present at the Sharon

Tate killings and had tried to stop the murders from taking place. She fled the Manson family shortly afterwards. Many critics have commented on the sadism inflicted on Sally by the cannibals (and, by inference, the film itself). The British Board of Film Classification refused a certificate to *Texas Chain Saw* for twenty-four years. They finally passed the film without cuts in 1998, but with misgivings:

> Possibly the most notorious feature is the relentless pursuit of the "Final Girl" throughout the last half hour or so of the film. The heroine in peril is a staple of the cinema since the earliest days. It is nonetheless legitimate to question the unusual emphasis *The Texas Chain Saw Massacre* places on the pursuit of a defenseless and screaming female over such an extended period.[71]

Carol J. Clover also comments that for nearly a third of the film "we watch [Sally] shriek, run, flinch, jump through windows, sustain injury and mutilation," but goes on to observe, "Her will to survive is astonishing: in the end, bloody and staggering, she finds the highway."[72] Sally's representation as the civilizing force, the anima, perhaps provides the key both to her astonishing will to survive and the unusual emphasis that the film places on her torment, although the film in the final analysis remains somewhat ambivalent about Sally's survival.

Westerns, of course, traditionally code their women characters as the civilizing force (even *Soldier Blue* does this) within the savagery-civilization dichotomy. In contrast, the apocalyptic western *The Wild Bunch* (1969), with its all-male cast, makes woman a Lacanian "structuring absence" within the film. Without the civilizing force of woman, the savage-in-man gradually takes over and this leads to bloodlust and ultimately self-destruction. *Texas Chain Saw* follows this same pattern with the all-male cannibals; however, they suffer from a weak link in the Old Man (Jim Siedow) who, like Franklyn, exhibits moral schizophrenia. He is half-savage, half civilized, but seemingly unable to control his conflicting impulses. As Henkel writes in the script, "He seems to enjoy torturing Sally but at the same time to be afraid that the torture will produce some terrible reaction with which he will be unable to cope." Again, the Nixon of Watergate and Vietnam springs to mind. The president's 1972 statement, through Henry Kissinger, "Peace is at hand," was shortly followed by the seemingly contradictory action of bombing North Vietnam on Christmas Day that year. Nixon's motivation for such a bizarre course of action has since become clear: His stated desire for peace was less an act of public conscience than one of personal ambition— Nixon wanted to be written into the history books as the great "peacemaker," and so leave his footprints in the sands of time. The Vietnam War had become an obstacle to détente with China and Russia. However, Nixon believed that winning the war was necessary so as to negotiate peace terms from a position of strength. At the time, however, his actions seemed inex-

Sally Hardesty (Marilyn Burns): the one survivor of *The Texas Chain Saw Massacre* (1974).

plicable. Likewise, in *Texas Chain Saw*, the Old Man's attempts at asserting authority and preserving order are undermined by his schizophrenia. His attempts at keeping order repeatedly dissolve because he can't keep himself in order; he cannot keep the malevolent forces within himself under control.

During the dinner scene, Sally witnesses the final breakdown, as civilized forces fully give way to barbaric ones. This final breakdown of sanity is logically presented as fundamentally absurd, as personified by Grandpa. Although mythologized by the Old Man as "the best killer that ever was," Grandpa is a mummification of the pioneer past, revived from its origins, but in shambolic form. Nevertheless, Grandpa conjures a history in which the slaughter of "beeves" might constitute the mass killing of the nation's youth in Vietnam; of the Indian massacres; of the whole bloody history of Texas-Mexican conflict. Sally becomes a symbol, then, of America's traumatized and bloody youth, but her survival instincts will not be quashed: "her struggles," as written in the script, "become superhuman" and she manages, against the odds, to escape.

But despite her powerful anima, one is left unsure whether by the end of the film Sally, in her fight to survive, has herself become dehumanized and regressed into savagery; whether barbarism has triumphed over the civilizing spirit once and for all. In the script, after she has escaped, and having exceeded the limits of human endurance, Sally sinks to the bed of the truck and huddles there, sobbing quietly. This response speaks of the trauma she has suffered, but at least leaves room for her recovery. However, in the film, Hooper changes her response to crazed, manic laughter, so that we are left doubting Sally's sanity. Has she become savage like the cannibals? ("Who will survive and what will be left of them?" asks the poster for the film.) Her hysterical laughter as she escapes in the back of the truck brings with it deep ambivalence, especially as this is closely followed by Leatherface's pirouette of death—a reference to Holbein's *Dance Macabre*, an allegory of the universality of death, celebrating the overpowering consciousness of the presence of death.

All in all, the sense of apocalypse in *The Texas Chain Saw Massacre* is even greater than that of *Last House on the Left*, due in part to its cosmic and historic dimension. As Sharrett observes of the film, the failure of the American civilizing experience is absolute, America's mythic past is perverted and there is nothing left but barbaric regression.[73] The apocalypse in *Texas Chain Saw* is non-regenerative and seemingly without hope.

7

COUNTERCULTURAL REVOLUTION
Shivers (1975), *Blue Sunshine* (1978)
and *Dawn of the Dead* (1978)

"Nobody should be alone tonight":
David Cronenberg and *Shivers*

Critic Ernest Mathijs has described *Shivers* as a film "dubiously torn between a sense of repulsion ... an unease with the discarding of taste, reason, conventions and cultural boundaries, and a sense of exhilaration for the liberating potential portrayed."[1] It is true that David Cronenberg's transgressive first feature, in which the bored residents of a sterile modern apartment complex are transformed into rampaging sex maniacs by a strain of mutant parasites, has divided critics in terms of its sexual politics, some seeing it as a deeply reactionary work, others arguing for its progressive potentials. Although ultimately remaining ambivalent about the countercultural sexual "revolution" that it depicts, *Shivers* does represent perhaps the first tentative step in modern horror towards the *possibility* of social change, a willingness to go beyond the apocalypse of Hooper and Craven, beyond the politics of pessimism and despair, to envision a new order alternative—albeit a tricky one.

In this way, *Shivers* arguably anticipates the more optimistic horror of *Blue Sunshine* and *Dawn of the Dead*; indeed the consumerist dystopia that America was rapidly turning into by the mid–1970s seems to have galvanized directors like Cronenberg, Lieberman and Romero into urgently revisiting and re-examining their 1960s countercultural beliefs in the bid to find an alternative to the modern age of shopping malls, discotheques, and credit card spending that threatened to turn the American public into soulless zombies. Thus, while the *process* of revolution, as depicted in *Shivers*, is viewed with a certain amount of horror and disgust, the need for it is presented as altogether necessary.

Shivers originated as Cronenberg's response to reading Norman O. Brown's *Life Against Death: The Psychological Meaning of History* (1959). Brown was an American classicist interested in the revolutionary potential of Freudian psychoanalysis. His call for sexual freedom through the resurrection of the body by Dionysian means both intrigued and disturbed Cronenberg. As the director recalled in 1986:

> [Brown] discussed the Freudian theory of polymorphous perversity—the kind of sexuality a child has, completely non-genital, and it's not focused and it's in everything—a suffusing sexuality or sensuality almost. Even Norman had trouble when it came to figuring out how that Dionysian consciousness would function in a society where you have to walk down the street,

cross the road and not get hit by a car. How does that all-enveloping sexuality work when you are just walking down the road? It's tricky.[2]

In *Shivers*, compartmentalized living as practiced by the residents of the apartment complex has resulted in an overwhelming sense of loneliness, isolation and ennui. Starliner Towers, as Mathijs notes, "is the site of total sexual repression."[3] The marriage of Janine and Nicholas Tudor (Susan Petrie and Alan Migicovsky) is on the verge of collapse: She is uptight and anxious, he is uninterested and uncommunicative. Free-spirited Betts (Barbara Steele) is bored stiff, and the nominal hero, Dr. Roger St. Luc (Paul Hampton), barely notices the advances of his nurse, Forsythe (Lynn Lowry). As Adam Lowenstein comments, Starliner Towers is clearly modeled on the "youth-orientated apartment complexes constructed in the 1970s to capitalize on the economic boom surrounding the new singles culture that glamorized the lifestyle of the unmarried."[4] The utopian promise, as held out by the sexual liberation of the late 1960s, Lowenstein observes, has given way to the "commodified excesses of the 'me' generation."[5]

In Brown's theory, repression during childhood results in sublimation of the sexual drive, the rerouting of frustrated libido. The libido becomes desexualized, and sublimation involves the negation of the body in favor of the intellect. Crucially, the child represses the urge to unite with others and with the world. In *Shivers*, the sexual isolation of the characters is, however, disrupted by the infiltration of the parasites, set loose by the quintessential Cronenbergian mad scientist Dr. Hobbes, who desires to turn the world into "one big beautiful orgy." (Naming the scientist after the 17th century philosopher implies comment on the Hobbesian belief that man's natural state is dissolute.) Brown saw in earliest infancy unrepressed sexuality as "polymorphous perversity," diffused around the body. In the natural state the infant does not distinguish between self and other but is one with the world. The sex drive, for Brown, is fundamentally the desire for union with the objects of the world. In *Shivers*, those infected by the parasite seek out others for a similar union and in the process they become "one" with the others in the apartment complex. This union brings a new sense of solidarity and with it liberation to Starliner residents. As Mathijs notes, a "rudimentary form of cooperation gives the revolution they start some appeal, as if it is not based on egoistic fulfillment of needs, but on some sort of solidarity, of units working together. Everyone is equal in the eyes of the infected."[6]

Cronenberg says that he wanted to suggest that "the proliferation of this strange disease was, on one strange level, liberating."[7] And so it is—up to a point. In the original script, the "benefits" of infection by the parasite to the occupants of Starliner Towers are made clear in the final pages:

> We find many of the residents we already know, now dressed to the teeth in their seductive best... Mr. Spergazzi and his wife stand and watch the spectacle canes in hand, with great dignity. With them stand others who are too old or too young to go into the night looking for new hosts for their parasites, content to remain incubators for the time being. The residents are full of bubbly anticipation in their cars... The driver of this first car is St. Luc, sleek and exuberant...[8]

The new-found "aliveness" that infection brings the residents by the end of the story is almost without question preferable to their ennui at the start. (The script is more optimistic than the film in this respect. At the end of the film, this exuberance is not so apparent as it is in the script; in the film the residents seem more benumbed and dehumanized, like the pod people in *Invasion of the Body Snatchers*, heightening the ambivalence at the heart of

Cronenberg's vision.) As Mathijs notes, in *Shivers*, by letting desires take over from needs, Cronenberg explores the "obliteration of the system" that placed the characters in a state of repression.[9]

The process of that liberation is, however, depicted as morally repulsive throughout the film, somewhat negating the optimism of its conclusion. Robin Wood, who has taken exception to Cronenberg's work generally, commented that his films dramatize "a horror of physicality, a great fear of repressed forces; a recurrent sexual disgust that recurs ... again and again."[10]

The parasite-infected Betts (Barbara Steele) seduces Janine Tudor (Susan Petrie) in *Shivers* (1975) (photograph courtesy Ronald V. Borst/Hollywood Movie Posters).

Cronenberg describes the liberation in *Shivers* as taking a form akin to polymorphous perversity. However, if we look closely at how this suffusing sexuality expresses itself in *Shivers*, the impression is one of almost puritanical disgust on the part of the director. We have fetishism and pederasty (Hobbes and Annabel); troilism (Kurt, the waiter in the elevator with the mother and daughter); attempted male-female rape (Kresimer's attack of Forsythe); attempted male rape (the black maintenance man's attack on St. Luc—the script makes it clear this is a sexual attack); non-consensual lesbianism (Betts' seduction of the vulnerable and confused Janine); and incest (the old man and his daughter Jessica). As Mathijs says of the sheer violence and distress of the sexual attacks inflicted on the residents of Starliner Towers, "In the interests of physical well-being, maybe some taboos about how human bodies can be approached, touched, groped, violated, need to remain."[11]

This seems to be Cronenberg's conclusion too. As he has commented in response to Wood's criticism: "There is an ambivalence on my part when it comes to preaching subversion because I'm aware that along with revolution of any kind comes destruction."[12] He has also expressed concerns of "the danger of replacing something ugly and repressive with something even more ugly and repressive," but to his credit he adds, "That doesn't mean that you stop, you keep going."[13]

Cronenberg defends his films against those who accuse him of being reactionary, claiming that they work on another level to the purely political—a visceral level. They are, he claims, thrilling and liberating to an audience, and thus beyond politics and beyond society. For Cronenberg, the process of imagining a world that is not necessarily better, just different, is in itself a threat to the status quo: "If you accept the Freudian dictum that repression is civilization, then unrepressed imagination is a threat to civilization."[14]

Cronenberg has also claimed, in relation to the modern horror film, "I don't want apocalypse in my life, I want epiphanies."[15] There is in Cronenberg's films an undeniable humanism (most apparent perhaps in his 1983 adaptation of Stephen King's *The Dead Zone*), with none of the pessimism of *Last House on the Left* or *The Texas Chain Saw Massacre*. Instead, as Christopher Sharrett has observed, there is the sense of a "rational consciousness" at work, giving the impression that the catastrophe facing mankind is ultimately surmountable "if human rationality is allowed to intervene."[16] Cautious optimism and incipient humanism *is* apparent at the end of *Shivers* (in the script at least) when, as the infected prepare to leave Starliner Towers in their cars to spread their infection to the outside world, one of them gives forth the rallying cry: "Nobody should be alone! Nobody should be alone tonight!" and the others pick up the cry and chant together, "Nobody alone! Nobody alone!"

Despite its ambivalence to "revolution," *Shivers* is the first horror film of the 1970s to employ such a rational consciousness in the face of apocalypse, a sense that catastrophe might be avoided if the forces of reason are allowed to step in and alter the course of events. As Mathijs comments: "What makes Cronenberg's body horror unique is that he takes the position of the philosopher: He does not take sides, but lets his stories and characters check the consequences of the possibilities; sometimes abandonment to desires seems worth the sacrifice, sometimes not."[17]

"We've lost a trust, a trust in ourselves, a trust in our fellow Americans and a trust in the leadership of our government"

Jeff Lieberman (perhaps best known for 1976's *Squirm*) remains an important director within the horror genre. Although not as well-known as George A. Romero, Wes Craven, John Carpenter, Tobe Hooper and David Cronenberg, his films have extended and enriched the subgenres made popular by these directors. *Squirm* is easily one of the best ecological horror films derived from Hitchcock's *The Birds* (1963); *Blue Sunshine* (1978) spans the zombie-satire gap between *Shivers* and *Dawn of the Dead*; *Just Before Dawn* (1981) develops the tropes of *The Texas Chain Saw Massacre* and *The Hills Have Eyes*; and *Satan's Little Helper* (2003) riffs intriguingly on *Halloween* (1978).

Perhaps more than any other director, Lieberman has the ability to crystallize the essence of a horror subgenre in a single striking image. In *Blue Sunshine* we have the murderous babysitter stalking her young charges with a large

Psychotic babysitter Wendy Flemming (Ann Cooper) rampages with a knife in *Blue Sunshine* (1978).

knife; her "invasion-metamorphosis" is signified by her bizarrely bald head, her "possession" by the visual reference to *Rosemary's Baby* (1968). In *Just Before Dawn*, Lieberman's heroine fends off her backwoods attacker by thrusting her fist down his throat—a gender subversion of the rape-violation imagery redolent in the urbanoia film (most notably the gun-in-the-woman's-mouth scene in *The Hills Have Eyes*). In *Squirm*, we have three such moments, neatly encapsulating the three stages of narrative progression in the apocalypse horror film identified by Charles Derry: proliferation—the scene where worms infest the face of the antagonist, Roger; besiegement—where the worms threaten to erupt from a showerhead on to the heroine (also, a sly nod to *Psycho*—linking via *The Birds* to Hitchcock); and finally annihilation—when the worms invade the house and engulf Roger, who sinks into them like a man disappearing into quicksand.

Like other horror film directors of the era such as Romero and Craven, Lieberman's political awareness has informed his work from the start. After cutting his directorial teeth on commercials and a documentary on abortion, he was invited to make an anti-drug film to be shown in American high schools. According to Lieberman:

> This was six years before *Blue Sunshine*, at the height of the drug hysteria. The government and corporations were pouring a lot of money into public service announcements, saying that it was the end of America because a whole generation was being lost to marijuana and LSD and Timothy Leary and all that. The Pepsi Cola Company was sponsoring ... these public service films that you would see in schools.[18]

The resulting short was *The Ringer* (1972), an anti-drug film that is not really anti-drug, but anti-corporate marketing. In the film, corporate organizations, including the Mafia, are shown to control music, fashion and drugs, and cynically market these as a package to America's young people. The central conceit of the film, that you can sell the kids anything if you market it correctly, is illustrated in an episode showing the launch of a new fashion accessory (the Ringer of the title) aimed at the youth. This episode is juxtaposed with a vignette showing Mafia types marketing drugs to kids by using a young person to do it. A third story strand shows a new pop group recording a record while music executives sit around planning how they are going to market the group as "hip." Lieberman managed to get the script past the production company, King Features, by justifying his approach as an analogy: "Kids are being force fed a lot of stuff they don't realize. I have nothing against the drugs themselves but if you're doing the drugs because of peer pressure, or for some other reason that isn't really your choice, then I'm against that."[19]

The Ringer shows a formal complexity that is astonishing for a first short by a 21-year-old director. Lieberman sets up the three stories and then has them intersect, as we see a group of young people taking drugs while discussing the latest fashion accessories and listening to the hot new music. Indeed, Lieberman punched home his anti–corporate marketing message with such force that high school students watching the film booed the Pepsi Cola Company logo at the end. Pepsi ended up taking their name off the film.

It is not surprising that Lieberman gravitated towards the horror film for the same reasons as Romero and Craven: "It's naturally subversive and allows you to say and do things that you can't do in other forms."[20] Belonging as he does to the subversive school of horror, Lieberman's cynicism—comparable to Craven's nihilism and Romero's guarded optimism—can perhaps be seen most clearly in *Blue Sunshine*, which depicts the baby boomers selling out their hippie values to the consumerism of the 1970s. The story concerns a group of college students who, in 1967, take a new form of LSD, the titular Blue Sunshine. Ten years later, now grown up and respectable, they discover that the drug has delayed side effects which cause its users to lose their hair and become homicidal maniacs.

Blue Sunshine is, first and foremost, socio-political satire playing on the paranoia of post–Watergate America. However, it also amalgamates elements of the psychedelic drug movie of the 1960s and the invasion-metamorphosis narratives of 1950s science fiction. Indeed, *Blue Sunshine*, as Lieberman acknowledges, is heavily indebted to the "radiation cinema" of the 1950s, such as *The Incredible Shrinking Man* (1957), which played on government-induced fears about the effects of atomic radiation during the Cold War; only instead of radiation, Lieberman plays on early 1970s fears about the effects of LSD: "The whole idea that LSD could cause chromosome damage, make people freak out and jump off roofs, came from the anti-drug government establishment," Lieberman told Rob Freese of *VideoScope* magazine in 2006. "Just saying 'what a load of crap' is not entertaining. But trying to visualize what it would look like if these bozos were right was a kick."[21] *Blue Sunshine* satirizes that point of view and sends up an entire generation in the process of crossing over to "the other side"—the "straight world" of the establishment they claimed to dread during the hippie heyday. "So it was a goof on the establishment's crazy drug views and a goof on my peeps at the same time, all tied together with a former baby boomer hippie drug dealer who cut off his 'freak flags' in order to run for Congress."[22]

In *Blue Sunshine,* protagonist Jerry Zipkin (played by Zalman King) goes on the run after becoming the prime suspect in a murder committed by a friend suffering the psychotic effects of the drug. Investigating the crime himself with the help of his girlfriend Alicia (Deb-

Alicia Sweeney (Deborah Winters) and Jerry Zipkin (Zalman King) read about murder in *Blue Sunshine* (1978).

orah Winters), Zipkin discovers that old college associate Ed Flemming (Mark Goddard), now a politician, is trying to cover up his past as the drug dealer who sold his friends the experimental Blue Sunshine. The film builds to a confrontation between Zipkin and Flemming's berserk henchman Mulligan (Ray Young) in a discotheque and shopping mall, symbolizing the new age of rampant consumerism that the baby boomers—having compromised the ideals of the 1960s for their own gain—helped to usher in.

Lieberman had originally set the film in New York, with elaborate flashback sequences showing the characters' college days. For budgetary reasons he ended up cutting those scenes and transposing the story to Los Angeles. In many ways that transposition helps the film. In *Shivers* and *Rabid* (1977) Cronenberg emphasizes the brutalist architecture of Montreal as a dehumanizing influence on the characters; in *Blue Sunshine* Lieberman uses the sterile modernity of Los Angeles, with its endless shopping centers and boutique malls, to similar effect, providing an ironic backdrop to the drug burn-out narrative.

The generic continuity between the Cronenberg films and *Blue Sunshine* is underlined by the similarity of several key scenes. In *Blue Sunshine*, Jerry anxiously watches his friend, Dr. Blume—whom he thinks might be affected by Blue Sunshine—perform surgery on a woman with cancer. The suspense is partly generated by Lieberman's playing on the audience's expectations; a similar scene appears in *Rabid*, in which a surgeon succumbs to the rabies virus while working on a patient and turns homicidal in the operating room. *Blue Sunshine*'s finest suspense sequence, the aforementioned moment when murderous babysitter Wendy, having taken Blue Sunshine years before, terrorizes the children with a knife, references *Shivers*: Wendy's apartment complex is strikingly similar to Starliner Towers, even down to the residents, such as the geriatric couple riding the elevators. By the same token, *Blue Sunshine* anticipates *Dawn of the Dead* in striking ways: There is a gun store scene very similar to that of *Dawn of the Dead*, in which Zipkin arms himself in defense against Mulligan; and their final showdown takes place in a shopping mall, in which the bald-headed mannequins are easily mistaken for "zombies." (Lieberman's film ends with a zombie being gunned down in a shopping mall.)

Blue Sunshine, thanks to Lieberman's genre savvy, places itself firmly alongside *Shivers* and *Dawn of the Dead* as an invasion-metamorphosis narrative. "Collectively, *we* have become potential victims, to be transformed into zombies, gibbering maniacs or diseased wrecks," Andrew Tudor writes of the invasion-metamorphosis subgenre. "Yet however vast its scale, the heart of this [type of] narrative lies in the emphatically *internal* quality of its threat. It is not simply that we may be destroyed, as we might have been by a score of traditional movie monsters. It is also that we will be fundamentally altered in the process; that our humanity itself is at risk."[23]

Ironically, the invasion-metamorphosis narrative, perhaps because of its emphasis on human transformation and social and political change, seems to form the basis of some of the more optimistic horror films of the 1970s, such as *Shivers*, *Blue Sunshine* and *Dawn of the Dead*. Whereas the savagery-civilization contradiction of *Last House on the Left*, *The Texas Chain Saw Massacre* and *The Hills Have Eyes* appears impassable (it is presented as essentially two sides of the same coin), the living-dead dichotomy of *Blue Sunshine* and *Dawn of the Dead* is surpassable, although, admittedly, it requires a fundamental shift in the values of society—which the films suggest nothing short of a countercultural revolution can bring about.

Accordingly, *Blue Sunshine*'s protagonist Jerry Zipkin is defined as a counterculture figure, an un-reconstituted hippie. Early in the story, it is revealed that, in the words of the detective following the case, Jerry is "erratic as hell." He graduated from Cornell but now, ten years later, "hasn't got a pot to piss in." He has gone through a number of jobs. "He quit his last one," we are told, "because the firm wouldn't hire enough women." Zipkin, because of his integrity, his adherence to the progressive values of his youth, his refusal to sell out, has become a "misfit." Hence, he finds himself the prime suspect in the murder investigation. Like David in *The Crazies*, Jerry seems immune to the psychosis spreading through the erstwhile peace and love generation (which is itself a metaphor for their selling-out to materialistic values). At times Lieberman asks us to question this immunity, as Jerry's own behavior becomes increasingly eccentric. (Lieberman attempts to play on our paranoia in a number of scenes, making us think that Jerry might be starting to suffer the effects of the drug. However, Zalman King's idiosyncratic performance makes this work less effectively than it might have.)

Zipkin's nemesis is Ed Flemming, the dealer turned politician. "We have lost a trust," Flemming announces in his campaign speech, "a trust in ourselves, a trust in our fellow Americans and a trust in the leadership of our government." Flemming is thus depicted as a hypocrite and self-serving parasite, part of the corruption that destroyed counterculture ideals in the 1960s, like the real-life drug dealers who moved into Haight-Ashbury after the Summer of Love. Fittingly, his election campaign rally is held at Shopper's World, a large mall in Topanga, which also houses a discotheque, thus aligning his values with those of consumerism. Disco, in *Blue Sunshine*, is seen as part of the ideological "superstructure" of 1970s consumer-capitalism, further evidence of the kind of commodified sexual freedom exemplified by Starliner Towers in *Shivers*. Incidentally, Lieberman attributes *Blue Sunshine*'s popularity among the underground hardcore punk scene to its discotheque sequences which, according to Lieberman, "shit over disco."[24] (One wonders if Lieberman—a lifelong Rolling Stones fan—was a supporter of the Disco Sucks! movement in the late 1970s.)

The conclusion of *Blue Sunshine* can be read as optimistic: Zipkin prevails and is vindicated. His defeat of Mulligan in the shopping mall is the triumph of integrity over corruption, of 1960s counterculture values prevailing in the age of consumerism; perhaps even the start of a backlash against the capitalist "reality" of the 1970s in favor of a return to flower-power idealism. Lieberman invites us to consider these possibilities as the camera tracks away from Jerry and the unconscious Mulligan, to retreat through the aisle of consumer goods, past televisions blaring out Flemming's campaign: "It's time to make America good again!" We need more people like Zipkin, the film seems to be saying, people immune to the lure of consumerism. Lieberman cannot resist a final irony, however, informing us in a title card that 255 doses of Blue Sunshine "still remain unaccounted for." The immediate threat may have been fended off, but the wider crisis remains. The need for progressive change is more urgent than ever.

"We whipped 'em and we got it all!": *Dawn of the Dead*

Dawn of the Dead opens in the midst of a full fledged apocalypse: It is three weeks into the crisis presented in *Night of the Living Dead*, and society is at the point of collapse. In this sense *Dawn of the Dead* is more than just a sequel; it is Romero's commentary on the apocalyptic horror film cycle itself, as it stood in 1977 when *Dawn of the Dead* was written.

Romero was and is a keen observer of the film industry and the genre; *Dawn of the Dead* assimilates what came before it, and serves as a culmination of 1970s apocalyptic horror.

More than that, however, it poses tentative ways forward for humanity, a glimpse at possible new ways of living, beyond apocalypse. As did Lieberman, Romero presents a parody of the consumer society that America had become in the late 1970s. The boutique shopping malls of LA that feature in *Blue Sunshine* have, however, given way to vast "cathedrals," "great symbols of a consumer society," as Romero describes them in the *Dawn of the Dead* script, "revealing the Gods and Customs of a civilization now gone."[25] And like the America that has been lost to the Native Indians, in *Dawn of the Dead*, the shopping mall is taken from the zombies, who are its original inhabitants, its "indigenous" peoples. Their ritualistic playing out of the frontier myth in the shopping mall proves to us, as it does to the film's surviving characters, once and for all, that the American pioneer values which led to the consumer-capitalist apocalypse are racist, destructive and must be rejected.

As in *Night of the Living Dead*, then, the nature of the apocalypse is essentially racial. In the early tenement sequence we are presented with a shocking vision of the racial divide facing America in the mid–1970s, with its consequent racial wars. The SWAT team, including the protagonists Roger (Scott H. Reiniger) and Peter (Ken Foree), are sent in to evacuate the tenement and arrest the Puerto Rican insurgents led by Martinez. The ensuing massacre is a result of the racism espoused by the trooper, Wooley (Jim Baffico), who uses the crisis as an excuse to go on a rampage of hatred and bigotry against the inhabitants of such ghettoes. In point of fact, the development of huge out-of-town shopping malls, like the one in *Dawn of the Dead*, were part and parcel of the urban decline that led to downtown areas becoming ghost towns inhabited by the forgotten, as *Dawn of the Dead* depicts. As family businesses and small retailers closed down as a result of mall development, inner city neighborhoods became increasingly poverty-stricken, and violence and shootings endemic—as happened in Detroit, the South Bronx and Washington, D.C. Romero's *Martin*, set in a poor suburb of Pittsburgh, dramatizes the economic decline of the 1970s in this way.

Like the characters in *Night of the Living Dead*, Peter and Roger, and the couple Frannie (Gaylen Ross) and Stephen (David Emge), are faced with a choice: adapt or die. They must find a new way of living that breaks with traditions of the past, or themselves be destined to join the ranks of the living dead. Essentially, *Dawn of the Dead* presents their spiritual journey towards this realization, and examines the ideologies that influence them in making those choices. Those who successfully complete the journey survive, and those who do not, perish.

As part of this process, as Linnie Blake observes, there is a re-enactment of the macho power of the gun, which defines the male order. Both Stephen and Frannie must master the art of the gun in order to gain a place within the power structure.[26] When the survivors first arrive at the mall by helicopter, their immediate decision is to colonize it, to exert this power. In the script, Romero likens this colonization to the winning of the Old West and the survivors to cowboys. However, their reasons for colonizing the mall are dubious; Romero suggests in the script that the items they pillage are "clearly not all functional. Some are representative of the luxuries considered necessary by a consumer society." As Linnie Blake comments: Pillaging non-essential items illustrates the "progressive degeneration of the pioneer ideal."[27] In the film, only Frannie appears to recognize this initially; at first she tries to persuade Stephen that the mall could be a "prison." "What happened to growing vegetables and fishing?" she asks him in the script. "What happened to the idea about the wilderness?" The opportunity for a new way of living that the crisis presents is initially quashed by the group who remain entrenched in their old ways; Frannie's voice, as the woman, is for the time being discounted. The men's decision is instead to fortify the mall, symbolizing their entrenchment in the old values. Frannie's strength as a character slowly grows throughout the film, as her viewpoint becomes increasingly acknowledged by the men as the voice of reason. In order to find this voice, however, she must first break free of her own cultural conditioning, her reliance upon the men and the protection that they provide and the security that the mall brings.

Underlying the urgency for ideological change is our growing realization that the main threat to the protagonists comes from within. As Blake points out, increasingly in the film Romero identifies the macho values of the group as an agent of infection[28]; both Roger and Stephen become infected by machismo which leads to their downfall. Stephen and Roger's machismo is thus another Romero "level of insanity" on which the characters operate that is "only clear to themselves"; but it is also tied to their material acquisitiveness as well. So while on one level the film plays on the audience's consumerist fantasies inherent in seizing the shopping mall, it also acknowledges the absurdity of such a "solution" to the zombie outbreak. The viewer instinctively knows that this is not a viable option for long-term survival even when the zombies are expelled from the mall.

Interestingly, one of the most-often censored sequences in *Dawn of the Dead* is the shopping mall massacre, where Frannie, Stephen, Roger and Peter slaughter the zombies in

Roger (Scott H. Reiniger), Fran (Gaylen Ross), Stephen (David Emge) and Peter (Ken Foree) **prepare to massacre the zombies in** *Dawn of the Dead* **(1978) (photograph courtesy Ronald V. Borst/Hollywood Movie Posters).**

order to claim the mall as their own. Prior to that we have seen Stephen and Peter raiding the mall's gun store and arming themselves. The tribal music that Romero plays over this scene emphasizes the frontiership theme that comes to the fore in this section of the film. In the script Romero comments, "We recognize the firepower in the arsenal that the two men accumulate." Indeed that firepower is such that the massacre of the zombies takes on a deeply ambivalent inflection when seen in the uncensored versions, bringing home the brutality of the slaughter. Instead of feeling exhilarated, as the group claims the mall from the zombies we feel a sense of moral disgust at the scale of the zombie massacre. "We see the men wheeling garden carts piled with corpses," Romero writes in the script. "The somber image is shocking as the figures move in silhouette against the bright store fronts with their displays of goods designed to attract shoppers to the sweet life the items pretend to represent." "We whipped them and we got it all!" the now infected Roger whoops ("like a cowboy," according to the script), but Romero makes him look pathetic as he lies alone in his deathbed in the group's stark hideout above the mall, emphasizing the wrong-headedness of such slaughter.

With the mall seized and "normality" restored, the rot soon sets in. The living space is equipped with the spoils of the mall and the survivors indulge their materialism. "The couple look like a pair of newlyweds who have just moved into a new house," Romero writes of Frannie and Stephen in the script, but ennui strikes almost immediately after Roger's death. Things are no longer the same, and the context of their attempt at maintaining a bourgeois existence in the mall only serves to heighten their realization that it is a sham. "It wouldn't be right," Frannie tells Stephen when he proffers a wedding ring, "not now." The hollowness of their consumerism is finally brought home to them. "The group has become a family," Romero writes in the script, "with all the disadvantages of comfortable living, including the inability to communicate." Again, it is Frannie who most clearly understands this. "What have we done to ourselves?" she asks despairingly. As Robin Wood comments, "With the defining motive—the drive to acquire and possess money, the identification of money with power, removed, the whole structure of traditional relationships, based on patterns of dominance and dependence, begins to crumble."[29]

Frannie learns to pilot the helicopter, a symbol of her step away from reliance upon Stephen, in favor of autonomy and self-awareness; she is able, like Peter, to escape her social conditioning. Stephen, however, is not. Stephen, Roger and the outlaw biker gang, in Blake's words, have "internalized the pervasive violence of the American endeavor to the extent that they have become inseparable from it."[30] Peter, however, along with Frannie, is finally able to relinquish the gun, realizing that he must find another way.

Dawn of the Dead, like *Shivers*, *The Hills Have Eyes*, and *The Texas Chain Saw Massacre*, has an ending that differs from the one originally written in the script. Unlike these other films, however, the ending finally committed on film is more optimistic than the one in the script. Whereas Craven, Cronenberg and Hooper changed their endings in favor of more pessimistic, apocalyptic or at best (in Cronenberg's case) ambivalent conclusions, Romero rejected his original ending—in which both Peter and Frannie committed suicide—in favor of a more optimistic one. Partly this was the result of a realization on Romero's behalf that he did not necessarily have to restore normality in order to allow his two protagonists to survive. More than this, however, is the fact that Peter and Frannie are able to fly off on equal terms, possibly to set up a new cooperative society based on what they have gained from their experiences: "the potential," as Romero has commented, "of a new kind of family."[31]

In a sense, the final scene in *Dawn of the Dead*, with the white woman and black man thrown together, mirrors the situation in *Night of the Living Dead* where Ben and Barbra are forced together in the farmhouse. However, whereas that relationship was marked by distrust and suspicion, we now have mutual trust and respect. America's minorities have finally risen to take control. *Dead of the Dead*, as it stands, is somewhat open-ended and inconclusive, but in its tentative suggestion of a possible new order based on alternative ideologies, it is, as Wood says, "curiously exhilarating,"[32] and remains the most progressive of horror films.

8

ANTI-"REAGANOMICS"
Henry—Portrait of a Serial Killer (1986)
and *American Psycho* (2000)

In 1979, a year after *Dawn of the Dead* was produced, Ronald Reagan was elected president of the United States, and in the UK, Margaret Thatcher was elected prime minister. Together they brought an agenda of right-wing neoconservatism—a return to family values and a move against liberalism. This was reflected in horror cinema entering a deeply conservative—some would say reactionary—phase in the late 1970s and early 1980s, as can be seen in the misogynistic slasher cycle which dominated the genre during the period from 1979 to 1983. At that time, subversive horror cinema seemed untenable. Romero continued to develop the themes of *Dawn of the Dead* in *Knightriders* (1981), a non-horror film, and then returned to the genre with the disappointingly safe anthology movie *Creepshow* (1982). Following the controversy of *Videodrome*, Cronenberg moved closer to mainstream horror with *The Dead Zone* (1983) and his 1986 remake of *The Fly*. Lieberman made the excellent *Just Before Dawn* (1981) and then quit the genre shortly afterwards to concentrate on science fiction and comedy (returning only in 2004 with *Satan's Little Helper*). It was only with the rise of body horror and "splatstick" later in the decade, that shock and transgression was celebrated by a new generation of filmmakers such as Frank Henenlotter, Sam Raimi, Stuart Gordon, Peter Jackson and Brian Yuzna (see next chapter).

One film produced in the middle of the 1980s (although not released until 1990) that used the genre consciously to directly challenge the political ideology of Reagan was *Henry—Portrait of a Serial Killer*, co-written and directed by John McNaughton. *Henry* was one of the first in the boom of serial killer films that started in the late 1980s (and continued well into the next decade), and in many ways set the template in terms of its docu-drama styling as well as its self-reflexivity, which anticipated films like *Natural Born Killers* (1994). It is, in other words, as much about the serial killer phenomenon, as it is about a serial killer. Indeed, its connection to the real-life killer Henry Lee Lucas is somewhat tenuous. Despite its apparent flatness as drama—its "slice of life" approach—*Henry* is very carefully constructed, like *Dawn of the Dead*, around a set of sociological concerns, specific to the time it was made: the height of the Reagan era.

Because it gained notoriety in the 1990s, several years after its production (due mainly to its censorship problems in Britain), McNaughton's specific political message in the film is often overlooked in favor of broader cultural readings. In fact, McNaughton's film represents a direct attack on Reagan's "trickle-down" economics and its effects on America's poor, which according to McNaughton was to create an economic underclass without hope, where for people like Henry, violence becomes the most viable method of getting by. As Linnie Blake has suggested, the prevalence of the serial killer in popular culture during the 1980s and 1990s is a result of the need in audiences to "engage psychologically and socio-culturally with the historic traumas of the Reagan years."[1] Thus, *Henry* deals with the shocking alienation and moral breakdown which results from the creation of a social underclass, and in doing so draws us into an uneasy sympathy with the serial killer.

As a flipside to *Henry*, *American Psycho* portrays the consumer capitalist excesses of the 1980s as a moral and spiritual vacuum driving the privileged Patrick Bateman to murder in an attempt to achieve some sense of personal identity. The consumer society that director Mary Harron depicts in this film is one where only the surface counts and "inside doesn't matter," and the narcissistic macho individualism of Reagan himself is condemned as a trait shared by serial killers. The serial killer (as personified by Hannibal Lector) became a cultural anti-hero by the mid–1990s. His radical individualism placed him above conventional laws and moralities, and in some respects grew out of the doctrines of neoconservatism with its elevation of the individual above society. Both *Henry* and *American Psycho* do a volte-face to shock the audience into facing uncomfortable truths about 1980s society and its role in creating such anti-heroes.

"A new sickness of our time": *Henry—Portrait of a Serial Killer*

When McNaughton co-wrote the *Henry* script in 1985, the phenomenon of the serial killer was relatively new. McNaughton claims not to have been aware of the term "serial killer" at the time, despite an interest in true crime. Figures for 1986 show a 95 percent increase in murder since 1966, with a 25 percent increase in apparently motiveless murders between 1966 and 1990, and an increasing number of murders committed by the same individuals.[2] In 1986, it was estimated by the United States Department of Justice that less than 100 serial killers were responsible for several thousand deaths annually.[3] In his introduction to the *Encyclopedia of Modern Murder*, Colin Wilson described this phenomenon as a "strange and frightening change in the patterns of violence in the civilized world" in which "an increasing number of crimes are characterized by a kind of motiveless viciousness."[4] McNaughton, for his part, saw the rise in random murder as "a new sickness for our time."[5]

In some ways we can see the mythology that has grown around the serial killer since the phrase was first coined circa 1984 as similar to the moral panics of the 1930s that gave rise to the sexual psychopath. The most common portrayal of the serial killer is of an unemployed, homeless drifter with a low IQ from a lower class background, often of degenerate heredity (usually the victim of a broken home and abusive alcoholic parents) committing thrill- killings. Like the psychopath, the serial killer is often described as lacking empathy but able to appear normal by adopting a "mask of sanity." As Estelle B. Freedman says of the 1930s moral panic over the sexual psychopath, suspicion was often cast upon non-conforming individuals such as vagrants and homosexuals (see Chapter 1). Such is the case with the serial killer in the 1980s and 1990s.

In *Summer of Sam* (1999), Spike Lee's crime drama based on the Son of Sam killings, the media hysteria surrounding the case results in the scapegoating of the film's nonconformist character (played by Adrien Brody) by the more right-wing members of his blue-collar community. He has committed no criminal act more serious than having sex with men for money in order to indulge his interest in attending punk rock gigs. In the same way, several key films of the 1980s played on the public's growing hysteria about a burgeoning degenerate and violent underclass as symbolized by the serial killer.

Films like *Blue Velvet, River's Edge* and *Something Wild* (all 1986) depict their lower-class characters as dangerously psychopathic and "other," helping to demonize America's poor in the process. In these films, membership in the underclass is intrinsically connected to crime, violence, drug abuse and deviancy.

McNaughton, however, has defended *Henry* against critics who read it as a similar right-wing sentiment on a violent underclass, instead claiming that the film is about the effects of social-exclusion caused by poverty in America. "If you prevent people from finding any path to fulfillment in their lives," McNaughton stated in 2003, "if their prospects are so bleak ... then some of them are going to become more antisocial, more destructive to society as a whole."[6] In this way, *Henry* adheres to the theory set out in the introduction to this book: Social collapse—in this case severe economic deprivation as a result of government social policy—gives rise to degenerate-regressive forces, here in the form of the serial killer Henry, whose recourse to violence is a failure to deal with the world in all but the most primitive and bestial of ways. The real war in the U.S., according to McNaughton, is against the poor, "but not just the poor—the whole underclass, right from the dismantling of the unions on up."[7]

"Open your eyes, Otis. Look at the world. It's either you or them"

In the United States under Reagan's presidency, unemployment peaked at 10.8 percent in December 1982—higher than at any time since the Great Depression. Reagan's policies proposed that economic growth would occur when marginal tax rates were low enough to encourage investment which would then lead to increased economic growth, higher employment and wages. This became known as "trickle-down economics," the belief that tax cuts would benefit the wealthy and create a "trickle-down" effect to the poor. With those tax cuts meaning reductions in spending on health care, housing and other aid to the poor and the disadvantaged, Reagan's policies clearly benefitted the wealthy much more than those living in poverty. Not surprisingly, many poor and minority citizens began to experience social exclusion and alienation, and homelessness increased, particularly in urban centers. Critics began to view Reagan as lacking empathy with America's poor, an attitude that the president did little to dispel by making repeated suggestions that jobless workers were unemployed by their own choice and that the homeless made it "their own choice for staying out there."[8] Reagan's policy approach to America's underclass was to see it as hopeless, unworthy of government aid: the so-called "laissez-faire" option.

"The American Dream is very contradictory," the archivist, writer and filmmaker Rick Prelinger observed in 2010. "It's built upon exclusion of all sorts of groups that weren't allowed in."[9] McNaughton has made the point that someone from the underclass is unlikely to rise to the same heights as someone with a middle-class upbringing, with the main routes of success for the lower classes being sports or entertainment (if they possess the talent) or crime. The real-life Henry Lee Lucas chose the latter route, McNaughton claims, achieving "success" and recognition through serial killing.[10]

McNaughton is from working class roots. Born in Chicago in 1950, he has worked in factories and steel mills, with people who have interesting lives, but nobody to "sing their songs."[11] McNaughton sings their songs. His films focus on unglamorous, often unsuccessful people and, like early Scorsese, he displays an unerring sense of the street, thanks in part to his background as a street photographer and an interest in cinéma vérité, both of which he draws upon in *Henry* to capture the texture and neighborhoods of blue collar Chicago. *Henry* was McNaughton's first feature film, shot on a budget of $100,000. Prior to that he studied film and photography, and after college worked in a factory on an assembly line on the south side of Chicago. When his marriage fell apart he hit the road and, like Tod Browning before him, joined a carnival. There he worked as a photographer. He ended up in New Orleans making sailboats and selling jewelry, before eventually returning to Chicago to join an audio-visual distribution business, while simultaneously working in construction. Eventually he was offered the chance to make a "true crime" documentary, and this then led to *Henry* for the same company, MPI Home Video. Michael Rooker, who plays Henry, had a similar lower-class background which he brings to bear in the role. Rooker had grown up in a welfare family in Alabama before moving to Chicago where he won a scholarship to drama school. When he met McNaughton he was working as a painter and decorator to make ends meet. According to Shaun Kimber, Rooker turned up at the audition "wearing his painting and decorating clothes" and was offered the part.[12]

One can see McNaughton drawing upon these formative experiences in *Henry*. His blue collar roots help lend the film its authenticity in terms of its locations, the dress and behavior of the characters, their use of language, their whole cultural milieu. As a former film student, McNaughton draws upon a sophisticated understanding of an audience's expectations when it comes to narrative and genre, often confounding these expectations and playing with the spectator's need to align with an empathetic character. To this end, *Henry* tricks its audience into identifying with the serial killer, only then to confront us with the moral emptiness that lies at the heart of Henry—as a direct result of Reagan's social policy.

John McNaughton (seated) directs Michael Rooker and Tracy Arnold in *Henry—Portrait of a Serial Killer* (1986).

"It's always the same and it's always different"

Henry infamously features a number of murder tableaux during its early scenes, depicting in shocking and graphic detail the aftermath of Henry's killings, showing the outrages he has performed upon his victims. From the outset, McNaughton emphasizes the social and economic context of these atrocities, by intercutting the tableaux with shots of Henry's movement through the city. Although these murders are purposefully shown as horrific, and we understand that Henry is the perpetrator, we are deliberately not shown him actually committing the murders. Instead the moment of killing is presented as audio accompanying the tableaux, in effect dissociating Henry from his actions, creating ambiguity in the character from the start. It seems as though the urban squalor in which *Henry* is located—the poverty and deprivation—might in some way be responsible for the atrocities. Increasingly, as the sequence progresses, the bodies seem to become part of the landscape. Like the discarded plastic container floating down the stream, or the cigarette butt that he flicks out of his car window, they are Henry's "garbage."

In the way McNaughton situates the serial killer narrative against a background of severe economic crisis, *Henry* resembles Romero's *Martin*, which set its serial killer–vampire story in a similar environment of urban decay. McNaughton's film seems to reference *Martin* explicitly in an early scene in which Henry scopes potential victims outside a mall. In *Martin* a very similar scene takes place in a supermarket car park, with the eponymous killer (John Amplas) watching shopping housewives load groceries into their cars. In *Wounds of Nations*, Linnie Blake discusses Romero's use of the city in *Martin* to symbolize the malaise of his characters, and her descriptions could equally apply to McNaughton's use of Chicago in *Henry*: "Outside stand the dispossessed, the disgruntled, the disposable by-products of American consumer capitalism, their lives symbolically encapsulated in the strip show and porn shops of ... less than salubrious side streets."[13] Thus in the early scenes when we see Henry drifting through Chicago's derelict neighborhoods, behind him are thrift stores and bookies and cheap furniture stores.

Like Romero, McNaughton uses the city setting to comment on the huge disparities between America's rich and poor. In a lengthy sequence, Henry follows a wealthy shopper to her bourgeois home in the leafy suburbs. The journey to the outskirts establishes a dividing line or perimeter fence between the impoverished inner city and its wealthy conurbations, between the two opposing sectors of American society. Henry's exclusion from such affluence is emphasized by the distance he must keep from her home to avoid detection, remaining in his car to watch her from afar. Like in *Martin* (which features

Henry (Michael Rooker) scouts for victims on Lower Wacker Drive in Chicago in *Henry—Portrait of a Serial Killer* (1986).

another similar scene in which Martin stakes out his victim's house), the use of point-of-view shots position us with the killer, who remains not only an outsider but an underdog, in the lowest class of the social hierarchy. Henry's only access into the bourgeois home is via his job as a pest exterminator (an apt if rather blatant metaphor)—the hired help. Thwarted in this first attempt, he later poses as a bug sprayer in order to invade the victim's home and leave his "mark." In another murder tableau the camera slowly encircles the woman's tastefully furnished living room to find her cigarette-burned body on the sofa. Henry has vented his class resentment on her.

James Marriott makes the point that Otis (Tom Towles) and Becky (Tracy Arnold) occupy the same economic dead end as Henry, and their lives have been similarly shaped by their environments.[14] As a child, Becky was abused by her father and is now fleeing her husband, leaving her daughter behind. She moves to Chicago to stay with her brother Otis and takes a job washing wealthy women's hair in a salon, which she sees as a step up from her previous job as a dancer in a men's club. Like Henry and his sister, for whom he harbors incestuous feelings, Otis relies on "trickle-down" wealth to survive. He works part-time in a garage, but deals "weed" to snotty college kids to eke out a living. Even his parole officer has little time to help him find more gainful employment, instead cutting short their meeting in order to take his son for oral surgery, the type of healthcare the likes of Otis, Becky and Henry—who probably lack medical insurance—are no doubt denied.

Throughout *Henry* there is distaste for poverty which at times verges on the reactionary: an equation of physical squalor (Otis's apartment) with moral squalor (Becky's profession as a stripper; Otis's lewdness; their lack of table manners). A slight sense of repugnance is also apparent in McNaughton's portrayal of Henry's illiteracy as a "poetry of idiocy"[15]: The poor verbal skills of Otis and Henry are shown in an absurd light. (Otis: "Where you goin'?" Henry: "Nowhere. You want to come?"). The same poetry of idiocy can be seen in other films of the period such as *Blue Velvet* and *Something Wild* (in the characters played by Dennis Hopper and Ray Liotta respectively), to equally heightened effect. (In *Blue Velvet* especially, delinquency and illiteracy merge to form a kind of scatological "meta-language.") However, McNaughton never turns his characters into grotesque, threatening representatives of a degenerate underclass as these two films do. He retains compassion for them and does not condescend. But depravity is never far from the surface, and that creates a certain ambivalence in *Henry* that some critics have found contentious.

"Did you really kill your momma?"

Henry forces empathy with its main character in order to make us face a fundamental question: How different am I from Henry? McNaughton's purpose in doing so, however, is not to suggest that such violence as Henry perpetrates is inherent in the human condition—quite the opposite. At the end of the film we realize that we have been misdirected by the filmmaker so that the rug might be pulled out from under our feet.

This misdirection can be seen as starting in the first kitchen scene between Becky and Henry as they swap childhood stories, encouraging the audience to begin to understand Henry and to see the possibility of redemption for him in his growing relationship with Becky, who senses that the two share a connection. Part of the trick that McNaughton plays lies in the ambiguity of Henry's changing story about how he killed his mother. Early in the conversation he confesses to Becky, "I stabbed her," only later to claim, "I shot her dead."

The audience, encouraged to read Henry's psychology, naturally assumes that his lapse reveals a clue to his reason for killing women: He is replaying the matricide over and over, killing and re-killing his momma in each and every victim in an attempt to overcome the trauma of his childhood. It is an oft-used piece of pseudo-psychology in serial killer films, derived from *Psycho*, and featuring in many slasher movies since, notably *Don't Go in the House* (1979), *Maniac* (1980) and, perhaps more self-reflexively, in *Santa Sangre* (1989). McNaughton's use of it is self-reflexive, but also a deliberate misdirection of audience expectations. "You think I'm lying?" Henry asks Becky somewhat defensively after he confesses that his prostitute mother abused him. That may indeed be closer to the truth; the story he tells Becky could well be a complete fabrication designed to throw her off the scent. The scene suggests that Henry possesses a degree of self-knowledge that he may not, in fact, have.

McNaughton uses the notion, common to the horror film—particularly those which exhibit a social conscience—of the sympathetic monster; but this is self-reflexive on McNaughton's part, and done for the purpose of ultimately wrong-footing the audience. We are led to believe that, like Frankenstein's Monster, there might be a little bit of goodness in Henry, deep down. The reference to Karloff's original sympathetic Monster is made in Rooker's physiological resemblance to Whale's creature. As discussed in relation to Whale's *Frankenstein* in Chapter 1 of this book, Karloff's makeup was based on the eugenicists' ideas of criminality being essentially an inherited trait, and that criminals could thus be detected by their visual appearance. Rooker, with his oddly shaped cranium and exposed forehead, would have fitted Cesare Lombroso's description of a "born criminal." This creates a certain degree of necessary ambiguity (the audience is invited throughout the film to entertain the various explanations for the serial killer phenomenon, including the idea of the "natural born killer") but it is the associations with Karloff's creature that ultimately sway the audience into believing that Henry is misunderstood. Ultimately, the key to Henry's character is that he cannot *be* understood—at least not in pop psychological terms.

"Otis, plug it in"

McNaughton knows that an audience needs to identify with a character, and that the horror film invites the blurring of the distinction between the normal and the monstrous so that fundamental values of a society can be questioned through the use of ideological shock. If the monster is cast as "victim," as Henry is, then identification becomes possible. But McNaughton takes the audience's sense of identification further in the contrast between Henry and Otis, to that point where Henry appears to recognize and reject the beast within himself, as we would wish him to do.

Henry initiates Otis in serial killing, drawing him into his own sickness, but in the process comes to see in Otis a psychopathology greater than his own. At least this is what McNaughton encourages us to think. Again, part of the film's power is that it tricks us into reading the film as a conventional morality tale: Henry, the damaged criminal, comes to recognize his wrong thinking that led him to commit murder and, through the redemptive power of love, overcomes this weakness in himself so that he can be reborn "good." The volte face ending ultimately belies this, shocking us into deeper realization. Moreover, the opening out of the narrative to include Otis, while tricking us into identifying more closely with Henry because he appears less depraved than Otis (at least Henry draws the line at necrophilia), also raises questions about serial killing as a wider social phenomenon rather than as a sickness that just affects isolated individuals like Henry. This, in effect, allows McNaughton to implicate the audience in the killings, as he does in the controversial sequence in which Henry and Otis invade the family home and videotape their murder in order to later watch it at their leisure. Like Michael Reeves did with *Witchfinder General*, McNaughton in *Henry* is challenging the audience to question the need for violent spectacle in our society, how entertaining violence really is. He does this shockingly but without condescension because that question is intrinsically tied to McNaughton's overarching concern of investigating the serial killer phenomenon as a "sickness of our time," a sickness that could potentially "infect" us all, as it has Henry and Otis.

Killing provides Otis with power (as it does for Henry), a way to assert his dominance in a world in which the lower classes are routinely victimized by society. ("It's either you or them, one way or the other," Henry tells Otis.) The randomness of the violence associated with serial killing is a result of what Colin Wilson termed "magical thinking," a generalized sense of resentment within society which results in the decision to scapegoat individuals because "someone deserves the blame."[16] Wilson attributes this resentment to unrealistic expectations about freedom and equality fostered by the likes of Rousseau and Karl Marx; in *Henry*, McNaughton, by contrast, presents society itself as an increasingly amoral landscape in which individuals inevitably get caught up in the machinations of violence. For example, we see Otis and Henry casually filming two bums assault a third in a park. It is a minor, seemingly inconsequential but, nevertheless, vicious and brutal scene—all the more so because of its everyday banality. Wilson's solution to the serial killer phenomenon is to discourage the teaching of Rousseau and Marx; McNaughton may not offer a solution but his view of society is somewhat less benign than that of Wilson, and his conclusion somewhat more subversive.

"Who do you think you're associating with, anyway?"

Thus, Henry offers Otis a way to get back at society, but Otis takes it too far. (Whether Henry truly objects to Otis's depravities on moral grounds, or simply because he fears that the modus operandi may result in their greater chance of being caught, is just one of the film's fascinating ambiguities.) Either way, the accidental breaking of the video camera symbolizes the beginning of the end for Henry and Otis as accomplices in serial killing.

This scene is immediately followed by Becky's inviting Henry to accompany her to Boston to live with her mother. Here McNaughton plays on our expectations of dramatic structure: We sense the movement towards a final act closure: Will Henry go with Becky and find redemption, and thus rehabilitation into normal society? The prospect of Henry living with three females including Becky's mother and her child, offers Henry the possibility of a positive relationship with mother figures, a potential healing. Henry offers to take Becky for a steak dinner and puffs up with pride when he reveals he has a new Visa card, linking potential redemption to a possible emergence from poverty and Henry no longer needing to murder. Reading *Henry* in this conventional way, one can see Becky's seduction as Henry's "supreme ordeal": the idea, derived from Joseph Campbell, that the hero must encounter his worst fear in order to emerge from the experience fundamentally changed for the better.[17] Thus the attempted seduction is followed by Henry's decision, having gone for a walk after Otis comes home, not to kill the tobacconist ("fuck the bears") or the woman out walking her dog who arouse his anger, but instead to return home, presumably having made the decision to accompany Becky to Boston.

8. Anti-"Reaganomics"

Why does Henry stop Otis from raping Becky? We have been led to believe that Henry, ironically, has a sense of morality, that incest and necrophilia, even to him, are wrong; that his misogynistic killings, depraved as they may be, are essentially born of anger, not of perversion. His fear of sex, inculcated in him by his mother, can be overcome by normal relations with Becky. Therefore, when he kills Otis, it appears that Henry is "killing" that side of himself, decapitating it. Although the murder scene is itself gruesome to the point of being repulsive, it is also cathartic. By now, the audience is reading the film as a purely redemptive tale: Henry defeats the killer inside him and is fleeing the city that fostered his murderous impulses.

The iconic image of Rooker as Henry contemplating his reflection in the motel mirror speaks of the essential ambiguity that the film plays upon in order to trick us into believing that Henry is indeed capable of such redemption. The "staring-at-himself-in-the-mirror-shot" in cinema is used inevitably to convey metaphorically the contemplation of personal identity and the facing-up to "truth." Characteristically, in *Henry*, even this moment is ambiguous. The camera does not linger on Henry in a scene of empathy but instead pans around to show that Henry is not alone; Becky is also in the room, playing a guitar. Henry does not need to reach a decision because the decision has already been made. His leaving with Becky is simply the fleeing of one more crime scene after murdering Otis. We realize finally that we have read into Henry's character a capacity for empathy—and thus for redemption—that he simply does not possess. Becky therefore is fated to become just another murder tableau: a body in a suitcase left by Henry at the side of the road.

In the final analysis, *Henry* subverts the usual message of crime films: that the criminal must atone for his crimes and seek rehabilitation into society. Henry's moral emptiness is

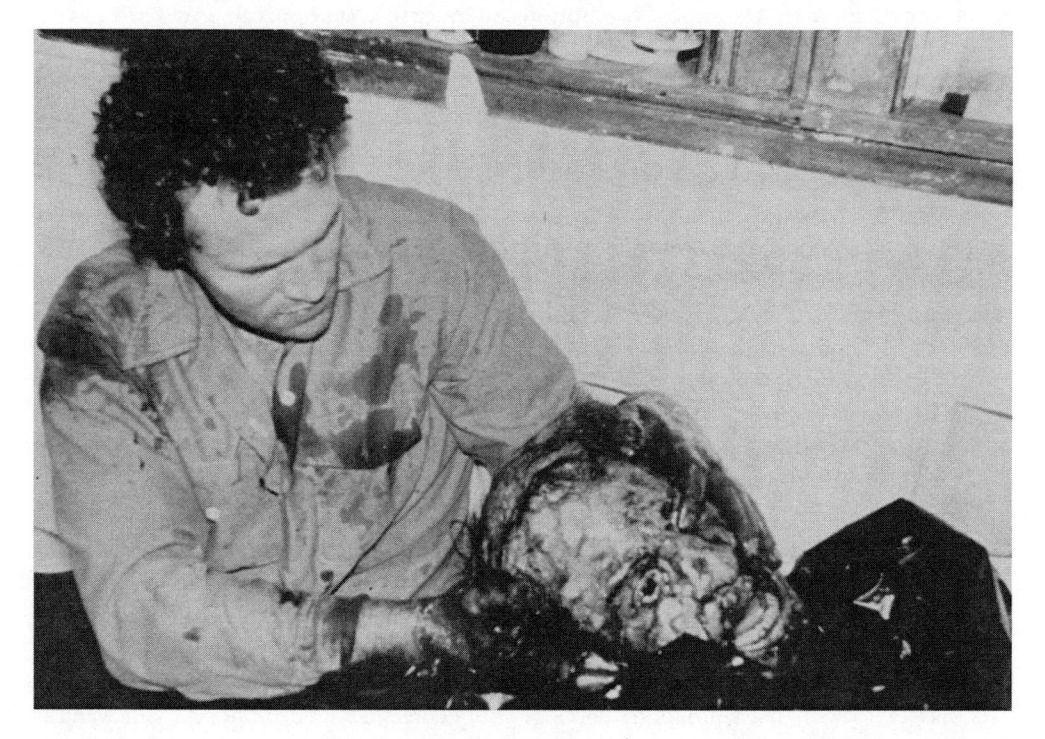

Henry (Michael Rooker) ends his short-term killing spree partnership with Otis (Tom Towles) in *Henry—Portrait of a Serial Killer* (1986).

such that he is beyond rehabilitation, beyond judgment. Furthermore, the film questions whether a society that could give rise to a Henry or an Otis is, itself, in need of rehabilitation. *How can Henry be cured*, McNaughton is saying, *when it is society itself that is sick*? The power of *Henry* is such that it shocks us into coming to this realization ourselves.

"Inside doesn't matter": *American Psycho*

Thanks largely to *Henry—Portrait of a Serial Killer*, the figure of the serial killer within popular culture came to embody social alienation and breakdown primarily among the lower classes during the Reagan era. However, in 1991 when Brett Easton Ellis published *American Psycho*, although the social satire inherent in it was not immediately appreciated, by relocating his serial killer within a milieu of wealth and privilege—as a flipside to *Henry*—Ellis created an equally potent metaphor for the moral and spiritual emptiness of the bankers and stockbrokers who benefitted from Reaganomics.

Ellis, by his own account, approached the idea of a yuppie serial killer not from any great desire to write an indictment of the "greed is good" philosophy of the 1980s, but from his own feelings of isolation and alienation at that point in his life. "I was living like Patrick Bateman," Ellis admitted in 2010. "I was slipping into a consumerist kind of void that was supposed to give me confidence and make me feel good about myself but just made me feel worse and worse and worse about myself."[18] In *American Psycho*, Patrick Bateman leads a double life: a wealthy investment banker by day, by night he stalks the streets of Manhattan as a serial killer. The novel parallels the material excess of Bateman's yuppie lifestyle—its designer clothes, endless cocaine consumption and expensive haute cuisine—with the pornographic violence that Bateman perpetrates on the prostitutes he regularly picks up, to create a catalogue of obscenity that is both morally and graphically shocking and repellent. At its heart *American Psycho* exposes the moral and spiritual vacuum of conspicuous consumption, where personal identity is based entirely on materialism, and where extreme narcissism encouraged by the culture becomes fascistic.

Although Mary Harron's film of *American Psycho* is set in 1987 (the year of Black Monday, the huge stock market crash that seemed to bring the yuppie boom to an abrupt halt), it was made in 2000. Because of its appearance post–*Scream* (1996), critics have described *American Psycho* as a "meta-slasher." Certainly it is self-reflexive in a similar way to *Henry—Portrait of a Serial Killer*, with intertextual references to *Psycho*, *Peeping Tom* and *The Texas Chain Saw Massacre*. However, in essence, *American Psycho* draws upon the short-lived cycle in 1980s American cinema known as yuppie horror or the yuppie nightmare movie, with such antecedents as *Something Wild* (1986), *After Hours* (1985) and, most notably, *Vampire's Kiss* (1988).

Both *Vampire's Kiss* and *After Hours* were written by Joseph Minion, who pretty much set the template for the yuppie nightmare movie in those two films: a young, upwardly mobile city dweller falls foul of a dark criminal underworld after being lured in by the promise of a woman. As a kind of Dante's Inferno for the Reagan era, the yuppie nightmare movie gave rise to some of the decade's most interesting films, playing on the white middle-class guilt of the affluent new breed of city professional profiting from short-term economic policies that led to stock market bubbles and a boom in consumer credit, but also widened the gap between the rich and poor, creating (particularly in the United States) a burgeoning underclass.

One of the criticisms of some yuppie nightmare movies is that the audience is encouraged to wallow in the grimy world of the criminal underclass while simultaneously encouraged to denounce it. In *Blue Velvet,* for example, the hero is recuperated into his middle-class world of white picket fences and healthy sex, cured of his fascination with the seedy underworld of gas-guzzling psychopathic gangsters and sexually alluring masochistic night club singers. But Minion's films refuse to recuperate their heroes in this way. In *Vampire's Kiss,* the protagonist, a Manhattan book publisher who believes himself to be *nosferatu* after having been bitten on the neck during a one-night stand, slides into madness, never to return. His decreasing ability to differentiate between what is real and what is imagined prefigures that of Patrick Bateman in *American Psycho,* whose hallucinatory experiences in the film become more and more bizarre until he loses his grip on reality completely.

Like Bateman, the protagonist of *Vampire's Kiss* (played by Nicolas Cage) has come to base his identity on popular culture. The similarities between the two characters are such that Christian Bale, who plays Patrick Bateman in *American Psycho,* is said to have modeled that performance on Cage's in *Vampire's Kiss.* Cage's character, in common with all yuppie nightmare movie protagonists and Patrick Bateman, is drawn to sleazy bars and squalid downtown environs in search of illicit thrills, even murder, in a bid to feel alive, to escape the confines of the consumerist void. Like Cage's character, Patrick Bateman longs for true identity, real individuality, but is trapped by his own conformity to Reagan-era ideology and his need for social status.

"I simply am not there"

Mary Harron saw in Ellis's novel an allegory of the 1980s, and approached her adaptation (co-written with Guinevere Turner) primarily as social satire mixed with horror genre elements. *American Psycho,* has been likened to David Fincher's *Fight Club* (1999) as a "genre-busting exploration of American maleness."[19] Throughout *American Psycho* these two genre strands run concurrently. On the one hand, Bateman represents the privilege and wealth of 1980s yuppie culture. He is caught up in a world obsessed with surfaces: restaurants, apartments, clothes and material acquisition. He embodies the perfect, desirable Calvin Klein–type male endorsed by the style magazines of the time: On the surface he is everything desirable in 1980s man. On the other hand, Bateman is a crazed serial killer given to committing the worst atrocities imaginable, and idolizes the likes of Ed Gein and Ted Bundy.

What draws these strands together is our realization, as the film progresses, that the murders Bateman commits may only be taking place in his imagination: He is likely a fantasist and mythomaniac who distorts reality in a bid to gain the attention of

"Inside doesn't matter": Patrick Bateman (Christian Bale), the investment banker-serial killer of *American Psycho* (2000).

others. In the film, Bateman finally feels compelled to confess his "murders" to his lawyer in a bid for recognition, which he is ultimately denied; sentenced instead to remain "the boring, spineless lightweight" that others perceive him as being, whose inner rage is vented only by doodling mutilated women in his diary—sick fantasies of murders that he might not, in reality, have had the actual "balls" to commit. Despite a background of wealth and privilege—Upper East Side upbringing, Harvard education, summers in the Hamptons—Bateman suffers from low self-esteem. Consumer excess has created in him a moral and spiritual void which is filled by narcissism and alpha male behavior.

As Harron has commented of the alpha male culture of the 1980s, its aggressive competitiveness creates feelings of panic and insecurity, both of which Bateman exhibits from the very start of the film.[20] Bateman is constantly worried about being outdone by others and is obsessed by how others see him. This obsession reaches absurd heights when Bateman's business card is "trumped" by those of his colleagues, whose designs surpass his own in terms of taste and elegance. This obsession is accompanied by the need, as established in the opening scene, not to transgress the social code. "You'll notice that my friends and I all look and behave in a remarkably similar fashion," Patrick informs us in his voiceover narration. Conversation in the scene revolves around the thorny question of whether wearing a sweater vest with a suit is "against the rules."

One-upmanship is the order of the day: Bateman establishes the moral high ground on the basis of political correctness by taking a colleague to task for making anti–Semitic comments; however in the next scene, the sexist comments of another colleague go unchallenged. Misogyny is accepted as part of the social code; and status is defined by the ability to score "hardbodies." Harron establishes the similar contempt with which the homeless (who are pointedly conspicuous in the film, emphasizing the immoral wealth and privilege of the yuppies) are treated by Patrick and his friends: It is considered acceptable to taunt a homeless man with the offer of an Amex card outside the nightclub. The social code requires the ritualized consumption of cocaine, which only serves to fuel the paranoia and aggression of the alpha males, some of whom are already pumped up on steroids. The sequence culminates in Patrick telling a bar girl that he wants to stab her to death and "play around in her blood." The girl's refusal to recognize Patrick's status creates a rage within him which, from the outset, we see as stemming from his deep insecurity, his fear that he is "simply not there."

American Psycho is, as David Robinson observes, "a powerful condemnation of consumption, both of products and of cultural narratives."[21] During the next sequence we see how Patrick constructs his identity through such products. The script describes his expensive Manhattan apartment as "oddly impersonal—as if it had

Bateman (Christian Bale) tops up his tan in *American Psycho* (2000).

sprung straight from the pages of a design magazine."[22] This use of consumer products to bolster a failing sense of self fosters an all-encompassing narcissism: Patrick's first action, upon urination in the morning, is to affirm himself by looking at his reflection in a poster of *Les Misérables* above the toilet. He explains to us in great detail his skin care regime which is highly ritualized and fetishistic, involving dozens of expensive creams, lotions and cleansers that produce, ironically, a bland face mask. Harron uses the mask as a metaphor both for the emptiness at Bateman's core—for there is nothing behind the mask—and for the "mask of sanity" which begins to slip as the film progresses. By admitting "I simply am not there," Bateman is referring both to his personal identity and his conscience.

That Bateman uses the *Les Misérables* poster as a mirror shows how he uses the narratives of popular culture and advertising to provide a sense of identity. He consumes pornography and horror films on home video, and attempts to buy into art (the script reveals that the Baselitz painting in his apartment is hung upside down), rhapsodizing about the artistic merits of MOR music (most absurdly Huey Lewis and the News), but appears to be merely reciting the reviews of rock journalists that he has read in style magazines. He has, as Harron points out, "constructed his identity from a lot of external images, from the reflection of how other people see him."[23] The purpose of this constructed identity, Harron suggests, is to "allow him to pass as a human being."[24] Thus, his haircut, tan and Armani suit provide the finishing touches to this construction: the uniform of the yuppie. Patrick's uniformity is emphasized in the script when, having approved himself in the mirror, he arrives at work where he passes a man who "looks just like him."

In many ways, Bateman is the monstrous embodiment of Reagan's neoconservative ideology: He is, as Harron observes, "less a real person than a collection of symptoms."[25] The film makes this clear in the scene where, having taken his fiancée Evelyn (Reese Witherspoon) to dinner with friends, Patrick launches into an extraordinary quasi-political speech that reveals the mass of contradictions and hypocrisies behind 1980s neoconservative thinking. On the one hand Patrick claims that "we have to provide food and shelter for the homeless" while on the other hand advocating the need to "stop people from abusing the welfare system"; and it is important to "protect the right to life" while somehow maintaining "women's right of choice." Also on Bateman's list of social policies is the importance of encouraging "a return to traditional moral values," to "curb the graphic sex and violence on TV, in movies, in pop music, everywhere." Finally, Bateman advocates the need to promote "less materialism in young people." The speech is the film's supreme moment of political satire, made all the more incongruous because Bateman's actions completely belie his words. Bateman may make those proclamations in a bid for legitimacy and acceptability in the eyes of others, as did the Reagan administration, but, as David Robinson observes, America's consumer-capitalist mindset, as embodied by Bateman, "taken to its logical extreme, exposes itself as inherently violent."[26]

"I'm in murders and executions"

Patrick's murders are attempts to achieve status and identity, and they are motivated by his frustration at not being recognized. The murder of the homeless man, Al (Reg E. Cathey), takes place immediately after Patrick's business card—a literal representation of his identity—has failed to impress his colleagues in terms of its individuality and taste. Murder, therefore, becomes a way for him to stamp his presence on the world around him. His killing of Al—and, later, various women of his acquaintance—is logical in terms of the contempt he and his friends have shown the women and the homeless in the film's early scenes.

Patrick continues to taunt Al, the way his friends taunted the other homeless man. At first Patrick appears to be sympathetic to Al's situation, offering him money for food. But as the scene progresses we see that he is merely treating Al with contempt. Ultimately Bateman blames Al for being out on the street with no job, telling him, "You've got a negative attitude ... you've got to get your act together." The neoconservative mindset of the 1980s favored initiative, ambition and responsibility but was unable to admit that the great disparity of wealth and opportunity that had arisen as the by-product of trickle-down economics had contributed to the increasing numbers of unemployed homeless. In Bateman's condescension and cruelty to Al we can see echoes of Reagan's blaming the homeless for their own misfortunes; and Bateman's murder of Al is both an extension of the contempt that the wealthy held for the poor under Reagan and a comment on the class tensions that developed in the decade as organized labor was systematically dismantled as a result of changed union laws.

Ellis's novel became infamous because of its extreme violence, much of which was highly sexualized and openly sadistic. Accusations of misogyny were leveled at Ellis, partly because the tone of the violence was such that irony became obscured by atrocity. The description of the violence was graphic to the degree that it produced such a high level of shock and outrage in the reader that it was always more likely to cause offense than provoke insight. The satire in Ellis's novel is extremely dark and lay for the most part in the paralleling of detailed physical description of the murders with the detailed description of consumer behavior. It is a catalogue of obscenity both in terms of the pornography of violence and the immorality of excessive consumption. In the novel, immediately after Patrick murders Al (which is described in nauseating detail), Ellis launches into Bateman's first-person rhapsodizing over the band Genesis. Bateman's pedantry as narrator produces the satire: Bateman is consumer-capitalism turned monstrous.

In the film, Mary Harron decided to play up the black comedy aspects. She goes less for graphic shock and more for broad satire in the Kubrick vein. But by combining the eulogizing over pop music with the murder and sadism—within the same scene—the satire becomes more apparent. Thus, Patrick's speech lauding the Huey Lewis and the News song "Hip to Be Square" as a statement about the "pleasures of conformity," delivered as he prepares to axe to death Paul Allen (Jared Leto) whom he deeply resents because Paul is perceived to be of the higher status, becomes comedic. However, his mania in doing so and the ludicrous nature of his claims for commercialized music as high art, show his incipient insanity: Consumption is literally driving him mad.

Bateman's lengthy descent into insanity in the second part of *American Psycho* is akin to that of Nicolas Cage's plunge into psychosis in *Vampire's Kiss*. In both films the behavior of the two characters becomes more extreme and ever more grotesque. In *Vampire's Kiss* Cage spirals into madness because he believes himself infected with the curse of the undead. Cage's image of what it is to be a vampire is entirely shaped by his exposure to popular media: He transforms himself into the vampire in F.W. Murnau's *Nosferatu* (1922), donning plastic fangs to stalk nightclubs in search of victims, leering crazily and walking stiffly in a psychotic parody of Max Schreck. However, underlying the insanity of both characters is, in fact, a deep-seated guilt.

In *Vampire's Kiss*, Cage's main victim is his Latino secretary (Maria Conchito Alonso)

Bateman (Christian Bale) loses his grip on reality in *American Psycho* (2000).

whom he bullies mercilessly. When she takes sick time due to the stress, Cage—in a particularly uncomfortable-to-watch scene—takes a cab to her house so that he can continue the harassment there. The film spends some time showing the life of the poor working immigrant through Alonso's character, in contrast to Cage's privileged Manhattanite lifestyle. This gives some context to Cage's peculiar guilt-based love-hate fixation on his secretary, whom he eventually attempts to rape: white middle-class guilt sublimated into victimizing the "despicable" migrant. In *American Psycho*, Patrick's relationship with Jean (Chloë Sevigny) is strikingly similar. His attitude towards her is completely male chauvinist despite the fact that she loves him. Patrick's turning point in the film occurs when he invites Jean into his apartment with the intention of murdering her. He thinks that she is just another victim for his insane bloodlust; however he finds that he cannot kill her and asks her to leave. It is at this stage in the film that Bateman realizes he can no longer control himself and is going insane.

Like Becky in *Henry—Portrait of a Serial Killer*, Jean offers Patrick an opportunity for redemption, and like Henry he is unable to take it. Unlike Henry, though, Patrick's sense of guilt ultimately delivers him to damnation. In *Vampire's Kiss*, Cage's character is not redeemed either. Instead, as *nosferatu*, he has to suffer the inevitable stake through the heart as punishment for his sins. The downward spiral for both his character in *Vampire's Kiss* and Bateman in *American Psycho* precludes a third act. Interestingly, both films are structured into two acts only and the third, which traditionally sees the errant protagonist recognize the error of his ways, redeem himself and restore order to his life, is noticeably missing. Instead, what we have in *American Psycho* is a volte-face conclusion that ultimately sees Patrick Bateman—and all that he stands for—condemned by the filmmaker.

"How can he lie like that?"

The implication in *American Psycho*—both in the novel and in the film—is that the murders may or may not have happened: They may merely be Bateman's fantasies about asserting an identity, or they may have happened and just not been recognized. Either way, Bateman's attempts at gaining an identity through serial killing fail. As David Robinson comments, the fact that the murders are not recognized in mutuality means that, even if they did happen, they might as well have not. In Bateman's world, Robinson points out, "interiority and self-knowledge are deemed irrelevant. Even that which one senses to be true must be confirmed by the pack in order to gain credence."[27] As Bateman himself comes to realize, "inside doesn't matter."

The volte-face that Ellis and Harron pull on the audience takes on allegorical meaning by the context of the scene, and is perhaps more pointedly political in the film. After Bateman confesses to his lawyer (the lawyer laughs it off as a prank, saying that one of the people Bateman claims to have killed was recently seen alive), Bateman returns to his friends who are watching Reagan's address on the Iran-Contra Affair. "How can he lie like that?" one of them asks, marveling at how composed Reagan is. In the Iran-Contra affair, one of the largest political scandals of the 1980s, it came to light that the proceeds of arms sales to Iran were used to fund Nicaraguan Contra rebels. Reagan claimed ignorance of the affair, but was later forced to explain the breaking of international law in the funding of the Contra militants. In his television address on the evening of August 12, 1987, Reagan justified his position through persuasive use of rhetoric, drawing on the American ideals of individualism and patriotism to argue that that "foreign policy can't be run by committee." Reagan's approval returns took an upturn after the speech, proving that indeed "inside doesn't matter." The perceptions of others, rather than one's own actual actions or thoughts, define one's identity: "The overwhelming force of public opinion" as Robinson points out, "is what creates truth."[28]

This realization on Bateman's part binds him and Reagan together ideologically. "There are no more barriers left to cross," he confesses in the final voiceover. "All I have in common with the uncontrollable and the insane, the vicious and the evil, all the mayhem I have caused and my utter indifference toward it, I have now surpassed..." Harron's subversive conclusion sees the narcissistic, macho individualism of the Reagan doctrine likened to that of the serial killer. Reagan's cowboy political persona, conveyed in his vows to "pursue a new, different direction for America," placed him, like Henry and Bateman, above conventional laws and moralities, but left America alienated, with its working class dissatisfied and its nouveau riche suffering a malaise of excess and narcissism.

On October 19, 1987, barely two months after Reagan's Iran-Contra speech, Reagonomics suffered an even harsher blow when the stock markets crashed as a result of program trading. Computerized systems of trading may have been blamed for the crash—something of a setback for economists like Alan Greenspan who saw computers as creating a stable form of capitalism free from the booms and busts of previous decades—but many commentators of the time predicted the end of Reagan's supply-side economics as a consequence. Writing in the *Florida Sun Sentinel*, Richard Reeves saw Black Monday as evidence that deferred taxation of the Reagan deficits had to end: "The credit card years of the anti-government, supply-side spree are over."[29] It was time, as Reeves suggests, for the Wall Street yuppies to grow up. Indeed the term yuppie started to be used more pejoratively after the 1987 crash, until, in 1991, *Time* magazine proclaimed the death of the yuppie in a mock obituary.[30] However, while the social-economic bubble might have burst for many, the appetite for materialism remained, and if anything increased in the next decade with the development of designer technology. Filmmakers like Brian Yuzna responded with a new subgenre of horror, termed splatstick, which celebrated the transgression of gooey bodily transformation.

9

ANTI–1990S MATERIALISM
Brian Yuzna and Splatstick

Although the stock market crash of 1987 brought the era of the yuppie to an end, youth materialism—which had been increasing over the generations—peaked in the late 1980s and early 1990s, staying at historically high levels into the new millennium. Consumerism had not gone away and the development of new technology, such as the mobile phone, only served to increase the public's appetite for material possessions and accumulated wealth. But with the material lifestyle came a higher incidence of depression, narcissism and paranoia, leading paradoxically to greater unhappiness in the population. When the transformation narrative that consumer-capitalism promised did not deliver, people began to seek it elsewhere, such as in New Age beliefs and alternative religions which promised spiritual growth.

In the 1980s and 1990s horror film, this yearning for transformation can be seen reflected in the satirical body-horror movies of Brian Yuzna, a filmmaker who remains largely neglected in film criticism. He is, however, a writer-producer-director who consistently uses the horror genre for social satire. In this sense he is comparable to Herman Cohen and indeed his films—which can also be described as B movies—share many of the same themes as Cohen's: Authority cannot be trusted—it creates monsters! However, for Yuzna, the process of bodily transformation (especially in *Initiation* [1990] and *Return of the Living Dead 3* [1993]) is potentially liberating, offering his characters (particularly women) the chance to escape the shackles of mainstream social norms and become who they really are. In contrast, Yuzna's *The Dentist* (1996) and *The Dentist 2* (1998) show their materialistic protagonist driven mad by his neurotic obsessions.

Yuzna's films belong to a cycle of surreal bad taste comedy horror often referred to as splatstick. The term, which fuses splatter horror and slapstick comedy, was first coined by Peter Jackson to describe his own brand of early horror-comedy that combined extreme gore and silent movie slapstick humor to shock effect. The splatstick cycle started in the early 1980s with Sam Raimi's *The Evil Dead* (1982) and *Basket Case* (1982); took shape as an identifiable subgenre in the mid–1980s (*Re-animator* and *Return of the Living Dead* [both 1985]) and peaked in the late 1980s and early 1990s (*Brain Damage* [1988], *Society,* [1989], *Dead Alive* [aka *Braindead*] [1992]). The comedy-horror hybrid has, of course, been a staple since silent days; splatstick combines the subversive aspects of both genres, with transgression, absurdity, bad taste and social satire forming the common ground. Not surprisingly, splatstick has its own particular auteurs who return to it repeatedly, most notably Frank Henenlotter, who, along with Yuzna, continued to make splatstick-inspired films after the main cycle had ended in the mid–1990s. A new wave of satirical J-splatstick has been underway in Japan since the mid–2000s led by director Noboru Iguchi (*Mutant Girls Squad* [2010], *Zombie Ass: Toilet of the Dead* [2011], *Dead Sushi* [2012]) whose work is directly influenced by the films of Raimi, Jackson, Henenlotter and Yuzna.

The use of splatter in horror has always had transgressive connotations: John McCarty described the splatter movie as breaking the "last taboo of the screen,"[1] although its origins can clearly be traced to Grand Guignol Theater, those short horror plays of the early twentieth century that featured realistic eye-gouging, decapitation and dismemberment. Herschell Gordon Lewis pioneered gore-horror in the early 1960s and subsequently based his career in splatter, bucking the Motion Picture Association of America by releasing his films (most notably *Blood Feast* [1963] and *Two Thousand Maniacs!* [1964]) in drive-ins. George A. Romero was the first major director to fully utilize the shock value of splatter (he invented the term) for the purposes of social satire in *Dawn of the Dead*, literalizing the metaphor of America's civic body eating itself alive in a gory excess of conspicuous consumption.

Splatstick has a number of discernible themes that are common to the satirical films of Jackson, Henenlotter and Yuzna in particular. Authority cannot be trusted. In splatstick, authority often takes the form of the military (the *Return of the Living Dead* series) and the medical establishment (the *Re-animator* series). In *Return of the Living Dead* and *Return of the Living Dead 3* the zombie outbreak is caused by the military's production of a chemical weapon, Trioxin. The *Re-animator* films memorably depict the medical establishment as driven by greed and vanity and populated by corrupt middle-aged doctors (such as the villainous Dr. Hill) who quash attempts at innovation by younger medical students. If authority creates monsters, the process of bodily transformation can, paradoxically, be seen as potentially liberating to the individual, bringing true identity. In *Return of the Living Dead* and

Curt Reynolds (J. Trevor Edmond) and Julie Walker (Mindy Clarke) are lovers on the run in *Return of the Living Dead 3* (1993).

Return of the Living Dead 3, becoming a zombie releases taboo female sexuality and latent feminine powers. Not surprisingly, Kafka-esque metamorphosis abounds in splatstick, but satirical references are also made to the cosmetic surgery boom of the 1990s. Body modification can be seen as a logical extension of materialism—whereby people relate to their bodies as they would to other "objects"—and splatstick satirizes both the desire and the fear of bodily transformation. Strong women characters often feature in splatstick and their bodily transformation can be a potentially progressive and liberating "monstrous-feminine" (*Initiation, Progeny, Bride of Re-animator, Return of the Living Dead 3, Frankenhooker, Bad Biology*). It follows that splatstick is often concerned with the changing relationships between men and women, as patriarchy gives way to feminism. This can be seen as an attempt to reset the balance in horror cinema after the misogyny of the slasher movie in the late 1970s and early 1980s.

Before exploring Yuzna's work in more detail, let's first look briefly at the careers of Peter Jackson and Frank Henenlotter, important directors within splatstick and subversive horror cinema generally. Their work is vital to our understanding of this transgressive horror subgenre.

Bad Taste: Peter Jackson

From 1987 to 1992, Jackson made three movies that pushed the boundaries of on-screen gore and shock about as far as they could go. *Bad Taste* (1987), *Meet the Feebles* (1990) and *Dead Alive* (aka *Braindead*) sent censors worldwide running for their scissors and audiences for their sick bags, and in the process turned Jackson into a cult director and a national hero.

Born into a working class family in the aptly named Pukera Bay, near Wellington, Jackson seemed determined from an early age to rebel against his parochial New Zealand background. Growing up on a diet of Ray Harryhausen movies, *Thunderbirds* and *Monty Python*, he started making films at the age of nine after he was given a Super 8 camera by a family friend. The results were a string of homemade Minotaur movies. Jackson's early films revel in special effects and DIY gore, often fashioned by his own hand. He lists Tom Savini—the special cosmetic effects artist of *Dawn of the Dead*—among his early influences.

Jackson had no formal training in film, but learned his craft in the doing. His first feature, *Bad Taste*, began life as a short film shot at weekends but gradually expanded. It grew over a period of four years into a full-length 35mm feature. *Bad Taste* can be described as a sci-fi splatter comedy: Aliens invade the small New Zealand town of Kaihoro to harvest humans for their intergalactic fast food franchise. The town is defended by a four-man army, Frank, Ozzy, Barry and Derek. Their unconventional military tactics include exploding sheep with a rocket launcher and alien dismemberment by chainsaw. Early in the film, Derek (played by Jackson) finds his own brain leaking from his skull after a head injury and he resorts to increasingly desperate measures to hold it in. When a hat doesn't work he tries a belt, and when that fails, he stuffs part of an alien's brain into his head to make up for what he's lost of his own.

The late 1980s was a watershed time for New Zealand film, with directors Geoff Murphy (*Goodbye Pork Pie* [1981], *Young Guns 2* [1990], *Free Jack* [1992]) and Vincent Ward (*The Navigator* [1988], *Map of the Human Heart* [1992], *What Dreams May Come*, [1998]) appearing on the national and international stage. *Bad Taste* caught the attention of the New Zealand Film Commission, who gave Jackson the funds to complete the film and send it to festivals—including Cannes—where it became an instant cult success.

After *Bad Taste*, Jackson began work, with Fran Walsh, Stephen Sinclair and Danny Mulheron, on a series of scripts including a sequel to *A Nightmare on Elm Street* (1984) and the screenplay to what would eventually become *Dead Alive*. When the finances for Jackson's proposed zombie movie fell through at the last minute, he set out to make a short film for television entitled *Meet the Feebles*. It was at first envisaged as a Muppet-style musical comedy, but Jackson quickly expanded the idea to feature length after he found a group of Japanese investors who evidently shared his bizarre sense of humor. The finished film has been accurately described as "Sex, Drugs and Soft Toys."

Meet the Feebles is the behind-the-scenes story of a theatrical troupe (the titular Feebles) and their backstage antics as they prepare for a live TV show that might make them rich and famous. They are a badly behaved bunch, indulging in vice, pornography and illicit sex. In many ways they are the Muppets' dark alter egos, with Heidi, the hippo, for example, taking the part of Miss Piggy. Only Miss Piggy doesn't actually have sex with Kermit the Frog, the way Heidi does with her love rat boyfriend Bletch in *Meet the Feebles*. And after Bletch does the dirty on Heidi with another Feeble, Heidi seeks solace in a giant chocolate cake that causes the hippo such flatulence that she lays waste to the television studio with her explosive wind. Other transgressive highlights include projectile vomiting by Harry the rabbit, suffering from a suspected STD. Critics called the film "disgustingly graphic, obscenely offbeat and caustically funny."[2] Jackson was clearly a filmmaker adept at using shock tactics. "You are showing something so extreme as to be ridiculous, that can't help but make people laugh,"[3] he has said of his work.

Extreme is certainly the word to describe Jackson's next film. After the financial success of *Meet the Feebles*, Jackson returned to *Dead Alive*, rewriting the script to top the shock value of his previous works. In *Dead Alive*, heads and arms are ripped off, flesh is torn from bone, zombie babies are liquidized, a reanimated human digestive system complete with farting rectum goes on the rampage, and hordes of the living dead are chopped to pieces by a lawnmower. The overall effect is akin to the absurd humor of Monty Python taken to bloody extremes. "I couldn't make a horror movie that scares people because I just can't take them seriously," Jackson said in 1988. "I find them hilarious."[4] Philip Brophy's term "horrality"[5] (the combination of horror, textuality, morality and hilarity) is wholly appropriate in relation to *Dead Alive*. Lampooning the splatter conventions of the zombie film to the umpteenth degree, the splatstick gags are both horrible and hilarious, eliciting a combined response of shock, disbelief, disgust and laughter, and there is political meaning to the film.

By *Dead Alive*, a theme was starting to emerge in Jackson's work: that of using outrageous shock and bad taste to strike out at the parochialism that had dogged his childhood in small town New Zealand. Set in 1957 Wellington, the film's timid hero Lionel (Timothy Balme) battles his domineering mother when he falls in love with the Hispanic shopkeeper's daughter, Paquita (Diana Peñalva). When the mother is bitten by a Sumatran Rat Monkey during a trip to the zoo, she succumbs to zombie contamination and is soon infecting everyone with the disease. Lionel is forced to take desperate measures to keep his monstrous mother—and the ever-growing band of her zombie victims—hidden away from prying eyes, locking them all in the cellar of his house, along with his other dirty secrets.

Dead Alive begins with a closeup of the New Zealand flag and then cuts to a shot of Queen Elizabeth riding a horse, with the British National Anthem playing in the background. It ends with Lionel's zombie mother—another monstrous matriarch—literally trying to stuff her son back into her uterus. What is Jackson saying about New Zealand under the British monarchy, you might wonder?

A gore-splattered Lionel Cosgrove (Timothy Balme) fights off the zombie hordes in *Dead Alive* aka *Braindead* (1992).

After the success of his "bad taste" trilogy, Jackson began to move in a different direction, away from the sick but funny splatter approach towards more serious subject matter. *Heavenly Creatures* (1994) was based on the true case of Pauline Parker and Juliet Hume, teenagers who committed murder as a result of the close, obsessive relationship they shared. Jackson surprised critics by eschewing the shock approach of his earlier films to present a more mature side as a filmmaker. *Heavenly Creatures* is above all a compassionate tale of two girls lost in a fantasy world of their own devising, created as a means of escaping the oppressive parochialism of their lives in 1950s Christchurch, New Zealand. Avoiding the sensational real-life aspects of the story, which the press at the time had exploited in their headlines about "school girl lesbian killers," Jackson instead tried to illustrate their inner lives of fantasy and magic, and he spent a year immersing himself in the girls' diaries and stories. In some ways *Heavenly Creatures* is a forerunner to *The Lovely Bones* (2009) in its portrayal of innocence corrupted and children trapped between patriarchy, parochialism and a fantasy world—themes, nonetheless, developed by Jackson during his splatstick phase.

"What's in the basket?": Frank Henenlotter

Unlike Peter Jackson, who eventually moved away from comedy-horror into fantasy and drama, Frank Henenlotter has remained true to his splatstick roots, repeatedly drawn to its potential for shock and subversion. As Donato Totaro has noted:

Henenlotter expresses a unique and, for some, uneasy blend of social conscience and exploitation cinema in the three *Basket Case* films (treatment of physical deformity), *Brain Damage* (substance addiction) and *Frankenhooker* (a feminist twist on the Frankenstein story).[6]

Filmed in 1981 on a budget of $35,000 as an extension of the backyard 16mm horror-exploitation home movies that he had been making since he was a teenager, the first *Basket Case* movie became an immediate cult hit following sellout midnight movie screenings in New York, taking its director completely by surprise and leaving him more than a little exasperated. It was conceived as a love letter to the grindhouse movie theaters of 42nd Street, Henenlotter's "second home" since the age of 15. Henenlotter originally thought his debut feature would play a couple of weeks in Times Square and then sink without a trace. But, in retrospect, it is not hard to see why the film became a massive hit on the midnight movie circuit and later on home video. Similar in theme to previous midnight movie greats *Freaks* and *Eraserhead* (1976), *Basket Case* is a celebration of freakishness and transgression—essential viewing for counterculture audiences of the late 1970s and early 1980s.

It is essentially the tale of a young man who is ultimately destroyed by his "dark half." One is tempted to read an element of autobiography into *Basket Case*: Duane Bradley (Kevin Van Hentenryck), the wide-eyed slightly goofy innocent, carries his deformed twin brother Belial in a basket through Times Square in much the same way that the teenage Henenlotter (who grew up in the clean environs of Long Island) carried around his love of exploitation movies. Duane and his brother are in hiding from the uncaring world that sought to separate them and consign the deformed Belial to the garbage. Their father's fear and hatred of their abnormality is aided and abetted by the medical establishment on whom Duane and Belial seek bloody revenge. The "what's in the basket?" refrain subsequently carries on this theme of betrayal: Those who open the basket to see what's inside rarely do so out of simple curiosity, but usually with the intention of stealing the contents. Duane and Belial are alone in the grim New York underworld of prostitutes and drug dealers with only each other. The women they meet are kind—like the matronly aunt who brought them up after the death of their father—but bring with them the threat of coming between Duane and his Siamese twin. (Separation as motif is even carried through to the killing of the various villains: Belial literally tears them in two.)

Sexual jealousy rears its ugly head when Duane falls for receptionist Sharon (Terri Susan Smith) and here *Basket Case* takes a turn into the dark and disturbing. Belial's sexual perversity gives the film a transgressive undercurrent that makes it more than just a bad taste romp and paves the way for Henenlotter's later *Frankenhooker* (1990) and *Bad Biology* (2008).

In *Basket Case,* Belial can be seen as the id, the dark side within us all. Duane is the eternal misfit who carries his monster—his darkness—around in a basket, afraid to let it out for fear of transgression. "Something we all fantasize about doing," the movie's star

"What's in the basket?" Belial, the deformed Siamese twin in *Basket Case* (1982).

Kevin Van Hentenryck comments, "but in the culture we've built for ourselves it's really impossible."[7] It is a powerful metaphor in the film, made all the more so by Henenlotter's ambivalence: In his films, transgression inevitably brings with it self-destruction.

Henenlotter's own cocaine addiction inspired the theme for his next film *Brain Damage* (1989), in which Brian (Rick Hearst) sees his life begin to fall apart when a brain-eating parasite called Aylmer attaches itself to him. In return for secreting a highly addictive but pleasurable hallucinogenic fluid into his brain, Brian has to supply Aylmer with victims, becoming an accomplice to murder in the process. The film is about the joys and perils of addiction, in whatever form that may take. "This is the start of your new life," Aylmer promises Brian at the start of their liaison, "a life without worry or pain or loneliness." The fact that Brian's life is already good at the start—he is affluent, with a good job, an apartment on the Lower East Side and a girlfriend—speaks to the hedonistic appeal of cocaine to young people like Brian during the late 1980s. By the end of *Brain Damage*, however, as befits a movie with an anti-drugs message (*The Man with the Golden Arm* [1955] comes to mind as an obvious influence on the film), Brian has hit bottom and is desperately trying to go cold turkey, which proves far from easy.

Henenlotter's tropes—which come to the fore in *Brain Damage*—involve a kind of 42nd Street surrealism, often including bizarre Svankmajer-esque stop frame animation, dream sequences, bodily transformation and gooey mutant sex. Here, the jerky stop motion puppetry of *Basket Case*, deliberately bad in that film, is used to create the penis-like Aylmer, which at one point emerges from Brian's trousers to enter his girlfriend's brain via her mouth; during a nightmare, Brian imagines his ear spurting blood as Aylmer attempts to fuse with him permanently; and in a romantic restaurant, meatballs and spaghetti on Brian's plate turn into pulsating brains. All of this helps make *Brain Damage* one of the most powerfully freakish movies about the highs and lows of drug addiction yet filmed.

After *Brain Damage*, Henenlotter made *Frankenhooker* (1990), in which a medical student, Jeffrey (James Lorinz), transplants the head of his dead girlfriend Elizabeth (Patty Mullen) onto the body of a hooker. In this intriguing reworking of *Bride of Frankenstein*, Henenlotter presents a surprisingly progressive tale which builds on the feminism of both Mary Shelley's original and James Whale's classic. Jeffrey is not prepared for the sexual liberation that the transformation brings as his previously monogamous Elizabeth spurns him in favor of picking up johns on the street. The young lovers are finally reunited, but only after Jeffrey is murdered by a pimp and has his head implanted on the body of a woman, adding a hint of bisexuality to the proceedings. Like the later *Bad Biology*, which picks up the theme of male-female compatibility, *Frankenhooker* is marred only by Henenlotter's occasional tendency towards self-indulgence and overlong sequences.

Basket Case 2 (1990) takes up where the first film left off but is altogether a lighter movie—despite the inevitable mutant sex scenes. Escaping from the hospital, the brothers (who are revealed to have survived the first film) meet up with Granny Ruth (Annie Ross) and are whisked off to live with her and her houseful of similarly adopted freaks. Henenlotter references Tod Browning's classic *Freaks* throughout, subverting normality and freakishness as the freaks in *Basket Case 2* become the heroes and the normals the villains. Belial becomes the more sympathetic of the brothers, falling in love with the mutant Eve, while Duane becomes deranged with jealousy. Things moved towards their logical conclusion in *Basket Case 3* (1992), which sees Belial becomes the proud father of twelve deformed progeny, and the series finally resolves the sibling rivalry between Belial and Duane.

"Exploitation films have an attitude that you don't find with mainstream Hollywood productions," Henenlotter has said. "They're a little ruder, a little raunchier, they deal with material people don't usually touch on, whether it's sex or drugs or rock and roll."[8] Working within exploitation, Henenlotter blends comedy, horror and sex with a delight in breaking cinematic taboo. One of the most shocking sequences in Henenlotter's films is Belial's rape of Sharon in *Basket Case*, a graphic and repellent mix of cold nudity, blood, goo and mutant bodies. Henenlotter's most taboo-breaking film is arguably *Bad Biology,* in which a woman with seven clitorises mates with a man whose monstrous penis has a mind of its own. Made at a time when, in some American states, images of the vagina were routinely censored in high school biology textbooks (as discussed in the next chapter), *Bad Biology* is more than simply a bad taste exercise in biological excess, interrogating as it does continuing taboos surrounding human genitalia and reproduction.

Set in New York's art underground (the protagonist is a photographer), *Bad Biology* references shock art in painting, sculpture, fashion and music, inviting comparisons with the Cinema of Transgression of the 1980s (the shock cinema of Nick Zedd, Lydia Lunch, Richard Kern and Beth B, among others). Zedd proclaimed in that movement's manifesto that "any film which doesn't shock isn't worth looking at."[9] This could indeed be Henenlotter's manifesto too. Like Zedd and his associates, Henenlotter is determined to break all the taboos of our age by "sinning" as much as possible.

"Life, sex and death": Brian Yuzna

Born in the Philippines in 1949, Brian Yuzna was inspired by art during his childhood, claiming an early interest in expressionism and surrealism, "this dream-like experience."[10] The son of a bridge engineer who worked for the United States government, he grew up in Nicaragua, Puerto Rico and Panama before moving with his family to Atlanta, Georgia, in the 1960s. He didn't have television in the Philippines so each Sunday he and his family went to the movies. Films like *Creature with the Atom Brain* (1955) and *The 7th Voyage of Sinbad* (1958) made a lasting impression; Yuzna attributes his interest in horror to this early viewing of fantasy and horror and to his Catholic upbringing which "is all about the transformative properties of the flesh."[11] At college in the States he majored in the phenomenology of religion and later studied art. He thought he might become a painter, moving briefly to Soho, but decided it wasn't for him: "it's too much about trying to get your friends to think you are God."[12]

A child of the 1960s, he spent most of his twenties living in hippie communes in North Carolina, where to make ends meet he sold his paintings, worked as a carpenter and also ran a restaurant. "At that time there was this idea about tune in, turn on, drop out. So I did that," he remembers, admitting that he had "not prepared at all for any sort of life."[13] He started making short experimental films with a 16mm Bolex camera; one particular amateur short grew into a ninety-minute feature. At that point, 1982, he married and deciding that filmmaking was his true vocation, Yuzna moved to Hollywood and set himself up as a producer. He put an ad in *Variety* saying he was looking for a director.

Exploitation movie legend Charles Band introduced him to Stuart Gordon, the artistic director of the Organic Theatre Company in Chicago (whose membership, incidentally, included Michael Rooker). Gordon had adapted H.P. Lovecraft's story "Herbert West—Reanimator" into a script for television. Yuzna liked the script and offered to produce, helping Gordon to develop the fifty-page treatment into a full-length feature. *Re-animator* (1985) is a film that Yuzna still regards as one of his most successful: Its slyly subversive anti-authority stance is in perfect keeping with the satirical sensibilities of Gordon and Yuzna. They followed it up with a second Lovecraft adaptation, *From Beyond* (1986), again directed by Gordon and produced and co-written by Yuzna. Although not as well-received, *From Beyond* remains an intriguing if slightly incoherent mix of Lovecraft, splatter horror, bizarre S&M and extreme bodily transformation. Yuzna and Gordon went on to make the subsequent Lovecraft adaptation *Dagon* (2001) as well as collaborating on the Yuzna-directed *Progeny* (1999) and the mainstream children's hit *Honey, I Shrunk the Kids* (1989), which Yuzna and Gordon co-wrote with Ed Naha.

In 1989, Yuzna made his directorial debut with *Society*, a class-conscious body horror in which the rich literally feed off the poor. Since then, as a producer-director-writer Yuzna has been prolific: He directed the *Re-animator* sequel *Bride of Re-animator* in 1990, followed by *Initiation, Return of the Living Dead 3, The Dentist, Progeny, The Dentist 2, Faust: Love of the Damned* (2000), a further *Re-animator* sequel called *Beyond Re-animator* (2003), *Rottweiler* (2004), *Beneath Still Waters* (2005) and *Amphibious* (2010). In addition Yuzna has produced and executive-produced films by Steve Miner (*Warlock* [1989]), Screaming Mad George (*The Guyver* [1991]), Tony Randel (*Infested* [1993]), Christophe Gans (*Crying Freedom* [1995]) and Jack Sholder (*Arachnid* [2011]), among others.

"As a former hippie," Yuzna told Emiliano Carpineta in 2006, "the idea of politics as being not only important but entertaining and inextricably linked to art was a part of my mentality."[14] In *Re-animator* we can already see the splatstick themes that Yuzna would develop in his later films. There is the portrayal of authority as depraved and corrupt, as personified by the villainous Dr. Hill (David Gale), who claims Herbert West's (Jeffrey Combs) discovery of a serum that can re-animate the dead as his own, despite the protests of West and the film's hero, lowly medical student Dan Cain (Bruce Abbott). Yuzna's anti-authority feeling, like those of his contemporaries, stems from his experiences in the 1960s, from demonstrating against the Vietnam War and belonging to the counterculture. In Yuzna's case, living an alternate lifestyle colored his beliefs: As a hippie he "thought the revolution was coming and we'd never have to work," that "theoretically, everything was going to change."[15] In Yuzna's film, patriarchal authority in all of its forms is open to question, whether it be the military (*Return of the Living Dead 3*), men's control of women's bodies (*Bride of Re-animator, Initiation, Progeny*) or masculinity itself (*The Dentist, The Dentist 2*); and his work is underscored by a strong current of feminism. Yuzna's films also display a developed class-consciousness colored by 1960s radicalism, as in *Society*. He sees capitalist society as a hidden oligarchy in which the majority of wealth is kept by a small minority of rich families while the poor are exploited and "fed upon." He has described the economic political system in perpetuating this as degenerate. "You've got to be paying something off to plug you into the system," he observes of the huge debts from medical insurance and college fees that most people have to service in order simply to take part in society, while the wealthy few retain political and economic control.[16]

Sex and death are important aspects of the horror film for Yuzna and we can already see this in *Re-animator*. For example, when Dr. Hill is decapitated by West and subsequently re-animated as a headless corpse, the corrupt and depraved Hill finally acts out his lustful obsession for Cain's girlfriend Megan (Barbara Crampton); abducting her and subjecting her to the sexual advances of his own disembodied head. This sequence was not in Gordon's original script; it was Yuzna who helped develop these aspects of the film: "I think if you try to take away sex and death from a horror movie, you don't have a horror movie."[17] Like

Herman Cohen, Yuzna identifies horror movies with a teenage audience because adolescence is when sex and death appear to us. In *Return of the Living Dead 3*, teenage protagonist Curt (J. Trevor Edmond) has a poster on his wall that says "Life, Sex + Death" and the film explores this triangulation throughout, ultimately reformulating it to Sex + Death = Life, as it is only in death that Curt and his girlfriend Julie (Mindy Clarke) become fully "alive."

The gory climax of *Re-animator*, which almost tops Peter Jackson's *Dead Alive* in terms of its extreme splatter, contains a strong element of carnivalesque: the "big, transgressive, crazy, orgiastic type scenes"[18] that would feature in all of Yuzna's future work including *Society, Initiation, Progeny, Return of the Living Dead 3* and *The Dentist* as well as *Bride of Re-animator* (in which the sympathetic "monstrous-feminine" Bride is climactically torn apart). Again, this was not in Gordon's original script but suggested by Yuzna, who felt the film needed more in the way of "real transgressive, bad sexuality."[19] These elements of Yuzna's films are akin to the Bacchanalia, the wild drunken orgies of ancient Rome. Interestingly, Yuzna traces the inclusion of such scenes in his own films to the influence of watching movies like *Ben-Hur* (1959) and *The Ten Commandments* (1956) as a child, the latter of which contains an "incredible orgy scene."[20]

Finally, in *Re-animator*, as in all of Yuzna's subsequent work, there is a fascination with bodily transformation and its political implications. *Re-animator* ends with the death of Megan, who is simultaneously the daughter of the dean of the medical school, the girlfriend of the hero Dan Cain, and the object of Hill's lust. She is injected with the reagent at the end, suggesting the possibility of transformation from male love object to something more. This raises questions about the future of her relationship with Dan Cain, which until now has followed fairly traditional gender patterns. The theme of bodily transformation as something potentially liberating to women would feature prominently in *Initiation, Progeny* and *Return of the Living Dead 3*; in each of these films bodily transformation brings liberation from patriarchy, a release of sexual power and a stronger sense of identity—opportunity to transcend the confines imposed by society.

Yuzna traces this interest in bodily transformation to his early Roman Catholicism, where transcendental belief in the flesh is embodied by the doctrine of transubstantiation—the idea of the Eucharist literally transforming into the blood and flesh of Christ. However, Yuzna also recognizes that there is a cultural fascination with transformation within modern secular society. "It could be a kind of symbol of our own psychology," he told Dejan Ognjanovic in 2008. "We all want to transform into something else."[21] It follows that the yearning for transformation in Yuzna's films is psychological and spiritual but rooted in the material. "This is what we try to express upon the physical flesh. And if you're a Westerner then you believe in the flesh.... So, if we

Julie (Mindy Clarke) is transformed into an S&M zombie in *Return of the Living Dead 3* (1993).

want to be free we have to transform the flesh."[22] In this way, Yuzna's narratives both reflect and critique the materialistic 1990s where happiness and fulfillment were sought through transformation by material means, including through cosmetic surgery and body adornment. For Yuzna, such transformation has political ramifications, as it represents changes in the balance of power between individuals and within society as a whole. The political aspects of body morphing are explored in *Society*.

"Feed the rich": *Society*

Society developed from Yuzna's satirical ideas about class and breeding. "One of the reasons the upper classes fail is because the gene pool gets too limited," Yuzna has said. "They need to spike the breed with the lower classes which is the same way they breed dogs, spike the breed with a mongel."[23] In *Society* the "mongrel" is Bill Whitney (Billy Warlock), who lives with his family in the wealth and splendor of Beverly Hills. Despite a life of privilege and popularity, Bill feels that he does not fit in with his family and begins to see them as increasingly sinister; he believes himself adopted and harbors incestuous feelings for his sister Jenny (Patrice Jennings). His paranoia turns out to be justified when he discovers that his family and their society friends belong to another race altogether, of decadent rich shape-shifters who feed off the poor in a body-melding process called "shunting." Worse yet, Bill is being nurtured as their next victim.

Society is one of several late 1980s films which portray America's fashionable, wealthy and influential elite as a race of aliens or monstrous parasites that leech off the lower classes while keeping their alien nature hidden. John Carpenter's *They Live* (1988) depicts those in authority as alien invaders controlling human affairs by the means of subliminal messaging; only by wearing special glasses is one able to see the "truth." Bob Balaban's *Parents* (1989), a variation of the theme, depicts the perfect suburban parents of the title feeding their increasingly suspicious son human meat. At the heart of these films seems to be the Marxist notion of false consciousness, that people are unable to see things—exploitation, oppression and social relations—as they really are because their world view is imposed upon them by the ruling classes. In *Society*, Bill becomes politically aware: He begins to see the true nature of privilege, and fights against it, in the end managing to free himself from the clutches of his wealthy but corrupt and depraved parents.

Yuzna draws on science fiction tropes in *Society* (a genre he considers especially political), particularly the paranoid scenarios of *Invasion of the Body Snatchers* and *Invaders from Mars*. The narrative is revealed through Bill's growing paranoia about his family (memorably depicted in an early scene in which his sister appears to mutate before his eyes). As Yuzna has noted, "The basis of the paranoia [in *Society*] was the unease of someone born into privilege."[24] The film's early sequences establish the materialism of the Beverly Hills lifestyle. Bill has his own Jeep Wrangler. His sister Jenny has a closet filled with expensive clothes. They live in a mansion. Bill and his girlfriend spend most of their time on the beach getting suntanned. Bill's parents constantly attend society dinners and fundraisers. Jenny is preparing for her "coming out," her formal entry into the society of the film's title. However, despite his wealth and privilege, Bill feels alienated. He tells his analyst Dr. Cleveland (Ben Slack) that he is afraid that "if I scratch the surface, there'll be something underneath." He has nightmares in which the mansion becomes alien and threatening. Gradually he begins to suspect that his family is not what they appear to be and is involved in some kind of conspiracy. The linchpin to this comes in the form of an audio recording of his parents and sister taking part in what seems to be an incestuous orgy, in which his father is heard to say, "First we dine, then we copulate."

Despite the SF tropes, Yuzna is careful within the film to emphasize that the society of the film's title is made up not of "alien scum" as Bill assumes, but instead that it is something that comes from within the Earth. The mutant rich have evolved alongside the human lower classes throughout history as natural rulers, with a "lineage that goes back to Julius Caesar." *Society* builds to this reveal with an extraordinary, justly celebrated final sequence in which the slimy leech-like society transforms and mutates as it feeds upon its victims. The sequence is splatstick at its most subversive. For these sequences, Yuzna draws directly on surrealism, particularly the paintings of Salvador Dali, to give form to the idea that the ruling classes inter-breed with the lower classes in order to prevent the gene-pool from getting too limited. The "shunting" sequences are big, transgressive, crazy and orgiastic and have the feel of Bacchanalia, depicting the act of shunting as akin to a decadent Roman orgy. At the same time, the participants are shown to appear and act like slugs, which according to Yuzna "have orgies. They're all kind of bisexual. When slugs have sex, they all sort of clump together."[25] A further aspect of the shunting is to reveal Bill's family in the grotesque, repulsive and debauched form that he really sees them. His mother and sister become melded together in one incestuous body, and his father becomes a literal "butt-face"—his face melding with a pair of buttocks.

Bill manages to escape being shunted himself, but the film makes it clear that, with its members already in Washington, society will continue. However, the suggestion is made that Bill will continue his fight against them by raising the political consciousness of his friends and peers. Earlier in the film we saw Billy running for college president, and he has already addressed the student audience during a debate with the news of a society that kills to keep its existence secret. *They Live* concludes in a similar manner: with the false consciousness of the human population lifted after the alien television transmitter is destroyed. *Society* remains equally outrageous and subversive in its treatment of class and the nature of material wealth.

Become Who You Are: *Initiation* and *Return of the Living Dead 3*

"You're one of us now," Fima (Maud Adams) tells Kim Levitt (Neith Hunter) in *Initiation*. "You're free of men and the parasite of fear that they bring us." The parasite in question is a gloopy Cronenberg-esque larva that Kim has possibly hallucinated since being drugged by a coven of witches who want to initiate her as one of their own. Like Cronenberg's parasite in *Shivers*, it is a literalism; as Fima explains, "You gave form to the fear inside you—you created these things from the power of magic within you."

While *Society* was about the material excesses of the 1980s and '90s, *Initiation* is about spirituality, feminism and the yearning for transcendence. Kim, an aspiring journalist, becomes entangled with the witches while investigating the death of Lilith, a girl who appears to have spontaneously combusted on a Los Angeles rooftop. The witch cult wants to transform Kim into Lilith—Fima's daughter—who was consumed in flames after her initiation by the cult. To prevent the same thing happening to her, Kim must complete her own initiation by killing a male.

Initiation presents two covens: the sealed-off men's club of the newspaper, a chauvinist workplace that excludes Kim and denies her opportunity, and the secret coven of men-hating witches who are equally concerned with power and want to initiate Kim as one of their own. Without her boss Eli's permission, Kim decides to follow the news story of Lilith's apparent suicide, which means going it alone and in secret. Her gesture of self-reliance is predictably taken as a betrayal, both by Eli and by her boyfriend Hank, who also works for the newspaper and seems to get all the breaks. "I'm ready for a change," Kim tells the coven during a picnic. Like Julie in *Return of the Living Dead 3* and Sherry (Jillian McWhirter) in *Progeny*, Kim is torn between her old existence as exploited female and her new one as initiate witch, with neither option satisfactory. The viewer longs for the coven to represent a truly progressive pathway (there are hints of lesbianism between Kim and Fima) but Yuzna seems to be warning against the opportunist powermongers who use radical causes to serve their own ends.

Initiation ends with Kim refusing to sacrifice Hank's little brother Lonnie to the cult, thereby not completing her initiation. The ensuing fire is revealed to be Fima's punitive power, which Kim turns back on the head witch, destroying her. Kim ultimately becomes "herself," freed of fear and wise to the chauvinism of men, but also willing to reject the men-hatred of the witches.

As Donato Totaro has suggested, the influence of Roman Polanski's *Rosemary's Baby* (1968) can be seen in many of Yuzna's films and *Initiation* is no exception.[26] Like *Society*, *Initiation* teems with the same paranoia and conspiracy as Polanski's film. The feminist subtext of *Rosemary's Baby* is also present in *Initiation*: Kim, like Rosemary (Mia Farrow), is subject to the controlling influences of others and has to reject those influences in order to find her own way. The body horror aspects of *Rosemary's Baby* in the 1960s paved the way for Cronenberg the following decade, and Cronenberg's influence on Yuzna has already been noted. The giant larva in *Initiation* gives flesh to Yuzna's ideas in a very Cronenbergian way while also playing to the body horror shock content inherent in the splatter film. The central shock sequence in *Initiation* sees the larva placed on Kim's bare stomach; it crawls under her skin and up inside her body, eventually emerging from her mouth as a giant cockroach. It is a sequence highly reminiscent of *The Fly* (1986) but with an incipient feminist sensibility largely absent in Cronenberg (with the exception, perhaps, of *Rabid* [1977]). In this way, it is possible to see Yuzna's work in the 1990s, particularly *Initiation* and *Return of the Living Dead 3*, as paving the way for the fully developed feminist body horror of *Teeth* (2008) and *American Mary* (2012), as discussed in the next chapter.

Initiation develops ideas of sexual rebirth into freedom. Yuzna based the script on the Biblical story of Lilith, Adam's wife before Eve, whom Adam rejected after she rebelled against him. "We tried to take the central female character through Lilith," Yuzna has stated.[27] The film opens with Kim having sex in a seedy hotel room, watching porn with Hank, a situation that she is not entirely comfortable with but agrees to in order to keep the man happy. Eventually, like Lilith, she rebels against the expectations placed upon her by a male society. Yuzna makes use of what he terms "simulacra" in the film, as projections of Kim's inner self (seen in images in trees and pictures of flames in spaghetti) force Kim to see her future transformation into "Lilith." She undergoes a literal rebirth when she finds herself breaking out of a larva cocoon; a fire later starts to engulf her legs. Finally she transforms both physically and spiritually and gains, in Yuzna's words, "the power of sex. So she's free, sexually."[28]

"The thing about *Initiation* for me is that it isn't well done formally speaking," Yuzna told Donato Totaro in 1999. "It's sort of sloppy. But what I really liked about it is that it really starts with these ideas and tries to give flesh to them."[29] Yuzna was to develop these ideas, arguably more successfully, in *Return of the Living Dead 3*. He approaches the film as a simple Romeo and Juliet story and imbues it with a truthfulness rare in B movie exploitation. Young lovers Curt and Julie break into a military establishment run by Curt's father, Colonel Reynolds (Kent McCord), where they discover that a chemical toxin is being used to bring corpses back to life as weapons. After a motorcycle accident in which Julie is killed, Curt returns to the military base and re-animates her corpse. They go on the run, but Julie begins to crave human flesh. To prevent herself from harming Curt, she adorns herself with S&M piercings and scars to cause herself pain. Eventually Curt and Julie are captured by the army and Julie is to be turned into a weapon like the other zombies. Curt and Julie are reunited when Curt frees all the zombies in the base, but is himself bitten in the process.

"It's a way of making identity," Yuzna commented on Julie's piercing and scarification in the film. "When somebody is piercing themselves or tattooing themselves, they're trying to make an identity. And I think S&M type activities also are very much about identity."[30] Julie in *Return of the Living Dead 3* is one of Yuzna's strong women. Like Kim in *Initiation* and Megan in *Re-animator* she lives in the shadow of men, conforming to their idea of how she should be. Although Curt loves her and she him, her sexual power is stifled within the relationship; we see glimpses of it early in the film when, aroused by the danger and excitement, she licks her credit card sensually before they use it to break into the military base and later, when they escape on the motorbike, as she grabs Curt's crotch, causing him to lose control of the bike.

After Julie is re-animated, the film very carefully takes us through the various stages that Julie goes through in dealing with her new identity as a zombie and realizing that she has changed. At first she is disgusted by herself, by what she has become and by her need for human flesh. She knows that Curt is disgusted also, but it is only when he voices his disgust that Julie takes action to transform herself fully, to release the sexuality that was stifled when she was alive. In the film's celebrated central sequence, Julie pierces and scarifies herself, and in doing so she comes to express her true sexual identity. "The pain," as she informs Curt, "makes the hunger go away." Here the "hunger" can be read as the emptiness caused by repression of her full sexuality and therefore of her true identity. Paradoxically it is only as a zombie that Julie becomes fully "alive," offering as it does the fullest possibilities of her expressing her sexuality, the possibility to become who she really "is." Confronted by this truth, Curt is forced to reassess the way he sees Julie. He comes to accept the true Julie, not the Julie he thought she was and thought he wanted her to be. Finally, at the climax, he chooses her above his conformist military father and the two perish together in a conflagration at the military base.

In *Return of the Living Dead 3* Yuzna creates in Julie a genuinely progressive monstrous-feminine, based on transgressive female sexuality. Julie is never anything less than completely sympathetic. Moreover, her relationship with Curt is credible: two young lovers who are in danger of one "outgrowing" the other, but who eventually learn to change with each other. It is the most powerful transformation narrative that Yuzna has yet filmed, fully expressing the spiritual, political and physical aspects of his cinema, dovetailed into a love story that has genuine feeling.

"The stench of decay": *The Dentist* and *The Dentist 2*

After *Return of the Living Dead 3*, Yuzna directed *The Dentist*, a biting satire of materialistic 1990s values, and a supreme piece of splatstick. Dr. Alan Feinstone (Corbin Bernsen) is the titular Beverly Hills dentist who appears to have every material success: the thriving practice, the 90210 mansion, the trophy wife. But when he discovers said wife, Brooke (Linda Hoffman), having sex with the pool cleaner, he snaps. The constant strain of maintaining a "veneer" sends him over the edge and he becomes homicidal: subjecting patients, enemies (including the IRS) and his treacherous wife to horrific surgical torture and mutilation. The film is reputedly based on a real-life case of a serial killer–dentist called Nick Rex, but Yuzna uses the film's premise to poke fun at the materialistic lifestyle of Beverly Hills surgeons and the neurotic need to create and maintain wealth. We are drawn into Feinstone's obsessive-compulsions and his subsequent spiral into paranoia and psychosis.

"I had a beautiful wife. We had a beautiful home. We had a perfect life together. But underneath that clean, white surface there was the stench of decay…" So begins Feinstone's voiceover narration that opens *The Dentist*. We are immediately introduced to the uptight, obsessive, controlling Feinstone, who is fixated on orderliness and cleanliness. He lives in an idealized world of his own making, one based on surface gloss and materialistic values. In his mind, tooth decay symbolizes his worst fears: that his world is subject to constant maintenance and if he does not remain in control, it will all "rot away."

His perfect life with Brooke is revealed early on to be merely a façade. In a brief but telling moment, when Brooke hangs up after speaking to Feinstone on the telephone, she mutters, "Asshole"; Yuzna then immediately cuts to Feinstone hanging up the phone on his end, murmuring, "Bitch." Husband and wife secretly despise each other and their marriage is nothing more than a business arrangement. Later, Feinstone muses to himself, "If I kick her out, she'll take everything." Feinstone is threatened by his wife's affair, not because of her emotional betrayal but because his masculinity (which is based on material success) is affronted. *The Dentist* and *The Dentist 2* are reminiscent of the Bunuel of *El* (1953) in their portrayal of machismo gone insane. As Feinstone extracts his wife's teeth in an act of revenge, "Tristan and Isolde" plays in the background, and one is reminded of the jealous revenge that Bunuel's macho men exact upon their women and the absurdity of doing so. "I am an instrument of perfection and hygiene," Feinstone declares after slashing his wife's lover to death, "the enemy of decay and corruption—a dentist!" Unhinged

In *The Dentist* (1996), Dr. Alan Feinstone (Corbin Bernsen) is driven insane by his obsession with order and cleanliness.

completely by the end of the film and plagued by visions of rotting teeth, Feinstone ends up in a psychiatric hospital where he is doomed to suffer endless hallucinations of his wife torturing him in the hospital's dentist chair.

Yuzna takes ondontophobia (and its underlying Freudian associations) to extremes in *The Dentist and The Dentist 2*: Teeth are drilled and pulled out; tongues sliced off; a man's jaw is cracked wide open with retractors; pliers and power drills are used in place of surgical equipment. Like all of Yuzna's films, *The Dentist* at times fails to transcend its B-movie origins: Feinstone's lapse into homicidal mania is too abrupt and the schlock elements are sometimes too prominent. However, despite its faults, *The Dentist* is an insightful look at male neurosis and its relation to ego and the desire for material possessions, money and self-achievement, made during a time when materialistic values in America seemed to reach a peak.

The Dentist 2 sees Feinstone escape the psychiatric hospital and flee to his hometown of Paradise, Missouri, in search of "honest people and clean living." He rents a cottage from Jamie (Jillian McWhirter), who bears more than a passing resemblance to Feinstone's wife Brooke, and it seems as though the doctor might make a new start now that he is returning to his roots and "fleeing a dream in search of a new reality." (He accepts that his previous life and marriage were based solely on material needs, remarking satirically, "We were the perfect couple for the perfect dinner party.") However, Feinstone's grip on reality is tenuous and when he loses a cap on his tooth, a visit to the town's inept dentist threatens to send him back into his psychosis.

Like Julie in *Return of the Living Dead 3*, Feinstone in *The Dentist 2* has to resort to self-mutilation to prevent himself from hurting those he cares about, in this case Jamie, with whom he has fallen in love (she reminds him of Brooke when they first met, before the "rot" set in). The pain of the flesh is necessary to prevent wrongdoing. From there Yuzna develops the theme of man's distrust of woman—his anger and uncontrollable jealousy—satirizing male attitudes to an absurd degree as Brooke transforms into Jamie in Feinstone's mind: Feinstone's insane distrust extends to all women. Alan Howarth's score reprises Bernard Herrmann's *Vertigo* (1958). Feinstone cannot help but slip back into his old ways: Like Scott Ferguson (James Stewart) in Hitchcock's classic he is damned by his own obsessions and compulsions. At the film's climax, he must face down both Jamie and Brooke (who brandishes a nail gun against him). The film ends memo-

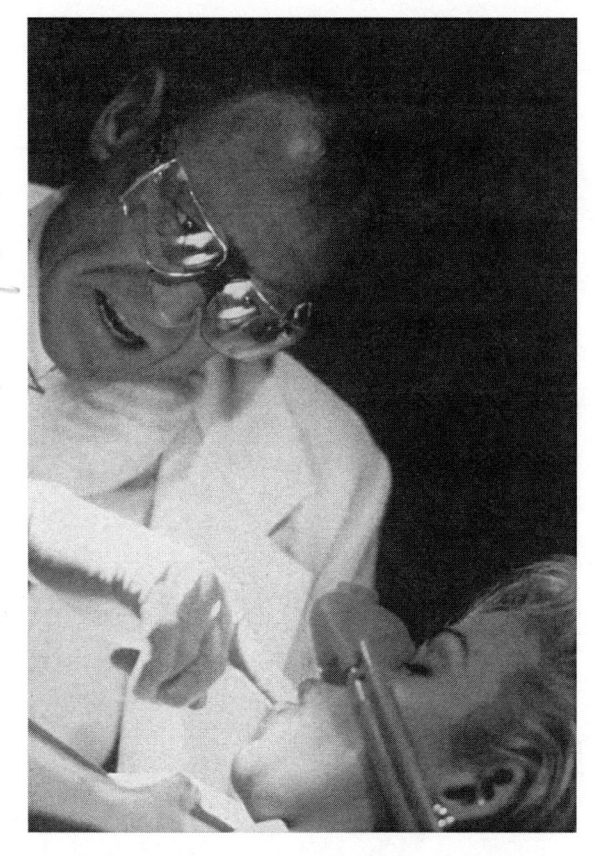

The unhinged Dr. Alan Feinstone (Corbin Bernsen) molests beauty queen April Reign (Christa Sauls) in *The Dentist* (1996).

rably: Feinstone escapes but not completely unscathed, and as he drives away with a headful of nails, he laughs uproariously at the absurdity of his predicament.

* * *

As the 1990s went on, splatstick petered out. In retrospect, it shares characteristics with another short-lived cycle within the horror genre, the youth horror films of the 1950s such as those produced by Herman Cohen and AIP (as discussed in Chapter 3). Like those movies, splatstick catered to a youth-orientated B-movie audience. Gradually in the 1990s, B movies became A movies. The tropes of cheap science fiction and horror—gore and nudity—were appropriated into larger-budget Hollywood product but without the transgressive element.

Moreover, splatstick appealed to an early 1990s youth audience keen to dissociate itself from the materialistic values of the "me" generation, seeking alternatives within art, music and film. The re-emergence of splatstick in Japan in the mid–2000s speaks to its transgressive, anti-materialistic, non-conformist, even feminist potential. Crucially, the legacy of splatstick in terms of its body mutations and transformations and its strong element of social satire can be seen in the recent body-horror satire of *Ginger Snaps* (2000), *Teeth, Jennifer's Body* (2009) and *American Mary*.

10

ANTI-NEW PURITANISM
Teeth (2007) and *American Mary* (2012)

In 2006, the Bush Administration increased funding for abstinence-only education in America, introducing courses to encourage un-married adults to remain abstinent until marriage. Abstinence-only education had expanded throughout the United States since it was first instituted under Reagan in 1981, but had been aimed mainly at teenagers, promoting strict abstinence from sexual behavior until marriage as the sexual norm. The expansion of such programs to include courses for the over–18s can be seen as evidence of a new puritanism that emerged in America in the wave of patriotism and increased conservatism following 9/11: Critics of abstinence-only education, such as the organization SIECUS, have described many such programs as relying on "fear, guilt and shame to try to control young people's sexual behaviour."[1]

Mitchell Lichtenstein's comedy horror shocker *Teeth* addresses themes of sexual conservatism in modern America in the style of black comedy reminiscent of the great American satirists. As an modern American independent film, *Teeth* approaches its subject matter very much in the vein of social satire that has become associated with the work of Todd Solondz, Todd Haynes and Ang Lee. Like Solondz's masterpiece *Happiness* (1998), it is a bleakly funny exposé of societal repression and its effects on the day-to-day life of the individual. But it also subverts the fear of female sexuality that perpetuates the myth of "vagina dentata," exploding taboos about female anatomy and female sexual empowerment along the way, placing it very firmly into the school of subversive horror cinema.

In *Teeth*, the central character, Dawn (Jess Weixler), has a toothed vagina, an anatomical aberration that has made her a stranger to her own body and an active participant in her local chastity group. However, she learns to embrace her uniqueness and the special power that it brings. In *Teeth,* the link is made between the inhibition of sexual knowledge and the persistence of the vagina dentata myth. In so doing, it speaks to the suppression of female sexual empowerment which continues in the United States in the form of the federal abstinence-until-marriage program.

Teeth is one of several recent films to have emerged under the loose umbrella term of new feminist horror, including *Jennifer's Body*, *The Woman* (2011) and *American Mary*, which have used the avenging angel plot motif to tackle themes of female sexual empowerment in subversive ways. These films can be seen as following in the footsteps of 1970s classics such as *Carrie* (1976) and *Rabid* (as well as the splatstick horror of Brian Yuzna and Frank Henenlotter as discussed in the previous chapter) but with a more overt feminism. *American Mary* takes the rape-revenge motif of films such as *I Spit on Your Grave* (1978) and *Ms. 45*

(1981) and locates it within the context of the body modification community. The central character, medical student Mary Mason (Katharine Isabelle), is an outsider within a corrupt patriarchal medical establishment which seeks to exploit and degrade her. Instead she finds a greater sense of belonging among the "sideshow freaks" of the body-mod community for whom she performs illegal body modification surgery. Rejecting the hypocrisy of her teachers and the puritanism of society as a whole, she finds empowerment in controlling her own sexuality and in helping others control theirs. Like Browning's *Freaks*, *American Mary* portrays a false and dangerous normal polite society mirrored by an outwardly freakish subculture that celebrates transgression and looks after its own.

According to critics of George W. Bush, his administration presided over possibly the most far-reaching campaign attacking sexual and reproductive rights for women that has yet been seen in the United States. His attempt to replace contraceptive choice, reproductive freedom and scientific fact with a conservative religious morality constitutes a new puritanism whose effects are still being felt throughout America. The new feminist horror of *Teeth* and *American Mary* can be seen as a direct challenge to these social policies that were part and parcel of the Bush era.

"A very precious gift": *Teeth*

The events of 9/11 gave rise to a wave of patriotism in America and with it a return to traditional family values, including the promotion of no sex before marriage, boosting the number of Christian chastity groups in the United States to record highs. Although Bill Clinton signed the act which resulted in the expansion of abstinence-only education into law, Bush, a fervent Christian, massively increased the funding for these programs. Under the terms of the multi-million dollar fund which Bush made available to schools and groups, sex education had to have the "exclusive purpose" of promoting abstinence. They had to make clear that sex before marriage was harmful, both physically and mentally, and that contraception could only be mentioned in terms of its fallibility.[2]

Critics of these programs were quick to see through the political rhetoric, however, pointing out that there was little evidence that the teenagers who took part in chastity groups actually abstained from intercourse longer and that abstinence-only education in schools did not result in a significant decrease in unwanted teenage pregnancies. Moreover, abstinence-only education, according to these critics, was potentially damaging, particularly to adolescents, denying young people the right to full information and freedom of expression.

Teeth director Mitchell Lichtenstein, while claiming to hold nothing against chastity groups in general, was concerned about the withholding of knowledge from young people. *Teeth* originated when he became aware of the censorship of textbooks by education authorities in places such as in Lynchburg, Virginia, where the school board censored an illustration of a woman's vagina in a high school biology textbook. Whereas the diagram of the penis was considered acceptable by the school board, the inner vagina drawing was deemed a "violation of a woman's natural modesty."[3] "It seemed to me that there was a connection between hiding the female reproductive system and genitalia, and the persistence of the myth of vagina dentata," Lichtenstein stated in his DVD commentary to *Teeth*.[4] Lichtenstein makes the exact nature of that connection explicit in his director's statement: masculine fear.

Teeth is essentially about the journey of its heroine, Dawn, from sexual repression to sexual empowerment, and at its heart is a subversion of the vagina dentata myth which traditionally symbolizes the power relationship between men and women, whereby the male hero must conquer the woman with the toothed vagina and render her powerless. In *Teeth*, by contrast, Dawn comes to see her anatomical uniqueness as a source of power against men who would seek to render her submissive and victimize her. She comes to see it, and not her chastity, as her "very precious gift" in a brutally patriarchal world. Intriguingly, the film suggests that while Dawn may be the first to be blessed with this special power, she may not necessarily be the last, and that her toothed vagina may be a biological adaptation to her hostile male environment.

Lichtenstein first became aware of the vagina dentata myth at Bennington College while taking a literature class taught by the author and critic Camille Paglia (famous for her book *Sexual Personae* which, similarly to *Teeth*, depicts human sexual nature as a brutal demonic force). In *Teeth*, Lichtenstein identifies the vagina dentata myth as having its basis in ancient masculine fears of the "unknown" of sexual congress. "The mystery of sexual union evokes fears of castration," Dawn reads in the film, "the loss of the penis during intercourse. Undoubtedly it relates to fears of weakness and impotence, destruction suffered during union." Variations on the vagina dentata myth have been used repeatedly in horror and science fiction film, as Lichtenstein (and others, most notably, Barbara Creed[5]) have observed. In horror cinema, the "she-monster" in particular (cf. *Alien* [1979], *Rabid* [1977], *Species* [1995]) can be seen as representation of the vagina dentata myth which, as Lichtenstein notes, is itself already a metaphor for male fear of women:

> [T]hat additional remove is what I always found disturbing because it masks the original fear, assuring that it never be resolved and allowing monstrous qualities to continue to be attributed to women.[6]

In contrast to most horror films, *Teeth* confronts the vagina dentata myth directly, through the use of dark satirical humor.

"Girls have a natural modesty. It's built into our nature"

Lichtenstein did not set out to make *Teeth* strictly as a horror film. Instead it is a combination of dark satirical comedy and horror with science fiction tropes. The comedy functions largely to counteract the male response to castration horror within the scenario by emphasizing the preposterous nature of the vagina dentata myth and men's fear of it. Furthermore, *Teeth* appropriates elements of the avenging angel plot motif (*Ms. 45*), the special gift scenario (*Carrie*) and the castration-revenge fantasy (*I Spit on Your Grave*) that are staples of the horror genre; but in some respects Lichtenstein subverts these elements. *Teeth* bears a marked resemblance to *Rabid*, for example, but unlike Rose (Marilyn Chambers), the similarly mutated heroine in Cronenberg's film, Dawn in *Teeth* ultimately gains control of her monstrous gift. In *Rabid* Rose never gains control of the mutation; it ultimately controls her and causes her destruction. In *Teeth* the mutation is never seen (in *Rabid*, the mutation is both graphic and horrific); therefore Dawn is never a "monster." Having said this, *Teeth* is not entirely immune to the reactionary inflection that is inherent (to use Wood's phrase) in the castration-revenge horror subgenre, and is in some ways constrained by this.

Teeth is, by virtue of its romantic subplot, a "coming of age" movie, but again, it subverts the messages usually to be found in such movies, especially those films (such as *Clueless*

Dawn's (Jess Weixler) natural modesty proves irresistible to fellow chastity group member Tobey (Haley Appleman) in *Teeth* **(2007).**

[1995]) that center on the female experience. In short, *Teeth* repudiates the romantic ideals of love and marriage—with their emphasis on heteronormativity—as espoused by the chastity- abstinence–only movement: the idea that a woman should save herself for the "right person" to whom she will eventually surrender her virginity. Dawn's coming of age disabuses her of these notions because, as she discovers, there are no such "knights in shining armor" forthcoming. Her potential suitors, such as the apparently respectful Tobey (Haley Appleman) and outwardly gentle Ryan (Ashley Springer), turn out to be deceitful and selfish. Indeed, all the men she encounters are abusers and/or rapists at heart. Instead, Dawn's true coming of age story is akin to that of a superhero origin narrative: Her special power is bestowed upon her, she comes to realize, so that she can fight the "bad guys." We bear witness to her journey from delaying confronting her difference; to her unwittingly activating her power, to her finally accepting her special gift, discovering it can be controlled, and using it—she appropriates the vagina dentata myth.

Lichtenstein very carefully structures his story around these various stages of Dawn's journey of self-discovery. *Teeth* is set in nondescript suburbia, a depressing working class America which Lichtenstein, in 2008, felt "so much of America seems to be becoming."[7] It is the America of advertising billboards and power stations: symbols of the destructive nature of late capitalism to man and his environment. The scantily clad women on the billboards that Dawn passes as she cycles home from school denote a patriarchal society which is, as James Gracey points out, hypocritically endorsing the commodification of female sexuality in the advertising of products while still to a large extent not willing to discuss sex, and particularly female sexuality, openly.[8] The nuclear power station near which Dawn lives is a possible cause of her mutation; it seems to have caused her mother's cancer. Lichtenstein never makes this definite, however. Instead the power station itself, with its giant teeth-like structure, is only one element in an environment that is intrinsically hostile, to which Dawn must adapt biologically and spiritually. (Dawn seems aware of the possibility that her biological uniqueness might be adaptationist in nature: When she goes to the Internet to research her special gift, her first Google search is for the word "adaptation.")

Dawn's high school is, like her doctor's surgery, sterile and corporate, suggesting a rigid adherence to transmitting the values of the State. Her sex education teacher, a respectably dressed middle-aged white male, falteringly delivers the ideologically approved lesson in human reproductive biology and the illustration of the female anatomy has been dutifully censored. The word "vagina" is itself taboo; the teacher is unable—or, indeed, not allowed—to say it; "privates" proves an acceptable euphemism. "We're talking about a word that some people are still uncomfortable saying out loud," Lichtenstein muses in the DVD commentary.[9] The students question why the vagina is censored in their textbook but not the penis. They are genuinely perplexed by this double standard, and the teacher, tellingly, is not able to give them a satisfactory explanation, beyond affirming that the distinction is morally "right."

Dawn speaks on behalf of the teacher, asserting that "girls have a natural modesty. It's built into our nature." Although she is upset that the other students laugh at her, Dawn's zealous beliefs in Bush-era chastity and modesty (which has led her to join the school chastity group) speaks to her subconscious desire to delay sexual knowledge and experience. Something inside her is different: Unconsciously she wants to delay knowledge of it. Moreover, this starting point of Dawn's total obedience to the doctrines of the State enables Lichtenstein to arc Dawn's character in a way that is both dramatic and politically subversive. Like the Peter Strauss character in *Soldier Blue* (discussed in Chapter 6), Dawn begins the story as naïve and institutionalized, but gradually begins to remove her ideological blinkers, journeying towards greater political awareness and a radical change of beliefs.

In this way, Dawn's political awareness is intrinsically linked to her self-knowledge and her burgeoning sexual identity. Her masturbation fantasy of Tobey—in which she imagines their wedding night—is based on her idealized and ideologically approved view of marriage and the complete sexual satisfaction that she has been told abstinence until marriage will bring. But Lichtenstein shows this as a charade, a state of repression, which her toothed vagina symbolically threatens to chase away. Therefore Dawn cannot allow herself even to masturbate without feeling a sense of guilt and sin. "What is wrong with me?" she despairs at having given in to lustful thoughts, reciting the affirmation, "Purity, purity."

"So no one's ever even touched your..."

Dawn, as Lichtenstein affirms, has been kept from knowing her body—"by her teachers, her peers, society, herself."[10] What knowledge she has of her anatomical uniqueness has been suppressed, and her views and understanding of sex have been shaped by Christian orthodoxy. It follows that her first sexual encounter should be portrayed as a Biblical fall of man: Dawn's first step from "innocent" obedience towards "guilty" disobedience. Lichtenstein plays the scene as a symbolic re-enactment of the Garden of Eden with Dawn as Eve and Tobey as Adam. Traditionally Eve was blamed for the fall, as she urged Adam to yield to temptation and eat the apple from the tree of knowledge of good and evil. In *Teeth*, it is the male who urges the female to sin, and when she resists, he rapes her anyway. The true "fall" in Lichtenstein's film is the inability of man to treat woman respectfully. Thus it is violence visited upon Dawn's body that activates her special power. However, just as Eve was blamed for the fall, in the vagina dentata myth the woman's body is given a menacing identity. "There is something inside of me that is lethal," Dawn observes after she unwittingly castrates her rapist Tobey, "but I don't know what it is."

Her first recourse is to observe vagina dentata mythology from its patriarchal viewpoint. This enables Dawn to begin to accept her difference, in the belief that her condition can be "cured" if she allows a male to conquer her. However, running parallel to this is Dawn's gradual realization that her toothed vagina only bites defensively. Dawn unconsciously knows she is being abused by the men she trusts, such as Tobey and Dr. Godfrey (Josh Pais). At first, the vagina dentata act upon this subconscious awareness of male power abuse; but after she faces up to the true nature of the men around her she is able to activate the vagina dentata at will.

Dawn's political awakening coincides with her first true experience of sexual intercourse and this also marks a significant advance in her self-knowledge. She goes to her friend Ryan, who poses as the hero who will conquer her vagina dentata. It is worth noting that the audience is fully positioned with Dawn throughout the film. As Lichtenstein notes, the actors remain truthful emotionally despite the film's "far-fetched ideas."[11] The film's satirical element does not detract from this positioning. This enables Lichtenstein to fully explore the vagina dentata myth before finally subverting it. We want to see how this plays out: Will Ryan (or another man) conquer Dawn's vagina dentata? Is the romantic love that Dawn dreams of a possibility? Only by the end can we be sure of the answer to these questions.

When Ryan makes love to her, Dawn is still not aware that she can control her special power. She fears that her vagina will bite Ryan regardless. When it doesn't, Dawn believes herself cured, that her vagina dentata has been conquered. At this moment, Dawn sees herself as a sexual person in a positive way for the first time. She surveys herself in the mirror and realizes that innocence has given way to experience, and that this is something to be celebrated. It is at this major turning point that Lichtenstein starts to subvert the myths, as political and sexual awareness, for Dawn, dovetail with self-knowledge.

During a second act of intercourse with Ryan, Dawn discovers that he is deceiving her; he has made a bet with his friend that he could "score" with a virgin. In anger, Dawn activates

Dawn (Jess Weixler) contemplates what lies beneath in *Teeth* (2007).

the vagina dentata, only afterwards realizing what she has done. But it is here that she becomes disabused of the notion, inherent in the vagina dentata myth, that a hero can conquer her power; and, crucially, she becomes aware that the dentata are under her control and can be used to fight back against attackers and violators.

"We all know who you've been saving yourself for…"

Teeth opens with a short prologue depicting Dawn as a small child first experiencing her special gift. It is in many ways the primal scene, and explores as an analogy the origins of the vagina dentata myth and male fears of it. It also introduces her same-age stepbrother Brad (John Hensley), whose story runs parallel with Dawn's throughout the film. The two children are in a paddling pool. Brad, in an act of curiosity, places his fingers between Dawn's legs, only to have them bitten. He withdraws his hand quickly, confused and afraid. From that point on, Brad views women as dangerous and frightening, and is compelled to treat them as objects in order to combat his fear. The adult Brad's world, as depicted vividly in the film, becomes one of sick sex and abuse. He can only relate to sex through pain inflicted either on his girlfriend Melanie (Nicole Swahn) or on himself through piercings and tattoos. As Lichtenstein observes in his notes to *Teeth*, Brad's preoccupation with anal sex is also "a result of that first scarring childhood contact with a vagina."[12] His childhood experience has left him obsessed with his stepsister, whom he both fears and desires. He, like Dawn, represses the memory of that childhood encounter, but that repressed memory creates a mystery that he feels compelled to solve (what is between a woman's legs?) and he becomes increasingly frustrated by his inability to possess Dawn.

Brad, in a confrontation with his father, reveals that he loves Dawn. Again, the film plays with notions of romantic love as a possible salvation for Dawn—and as redemption for her tarnished knight Brad—only to finally and irrefutably reject these notions in the penultimate sequence. We know that Dawn has gone to Brad to castrate him as punishment for his part in the death of Dawn's mother (he ignored her screams when she collapsed as he was busy having sex). We also know that Brad's misogyny arises from fear and ignorance. However, that fear is not dispelled during the act of intercourse (if anything, it is intensified as it brings the childhood memory to the forefront of Brad's mind) and Brad finally gets to exert his power over Dawn, which the film suggests was what he (and the other men in the film) really wanted all along: domination in the guise of romantic love. The conclusion of *Teeth* seems to be that the vagina dentata will persist as long as men continue to try to exert their power over women; it is men, rather than women, who need to undergo transformation.

The castration scenes are graphic and bloody, and darkly comedic. Lichtenstein fully exploits the shock value and taboo inherent in the material to subversive effect. The men in *Teeth* are quite literally cut down to size. In Brad's case, his sacred appendage, complete with piercing, is dropped unceremoniously on the carpet between Dawn's legs, and is eaten by Brad's pet dog before Brad has the chance to retrieve it.

"I definitely don't want her to become Aileen Wuornos"

Teeth was very favorably received upon its release in 2008. Critics responded to its subversive elements and its combination of genres, seeing it as part horror film, part myth, part cautionary tale, part rape-revenge fantasy and part superhero origin. This led some critics to claim that *Teeth* transcends the horror film.

Despite its appropriation of a variety of genres, *Teeth is*, at heart, a horror film—albeit a subversive one, and as such grapples with what Robin Wood terms "the essential dilemma of the horror genre."[13] In other words, is a truly positive conception of the "monster" logically possible within the horror genre? Granted, by combining genres, Lichtenstein partially circumvents the reactionary inflection that Wood claims the horror genre carries within itself, to which, as Wood says, perhaps no horror film is entirely immune. The appropriation of the superhero movie conventions and a "coming of age" narrative enables Lichtenstein to make his heroine wholly sympathetic and sweet, without her ever becoming monstrous. However the film's avenging angel motif, with its castration-revenge subtext, remains problematic.

In interview with Ain't It Cool News, Lichtenstein reflected on the issue of Dawn using her vagina dentata to exact revenge on her abusers at the end of *Teeth*: "I definitely don't want [Dawn] to become Aileen Wuornos," he told the interviewer. "It's tricky because, as you say, where she is at the end of the movie, you're about to lose sympathy for her maybe, and I don't want you to. So, it's tricky."[14]

In the film's coda, Dawn is shown to be fully in control of her special power and willing to use it on any would-be abuser. She hitches a ride out of town with an old man who refuses to let her out of his car until she performs a sexual favor. The film ends with a closeup of Dawn smiling seductively at the old man. The film suggests that she is ready to turn the tables on men and make them *her* victims. Dawn veers close to the monstrous feminine of *Species* in this final section. She is filmed in such a way as to appear Medusa-like, somewhat negating Lichtenstein's aim of not portraying Dawn as a monster. The danger, inherent in the film's premise, perhaps resides in its "duplicity," its simultaneously progressive and reactionary message: Dawn *is* the vagina dentata myth personified. In the very final moments she becomes the castrating monster that men fear. We need to know where Dawn's journey goes next now that she is control of her precious gift; instead we are left with a final image which takes us worryingly close to the Aileen Wuornos–type scenario that Lichtenstein was keen to avoid. Is Dawn destined to spend the rest of her life caught in a cycle of rape-revenge, as was Wuornos?

Until Lichtenstein clarifies this by producing a sequel, we must take consolation in the knowledge that, while *Teeth* might not fully transcend the horror genre as some critics have claimed, it comes admirably close to doing so. It certainly remains one of the most subversive horror films of recent years.

Physician Heal Thyself: *American Mary*

The male double-standard is also at the heart of Mary Mason's dilemma in *American Mary*. Abused by her male mentors with the medical establishment, med student Mary (Katharine Isabelle) takes her surgical skills into the underground body commodification community where she is able to pursue her ambition to become a highly paid surgeon *and* exact retribution on the men who wrongly judged her. But this empowerment comes at a price, as Mary becomes increasingly compromised by the situation that has been imposed upon her and her inability to fully heal because of it. Jen and Sylvia Soska, who wrote and directed the film, have described themselves as third wave feminists, and the film is much concerned with the need for women to fight against being treated as sex objects by reclaiming their sexuality and their right to freedom of sexual expression. In this way *American Mary* can be seen as growing out of the Soskas' own experience as filmmakers and as women.

As filmmakers, they have found acceptance within the horror genre that was denied them in the male-dominated mainstream Hollywood industry. Their first film, *Dead Hooker in a Trunk* (2009), is a splatstick variation on *Weekend at Bernie's* (1989) that also owes much to the Cinema of Transgression of the 1980s. Its genre subversion proved a difficult sell to distributors, and the experience of shopping it around was instructive to the Soskas, not only in terms of how their work was looked upon by Hollywood, but how they themselves were regarded by men in positions of power within the mainstream film industry. (Sylvia subsequently described these men as "horrendously awful human beings."[15]) They were shunned, sexualized and not taken seriously by Hollywood. ("I blame *Penthouse*," Sylvia has remarked. "People take identical twins in the worst possible way."[16]) Then they found a home for the film in the horror genre, whose community embraced them, celebrated their transgression and subsequently helped to elevate both *Dead Hooker in a Trunk* and *American Mary* to cult status.

The celebration of difference is, of course, a staple of subversive horror cinema. *American Mary* draws parallels between the "freakishness" of the body horror community and that of the horror film audience. Fandom has been instrumental in raising the profile of individual films and filmmakers belonging to the genre based on their transgression and alternative ideologies, their underground appeal; horror fans themselves are often considered as separate from the mainstream, and belonging to a "disreputable" subculture. Part of the genesis of *American Mary* was Jen and Sylvia Soska's fascination with body modification community websites—an interest which, it must be said, was limited to casual observation, rather than active participation, although their own "freakishness" as identical twins (and our culture regrettably persists in viewing twins in these terms) no doubt provided a frame of reference and an empathy with the need for independence of expression. As the first film to focus on body modification culture, the Soskas wanted *American Mary* to provide a fair and honest representation and their portrayal of that subculture is largely sympathetic. However, the film also addresses the problem of self-expression being driven underground. The desires of the female body modification characters to radically alter their appearances are largely motivated by a profound sense of alienation from a society that promotes the sexual objectification of the female. Beatrice Johnson (Tristan Risk), a stripper at the club where Mary works, wants to transform herself into Betty Boop, the highly sexualized fetish figure of the 1930s cartoon/1940s animation films; only by acquiescing entirely to male voyeurism can she gain control of her sexual identity and thereby achieve any sense of inner peace. Conversely, Ruby Realgirl (Paula Lindberg) seeks to desexualize herself completely in the eyes of others by transforming herself into a Barbie doll without nipples or a vagina.

While the film champions the right of these women to modify their bodies in whichever way they choose, it also sees their need to do so as regrettable. The objectification of women within a patriarchal society is all-pervasive, such that it proves impossible for Beatrice and Ruby to define their sexual identity away from the male gaze. Their only recourse is to transform themselves into literal objects: complete acquiescence (Beatrice), total defiance (Ruby). It is the sort of defiance that Ruby Realgirl practices that provides Mary with a sense of empowerment as she takes control of her body and her image after being raped. Her dress code becomes increasingly fetishistic, but not sexually provocative, done for herself and not others, but at the same time done defiantly: proof that she, and not men, owns her sexuality.

It is, as Sylvia says, a case of "girls always have this little black dress in their closet and when they've had a shitty day they put it on and they're like, 'I'm awesome.'"[17]

"I'm lucky enough to be able to afford to make myself look on the outside the way I feel on the inside"

Her mentors in the "respectable" world of the medical establishment assume that Mary is a prostitute, and so she dresses like one. However, in order to find her identity, Mary must descend into the underworld. In some respects, *American Mary* can be seen as a feminine disruption of the classic narrative form: Mary, in her relentless pursuit of the American Dream, is an archetypal striving protagonist; however, she becomes somewhat diminished as the story progresses, until she appears to have lost all sense of herself. Her death thus becomes almost a case of *deus ex machina*. The forces of patriarchy remain entirely outside her control. Her journey from girl to woman involves empowerment but not spiritual growth—quite the opposite, in fact, because Mary regresses. The film ends with her realization that she has been forced into a dead end with nowhere to go. *American Mary* compares intriguingly with *Teeth* in this respect: Both protagonists become empowered but only Dawn "grows." Having said that, of the two films, *American Mary* is perhaps more devastating in its willingness to confront how woman are trapped by patriarchal values because of its refusal to invoke wish fulfillment. *Teeth*, no matter how "progressive" (or otherwise) its conclusion, makes clear that Dawn is in complete control of her destiny aided by her special gift. Mary has no such control of her life.

Screenwriting teacher Cherry Potter has spoken of feminine archetypes in terms of their encompassing an awareness of the magical, mythological and unconscious which can neither be totally controlled nor fully understood, and which is therefore threatening to the masculine ego:

> Although the descent into the underworld, or unconscious, can be frightening, and destructive, the magical and mythological is also an essential part of the transformative experience and as such crucial to the process of change in the "feminine" creative cycle of growth.[18]

Reading *American Mary* in these terms, it is possible to see Mary's descent into the underworld of the strip club as a descent into the "masculine" unconscious where Mary is forced to adopt masculine traits: dispassion, cruelty, hardness. Her transformation, such as it is, enables her to recognize these traits as essentially destructive to the self.

Jen and Sylvia Soska have discussed their screenwriting process in terms of utilizing the classical three-act structure. In *American Mary*, they set up our expectation of this paradigm: Mary, for example, receives a call to adventure in the form of Beatrice's proposal to perform surgery on Ruby. This precipitates Mary's entrance into the special world of the strip club and body modification and is a typical end-of-first-act solution: It will solve her money problems. The midpoint of the story coincides with her rejection of the respectable medical world for a total descent into the violence of the strip club and the darker side of body modification (physical torture). However, like in *American Psycho* (which *American Mary* obliquely references), there is no third act redemption: Mary is not recuperated into the respectable medical world, healed and chastened by her experiences (but a better person for it). Instead she dies without being able to reconcile this sense of dualism between the masculine and the feminine.

Mary begins the story characterized by a sense of girlishness. In her dealings with her mentor, Dr. Grant (David Lovgren), as well as with Beatrice and Ruby, she is unsure of herself, somewhat "goofy." After she is raped, this changes dramatically as she locks down any former display of vulnerability; she becomes immediately self-composed and cold. The abruptness of her change is paralleled by the disorientating speed in which she exacts her revenge on Dr. Grant. There is no soul-searching leading to a decision to act; instead, Mary immediately adopts the avenging angel persona. The rape and Mary's subsequent torturing of Dr. Grant are collapsed almost into one sequence of "dual" events.

This sense of dualism in the narrative is heightened by the use of mirroring in other aspects of the film. As mentioned before, Beatrice and Ruby are polarized versions of each other; Mary has two potential male "suitors," Billy Barker (Antonio Cupo), the club owner, and Detective Dolor (John Emmet Tracey), the understanding policeman investigating Dr. Grant's disappearance. In other aspects of the film, this dualism is reinforced: in the chiaroscuro lighting of cinematographer Brian Pearson and set design of Tony Devenyi and Courtney Stockstad which combine reds and blues; and in the cameo roles of Jen and Sylvia Soska as the German identical twins who wish to become conjoined. In Mary's case the dualism in her psyche refuses such conjunction, although her vulnerability and self-doubt make fleeting reappearances before disappearing for good, together with her conscience.

This quick glimpse of the Mary that was adds a poignancy that makes Mary's loss of

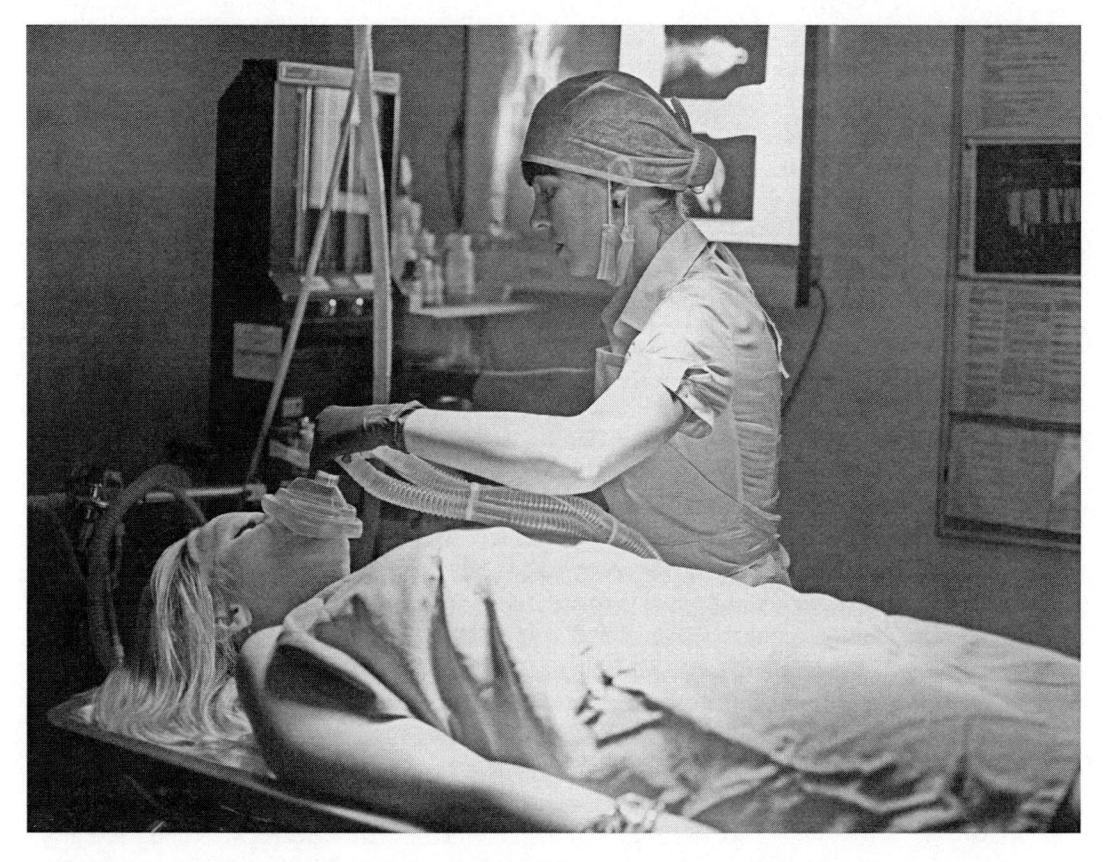

Medical student Mary Mason (Katharine Isabelle) prepares Ruby Realgirl (Paula Lindberg) for body-modification surgery in *American Mary* (2012).

self all the more tragic. Towards the end, Mary voices her self-doubt to Lance (Twan Holliday), Billy's henchman at the strip club. She confesses that she feels upset and affected by what she has done. When she sips the milkshake that Lance offers her as comfort, we glimpse for the last time the inner child that Mary has learned to suppress. After that, we see only Mary, the avenging angel, the torturer, who instills terror in others, both physically (in the case of the blonde girl whom she terrorizes in the rest room after discovering her fellating Billy) and "sexually" (Billy both desires and fears her).

"I wanted to be a surgeon for as long as I could remember"

The rape-revenge motif in *American Mary* is intrinsically linked to its treatment of the American dream (another instance of the film's dualism): Both are seen as corrosive to Mary's sense of self. The Soskas, who are Canadian, have spoken of the glass ceiling that exists in Canadian filmmaking, their need to do as Cronenberg and Mary Harron did and move to Hollywood in order to pursue a career. Unsurprisingly, given their background and circumstances, their views on the American dream are ambivalent. They cite Ruby Realgirl—a blonde with large breast implants—as the expected form of beauty in a land where appearance, as they have discovered to their distaste, means everything. "There's a lot of self-sacrifice to get to the American dream," Jen has said, "and you see Mary make sacrifice after sacrifice of her own morality and the person that she is, and it's just about how far you will go to reach your own American dream."[19]

In *American Mary*, Mary's pursuit of easy money and her desire for acceptance into the patriarchal medical world lead to her eventual undoing. Her immediate solution to the need to earn money to continue her studies is to apply for work in the strip club. This speaks not necessarily to any moral shortcoming on Mary's part but to the ready acceptance of sex as a commoditized "asset" as engendered by our culture. As Sylvia has commented:

> In the scene where she clomps around in the strip club, auditioning—"You may want to walk a little sexier, Mary"—after that one scene happens, she doesn't do anything but have these beautiful, really strong, sexy moves and it's like, you lose a lot of the real person that she is because she puts on this front instead of what she thinks everyone perceives her as.[20]

The question facing Mary is: How far is she willing to compromise her own sense of morality in order to fulfill her career ambition? Interestingly, even before Mary has performed body modification, we can already see how her career as a "respectable" surgeon might corrode her psyche. During her hospital residency she is asked by the cynical and callous Dr. Walsh (Clay St. Thomas) to deliver repeated bad news to a patient in order to practice her "bedside manner." We are not sure whether the situation is genuine or whether Mary is being manipulated by the egocentric Walsh, but it gives us an early glimpse of the dehumanized medical environment that Mary is entering and how she will become hardened by it.

And yet her ambition is such that she readily accepts the offer of money to perform illegal body modification on Ruby Realgirl, despite her obvious distaste for it. Her hypocrisy is tellingly highlighted in the scene where, after dressing for Dr. Walsh's party (she takes the invitation as tacit acceptance into the elitist patriarchal world of the surgeon, her opportunity to become, as it were, "one of the boys"—it is an invitation that she eagerly accepts), she disgustedly slams her laptop shut on a body mod website, cynically rejecting that community in favor of the morally dubious world of the highly paid surgeon.

The correlation between rape-and-revenge and the pursuit of the American dream becomes clear when Mary continues to engage in both. She keeps Dr. Grant alive over time so that she can systematically torture him (reducing him to a human torso without arms or legs) as punishment for raping her, while simultaneously building a lucrative career as a willing surgeon among the body modification community. She earns enough by doing this body-mod surgery to buy herself expensive clothes and to move into a more up-market apartment, where she sets up her practice. But she becomes more glazed throughout the rest of the film, and is dying inside.

Her Hungarian grandmother is the last reminder of her old life, who she was before she became "American" Mary. But Grandma is nothing more than a distant voice on the telephone, so that by the time she passes away, she is merely a contact to be deleted from Mary's cell phone, Mary hasn't seen her in so long. However, the death of Mary's grandmother is highly symbolic: On the one hand it marks Mary's achievement of the American dream, her final escape from poverty, but it also represents the end of the only close relationship Mary has—perhaps ever had. Without that, Mary becomes irretrievably lost. Her roots are gone forever, and with them, her sense of self.

A blood-soaked Mary (Katharine Isabelle) in *American Mary* (2012).

"Maybe I need a change of pace too"

In the final sequences it becomes clear that Mary's attempts to heal herself are failing. If we compare *American Mary* to another rape-revenge drama, Tony Garnett's *Handgun* (1981), the reasons for Mary's failure to heal become clear. In *Handgun*, the victim of rape, Kathleen (Karen Young), exacts an elaborate revenge on her gun-obsessive attacker: She hunts him down with a handgun so that he becomes a victim of the very gun culture which he espouses. However, Karen falls short of actually shooting her rapist; instead her "big game"–hunting him turns out to be a terrifying practical joke intended to teach him a lesson. Actual violence, as Karen understands, will solve nothing; but Karen is vindicated at the end and is, therefore, able to get on with her life again as the loving, compassionate person she really is. Mary, by contrast, is unable to heal precisely because she has become what Karen was not: a murderer. Indeed, Mary begins to really lose all sense of who she once was when she is driven to murder the innocent security guard who discovers her torture chamber. The killing is brutal and shocking: Mary bludgeons him repeatedly, symbolically bloodying herself in the process. Although she appears to show remorse later (in the scene with Lance), this becomes the final ruinous compromise of her morality from which she cannot recover.

After this, there is nowhere for her to go. The only hope left for her redemption is through her relationships. The film moots this as a possibility, but only fleetingly. Detective Dolor offers understanding and compassion. She recognizes this in him but is unable to accept it without telling him the truth, which she is unwilling to do. That leaves Billy, the strip club owner, who is obsessed with her. The film shows us that Billy, like the other men, objectifies Mary, fantasizing about her sexually. However, Billy is, himself, searching for redemption, a way out of his own demeaning lifestyle of violence and commoditized sex. His offer to drive with Mary to Los Angeles, though gauchely delivered, is apparently genuine, as perhaps is his affection for her. But by this point Mary is completely blank. "Do you think I'm crazy?" she asks Billy emotionlessly. To his invitation she answers in a parting shot, "I'll think about it. Maybe I need a change of pace too." But we can tell by her toneless voice, her glazed expression, that Mary has finally lost all sense of self. It is a case of "physician, heal thyself," but for Mary, alas, it is too late. Patriarchy has destroyed her. She cannot sew herself up after the final symbolic wound is inflicted.

AFTERWORD
Subversive Horror Cinema Post–9/11

The actual images of the Twin Towers falling and the destruction to Manhattan have become iconic to the age, just as the mushroom cloud was to the dawn of the atomic age in the 1950s, and science fiction–horror films made since 2001 have been replete in imagery of a destroyed New York. *Cloverfield* (2008), for example, in its lo-fi handicam presentation of the city under attack, echoed the video footage of the Twin Towers at the point the planes hit—the chaos, the panic, the flight from Ground Zero and the response of the emergency services in the moments that followed. The immediacy of the "actuality" footage in *Cloverfield* seemed therapeutic in revisiting the trauma of 9/11 and contributed towards the film's popularity.

According to Joseph Stiglitz, America's handling of globalization had contributed to the wave of anti–American feeling that led to the 9/11 attacks: "By pushing poor countries to eliminate trade barriers while keeping up their own barriers," writes Stiglitz in *Globalization and Its Discontents*, "the West has ensured it garners a disproportionate share of the benefits, at the expense of the developing world."[1] This hypocrisy on the part of the West led to social collapse in countries such as Thailand and South Korea and a subsequent wave of hostility towards the West, a rise of regressive-degenerate forces (Al Qaeda), culminating in the September 11 attacks on America. Bush subsequently escalated these hostilities in his invasions of Afghanistan and Iraq. Two films that dealt allegorically with the War on Terror—particularly the invasions of Afghanistan and Iraq—highlighted the shortcomings of the Bush administration and its militaristic foreign policy.

28 Weeks Later (2007) depicted an Iraq-like Green Zone and its breach by violent insurgents. The film focuses (as does Romero's *The Crazies*—an obvious influence on *28 Weeks Later*) on the military's botched response to the outbreak of the "rage" virus which threatens to infect everyone in the zone. Unable to contain the outbreak, the military escalates the violence to the point where their only solution is to carpet bomb the whole area, killing everyone in it. The film makes the point that responsibility is not always taken seriously by those who hold power. This theme of the irresponsibility of patriarchal authority is eloquently developed by director Juan Carlos Fresnadillo and resonates on many levels. The lead character Don (Robert Carlyle) abandons his wife during a zombie attack and subsequently lies to his children about their mother's death. Later, as one of the "infected," he is driven by the need to destroy his children in order to erase his guilty feelings at having shirked his responsibility as husband and father. The conclusion of the film seems to say: Militaristic violence comes from male irresponsibility and the guilt arising from it which is directed as rage against others—and starts in the family.

Jane O'Flynn (Kathleen Munroe) attacks Chuck (Joris Jarsky) during the final zombie uprising of George A. Romero's *Survival of the Dead* (2009).

Romero made the same point in *Land of the Dead* (2005). But whereas *28 Weeks Later* offered a withering critique of America's foreign policy, *Land of the Dead* criticizes Bush's domestic policy in the aftermath of 9/11. "We do not negotiate with terrorists," states the Rumsfeld-like plutocrat Kaufman (Dennis Hopper) when faced by a revolt headed by the ethnic military man, Cholo (John Leguizamo) (read Bin Laden, Saddam Hussain, Gaddafi), who, up until then, had been doing his dirty work. In the face of the zombie crisis, Hopper's character has been feathering his own nest—and those of his cronies—Enron-like in a literal tower while the ordinary people over whom he rules are left to fend for themselves on the ground. Romero's conclusions—that those in power during 9/11 have acted only to serve themselves—firmly echo those of Michael Moore in *Fahrenheit 9/11* (2004).

Land of the Dead's protagonist, Riley (Simon Baker) is a moral, decent man, skeptical of politicians: a similar character to David in *The Crazies*. But unlike David, whose downfall is caused by his inability to give up his rugged individualism, Riley learns that community is the future. *Land of the Dead* may be Romero's most optimistic film yet; the removal of tyranny enables the survivors of the colony to move forward in a new spirit of cooperation, and there are indications that man and zombie may yet learn to co-exist.

Survival of the Dead (2009) developed this theme of co-existence: The survivors discover that zombies can be fed on horseflesh, thus potentially neutralizing their threat. But tribal factions among the survivors once again prevent cooperation among the living in their war with the dead. As he did in *Dawn of the Dead*, Romero utilizes the tropes of the classic western, but more overtly so, to comment on tribalism post–9/11 and its standing in the way of peace and the rebuilding of society. Made in the year of Obama's inauguration as president, *Survival of the Dead* tempers the optimism of *Land of the Dead*'s co-existence message with a cautionary warning about the dead weight of the past hanging heavy on future prospects for cooperative social endeavor.

Other horror films after 9/11 have addressed the issue of America's War on Terror more obliquely. The backwoods horror films *Wrong Turn* (2003), *The Texas Chain Saw Massacre* (2003) and *The Hills Have Eyes* (2006) spoke of the curtailing of liberties following 9/11 and, according to critic Linnie Blake, the demonization of difference: The hillbilly figure in these films is presented both as a savage aggressor and a victim of the nation's attempts to marginalize those in society who refused to be assimilated into the dominant ideology.[2]

The international instability post–9/11 has thus created a context for the re-emergence of subversive horror cinema in the last ten years, a flourishing which has, if anything, intensified since the economic "banking" crisis of 2008 and subsequent global recession. The sense of societal collapse is at the heart of all of these films. To conclude then, let us consider the recent subversive horror cinema of America and Great Britain in more detail, with a particular focus on films which might be seen as indicators of its future direction.

Red, White and Blue (2010) was British director Simon Rumley's first film after *The Living and the Dead* (2006) and his first set in the United States. A commentary on America, it plays equally well as an intimate tale of love and revenge. Rumley has described it as a "slacker revenge movie,"[3] and in many ways it is similar in theme and feel to Shane Meadows' *Dead Man's Shoes* (2004), only instead of dealing with the British underclass, Rumley casts his sights on small town America. This is not the romanticized Americana of Frank Capra, George Lucas or even David Lynch, but an honest depiction of a modern small town America where FM Rock plays 24–7; where Axl Rose lookalikes in denim cut-offs and bandanas, just out of the state pen after beating up or shooting their wives or girlfriends, spend most of their time in gloomy downtown bars; where Main Street stands deserted and the only thing that moves is the traffic lights changing colors.

The last film before *Red, White and Blue* to portray small town America so unflinchingly was probably Darren Aronofsky's *The Wrestler* (2008). This is a place where community has more or less broken down and alienation is a way of life. *The Last Picture Show* (1971) captured the decline of small town life of the 1950s; films like *Red, White and Blue* attest to its further deterioration.

The plot is minimal: Erica (Amanda Fuller), an emotionally damaged twenty something, engages in endless casual sex to numb the pain of her existence, until she strikes up a close platonic friendship with Nate (Noah Taylor), an Iraq war veteran who has drifted into town. But when one of Erica's casual flings, Franki (Marc Senter), discovers he has contracted HIV from Erica, he abducts her, spurring Nate to exact terrible, bloody vengeance.

Rumley has spoken about *Red, White and Blue* as being a commentary on America's violence culture: "It seems nothing was learned from Vietnam and there are lots of countries, but particularly America, that seem to have violent knee-jerk reactions to situations, so it was a comment on that."[4] Nate is an ambiguous figure in this respect. He is gentle, patient and protective of Erica, but when it comes to avenging her mistreatment by Franki and his friends, Nate's propensity for sadistic violence is released and he shows no mercy. Rumley is careful to portray Franki as a gentle and empathetic character too. He lives with his mother who has had cancer, aspires to be a rock star and has a steady girlfriend whom he is respectful towards. When he learns that Erica has given him HIV, he initially reacts with understanding. Tragically he tries to connect to Erica and even proposes marriage. When she rejects him, however, his response gradually turns to violence.

Because Rumley makes his characters empathetic (structuring the film very specifically so that we follow Erica first, then switch attention to Franki before centering on Nate), Nate's vengeance on Franki, in particular, becomes alienating in itself, ultimately making the violence abhorrent. Nate becomes an emblem of America, or at least of violence within American culture (he even wears a stars and stripes on the back of his cut-off denim jacket). The violent streak within him has partly been inculcated by the army (as with the Paddy Considine character in *Dead Man's Shoes*) but there is also despair at his blue collar existence, a sense that violence is all he has. Erica, too, is aimless; she suffered abuse as a child at the hands of her stepfather. Even Franki, who at first seems well adjusted, despairs at his life and feels alienated from other people.

The violence in *Red, White and Blue* is disturbing, but we are never encouraged to view the characters as debased or degraded, and we don't feel demeaned or degraded by watching it. We do not share the glee with which Nate carries out his punishment, but we understand how emotionally dead inside he has become to act the way he does.

Simon Rumley more than fulfilled the promise of *The Living and the Dead* in this film; he has a Wim Wenders–like eye for America, but with a harsher outlook. All the iconography is there (the diners, the bars, the Texas landscape) but Rumley makes it look bleak, with none of the enchantment of *Paris Texas* (1984). The ending, too, is quietly devastating: a simple scene with Nate alone by a campfire looking at a photograph of himself and Erica, which he then burns. But it says everything about the futility of love in such a bleak emotional environment.

* * *

The Butcher Brothers is the AKA for Mitchell Altieri and Phil Flores. *The Hamiltons* (2006) is their little-seen but well-received debut as a producing-directing team. It won awards at the Santa Barbara and Malibu film festivals but only received a limited theatrical release by Lionsgate before its DVD release in 2007.

Following the mysterious death of their parents, a family of orphans moves into a house in a small Midwest industrial town. David (Samuel Child), the eldest, has taken on the responsibility of care for his siblings: twins Darlene (Mackenzie Firgens) and Wendell (Joseph McKelheer), and Francis (Cory Knauf), the youngest. Things are not easy after the loss of both parents, and David struggles to hold the family together. Francis is making a video about them all and harbors his own doubts: Will they be able to stay together now that Mom and Dad are gone? Things are made even harder by the fact that Wendell has kidnapped two girls and is holding them captive in the basement, where something hungry and maybe not human is also being kept under lock and key.

The Hamiltons starts off resembling a piece of torture porn but emerges as something else entirely. The degeneracy of the Hamiltons is shown to be an extension of normal family values rather than a deviation from them. "The family that slays together stays together," as it were. At first it appears that Wendell is the cause of all the family's problems, but the film reveals that there is more to it than that. He is hot-headed and compulsive, a sexual psychopath, and David covers up for him, hiding the truth from the world in order to protect his siblings so that they can stay together. But then we begin to realize that David is more involved than we first thought—and shares in his brother's bloodlust. David seeks out his own victims in the young men he lures home and buries under the house. And we already know that Darlene is twisted and enjoys an incestuous relationship with her twin brother Wendell to boot.

Only Francis, the youngest, seems untouched by the family's psychopathology. He is just trying to figure out where he belongs. Camcording his siblings shows his alienation. He cannot help but empathize with Samantha (Rebekah Hoyle), the only surviving girl in the cellar. Like Junior in *Last House on the Left* (1972) and Ruby in *The Hills Have Eyes* (1976) he represents the possibility of change, of breaking away from the family pathology. As far as Wendell is concerned, Francis has yet to "pop his cherry": "We do what we do to survive," Wendell tells him. The bleak barren industrial landscape corroborates his sentiment. In some respects, the Hamiltons are just another family struggling to survive in modern America, and their attitude that family comes first, even if it is at the cost of society as a whole, is redolent of the individualism inherent in the American way. Francis, it seems, is going to be forced to make a choice: stay true to his family or stay true to himself.

At least that is how it appears until he helps Samantha escape and we discover that it was the Hamiltons' father who first taught them how to take what they need from their victims. Francis battles his nature when he sees that Sam is bleeding. "We're born, not made," he tells her. But finally even Francis can't fight against who, or what, he really is.

In many ways, *The Hamiltons* is part of the pastiche movement of the modern horror film. It resembles, in its harsh, flatly lit look, rough-hewn 1970s horrors like *Three on a Meathook* (1972) and *Deranged* (1974). After *The Hamiltons*, the Butcher Brothers went on to remake Fred Walton's 1986 *April Fool's Day*, and they have a foot in the modern horror industry of remakes, pastiches and sequels. But, overall, this is more intelligent than the average pastiche. For the most part, *The Hamiltons* critiques the idea of family survival at any cost—presenting it as a "feeding" on the rights of others. The film falters, though, in its final reveal. Francis cannot change because of what is revealed as his nature. He must, therefore, accept who he is. The problem is that the film then conveniently forgets the degeneracy of the family and asks us to sympathize with the Hamiltons who, after all, can't help what they are and are "just trying to fit in." (It is revealing, perhaps, that David's homosexuality is coding for his sexual psychopathology.)

It is a shame that the Butcher Brothers ultimately settle for the more conservative message: Their sequel to *The Hamiltons*, *The Thompsons* (2012), went further in turning the characters into full-blown antiheroes in the mode of *The Devils Rejects* (2005), an indication perhaps of the tendency towards empty nihilism inherent in the modern horror pastiche-remake.

The Violent Kind (2010), the Butcher Brothers' next film after *The Hamiltons*, divided critics and fans alike: Some saw it as an original and highly unpredictable genre "mash-up" combining elements of the bike movie, Lovecraftian horror and alien invasion sci-fi; others as a rambling, incoherent mess that merely leaves viewers scratching their heads. I watched the film with limited knowledge of it, expecting a cross between the TV series *The Sons of Anarchy* and *The Devil's Rejects* (which it is—and more). *The Hamiltons* was an incisive look at violence as inherent in the American family. This led me to expect *The Violent Kind* to be a study of violence ingrained within the American psyche as engendered in popular culture by the Hells Angels movement. Having seen the film, I still think that this is, at heart, what *The Violent Kind* is about, and the genre-bending in the movie makes sense, at least for me, when the film is read this way.

A pre-credits sequence establishes the bikers as the "violent kind." Cody (Cory Knauf), the antihero and deputy of The Crew, a second-generation Californian biker gang, is waiting with his cronies outside a house while their leader Q (Bret Roberts) finishes having sex with his girlfriend (an act that climaxes with the girlfriend punching him in the face). Two hicks arrive in their pick up, looking for Q, a drug dealer. They have a beef with him, which is swiftly settled by violence, coldly meted out on the hicks by Q and Cody. Afterwards, Q ensures that the hicks are safely returned to their truck so they can drive off. No hard feelings. Violence is clearly a way of life for this gang.

The gang goes to Cody's mother's old house in the woods to celebrate her 50th birthday in typical biker fashion. Here there are some soap opera elements typical of a biker movie. Cory's ex-girlfriend, Michelle (Tiffany Shepis), has a new boyfriend. Cody is not happy. He gets to talking to Michelle's younger sister Megan (Christina Prousalis), who always liked him and wrote to him while he was in prison. There is also unresolved sexual tension between Cody and Shade (Taylor Shade), Q's aforementioned girlfriend with the right hook. So far so *The Wild Angels* (1966). Cody is exactly the type of character that Jack Nicholson would have played in Roger Corman's 1960s biker movies.

Then the film takes a turn towards genre shifting, as Michelle returns to the house, having previously left with her boyfriend, all beaten and bloody. She has been viciously attacked but we are not sure by whom or what. While the others go to investigate, one of the gang sexually assaults Michelle while she sleeps (further developing the violence and depravity theme) and she appears to respond to his advances, but then attacks him, biting into his face (a shocking scene of cannibalism reminiscent of Claire Denis's *Trouble Every Day* [2001]). It soon becomes apparent that Michelle has become possessed. We seem to be moving into *The Evil Dead* territory at this point.

The Butcher Brothers wrong-foot us again shortly afterwards by introducing a home invasion scenario, as a bizarre retro-gang of rockabillies imprisons Cody, Shade, Megan and Q. They claim to have come to retrieve "what is inside Michelle" (and later perform a bizarre ceremony that is part demon invocation, part extraterrestrial encounter *a la The Fourth Kind* [2009]). For the most part however, their motives are to torture and torment the bikers.

This constant genre-shifting makes *The Violent Kind* either engrossing or infuriating, depending on your point of view. It may appear an arbitrary mix at first, but its setting provides a unifying context. California, and particularly the San Francisco area and Sonoma Valley where *The Violent Kind* was filmed, has a history of cultism spanning the Hells Angels, the Manson Family and UFOlogy, all of which *The Violent Kind* references. The Californian counterculture of the 1960s (as discussed in Chapter 6), which gave rise to the Haight-Ashbury hippie movement, also involved the Hells Angels, Charles Manson and alien abductions. *The Violent Kind* links these three areas of cultism as holding a particular cultural fascination in the American psyche because of their inherent violence.

The cultural firmament that gave rise to the Manson killings in the 1960s still troubles modern America. This trauma continues to be played out in home invasion horror films as recent as *The Strangers* (2008), *Mother's Day* (2010) and *You're Next* (2012). Interestingly, *The Violent Kind* subverts the usual scenario, as the representatives of the dark counterculture (the bikers) are the victims in the story rather than the victimizers. Their attackers are "them" in a sense but fifty years before: a biker gang from the 1950s who disappeared mysteriously years ago. That this 1950s gang should engage in the same violent behavior as the modern bikers (using switchblades rather than sheaf knives) is befitting in terms of the film's theme: *Violence is inherent in the American subculture—always has been, always will be*. The fact that this 1950s gang has been a victim of alien abduction and body invasion, is also telling in terms of UFOlogy, which at its heart is obsessed by violence done towards the human body by extraterrestrial beings: the notion of being abducted for human experiments.

These themes are bound together by the central section of the film that presents the possession scenario, in which an invading entity takes control of the body and compels it towards violence. *The Violent Kind* is ultimately presenting the American counterculture of

Cody (Cory Knauf) and Megan (Christina Prousalis) attempt to escape in 2010's *The Violent Kind* (photograph by Michael Jang, courtesy San Francisco Independent Cinema and Compound B).

the 1950s, '60s and '70s as possessed by a "force" that leads it into violence. That force might be alien or it might be inherent, but it has become deeply ingrained in the American psyche, passed down through the generations, and is likely to explode again as it did in the late 1960s. The ending of *The Violent Kind* suggests that this violence may begin within the subculture but it eventually spills out into the American mainstream as it did at Altamont in 1969 and at Kent State in 1970.

* * *

On the surface, Lucky McKee's *The Woman* (2011) raises questions about gender relations in modern society, while comparing notes with *Deliverance* (1972) in portraying civilization as a thin veneer for the beast that lurks within. The premise is a variation of the German fairytale "Iron John," about a wild man discovered in the woods, captured by soldiers, imprisoned and "tamed." Iron John also became the basis for a famous book of the same name by Robert Bly,[5] which led to the 1990s masculinist movement in the United States: a grassroots movement claiming that masculinity was in crisis due to social and family breakdown and advocating that men should concentrate on developing masculine traits in themselves and their sons. Although not necessarily seen as a backlash against feminism, the masculinist movement in popular culture is evident in the surfeit of survivalist game shows and boys adventure stories on TV, and also in the "lads mags" culture in Great Britain, which tends to show men as half adults, trapped somewhere between childhood and maturity—a state in which they find it hard to become responsible leaders, carers and fathers, and which in turn leads to the passing down of that immaturity through the generations.

In part, *The Woman* satirizes this through its portrayal of the main character, Chris

Cleer (Sean Bridgers), a man who feels that his masculinity is constantly under threat and who goes to increasingly desperate lengths to protect it. As a study of such a male, *The Woman* succeeds admirably for the most part. In other respects, though, McKee's film is less clear in what it is trying to say.

The Woman (Pollyanna McIntosh) functions in a similar way to the Terence Stamp character in Pasolini's *Theorem* (1968), in that she forces each of the family members to confront what until now they have tried to conceal in order to function as a family. To Chris she represents what he would like to achieve through his hunting trips but fails to do: to be at one with nature. His attempt to "civilize" the Woman is a really a desire to subjugate her to his will absolutely, to achieve a complete domination over her that is impossible to do with his family without the family unit breaking down (which is, of course, what happens in the end when he finally loses control of himself and beats up his wife). Not only does the Woman represent the complete self-awareness that Chris lacks, she ultimately embodies the perceived threat that women pose to his masculinity. Throughout the film, Chris increasingly resents his actions being questioned by the women around him, and finally explodes when the young teacher, Ms. Raton (Carlee Baker), appears to question his abilities as a father. His failings have clearly been passed down to his alienated son (whom he refuses to take on his hunting trips). The son, disturbed by the gradual disintegration of the family, also chooses to blame women for his problems, using the captive Woman as an outlet for his sadism. The mother (Angela Bettis) represses her anger at her husband's increasingly unreasonable behavior towards the Woman out of her sense of responsibility towards her children. She does not want to rock the boat. Meanwhile, the eldest daughter holds deep misgivings towards her father, which the Woman brings to the fore.

Gradually, the family is forced, through Chris's behavior, to confront these things, and *The Woman* builds a tremendous head of steam, as each family member is forced to choose his or her allegiances. Frustratingly, though, the film suddenly unravels, losing its way in the final sequences. Firstly, McKee gets across the idea that Chris may be the father of his daughter's child, something suggested but not confirmed. Second, we learn that Chris is keeping a second feral child, "Socket," captive. What are we to make of this? Is Socket another member of the Woman's clan? The Woman's child? Or is she the child of Chris and his wife that they have rejected due to birth defects? The film does not make this clear. Then the film climaxes in a sequence of extreme (and slightly ludicrous) gore, which also tends to undermine what has gone before. The savagery, indiscriminately meted out by the feral Woman, feels like a descent into fashionable nihilism. Like the grunge soundtrack, it may simply be an attempt to please the gore fans. In particular, the fate of the mother seems ill-judged. She has clearly made a journey from subjugation to strength, and yet is punished for it (presumably for her complicity in the incest). The killing of the female teacher feels like a scapegoat or sacrificial killing on the part of McKee and his writer Jack Ketchum. Finally, the Woman and "Socket" are revealed as cannibals but to what purpose?

As a director, McKee makes sometimes bold stylistic choices, but there are times when his uncertainty also shows in his storytelling devices. Early sequences use dissolves whose purpose is unclear. Some of the early scenes are confusing. His use of grunge songs instead of a traditional score is sometimes striking, but more often gets in the way. Again, their purpose is unclear; perhaps they are an attempt to "counterpoint" the action, but mostly fail to do this. Most of the story is up-front which tends to underplay mystery and suspense in the earlier sequences. However, the filmmakers are deliberately showing their hand in adopting these stylistic choices, alerting us to their presence, and this invites us to read *The Woman* as the desire to make a statement even if, at times, it is unclear exactly what the statement is.

* * *

Stake Land (2010), directed by Jim Mickle, succeeds through its mix of cultural references to be very insightful indeed. It is difficult to recall another horror film which makes such strong connections to the Great Depression through cultural references to that period of American history as represented in film, photography and literature. No surprise that one of the creative forces behind the film was Larry Fessenden, a producer-writer-director-actor who has probably done more than anyone to promote independent horror production in the last ten years, and has a genuine sense of the subversive potential of the genre.

The story is very similar to that of *Zombieland* (2009). Martin (Connor Paolo), a teenage boy who has lost his family, teams up with a grizzled vampire-hunter known only as "Mister" (Nick Damici), and together they embark on a road trip through an apocalyptic landscape, heading towards what they hope will be a better place in Canada. Along the way they experience hardship, loss, human kindness (in some of the encampments they stop at) and its opposite (in their encounters with the Brotherhood, the right-wing fundamentalist group ruling the South). The vampire threat (like the zombie threat in Romero's films) is largely secondary. The main concern of the film is survival in a bleak landscape following social collapse, where humanity is at a premium.

Co-writer–director Mickle consciously referenced the Great Depression in choosing to set much of the film in rural Pennsylvania, giving it "a dustbowl depression look, not some futuristic, apocalyptic look, but more little kids running around in potato sacks."[6] As the film unfolds, the viewer becomes aware of images that strongly invoke the famous Depression-era photography of Dorothea Lange. We see families stranded at the side of the road in broken-down cars; people living in shanty towns; possessions and clothes being bartered in street markets. This invites an allegorical reading of the film, which Mickle has welcomed. "People have seen the film as a critique of capitalism, greed or extremism, and I'd agree that it's meant to be a cautionary tale."[7]

The film is beautifully photographed by Ryan Samul. His approach strongly echoes the work of cinematographer Nestor Almendros in Terrence Malick's Depression-era drama *Days of Heaven* (1978), especially in the use of "magic hour" filming. *Stake Land*'s bleached landscapes also owe a great deal to that film. The Malick influence can also be felt in *Stake Land*'s use of voice-over narration by a teenager, which forms the emotional core of the film.

However, the overriding reference in *Stake Land* is to *The Grapes of Wrath* (1940), John Ford's film based on Steinbeck's classic novel, and the plot echoes that of Steinbeck in several ways. In Ford's film, unemployed Oklahoma farm workers travel to California in search of work in the fields. This is similar to the protagonists' plight to reach the "New Eden" in *Stake Land*. The hardships along the way threaten, in Steinbeck's story, to erode the family and with it the very fabric of American society. In *Stake Land*, the protagonists form a ramshackle family which is constantly undermined by the vampires, the Brotherhood, and the day-to-day hardship of survival. Martin briefly finds a surrogate mother in a nun (Kelly McGillis) they rescue from the Brotherhood, but she is taken from him almost as soon as he finds her, and not once but twice. Other family members come and go, but in the end, it is always only Martin and "Mister" left, and it seems, like in Steinbeck, that any form of normal family life is going to remain impossible. Steinbeck, in 1939, was talking about the break-up of thousands of families during the Depression, caused by mass migration. In *Stake Land*, "Mister" repeatedly voices the impossibility of maintaining family ties in a survival situation: "I'm not your father," he reminds Martin constantly.

And yet there is a rich seam of humanity that runs through *Stake Land*. In a scene which closely mirrors a section in *The Grapes of Wrath*, the survivors chance upon an encampment where they briefly experience human hope again for the first time in months. Strangers in the camp revel in each other's company; social contact is renewed; people dance together in the street. This is the Weedpatch Camp of Steinbeck's novel: housing built for migrant workers by the government's Farm Security Administration to provide a decent hygienic environment for families—an alternative to the dirty, squalid camps established by the farmers and growers. In Ford's film, a group of deputies attempt to have Weedpatch Camp closed down, so that their bosses—the farmers and growers—can once again exploit and harass the farm workers. In *Stake Land*, no sooner has the human spirit re-established itself in the encampment, than the reactionary Brotherhood seeks to destroy it. The means by which they do so is one of the film's most astonishing moments. We, the audience, as well as Martin and "Mister," struggle at first to understand what is happening. Then the sheer malice of it is brought home, in the same way as, in *The Grapes of Wrath*, the malice of the bosses is underlined by their desire to wreck the Weedpatch Camp. *Stake Land*'s conclusion is similar to Steinbeck's in that respect: It is not the vampires or the Depression that cause the greatest threat to humanity, but those who would seek to exploit the disaster to increase their own power and/or fortunes.

Whether this is currently true in the United States with regards to Christian fundamentalism, as Mickle seems to suggest, is open to debate. One of the criticisms of *Stake Land* is that it perhaps tries to reference too many things at once. Not only are there the references to the Great Depression and Christian fundamentalism, but also to the conventions of the western genre. This leads to some messiness in the plot development towards the end. To reach a logical conclusion in terms of the apocalyptic–Steinbeck storyline, the family must perish, with only Martin and "Mister" left to roam the country alone in perpetuity. However, traditional western movie tropes call for the family to be preserved and for the individuality of the "pioneer spirit" to be reaffirmed. In *Stake Land*, this means that there is a bit of to-ing and fro-ing in the final scenes, as a new character is introduced to take over from "Mister" as Martin's "family," so that Mister can do the Ethan Edwards (John Wayne) thing from *The Searchers* and continue to roam.

With that said, however, *Stake Land* shows that great insight in horror films comes, not necessarily from "self-reflexivity" within the genre, but by a film combining cultural and historical references in a meaningful way.

* * *

Brad Anderson is one of the best—if not *the* best—directors working in psychological horror today. *The Machinist* (2004) is already an acknowledged classic. *Session 9* (2001) continues to disturb, intrigue and mystify. *Sounds Like* (2006) is, along with John Carpenter's *Cigarette Burns* (2005), the strongest of the *Masters of Horror* series. Anderson combines the best of Hitchcock and Polanski in his ability to use pure cinema to unsettle and unnerve. He is so adept at psychological horror that the social commentary in his films often passes unnoticed by critics. It is there. In *Session 9* there is the abandoned asylum, a relic from a time when people would be incarcerated against their will simply because they were considered too burdensome to remain in society. Dozens of huge asylums like the one in *Session 9* stand abandoned in the United States and Britain, a shameful reminder of our less-than-tolerant past when it came to treating mental illness. In *Session 9*, this sense of horror and shame—akin to that one senses in concentration camps—pervades the film.

In *Vanishing on 7th Street* (2010), a group of characters band together in a Detroit bar to fight against an inexplicable enemy. When darkness comes, those who are not protected by a light source—such as a torch—simply vanish, leaving only their clothes behind. The film opens in a cinema. Projectionist Paul (John Leguizamo) is changing the reels when the lights suddenly go out. When he investigates, he finds the entire movie house suddenly empty, except for clothes and possessions left on the seats and in the aisles. Where has everyone vanished to? It is a surreal premise—one that begs a metaphorical or even philosophical meaning. The setting of Detroit, in particular, has allegorical resonance. In real life, as well as on film, the once thriving Motor City is now a ghost town; industry has ended there. Houses stand empty. People have left. Like in *Vanishing on 7th Street*, only shadows remain. And the creeping darkness threatens to encroach into other cities, with similar results.

In Anderson's films, the inexplicable only happens to the workers: the blue collar stiff in *The Machinist*, the office drone *in Sounds Like*, the tradesmen builders in *Session 9*. In these films, the workplace itself becomes a site of horror. The personal insanity of the characters is possibly caused by their working environment, certainly is made worse by it. The mundane yet highly stressful job of the machinist (Christian Bale) seems at first to be the thing that is tipping him over the edge. In *Session 9*, the impossibly short timescale of the building contract pressures the men unduly, making them tired and disorientated–and susceptible to the influence of the asylum and the malignant forces housed within its walls. In *Vanishing on 7th Street* all the characters are separated from loved ones because of the pressures of work. Rosemary (Thandi Newton) is a junior doctor forced to leave her baby at home while she works her shift. Luke (Hayden Christensen) is a news reporter whose job takes him away from home, only to find his girlfriend vanished once he returns. For these characters, their lives are vanished and now their very existence is at stake. In fact, their final line of defense against vanishing is to protest their existence, as Leguizamo attempts to do. As the workers in real-life Detroit tried to do—by attempting to rebuild their communities, turning empty real estate into farms and social housing.

Vanishing on 7th Street borrows heavily from *Night of the Living Dead* in this sense. A small group of characters is besieged by an inexplicable, even absurd apocalypse. Both films share the absurdist approach of the playwright Eugene Ionesco, whose work (as discussed in Chapter 5) spoke to the absurdity of the 1950s nuclear age; similarly, Romero's film spoke to the absurdity of intergenerational conflict in the 1960s and Anderson's film speaks to the absurdity of economic collapse in present-day America.

Anderson has an uncanny ability to take the familiar environments of American towns and cities and make them impersonal and strange. In *Vanishing on 7th Street*, the abandoned Detroit streets take on an unreal sheen. In *The Machinist*, West Coast American details—cars, phone kiosks—were added to Barcelona Streets (where the film was shot) to disorientate the viewer. The film is set in America and it looks like America—and yet it doesn't quite.

This sense of jet-lagged disorientation is heightened by Anderson's masterful use of sound. Anderson often drops out the atmosphere track, leaving only a single sound source in isolation. The effect is to create a dislocated state of mind like that of descending in a plane when your ears pop, leaving everything slightly surreal. In *Sounds Like*, Anderson made this sense of heightened sound the basis of the story.

Even in an indifferent Anderson film like *Vanishing on 7th Street*, all of these characteristics are present. Despite the lackluster script, his gift for subtle psychological horror—and his peerless ability to render it on film—shines through. As does his social subtext.

* * *

A recent and powerful film about a degenerate family is *Mum and Dad* (2008), the feature debut of British writer-director Steven Sheil. Produced for £100K, it's an outstanding example of edgy low-budget horror. Sheil consciously draws on British domestic horror of the 1970s such as *Frightmare* (1974) and *Mumsy, Nanny, Sonny and Girly* (1970) to create a "fucked-up family" horror par excellence. He has discussed the influence of these earlier films on *Mum and Dad* in terms of both having the same sort of "twisted families, with twisted family values."[8]

Sheil's film closely mirrors the theme and plot of *Mumsy, Nanny, Sonny and Girly*: Airport workers Birdie (Ainsley Howard) and her silent brother, LB (Toby Alexander) bring home unsuspecting waifs and strays to Mum and Dad (played by Dido Miles and Perry Benson), who force them into perverse role-playing games in which they pretend to be the "perfect" family. Those who refuse to obey the rules or try to escape are ritualistically murdered. One day they bring home a Polish migrant, Lena (Olga Fedora), who turns out to be more than a match for the family in her determination to survive.

Both *Mumsy, Nanny, Sonny and Girly* and *Mum and Dad* are concerned with the threat posed to the traditional family by social change. But whereas in Freddie Francis's film it was the alternative lifestyle of the hippie and the drifter that threatened the family structure, Sheil's film draws on contemporary fears of mass immigration and its challenge to British identity for its subtext.

The film quickly gets down to business. As soon as Lena enters the home of Mum and Dad, she is knocked unconscious, drugged and imprisoned. Mum takes sexual gratification by scarifying her with a scalpel. Dad's proclivities are even more degenerate: He likes to dismember his victims and masturbate with their body parts. Sheil plunges us so suddenly into depravity that, for a moment, it becomes unclear where he could possibly take us next. It is a risky ploy (the torture porn scenario immediately threatens to turn the viewer off), but Sheil makes it work, taking us into a parody of family domesticity made all the more perverse by the knowledge of Mum and Dad's true nature.

Mum and Dad attempt to play the roles of parents to Lena. She is given a pet name, "Angel," and the rules of the house are explained. In effect, she must submit completely to the will of Mum and Dad if she wishes to survive. It becomes clear that everyone in this family is merely playing a role: Mum is emotionally needy and overbearing; Dad makes the rules and punishes those who disobey; Birdy is the favored sibling who feels in danger of being usurped by "Angel"; and LB is "Little Brother," the dogs-body. Both Mum and Dad spout clichés of parent-ism ("If you live under my roof, you'll abide by my rules"), and Sheil plays up the parody with soap opera–sitcom–like scenes set around the breakfast table.

The falsity of the situation is not lost on Lena or the viewer: None of these relationships are real (except, perhaps, the relationship between Mum and Dad) and there is no real emotion except the desire to control. At first, Lena attempts to play along in an effort to win the favor of Mum and Dad, but it soon becomes clear that they see through this. "You have to make them love you," Birdie tells LB, but here love is a masquerade for hatred. Birdie understands that perhaps the only way to gain the approval of Mum and Dad is by becoming like them. LB understands this too, but his sensitive nature precludes him becoming like Dad. And Lena's strong instincts for self-preservation secretly reawakens hope in LB that he too might escape the clutches of Mum and Dad.

As they so often do, family tensions come to a head at Christmas. The parody of the typical British family Christmas in *Mum and Dad* is scathing and disturbing: Lena has it spelled out to her that she is merely the family pet (her outsider status as a Polish immigrant precludes her assimilation into the family—she remains an object of loathing, a perceived threat to the family structure). Realizing that her time is almost up, she makes a desperate bid to escape, and as a result, all allegiances in the family are laid bare.

Sheil has remarked that much of *Mum and Dad* arose from thinking about the implications of Margaret Thatcher's dictum that "there is no such thing as society. There are individuals, and there are families." (In *Mum and Dad* it is therefore left up to Mum and Dad to make the rules, and there is no wider community to tell them that those rules are unacceptable.) In the light of a recent crop of true-life cases of abduction, imprisonment and torture such as that of Josef Fritzl in Austria, Sheil's film serves as a chilling reminder of how depravity can develop when a society is dismantled by the politicians.

* * *

Another recent British film that shows the damaging effects on the psyche of economic and social collapse is *Tony: London Serial Killer* (2009). Directed by Gerard Johnson on a tiny budget, it was shot on location in Dalston, Hackney, one of London's poorest and most deprived areas. It follows the life of the socially inadequate Tony as he tries to connect with the people around him in the bleak urban environment of London's East End. The only way he seems able to do this is through murder.

Tony: London Serial Killer has been compared to *Taxi Driver* (1976) and *Henry—Portrait of a Serial Killer* as a study of social alienation, and is worthy of the comparison. At its heart is a startling performance by Peter Ferdinando as Tony, a character loosely based on real-life London serial killer Dennis Nilsen. But whereas Nilsen was by all accounts a dominant personality, Ferdinando plays Tony as a timid, passive-aggressive, rather nerdish man who vents his anger and frustration by quietly, and sometimes unexpectedly, hammering, strangling and suffocating his victims to death.

Like Nilsen, however, Tony seems both sexually and socially confused. One is never quite sure of his orientation—if he has one—and over the course of the film we see him variously trying to make sexual or social contact with a prostitute and later with a gay man who picks him up in the pub he frequents. What Tony clearly is, though, is desperately lonely; and the great insight of the film is that it makes clear how human relations suffer in such dire economic circumstances. The only people Tony encounters are all as desperate as he is and see him as someone to use and abuse. In a darkly humorous sequence, Tony tags along with two junkies as they go to score some heroin and then invites them back to his flat for a beer and a smoke. By the time the two addicts have passed out on the settee, Tony has had enough of them abusing his hospitality and suffocates them both.

The theme of exploitation is extended to the portrayal of authority. In one of the most effective sequences, Tony (who is long-term unemployed) is sent for an interview by the employment bureau to work as a billboard man for a tanning shop. The shop owner wants Tony to work fourteen hours a day for a pittance and threatens to have his welfare benefits cut off if he refuses. In the next scene, Tony visits an East European prostitute who rebukes his offer of five pounds for a "cuddle." The clever juxtaposition of these two scenes deftly underlines the exploitation that faces people like Tony and the prostitute who are living on the fringes of society.

Although Gerard Johnson shies away from labeling *Tony: London Serial Killer* as a horror film, preferring instead to describe it as a work of social realism, the film quietly gets under the skin. Less overtly shocking, perhaps, than *Henry—Portrait of a Serial Killer*, the shock in Johnson's film is ideological nonetheless, and creeps up on you. As Tony wanders aimlessly through London's Kings Cross at the film's conclusion, destined only to repeat his actions, one is left fearing for the future of society.

Chapter Notes

Introduction

1. Elliot Stein, "Tod Browning," in Richard Roud, ed., *Cinema: A Critical Dictionary* (London: Secker & Warburg, 1980), 162.
2. "Wes Craven Interview." Adam Simon, *The American Nightmare*, 1999 (documentary).
3. Christopher Sharrett, "The Horror Film in Neoconservative Culture," in Barry Keith Grant, ed., *The Dread of Difference* (Austin: University of Texas Press, 1996), 254.
4. See Colin Odell and Michelle Le Blanc, "Sex and Death in the Horror Film," *Kamera*, accessed August, 11, 2012, http://www.kamera.co.uk/article.php/648.
5. "Tobe Hooper Interview," accessed September 9, 2012, http://www.avclub.com/articles/tobe-hooper,13680/.
6. "Jeff Lieberman Interview," *Rue Morgue* magazine podcast, accessed October 19, 2012, http://www.rue-morgue.com/2011/06/rue-morgue-podcast-jeff-lieberman/.
7. Quoted in Paul R. Gagne, *The Zombies That Ate Pittsburgh: The Films of George A. Romero* (New York: Dodd, Mead, 1987), 9.
8. Alice L. George, *Awaiting Armageddon: How Americans Faced the Cuban Missile Crisis* (Chapel Hill: University of North Carolina Press, 2003), 11.
9. The Gaither Report, accessed August 19, 2012, http://www.gwu.edu/~nsarchiv/NSAEBB/NSAEBB139/nitze02.pdf.
10. "Jeff Lieberman Interview," *Rue Morgue* magazine podcast.
11. Tony Williams, "Wes Craven: An Interview," *Journal of Popular Culture and Television* 8, No. 3 (1980): 12.
12. Robin Wood, *Hollywood from Vietnam to Reagan* (New York: Columbia University Press, 1986, reprint 2003), 107.
13. Andrew Tudor, *Monsters and Mad Scientists: A Cultural History of the Horror Film* (Oxford: Basil Blackwell, 1989), 189.
14. "The Monsters Chat with Jeff Lieberman," accessed October 19, 2012, http://www.monstersatplay.com/features/interviews/jeff-chat.php.
15. See Wood, *Hollywood from Vietnam to Reagan*, 63–84.
16. Indeed he has stated this on several occasions—see for example, Larry Getlin, "Return of 'Living Dead,'" *The New York Post*, May 18, 2008. http://www.nypost.com/p/entertainment/movies/item_GOZg54FUU8WNmSsP5eBk9N.
17. Dennis Fischer, "George Romero on *Bruiser*, Development Hell and Other Sundry Matters," in Tony Williams, ed., *George A. Romero: Interviews* (Jackson: University Press of Mississippi, 2011), 132.
18. See Susan Sontag, "The Imagination of Disaster," in *Against Interpretation and Other Essays* (New York: Farrar, Straus & Giroux, 1966), 208–225.
19. Wood, *Hollywood from Vietnam to Reagan*, 97.
20. Ibid., 63–84.
21. See Colin Campbell, "On Intellectual Life, Politics and Psychoanalysis: A Conversation with Gad Horowitz," *Ctheory.net*, accessed October 8, 2012, http://www.ctheory.net/articles.aspx?id=397.
22. Wood, *Hollywood from Vietnam to Reagan*, 170.
23. Ibid., 63–84.
24. Tom Seligson, "George Romero: Revealing the Monsters Within Us," in Williams, *George A. Romero: Interviews*, 78.
25. Carl Plantinga, "The Scene of Empathy and the Human Face on Film," in Carl Plantinga and Greg M. Smith, eds., *Passionate Views: Film, Cognition, and Emotion* (Baltimore: Johns Hopkins University Press, 1999), 239–55.
26. Wood, *Hollywood from Vietnam to Reagan*, 112.
27. Rick Worland, *The Horror Film: An Introduction* (Oxford: Blackwell, 2007), 21.
28. See, for example, Christopher Sharrett, "Apocalypticism in the Contemporary Horror Film: A Typological Survey of a Theme in the Fantastic Cinema, Its Relationship to Cultural Tradition and Current Filmic Expression," Ph.D. dissertation, New York University, 1983.
29. "Wes Craven Interview," *The American Nightmare*.

Chapter 1

1. "The Letchworth Village Freakshow," accessed January 22, 2012, http://www.eugenicsarchive.org/html/eugenics/static/images/1087.html.
2. "Genes and Eugenics." *New York Times*, August 24, 1932, accessed June 6, 2011, http://www.dnalc.org/view/11720—Genes-and-Eugenics-New-York-Times-

8-24-1932-critical-review-of-Third-International-Eugenics-Congress.html.

3. Since this chapter was written, Angela Smith has published *Hideous Progeny: Disability, Eugenics and Classic Horror Cinema* (New York: Columbia University Press, 2012). The book addresses the cultural fascination of disability during the eugenics era, as exploited by classic horror cinema.

4. There was an opinion held by some in Hollywood that Browning was a "ghoul." Screenwriter Budd Schulberg, for example, in his autobiography *Moving Pictures,* describes Browning during the filming of *Freaks* as "Count Dracula on Stage Ten." See Budd Schulberg, *Moving Pictures: Memories of a Hollywood Prince* (New York: Stein and Day, 1981), 314.

5. David J. Skal and Elias Savada, *Dark Carnival: The Secret World of Tod Browning, Hollywood's Master of the Macabre* (New York: Anchor Books, 1995), 100.

6. Ibid., 166.

7. Ibid.

8. David J. Skal, *The Monster Show: A Cultural History of Horror* (London: Plexus, 1993), 147–148.

9. See Christine Rosen, "The Democratization of Beauty," *The New Atlantis: A Journal of Technology and Society* No. 5 (Spring 2004): 19–21.

10. Cited by Nancy Pedri, "Portraiture's Unruly Faces," in Leslie Boldt-Irons, Corardo Federici, Ernesto Virgulti, eds., *Beauty and the Abject: Interdisciplinary Perspectives* (New York: Peter Lang, 2007), 131.

11. See Rosen, "The Democratization of Beauty," 19–21.

12. Ibid., 20.

13. Rachel Adams, *Sideshow USA: Freaks and the American Cultural Imagination* (Chicago: University of Chicago Press, 2001), 31.

14. Skal and Savada, *Dark Carnival: The Secret World of Tod Browning, Hollywood's Master of the Macabre*, 23.

15. See David Micklos, *Eugenics Research Methods,* accessed January 22, 2012, http://www.eugenicsarchive.org/html/eugenics/essay3text.html.

16. Adams, *Sideshow USA: Freaks and the American Cultural Imagination*, 67.

17. Rosen, "The Democratization of Beauty," 21.

18. Elias Savada, "The Making of *Freaks*," accessed January 22, 2012, http://www.olgabaclanova.com/the_making_of_freaks.htm.

19. Adams, *Sideshow USA: Freaks and the American Cultural Imagination*, 64.

20. See Paul Lombardo, *Eugenic Laws Against Race Mixing*, accessed January 22, 2012, http://www.eugenicsarchive.org/html/eugenics/essay7text.html.

21. See Paul Lombardo, *Eugenic Sterilization Laws*, accessed January 22, 2012, http://www.eugenicsarchive.org/html/eugenics/essay8text.html.

22. John Russell Taylor, "James Whale," in Richard Roud, ed., *Cinema: A Critical Dictionary* (London: Secker & Warburg, 1980), 1074.

23. Interview with Paul M. Jensen in "She's Alive! Creating The Bride of Frankenstein," DVD extra on *The Bride of Frankenstein*, 2008.

24. James Curtis, *James Whale: A New World of Gods and Monsters* (London: Faber, 1998), 143.

25. Ibid., 153.

26. Ibid.

27. Ibid., 154.

28. Russell D. Covey, "Criminal Madness, Cultural Iconography and Insanity," *Stanford Law Review* 6, No. 6 (2009): 1387.

29. Wood, *Hollywood from Vietnam to Reagan*, 72.

30. Covey, "Criminal Madness, Cultural Iconography and Insanity," 1388.

31. Curtis, *James Whale: A New World of Gods and Monsters*, 133.

32. Ibid., 145.

33. Ibid., 146.

34. Martin Tropp, "Recreating the Monster: Frankenstein and Film" in Barbera Tepa Lupack, ed., *Nineteenth Century Women and The Movies: Adapting Classic Women's Fiction to Film* (Bowling Green: Bowling Green State University Popular Press, 1999), 33.

35. Wood, *Hollywood from Vietnam to Reagan*, 68.

36. See Estelle B. Freedman, "Uncontrolled Desires: The Response to the Sexual Psychopath, 1920–1960" in *Feminism, Sexuality and Politics: Essays* (Chapel Hill: University of North Carolina Press, 2006), 121–139.

37. Quoted in Curtis, *James Whale: A New World of Gods and Monsters*, 154.

38. Ibid., 157.

39. Scott MacQueen DVD commentary, *Bride of Frankenstein*, 2008.

40. Quoted in Curtis, *James Whale: A New World of Gods and Monsters*, 381.

41. Quoted in Skal and Savada, *Dark Carnival: The Secret World of Tod Browning, Hollywood's Master of the Macabre*, 206.

42. Ibid.

43. Ibid., 228.

44. See Curtis, *James Whale: A New World of Gods and Monsters*, 343.

45. Ibid., 336.

Chapter 2

1. Wood, *Hollywood from Vietnam to Reagan*, 77.

2. Skal, *The Monster Show*, 212.

3. Ibid., 217.

4. Ibid., 215.

5. Martin Scorsese's DVD narration in *Val Lewton—The Man in the Shadows*, DVD, Turner Classic Movies, Sikelia Productions, 2007 (dir. Kent Jones).

6. Edmund G. Bansak, *Fearing the Dark: The Val Lewton Career* (Jefferson, NC: McFarland, 2003) 91–92.

7. Peter Hutchings, *The Horror Film* (London: Longman, 2003), 176.

8. Joel Siegel, *Val Lewton—The Reality of Terror* (New York: Viking Press, 1972), 23.

9. Bansak, *Fearing the Dark: The Val Lewton Career*, 8.

10. Quoted by Greg Mank, DVD commentary to *Cat People*, Warner Bros, 2005.

11. Bansak, *Fearing the Dark: The Val Lewton Career*, 12.

12. Mank, *Cat People* DVD commentary.

13. Annette Kuhn, "Genre, the Woman's Picture and the Female Audience." Film Reference, accessed Febru-

ary 16, 2013, http://www.filmreference.com/encyclopedia/Romantic-Comedy-Yugoslavia/Woman-s-Pictures-GENRE-THE-WOMAN-S-PICTURE-AND-THE-FEMALE-AUDIENCE.html.
14. Mank, *Cat People*, DVD commentary.
15. Siegel, *Val Lewton—The Reality of Terror*, 31.
16. Alice Kessler-Harris, "War, Work and the Culture of Gender," *Labour/LeTravail* 19 (Spring 1987): 163–167.
17. See Maureen Honey, *Creating Rosie the Riveter: Class, Gender and Propaganda During World War II* (Amherst: University of Massachusetts Press, 1985).
18. "Victory Girls," *Encyclopedia of Children and Childhood in History and Society*, accessed February 16, 2013, 2013http://www.faqs.org/childhood/Th-W/Victory-Girls.html.
19. J. P Telotte, *Dreams of Darkness: Fantasy and the Films of Val Lewton* (Urbana: University of Illinois Press, 1985), 14.
20. Ibid.
21. Ibid.
22. Ibid., 24.
23. Quoted in Scorsese's DVD narration, *Val Lewton—A Man in the Shadows*.
24. Carl J. Jung, "Marriage as a Psychological Relationship," in *Aspects of the Feminine* (London: Routledge, 1982), 41–54.
25. Lyn Davis Genelli and Tom Genelli, "The Return of *The Curse of the Cat People*," *Conflict Alchemy*, accessed February 5, 2013, http://www.conflictalchemy.com/includes/download.php?p=publications&id=10.
26. Mank, *Cat People*, DVD commentary.
27. Alexander Nemerov, *Icons of Grief: Val Lewton's Home Front Pictures* (Berkeley: University of California Press, 2005).
28. Mank, *Cat People*, DVD commentary.
29. Mary Ann Doane, *The Desire to Desire: The Woman's Film of the 1940s* (Bloomington: University of Indiana Press, 1987), 46.
30. Bruce Kawin, *Horror and the Horror Film* (London: Anthem Press, 2012), 138–139.
31. There is indeed a brief shot of a black panther later in the attack sequence shown pouncing on Dr. Judd's inert body. I would suggest that this was a shot included in the film at the behest of the studio, and went against Lewton's original intention not to show Irena in panther form.
32. Steve Haberman, *The Seventh Victim*, DVD commentary, Warner Bros., 2005.
33. Danny Peary, "Mark Robson Remembers RKO, Welles, and Val Lewton," *Velvet Light Trap* No. 10 (Fall 1993): 31.
34. Greg Mank, *Curse of the Cat People*, DVD commentary, Warner Bros., 2005.
35. Ibid.
36. Cited in Nemerov, *Icons of Grief: Val Lewton's Home Front Pictures*, 10.
37. Mank, *Curse of the Cat People*, DVD commentary.
38. Ibid.
39. Genelli and Genelli, "The Return of *The Curse of the Cat People*."
40. See Bansak, *Fearing the Dark: The Val Lewton Career*, 243–245.
41. Tom Weaver, *Bedlam*, DVD commentary, Warner Bros., 2005.
42. Ibid.

Chapter 3

1. Timothy Shary, *Teen Movies: American Youth on Screen* (London: Wallflower Press, 2005), 35.
2. Ibid., 33.
3. Ibid.
4. Tom Weaver, "Herman Cohen," in *Attack of the Monster Movie Makers: Interviews with Twenty Genre Giants* (Jefferson, NC: McFarland, 1994).
5. Samuel Z. Arkoff, *Guardian* Interview, British Film Institute South Bank, August 11, 1991. DVD extra on *Blood of Dracula*, Arkoff Film Library, 2003.
6. See, for example, Thomas Doherty, *Teenagers and Teenpics: The Juvenilization of American Movies in the 1950s* (Philadelphia: Temple University Press, 2002).
7. Garry Mulholland, *Stranded at the Drive-In: From* The Breakfast Club *to* The Social Network: *The 100 Best Teen Movies* (London: Orion Ebook, 2011).
8. Gary Morris, "Beyond the Beach: AIP's Beach Party Movies," *Bright Lights Film Journal* 21. (May 1998), accessed February 13, 2013, http://brightlightsfilm.com/21/21_beach.php.
9. Shary, *Teen Movies: American Youth on Screen*, 19.
10. Doherty, *Teenagers and Teenpics: The Juvenilization of American Movies in the 1950s*, 132.
11. Quoted by Morris, "Beyond the Beach: AIP's Beach Party Movies."
12. Cited in Cyndy Hendershot, *I Was a Cold War Monster: Horror Films, Eroticism and the Cold War Imagination* (Bowling Green: Bowling Green State University Popular Press, 2001), 107.
13. Ken Smith, "Mental Hygiene: The Dos and Don'ts of the Doo-Wop Age," *New York Times*. January 2, 2000, accessed February 13, 2013, http://www.nytimes.com/2000/01/02/movies/film-the-dos-and-don-ts-of-the-doo-wop-age.
14. Ibid.
15. Ibid.
16. Shary, *Teen Movies: American Youth on Screen*, 24.
17. Hendershot, *I Was a Cold War Monster: Horror Films, Eroticism and the Cold War Imagination*, 114.
18. Ibid., 115.
19. Ibid.
20. See Albert E. Kahn, *The Game of Death: Effects of the Cold War on Our Children* (New York: Cameron and Kahn, 1953), 10.
21. Hendershot, *I Was a Cold War Monster: Horror Films, Eroticism and the Cold War Imagination*, 115.
22. Winston Wheeler-Dixon, "Fear and Self-Loathing: Horror and Homophobia in the Films of Herman Cohen," *Senses of Cinema* Issue 49 (February 2009), accessed February 13, 2013, http://sensesofcinema.com/2009/feature-articles/herman-cohen/#1.
23. Oren Shai, "The Women in Prison Film: From Reform to Revolution, 1922–1974," *Bright Lights Film Journal* Issue 79 (February 2013), accessed February 13, 2013, http://brightlightsfilm.com/79/79-women-in-prison-movies-cinema-genre-caged_shai.php.

24. Ibid.
25. See Wheeler-Dixon, "Fear and Self-Loathing: Horror and Homophobia in the Films of Herman Cohen."
26. Shai, "The Women in Prison Film: From Reform to Revolution, 1922–1974."
27. Wheeler-Dixon, "Fear and Self-Loathing: Horror and Homophobia in the Films of Herman Cohen."
28. Ibid.

Chapter 4

1. Benjamin Halligan, *Michael Reeves* (British Film Makers) (Manchester: Manchester University Press, 2003), 153.
2. Quoted in John B. Murray, *The Remarkable Michael Reeves: His Short and Tragic Life* (Baltimore: Luminary Press, 2004), 210.
3. Erich Fromm, "The Nature of Violence," *The Collier's 1969 Year Book, Covering the Year 1968* (New York: Crowell-Collier Educational Corporation, 1969).
4. Leon Hunt, "*Witchfinder General*: Michael Reeves' visceral classic," in Andy Black, ed., *Necronomicon Book 1: The Journal of Horror and Erotic Cinema* (London: Creation Books, 1996), 124.
5. "Friday Night Frights—Episode 22: Kim Newman," *Starburst Magazine*, accessed April 16, 2013, http://www.starburstmagazine.com/podcasts/horror-podcast.
6. "Prurience Proves an Irritant to Democracy," *The Independent*, February 12, 1994. http://www.independent.co.uk/voices/leading-article-prurience-proves-an-irritant-to-democracy-1393544.html.
7. Halligan, *Michael Reeves*, 60.
8. Ibid., 63.
9. Iain Sinclair, *Lights Out for the Territory* (London: Granta Books, 1997), 296.
10. Murray, *The Remarkable Michael Reeves: His Short and Tragic Life*, 107.
11. Reeves in interview in "Blood Beast: The Films of Michael Reeves," documentary DVD extra on *Witchfinder General: Special Edition*, Metrodome, 2003.
12. Sinclair, *Lights Out for the Territory*, 301.
13. Kim Newman, "Production Notes," DVD extra on *The Sorcerers*, 2003.
14. Robin Wood, "In Memoriam: Michael Reeves," *Movie* 17 (Winter 1969–70): 5.
15. Fromm, "The Nature of Violence."
16. Sinclair, *Lights Out for the Territory*, 300.
17. Ingrid Cranfield, *At Last Michael Reeves: An Investigative Memoir of the Acclaimed Filmmaker* (Lightening Source Incorporated/ Ingrid Cranfield, 2007), 16.
18. Fromm, "The Nature of Violence."
19. "History of London: Swinging 60s—Capital of Cool," *History*, accessed April 16, 2013, http://www.history.co.uk/explore-history/history-of-london/swinging-london.html.
20. Murray, *The Remarkable Michael Reeves: His Short and Tragic Life*, 210.
21. Quentin Turnour, "Witchfinder General." *Senses of Cinema* Issue 31 (April 2004), http://sensesofcinema.com/2004/cteq/witchfinder_general/.
22. Fromm, "The Nature of Violence."
23. Ibid.
24. Ibid.
25. Halligan, *Michael Reeves*, 108.
26. Ibid., 189.
27. Ibid., 195.
28. Ibid., 172.
29. Ibid.
30. Sinclair, *Lights Out for the Territory*, 304.
31. Wood, "In Memoriam: Michael Reeves," 5.
32. Cited in Murray, *The Remarkable Michael Reeves: His Short and Tragic Life*, 210.
33. Quoted in Chris O'Loughlin, "Michael Reeves and *Witchfinder General*," *We Belong Dead* Issue 9 (Spring 2013): 72.
34. Quoted in Murray, *The Remarkable Michael Reeves: His Short and Tragic Life*, 218.
35. Halligan, *Michael Reeves*, 198.
36. Ibid., 188.
37. Wood, "In Memoriam: Michael Reeves," 6.
38. Cited in Cranfield, *At Last Michael Reeves: An Investigative Memoir of the Acclaimed Filmmaker*, 92.
39. Halligan, *Michael Reeves*, 217.
40. Cranfield, *At Last Michael Reeves: An Investigative Memoir of the Acclaimed Filmmaker*, 55.
41. "Wes Craven Interview," Adam Simon, *The American Nightmare*, 1999, documentary.
42. Cranfield, *At Last Michael Reeves: An Investigative Memoir of the Acclaimed Filmmaker*, 58.
43. See Steve Chibnall, *Making Mischief: The Cult Films of Pete Walker* (Guildford: FAB, 1998).
44. Ibid., 10.
45. Steve Chibnall, "A Heritage of Evil: Pete Walker and the Politics of Gothic Revisionism," in Steve Chibnall and Julian Petley, eds., *British Horror Cinema* (British Popular Cinema) (London: Routledge, 2002), 159.
46. Ibid.
47. "Friday Night Frights—Episode 3: Steven Sheil," *Starburst Magazine*, accessed October 12, 2012, http://www.starburstmagazine.com/podcasts/horror-podcast/4707-friday-night-frights-episode-3-steven-sheil.
48. Wood, *Hollywood from Vietnam to Reagan*, 76.
49. "Friday Night Frights—Episode 3: Steven Sheil."
50. Pete Walker, Q&A, BFI South Bank, March 12, 2009.
51. Quoted in Will Hodgkinson, "God, What a Terrible Film," *The Guardian*, March 11, 2005.
52. Chibnall, *Making Mischief*, 79.
53. Ibid., 21.
54. Ibid.
55. Pete Walker interview in *Courting Controversy: An Insider's Look at the Work of Pete Walker*, Nucleus Films, 2005, DVD extra, The Pete Walker Collection, Anchor Bay Entertainment.
56. Pete Walker, Q&A, BFI South Bank, March 12, 2009.
57. Quoted in Chibnall, *Making Mischief*, 22.
58. Ibid., 18–22.
59. Harvey Fenton, screen notes, DVD extra, The Pete Walker Collection, Anchor Bay Entertainment.
60. Chibnall, *Making Mischief*, 119.
61. Ibid.
62. David Pirie, *A Heritage of Horror* (London: Gordon Fraser, 1973), 18.

63. Quoted in Chibnall, *Making Mischief*, 121.
64. Steve Chibnall, Peter Jessop, and Pete Walker, *House of Whipchord*, DVD commentary, Anchor Bay Entertainment, 2005.
65. Harvey Fenton, screen notes, DVD extra, The Pete Walker Collection.
66. Shai, "The Women in Prison Film: From Reform to Revolution, 1922–1974."
67. Chibnall, *Making Mischief*, 16.
68. Steve Chibnall, Peter Jessop, and Pete Walker, *Frightmare*, DVD commentary, Anchor Bay Entertainment, 2005.
69. Chibnall, *Making Mischief*, 128.
70. Carol Ryan, "Irish Church's Forgotten Victims Take Case to U.N.," *New York Times*, May 25, 2011.
71. Chibnall, *Making Mischief*, 11.
72. Quoted in Chibnall, *Making Mischief*, 149.
73. Wood, *Hollywood from Vietnam to Reagan*, 75–78.
74. Ibid., 77.
75. Fergus Cashin, *The Sun*, July 12, 1974, cited in Chibnall, *Making Mischief*, 146.
76. Ibid.
77. Chibnall, Jessop and Walker, *Frightmare*, DVD commentary.
78. Chibnall, *Making Mischief*, 145.
79. Wood, *Hollywood from Vietnam to Reagan*, 82–83.
80. Chibnall, *Making Mischief*, 143.
81. Chibnall, Jessop, and Walker, *Frightmare*, DVD commentary.
82. Wood, *Hollywood from Vietnam to Reagan*, 83.
83. Chibnall, *Making Mischief*, 159.
84. Quoted in Chibnall, *Making Mischief*, 156.
85. Ibid.

Chapter 5

1. George A Romero, preface to John A. Russo, *Night of the Living Dead* (New York: Pocket Books, 1974).
2. "Detroit Race Riots," *Time Magazine*, August 4, 1967, accessed June 8, 2013, http://www.time.com/time/covers/0,16641,19670804,00.html.
3. "The People: A Time of Violence and Tragedy," *Time Magazine*, August 4, 1967.
4. Alex Ben Block, "Filming *Night of the Living Dead*: An Interview with Director George Romero," *Filmmakers Newsletter* 5, No. 3 (January 1972), reprinted in Williams, ed., *George A. Romero: Interviews*, 10–11.
5. Quoted in Joe Kane, Night of the Living Dead: *Behind the Scenes of the Most Terrifying Zombie Movie Ever* (London: Aurum Press, 2010), 54.
6. Sean O'Hagen, "Everyone to the Barricades," *The Observer*, January 20, 2008.
7. "A History of the Horror Film," season program, British Film Institute, 2004.
8. "George A. Romero Interview," Adam Simon, *The American Nightmare*, 1999, documentary.
9. Barry Keith Grant, "Introduction," in Barry Keith Grant and Christopher Sharrett, eds., *Planks of Reason: Essays on the Horror Film* (revised edition) (Metuchen, NJ: Scarecrow, 2004), 15.

10. Charles Derry, *Dark Dreams 2.0: A Psychological History of the Modern Horror Film from the 1950s to the 21st Century* (Jefferson, NC: McFarland, 2009), 55–87.
11. R.H.W Dillard, "Night of the Living Dead: It's Not Just Like a Wind That's Passing Through," in Gregory A. Waller, ed., *American Horrors: Essays on the Modern American Horror Film* (Chicago: University of Illinois Press, 1987), 23.
12. Tony Williams, *Hearths of Darkness: The Family in the American Horror Film* (Madison, NJ: Associated University Presses, 1996), 134–135.
13. Speech delivered by Dr. Martin Luther King, Jr., on April 4, 1967, at a meeting of Clergy and Laity Concerned at Riverside Church in New York City.
14. George Romero, "Speak of the Dead: Interview with Stuart Andrews," Bloor Cinema, Toronto, August 26, 2007, DVD extra on *Diary of the Dead*, Optimum Releasing, 2008.
15. Lee Karr, "Speaking of the Dead: An Interview with George A. Romero," www.Homepageofthedead, accessed June 12, 2013, http://www.homepageofthedead.com/baps/romero_interview.html.
16. Williams, *Hearths of Darkness*, 134–135.
17. Fischer, "George Romero on *Bruiser*, Development Hell and Other Sundry Matters," 130.
18. Richard Lippe, Tony Williams, and Robin Wood, "The George Romero Interview, Toronto Film Festival, September 15th, 1979," *Cinema Spectrum* 1 (1980), reprinted in Williams, ed., *George A. Romero: Interviews*, 64.
19. Tony Williams, *The Cinema of George A. Romero: Knight of the Living Dead* (London: Wallflower Press, 2003), 32.
20. Wood, *Hollywood from Vietnam to Reagan*, 102.
21. Williams, *Hearths of Darkness*, 135.
22. George Romero, "Speak of the Dead: Interview with Stuart Andrews."
23. Williams, *Hearths of Darkness*, 130.
24. Taken from "The Winter Soldier," found in the FBI file on the Winter Soldier Investigation, obtained through the Freedom of Information Act, accessed June 7, 2013, http://www.wintersoldier.com/index.php?topic=VVAWFBI.
25. As stated by John Kerry in *The Winter Soldier* press kit, Milliarium Zero, 2005, accessed June 7, 2013, http://www.wintersoldierfilm.com/.
26. Ellie Lachman, *The Winter Soldier* press kit, Millarium Zero, 2005, accessed June 7, 2013, http://www.wintersoldierfilm.com/.
27. See *The Winter Soldier*, Millarium Zero and the Winterfilm Collective, 2005, accessed June 7, 2013, http://www.wintersoldierfilm.com/.
28. Wood, *Hollywood from Vietnam to Reagan*, 114.
29. Alan Ormsby, *Deathdream*, DVD commentary, Blue Underground, 2004.
30. Ibid.
31. Ibid.
32. Wood, *Hollywood from Vietnam to Reagan*, 118.
33. Ibid., 118–119.
34. Ormsby, *Deathdream*, DVD commentary.
35. Ibid.
36. Bob Clark, *Deathdream*, DVD commentary, Blue Underground, 2004.

37. Williams, *Hearths of Darkness*, 141.
38. Dan Yakir, "Morning Becomes Romero," *Film Comment* 15, No. 3 (1977), reprinted in Williams, ed., *George A. Romero: Interviews*, 56.
39. Tom Seligson, "George Romero: Revealing the Monsters Within Us," in *Rod Serling's The Twilight Zone Magazine,* August 1981, reprinted in Tony Williams, ed., *George A. Romero: Interviews*, 77.
40. Ibid., 78.
41. Ibid., 78–79.
42. Linnie Blake, *The Wounds of Nations: Horror Cinema, Historical Trauma and National Identity* (Manchester: Manchester University Press, 2008), 85.
43. Ibid.
44. Ibid., 82.
45. Williams, *Hearths of Darkness*, 142.
46. Ibid.
47. Vincent Canby, "Review of *The Crazies*," *New York Times*, March 1973.
48. Steven Pinker interview, BBC Radio 4, *Thinking Aloud*, November 7, 2011.
49. Williams, *The Cinema of George A. Romero: Knight of the Living Dead*, 68.
50. Ibid., 69.
51. Blake, *The Wounds of Nations: Horror Cinema, Historical Trauma and National Identity*, 84.
52. Ibid.
53. Ibid., 85.

Chapter 6

1. Hutchings, *The Horror Film*, 172.
2. Ibid.
3. Angela Aleiss, *Making the White Man's Indian: Native Americans and Hollywood Movies* (Westport, CT: Praeger, 2005), 127.
4. Quoted in Aleiss, *Making the White Man's Indian: Native Americans and Hollywood Movies,* 127.
5. Ibid.
6. Sharrett, *Apocalypticism in the Contemporary Horror Film*, 55.
7. Ibid., 13.
8. "The My Lai Story," NBC News, New York: NBC Universal, March 29, 1971, accessed September 5, 2012 from NBC Learn: https://archives.nbclearn.com/portal/site/k-12/browse/?cuecard=516.
9. "Wes Craven Interview," *The American Nightmare*.
10. Ibid.
11. Quoted in David A. Szulkin, *Wes Craven's Last House on the Left: The Making of a Cult Classic* (Guildford: FAB, 1997), 15.
12. See Daniel C. Hallin, *The Uncensored War: The Media and Vietnam* (Berkeley: University of California Press, 1989).
13. Wes Craven interview, *Celluloid Crime of the Century*, Blue Underground, 2003.
14. Quoted in Szulkin, *Wes Craven's* Last House on the Left: *The Making of a Cult Classic,* 15.
15. Ibid.
16. Ibid.
17. Adam Lowenstein, *Shocking Representation: Historical Trauma, National Cinema, and the Modern Horror Film* (New York: Columbia University Press, 2005), 131.
18. Williams, "Wes Craven: An Interview," *Journal of Popular Culture and Television*, 11–14.
19. Wes Craven interview, *Celluloid Crime of the Century*.
20. Williams, "Wes Craven: An Interview," *Journal of Popular Culture and Television*, 12.
21. Clive Bloom, *Violent London: Two Thousand Years of Riots, Rebels and Revolts* (London: Sidgwick and Jackson, 2003), 461.
22. "Nation: Hippies and Violence," *Time Magazine*, December 12, 1969, 24.
23. Sharrett, *Apocalypticism in the Contemporary Horror Film*, 55.
24. Curt Rowlett, "The Summer of Love Breeds a Season of Hate: The Effects of the Manson Murders on Public Perceptions of the Hippie Lifestyle," www.Steamshovelpress.com, accessed June 19, 2013, http://www.steamshovelpress.com/fromeditor48.html.
25. Ibid.
26. See Katherine Powell Cohen, *The Haight Ashbury Map and Guide* (San Francisco: Reineck and Reineck, 2010).
27. See Williams, "Wes Craven: An Interview," *Journal of Popular Culture and Television*, 11–14.
28. Ibid., 14.
29. James Greenburg, "Freddie Kruger's Creator Breaks Out of His Genre," *New York Times*, October 9, 1994.
30. Jason Zinoman, *Shock Value: How a Few Eccentric Outsiders Gave Us Nightmares, Conquered Hollywood, and Invented Modern Horror* (New York: Penguin, 2011), 72.
31. See Williams, "Wes Craven: An Interview," *Journal of Popular Culture and Television*, 11–14.
32. Sharrett, *Apocalypticism in the Contemporary Horror Film*, 93.
33. See Williams, "Wes Craven: An Interview," *Journal of Popular Culture and Television*, 11–14.
34. Ibid.
35. Sharrett, *Apocalypticism in the Contemporary Horror Film*, 93.
36. Quoted in Szulkin, *Wes Craven's* Last House on the Left: *The Making of a Cult Classic*, 15.
37. David Hess, *Last House on the Left*, DVD commentary, Metrodome, 2007.
38. Ibid.
39. See Williams, "Wes Craven: An Interview," *Journal of Popular Culture and Television*, 11–14.
40. Ibid.
41. Quoted in Szulkin, *Wes Craven's* Last House on the Left: *The Making of a Cult Classic,* 101.
42. Jonathan L. Crane, "Come On-A My House: The Inescapable Legacy of Wes Craven's *Last House on The Left*," in Xavier Mendik, ed., *Shocking Cinema of the Seventies* (Hereford: Noir Publishing, 2002), 173.
43. See Campbell, "On Intellectual Life, Politics and Psychoanalysis: a Conversation with Gad Horowitz."
44. Sharrett, *Apocalypticism in the Contemporary Horror Film*, 13.
45. See Stefan Jaworzyn, *The Texas Chain Saw Massacre Companion* (London: Titan Books, 2003), for a comprehensive account of the film's production.

46. See Jaworzyn, *The Texas Chain Saw Massacre Companion*, 38.
47. See Zinoman, *Shock Value: How a Few Eccentric Outsiders Gave Us Nightmares, Conquered Hollywood, and Invented Modern Horror*, 134.
48. See "Tobe Hooper Interview," *The American Nightmare*.
49. See, for example, Wood, *Hollywood from Vietnam to Reagan*, 79–84; Mikita Brottman, "Once Upon a Time in the West: *The Texas Chain Saw Massacre* as Inverted Fairytale," in Andy Black, ed., *Necronomicon 1: The Journal of Horror and Erotic Cinema* (Hereford: Creation Books, 1996), 7–21; Christopher Sharrett, "The Idea of Apocalypse in *The Texas Chain Saw Massacre*," in Barry Keith Grant, ed., *Planks of Reason* (Metuchen, NJ: Scarecrow, 1984), 255–276; Williams, *Hearths of Darkness*, 183–193.
50. Quoted by John Bloom, "They Came. They Sawed," *Texas Monthly*, November 2004, accessed June 30, 2013, http://www.texasmonthly.com/content/they-came-they-sawed?fullpage=1.
51. Zinoman, *Shock Value: How a Few Eccentric Outsiders Gave Us Nightmares, Conquered Hollywood, and Invented Modern Horror*, 134.
52. Kim Henkel and Tobe Hooper, "*Leatherface*," 1973.
53. Quoted by Marjorie Baumgarton, "Tobe Hooper Remembers *The Texas Chain Saw Massacre*," *The Austin Chronicle*, October 27, 2000, accessed June 30, 2013, http://www.austinchronicle.com/screens/2000-10-27/79177/.
54. Quoted by Zinoman, *Shock Value: How a Few Eccentric Outsiders Gave Us Nightmares, Conquered Hollywood, and Invented Modern Horror*, 134.
55. Ibid.
56. Sharrett, "The Idea of Apocalypse in *The Texas Chain Saw Massacre*," 270.
57. Ibid., 256.
58. Ibid., 272.
59. Tobe Hooper interview, *Boogeymen 2: Masters of Horror*, documentary, 2002.
60. "Friday Night Frights: Episode 9—Gunnar Hansen," *Starburst Magazine*, accessed October 24, 2012. http://www.starburstmagazine.com/podcasts/horror-podcast-episode-9-gunnar-hansen.
61. Sharrett, "The Idea of Apocalypse in *The Texas Chain Saw Massacre*," 259.
62. Quoted by Baumgarton, "Tobe Hooper Remembers *The Texas Chain Saw Massacre*."
63. Quoted by Bloom, "They Came, They Sawed."
64. Ibid.
65. Quoted by Baumgarton, "Tobe Hooper Remembers *The Texas Chain Saw Massacre*."
66. Quoted by John Pym, "The Texas Chain Saw Massacre," *Monthly Film Bulletin* 43 (December 1976): 258.
67. Naomi Merritt, "Cannibalistic Capitalism and Other American Delicacies: A Bataillean Taste of *The Texas Chain Saw Massacre*," *Film-Philosophy* 14, No. 1 (2010), accessed June 30, 2013, http://www.film-philosophy.com/index.php/f-p/article/view/190.
68. "Friday Night Frights: Episode 9—Gunnar Hansen," *Starburst Magazine*.
69. Quoted by Jaworzyn, *The Texas Chain Saw Massacre Companion*, 45.
70. Sharrett, "The Idea of Apocalypse in *The Texas Chain Saw Massacre*," 271.
71. See "*The Texas Chainsaw Massacre* Rated 18 by the BBFC," accessed June 30, 2013, http://www.bbfc.co.uk/website/Classified.nsf/0/d35ce290a629176b80256737002b7882?OpenDocument&ExpandSection=4.
72. Carol J. Clover, "Her Body, Himself: Gender in the Slasher Film," in R. Howard Bloch and Frances Ferguson, eds., *Misogyny, Misandry and Misanthropy* (Berkeley: University of California Press), 1989, 202.
73. See Sharrett, *Apocalypticism in the Contemporary Horror Film*, 23–56.

Chapter 7

1. Ernest Mathijs, *The Cinema of David Cronenberg: From Baron of Blood to Cultural Hero* (London: Wallflower Press, 2008), 35.
2. Cronenberg interview in Laurens C. Postma, *Long Live the New Flesh: The Films of David Cronenberg*, documentary, 1986.
3. Mathijs, *The Cinema of David Cronenberg: From Baron of Blood to Cultural Hero*, 36.
4. Lowenstein, *Shocking Representation: Historical Trauma, National Cinema, and the Modern Horror Film*, 155.
5. Ibid.
6. Mathijs, *The Cinema of David Cronenberg: From Baron of Blood to Cultural Hero*, 37.
7. Cronenberg interview in Nick Freand Jones, *David Cronenberg and the Cinema of The Extreme*, BBC, 1997.
8. David Cronenberg, *Shivers*, 1975.
9. Mathijs, *The Cinema of David Cronenberg: From Baron of Blood to Cultural Hero*, 32.
10. Wood interview in Postma, *Long Live the New Flesh: The Films of David Cronenberg*.
11. Mathijs, *The Cinema of David Cronenberg: From Baron of Blood to Cultural Hero*, 37.
12. Cronenberg interview in Postma, *Long Live the New Flesh: The Films of David Cronenberg*.
13. Ibid.
14. Ibid.
15. Cronenberg interview in Paul M. Sammon, "David Cronenberg," *Cinefantastique* 10, No. 4 (Spring 1981): 23.
16. See Sharrett, *Apocalypticism in the Contemporary Horror Film*, 98–100.
17. Mathijs, *The Cinema of David Cronenberg: From Baron of Blood to Cultural Hero*, 32.
18. Lieberman interview with *Rue Morgue* magazine podcast.
19. Ibid.
20. "The Monsters Chat with Jeff Lieberman."
21. Rob Freese, "Filmmakers in Focus! Jeff Lieberman—Cult Cut Up!" *Videoscope* 57 (2006): 46–49. My thanks to Joe Kane at *Videoscope* for providing a transcript of this interview.
22. Ibid.
23. Tudor, *Monsters and Mad Scientists: A Cultural History of the Horror Film*, 97.
24. "The Monsters Chat with Jeff Lieberman."
25. George A. Romero, *Dawn of the Dead*, 1977.

26. See Blake, *The Wounds of Nations: Horror Cinema, Historical Trauma and National Identity*, 93.
27. Ibid., 95.
28. Ibid., 93.
29. Wood, *Hollywood from Vietnam to Reagan*, 106.
30. Blake, *The Wounds of Nations: Horror Cinema, Historical Trauma and National Identity*, 95–96.
31. Lippe, Williams, and Wood, "The George Romero Interview, Toronto Film Festival, September 15th, 1979," 63.
32. Wood, *Hollywood from Vietnam to Reagan*, 107.

Chapter 8

1. Blake, *The Wounds of Nations*, 103.
2. Quoted in Dennis Duclos, *The Werewolf Complex: America's Fascination with Violence* (Oxford: Berg, 1998), 1.
3. Quoted in Elliot Leyton, *Hunting Humans: The Rise of the Modern Multiple Murderer* (New York: Penguin, 1986), 12.
4. Colin Wilson and Donald Seaman, *The Encyclopaedia of Modern Murder* (London: Pan, 1989), 1.
5. Interview with John McNaughton, *Henry—Portrait of a Serial Killer, Collector's Edition*, DVD extra, Cult Epics, 1999.
6. Neil Young, "John—Portrait of a Film Director: Interview with John McNaughton," accessed July 30, 2013, http://www.jigsawlounge.co.uk/film/reviews/john-portrait-of-a-film-director-interview-with-john-mcnaughton/.
7. Ibid.
8. Steven V. Roberts, "Reagan on Homelessness: Many Chose to Live in the Streets," *New York Times*, December 23, 1988.
9. Peter Molloy, interview with Rick Prelinger in *An American Dream: A Dream Denied*, BBC, 2010.
10. See Young, "John—Portrait of a Film Director: Interview with John McNaughton."
11. Ibid.
12. Sean Kimber, *Henry—Portrait of a Serial Killer*, Controversies Series (London: Palgrave Macmillan, 2011), 8.
13. Blake, *The Wounds of Nations*, 87.
14. James Marriot, *Horror Films*, Virgin Film Series (London: Virgin Books, 2007), 289.
15. Quoted by Adrian Gargett, "Henry—Portrait of a Serial Killer," accessed July 30, 2013, http://www.kamera.co.uk/reviews_extra/henry_portrait_of_a_serial_killer.php.
16. See Wilson and Seaman, *The Encyclopaedia of Modern Murder*, 1–17.
17. See, for example, Joseph Campbell, *The Hero with a Thousand Faces* (London: Fontana Press, 1993).
18. Jeff Baker, "Q&A: Bret Easton Ellis Talks About Writing Novels, Making Movies," *The Oregonian*, accessed August 3, 2013, http://www.oregonlive.com/books/index.ssf/2010/07/qa_bret_easton_ellis_talks_abo.html.
19. See Serena Donadoni, "*American Psycho*: Writer and Director Mary Harron," *The Cover Girl*, accessed August 3, 2013, http://www.thecinemagirl.com/text/h/harron_psycho.htm.
20. Ibid.
21. David Robinson, "The Unattainable Narrative: Identity, Consumerism and the Slasher Film in Mary Harron's *American Psycho*," *CineAction* No. 68 (Winter 2006): 26–35.
22. Mary Harron and Guinevere Turner, *American Psycho*, 1999.
23. Quoted in Donadoni, "*American Psycho*: Writer and Director Mary Harron."
24. Ibid.
25. Ibid.
26. Robinson, "The Unattainable Narrative: Identity, Consumerism and the Slasher Film in Mary Harron's *American Psycho*," 32.
27. Ibid., 30.
28. Ibid., 33.
29. Richard Reeves, "Black Monday Is the Day Wall Street Yuppies and Reagan Grew Up." *SunSentinel*, October 25, 1987, accessed August 3, 2013, http://articles.sun-sentinel.com/1987-10-25/news/8702010935_1_mark-mehl-government-new-yorkers.
30. See Walter Shapiro, "The Birth and—Maybe—Death of Yuppiedom." *Time Magazine*, April 8, 1991, accessed August 3, 2013, http://www.time.com/time/magazine/article/0,9171,972695-1,00.html.

Chapter 9

1. See John McCarty, *Splatter Movies: Breaking the Last Taboo of the Screen* (New York: St. Martin's Press, 1984).
2. James Berardinelli, "Meet the Feebles," accessed August 12, 2013, http://www.reelviews.net/php_review_template.php?identifier=390.
3. Peter Jackson interview in Tony Hiles, *Good Taste Made Bad Taste*, documentary, 1988.
4. Ibid.
5. See Philip Brophy, "Horrality: The Contextuality of Contemporary Horror Films," *Screen* 27, No. 1 (1986): 2–13.
6. Donato Totaro, "Your Mother Ate My Dog! Peter Jackson and Gore-Gag Comedy," *Offscreen* 5, No. 4 (2001), accessed August 12, 2013, http://www.horschamp.qc.ca/new_offscreen/goregag.html.
7. Jon Towlson, "Interview with Kevin Van Hentenryck, Star of *Basket Case*," *Starburst Magazine*, accessed August 12, 2013, http://www.starburstmagazine.com/features/interviews/3641-interview-kevin-van-hentenryck-star-of-basket-case-.
8. Matt McAllister, "Frank Henenlotter: Born to Be Bad Interviews," *Total Sci-Fi*, accessed August 12, 2013, http://totalscifionline.com/interviews/3153-frank-henenlotter-born-to-be-bad.
9. Nick Zedd, *Cinema of Transgression Manifesto*, accessed August 12, 2013, http://www.nickzedd.com/.
10. Dejan Ognjanovic, "Interview: Brian Yuzna," accessed August 12, 2013, http://www.beyondhollywood.com/interview-brian-yuzna/.
11. Ibid.
12. Donato Totaro, Interview with Brian Yuzna and Jillian McWhirter, *Offscreen* 3, No.2 (1999), accessed August 12, 2013, http://www.horschamp.qc.ca/9902/offscreen_columns/yuzna2.html.

13. "Interview: Director Brian Yuzna at *Terror in the Aisles* with *Society*" *Midnight Ticket.Com,* accessed August 12, 2013, http://www.midniteticket.com/blog/interview-director-brian-yuzna-chicago-portage-theater-terror-in-the-aisles-society-part-1.
14. Emiliano Carpineta, "Interview with Brian Yuzna," accessed August 12, 2013, http://www.occhisulcinema.it/Dos-Brian percent20Yuzna percent20USA.htm.
15. "Interview: Director Brian Yuzna," *Midnight Ticket. Com.*
16. Ibid.
17. Ognjanovic, "Interview: Brian Yuzna."
18. "Interview: Director Brian Yuzna," *Midnight Ticket. Com.*
19. Ibid.
20. Ibid.
21. Ognjanovic, "Interview: Brian Yuzna."
22. Ibid.
23. Stephen Cremin, "Loving the Dead: Interview with Brian Yuzna," *Divinity* 7 (1994): 50.
24. Carpineta, "Interview with Brian Yuzna."
25. "Interview: Director Brian Yuzna," *Midnight Ticket. Com.*
26. See Totaro, "Interview with Brian Yuzna and Jillian McWhirter."
27. Ibid.
28. Ibid.
29. Ibid.
30. Cremin, "Loving the Dead: Interview with Brian Yuzna."

Chapter 10

1. See SIECUS website, "Abstinence-Only-Until-Marriage Q&A," accessed August 30, 2013, http://www.siecus.org/index.cfm?fuseaction=page.viewpage&pageid=522&grandparentID=477&parentID=523.
2. See Clare Murphy, "Chastity Pressed on U.S. Teens," *BBC News Online,* September 18, 2003, accessed August 30, 2013, http://news.bbc.co.uk/1/hi/world/americas/3117108.stm.
3. As stated in the *Teeth* press kit, courtesy of Pierpoline Films.
4. Mitchell Lichtenstein, *Teeth*, DVD commentary, Momentum Pictures, 2008.
5. See Barbara Creed, *The Monstrous-Feminine: Film, Feminism, Psychoanalysis* (London: Routledge, 1993).
6. As stated in the *Teeth* press kit.
7. Ibid.
8. See James Gracey, "Vicious Cunts: Transgressive Sexuality & Monstrous Femininity in *Ginger Snaps* and *Teeth*," *Paracinema* Issue 5 (February 2009). I would like to thank James Gracey for making a copy of this essay available to me.
9. Lichtenstein, *Teeth,* DVD commentary.
10. As stated in the *Teeth* press kit.
11. Ibid.
12. Ibid.
13. Wood, *Hollywood from Vietnam to Reagan*, 97.
14. "Capone Interviews Mitchell Lichtenstein, Director of *Teeth*," *Ain't It Cool News,* January 19, 2008, accessed August 30, 2013, http://www.aintitcool.com/node/35329.
15. Henry Northmore, "Interview—Horror Directors Jen and Sylvia Soska," *The List,* January 20, 2013, accessed February 6, 2013, http://film.list.co.uk/article/48419-interview-horror-directors-jen-and-sylvia-soska/.
16. Ibid.
17. Alan Bett, "Twisted Sisters: An Interview with the Soska Siblings," *The Skinny,* January 21, 2013, accessed February 6, 2013, http://www.theskinny.co.uk/film/features/303903-twisted_sisters_interview_with_soska_siblings.
18. Cherry Potter, *Screen Language: From Film Writing to Film-Making* (London: Methuen, 2001), 198–199.
19. Paul Risker, "The Gospel of American Mary—The Twisted Twins Interview," *Flickering Myth.com,* January 23, 2013, accessed February 6, 2013, http://www.flickeringmyth.com/2013/01/the-gospel-of-american-mary-review.html.
20. David Watson, "The American Mary Interview," *FilmJuice,* accessed February 6, 2013, http://www.filmjuice.com/the-american-mary-interview/.

Afterword

1. Joseph Stiglitz, *Globalization and Its Discontents* (London: Allen Lane, 2002), 7.
2. See Blake, *The Wounds of Nations,* 147.
3. See http://www.simonrumley.com/films/, accessed August 31, 2013.
4. Rob Daniel, "Simon Rumley on Turning Cinema Red, White & Blue," accessed August 31, 2013, http://skymovies.sky.com/simon-rumley-on-turning-cinema-red-white-blue.
5. See Robert Bly, *Iron John: Men and Masculinity* (Reading: Addison Wesley, 1990).
6. Eddie Harrison, "Profile: Jim Mickle, Director of Vampire Horror, *Stakeland*," *The List,* May 23, 2011, accessed August 31, 2013, http://film.list.co.uk/article/34544-profile-jim-mickle-director-of-vampire-horror-stake-land/.
7. Ibid.
8. "Friday Night Frights: Episode 3—Steven Sheil," *Starburst Magazine.*

Bibliography

"Abstinence-Only-Until-Marriage Q&A." Accessed August 30, 2013, http://www.siecus.org/index.cfm?fuseaction=page.viewpage&pageid=522&grandparentID=477&parentID=523.

Adams, Rachel. *Sideshow USA: Freaks and the American Cultural Imagination*. Chicago: University of Chicago Press, 2001.

Aleiss, Angela *Making the White Man's Indian: Native Americans and Hollywood Movies*. Westport, CT: Praeger, 2005.

Baker, Jeff. "Q&A: Bret Easton Ellis Talks About Writing Novels, Making Movies." *The Oregonian*. Accessed August 3, 2013, http://www.oregonlive.com/books/index.ssf/2010/07/qa_bret_easton_ellis_talks_abo.html.

Bansak, Edmund G. *Fearing the Dark: The Val Lewton Career*. Jefferson, NC: McFarland, 2003.

Baumgarton, Marjorie. "Tobe Hooper Remembers *The Texas Chain Saw Massacre*." *The Austin Chronicle*. October 27, 2000. Accessed June 30, 2013, http://www.austinchronicle.com/screens/2000-10-27/79177/.

Berardinelli, James. "Meet the Feebles." Accessed August 12, 2013, http://www.reelviews.net/php_review_template.php?identifier=390.

Bett, Alan. "Twisted Sisters: An Interview with the Soska Siblings." *The Skinny*. January 21, 2013. Accessed February 6, 2013, http://www.theskinny.co.uk/film/features/303903-twisted_sisters_interview_with_soska_siblings.

Blake, Linnie. *The Wounds of Nations: Horror Cinema, Historical Trauma and National Identity*. Manchester: Manchester University Press, 2008.

Block, Alex Ben. "Filming *Night of the Living Dead*: An Interview with Director George Romero." *Filmmakers Newsletter* 5, No. 3 (January 1972) reprinted in Tony Williams, ed., *George A. Romero: Interviews*, 8–17.

Bloom, Clive. *Violent London: Two Thousand Years of Riots, Rebels and Revolts*. London: Sidgwick and Jackson, 2003.

Bloom, John. "They Came. They Sawed." *Texas Monthly*. November 2004. Accessed June 30, 2013, http://www.texasmonthly.com/content/they-came-they-sawed?fullpage=1.

Bly, Robert *Iron John: Men and Masculinity*. Reading: Addison Wesley, 1990.

Brophy, Philip. "Horrality": The Contextuality of Contemporary Horror Films." *Screen* 27, No. 1 (1986): 2–13.

Brottman, Mikita. "Once Upon a Time in the West: *The Texas Chain Saw Massacre* as Inverted Fairytale," in Andy Black, ed., *Necronomicon 1: The Journal of Horror and Erotic Cinema*, 7–21. Hereford: Creation Books, 1996.

Campbell, Colin. "On Intellectual Life, Politics and Psychoanalysis: A Conversation with Gad Horowitz." *Ctheory.net*. Accessed October 8, 2012, http://www.ctheory.net/articles.aspx?id=397.

Campbell, Joseph. *The Hero with a Thousand Faces*. London: Fontana Press, 1993.

"Capone Interviews Mitchell Lichtenstein, Director of *Teeth*." *Ain't It Cool News*. January 19, 2008. Accessed August 30, 2013, http://www.aintitcool.com/node/35329.

Carpineta, Emiliano. "Interview with Brian Yuzna." Accessed August 12, 2013, http://www.occhisulcinema.it/Dos-Brianpercent20Yuznapercent20USA.htm.

Chibnall, Steve. "A Heritage of Evil: Pete Walker and the Politics of Gothic Revisionism." In Steve Chibnall and Julian Petley, eds., *British Horror Cinema* (British Popular Cinema), 156–71. London: Routledge, 2002.

_____. *Making Mischief: The Cult Films of Pete Walker*. Guildford: Fab Press, 1998.

Clover, Carol J. "Her Body, Himself: Gender in the Slasher Film." In R. Howard Bloch and Frances Ferguson, eds., *Misogyny, Misandry and Misanthropy*, 187–228. Berkeley: University of California Press, 1989.

Covey, Russell D. "Criminal Madness, Cultural Iconography and Insanity." *Stanford Law Review* 6, No. 6 (2009): 1375–425.

Crane, Jonathan L. "Come On-A My House: The

Inescapable Legacy of Wes Craven's *The Last House on the Left*." In Xavier Mendik, ed., *Shocking Cinema of the Seventies*, 166–77. Hereford: Noir, 2002.

Cranfield, Ingrid. *At Last Michael Reeves: An Investigative Memoir of the Acclaimed Filmmaker.* Lightening Source Incorporated/ Ingrid Cranfield, 2007.

Creed, Barbara. *The Monstrous-Feminine: Film, Feminism, Psychoanalysis.* London: Routledge, 1993.

Cremin, Stephen. "Loving the Dead: Interview with Brian Yuzna." *Divinity* 7 (1994): 50.

Curtis, James. *James Whale: A New World of Gods and Monsters.* London: Faber, 1998.

Daniel, Rob. "Simon Rumley on Turning Cinema Red, White & Blue." Accessed August, 31, 2013, http://skymovies.sky.com/simon-rumley-on-turning-cinema-red-white-blue.

Davis Genelli, Lyn, and Tom Genelli, "The Return of *The Curse of the Cat People*." *Conflict Alchemy.* Accessed February 5, 2013, http://www.conflict alchemy.com/includes/download.php?p=publ ications&id=10.

Derry, Charles. *Dark Dreams 2.0: A Psychological History of the Modern Horror Film from the 1950s to the 21st Century.* Jefferson, NC: McFarland, 2009.

Dillard, R.H.W. "*Night of the Living Dead*: It's Not Just Like a Wind That's Passing Through." In Gregory A. Waller, ed., *American Horrors: Essays on the Modern American Horror Film*, 14–29. Chicago: University of Illinois Press, 1987.

Doane, Mary Ann. *The Desire to Desire: The Woman's Film of the 1940s.* Bloomington: University of Indiana Press, 1987.

Doherty, Thomas. *Teenagers and Teenpics: The Juvenilization of American Movies in the 1950s.* Philadelphia: Temple University Press, 2002.

Donadoni, Serena. "*American Psycho*: Writer and Director Mary Harron." *The Cover Girl.* Accessed August 3, 2013, http://www.thecinemagirl.com/text/h/harron_psycho.htm.

Duclos, Dennis. *The Werewolf Complex: America's Fascination with Violence.* Oxford: Berg, 1998.

Elias Savada, "The Making of *Freaks*." Accessed January 22, 2012, http://www.olgabaclanova.com/the_making_of_freaks.htm.

Fischer, Dennis. "George Romero on *Bruiser*, Development Hell and Other Sundry Matters." In Williams, *George A. Romero: Interviews*, 122–33.

Freedman, Estelle B. "Uncontrolled Desires: The Response to the Sexual Psychopath, 1920–1960." In Estelle B. Freedman, *Feminism, Sexuality and Politics: Essays*, 121–139. Chapel Hill: University of North Carolina Press, 2006.

Freese, Rob. "Filmmakers in Focus! Jeff Lieberman—Cult Cut Up!" *Videoscope* 57 (2006): 46–49.

Fromm, Erich "The Nature of Violence." *The Collier's 1969 Year Book, Covering the Year 1968*, New York: Crowell-Collier Educational Corporation.

Gagne, Paul R. *The Zombies That Ate Pittsburgh: The Films of George A. Romero.* New York: Dodd, Mead, 1987.

"The Gaither Report." Accessed August 19, 2012, http://www.gwu.edu/~nsarchiv/NSAEBB/NSAEBB139/nitze02.pdf.

Gargett, Adrian. "Henry—Portrait of a Serial Killer." Accessed July 30, 2013, http://www.kam era.co.uk/reviews_extra/henry_portrait_of_a_serial_killer.php.

"Genes and Eugenics." *New York Times*, August 24, 1932. Accessed June 6, 2011, http://www.dnalc.org/view/11720—Genes-and-Eugenics-New-York-Times-8-24-1932-critical-review-of-Third-International-Eugenics-Congress.htm.

George, Alice L. *Awaiting Armageddon: How Americans Faced the Cuban Missile Crisis.* Chapel Hill: University of North Carolina Press, 2003.

Getlin, Larry. "Return of 'Living Dead.'" *The New York Post*, May 18, 2008, http://www.nypost.com/p/entertainment/movies/item_GOZg54F UU8WNmSsP5eBk9N.

Gracey, James. "Vicious Cunts: Transgressive Sexuality & Monstrous Femininity in *Ginger Snaps* and *Teeth*." *Paracinema*. Issue 5, February 2009.

Grant, Barry Keith, and Christopher Sharrett, eds. *Planks of Reason: Essays on the Horror Film* (revised edition). Metuchen, NJ: Scarecrow, 2004.

Greenburg, James. "Freddie Kruger's Creator Breaks Out of His Genre." *New York Times*. October 9, 1994.

Halligan, Benjamin. *Michael Reeves* (British Film Makers). Manchester: Manchester University Press, 2003.

Hallin, Daniel C. *The Uncensored War: The Media and Vietnam.* Berkeley: University of California Press, 1989.

Harrison, Eddie. "Profile: Jim Mickle, Director of Vampire Horror, *Stakeland*." *The List*. May 23, 2011. Accessed August 31, 2013, http://film.list.co.uk/article/34544-profile-jim-mickle-dire ctor-of-vampire-horror-stake-land/.

Hendershot, Cyndy. *I Was a Cold War Monster: Horror Films, Eroticism and the Cold War Imagination.* Bowling Green: Bowling Green State University Popular Press, 2001.

"History of London: Swinging 60s—Capital of Cool." *History*. Accessed April 16, 2013, http://www.history.co.uk/explore-history/history-of-london/swinging-london.html.

Hodgkinson, Will. "God, What a Terrible Film." *The Guardian*. March 11, 2005.

Honey, Maureen. *Creating Rosie the Riveter: Class, Gender and Propaganda During World War II.*

Amherst: University of Massachusetts Press, 1985.
Hunt, Leon. "*Witchfinder General*: Michael Reeves' Visceral Classic." In Andy Black, ed., *Necronomicon Book 1: The Journal of Horror and Erotic Cinema*, 123–30. London: Creation Books, 1996.
Hutchings, Peter. *The Horror Film*. London: Longman, 2003.
"Interview: Director Brian Yuzna at *Terror in the Aisles* with *Society*." *Midnight Ticket.Com*. Accessed August 12, 2013, http://www.midniteticket.com/blog/interview-director-brian-yuzna-chicago-portage-theater-terror-in-the-aisles-society-part-1.
Jaworzyn, Stefan. *The Texas Chain Saw Massacre Companion*. London: Titan Books, 2003.
Jung, Carl J. "Marriage as a Psychological Relationship." In C.G. Jung, *Aspects of the Feminine*, 41–54. London: Routledge, 1982.
Kahn, Albert E. *The Game of Death: Effects of the Cold War on Our Children*. New York: Cameron and Kahn, 1953.
Kane, Joe. Night of the Living Dead: *Behind the Scenes of the Most Terrifying Zombie Movie Ever*. London: Aurum Press, 2010.
Karr, Lee. "Speaking of the Dead: An Interview with George A. Romero." Homepageofthedead-www. Accessed June 12, 2013, http://www.homepageofthedead.com/baps/romero_interview.html.
Kawin, Bruce. *Horror and the Horror Film*. London: Anthem Press, 2012.
Kessler-Harris, Alice. "War, Work and the Culture of Gender." *Labour/LeTravail* 19 (Spring 1987): 163–167.
Kimber, Sean. *Henry—Portrait of a Serial Killer* (Controversies Series). London: Palgrave Macmillan, 2011.
Kuhn, Annette. "Genre, the Woman's Picture and the Female Audience." *Film Reference*. Accessed February 16, 2013, http://www.filmreference.com/encyclopedia/Romantic-Comedy-Yugoslavia/Woman-s-Pictures-GENRE-THE-WOMAN-S-PICTURE-ANDTHE-FEMALE-AUDIENCE.html.
Leyton, Elliot. *Hunting Humans: The Rise of the Modern Multiple Murderer*. New York: Penguin, 1986.
Lippe, Richard, Tony Williams, and Robin Wood. "The George Romero Interview, Toronto Film Festival, September 15th, 1979." *Cinema Spectrum* 1 (1980), reprinted in Williams, *George A. Romero: Interviews*, 59–68.
Lombardo, Paul. "Eugenic Laws Against Race Mixing." Accessed January 22, 2012, http://www.eugenicsarchive.org/html/eugenics/essay7text.html.
Lombardo, Paul. "Eugenic Sterilization Laws." Accessed January 22, 2012, http://www.eugenicsarchive.org/html/eugenics/essay8text.html.
Lowenstein, Adam. *Shocking Representation: Historical Trauma, National Cinema, and the Modern Horror Film*. New York: Columbia University Press, 2005.
Lupack, Barbara Tepa. *Nineteenth Century Women at the Movies: Adapting Classic Women's Fiction to Film*. Bowling Green: Bowling Green State University Popular Press, 1999.
Marriot, James. *Horror Films* (Virgin Film Series). London: Virgin Books, 2007.
Mathijs, Ernest. *The Cinema of David Cronenberg: From Baron of Blood to Cultural Hero*. London: Wallflower Press, 2008.
McAllister, Matt. "Frank Henenlotter: Born to Be Bad Interviews." *Total Sci-Fi*. Accessed August 12, 2013, http://totalscifionline.com/interviews/3153-frank-henenlotter-born-to-be-bad.
McCarty, John. *Splatter Movies: Breaking the Last Taboo of the Screen*. New York: St. Martin's Press, 1984.
Merritt, Naomi. "Cannibalistic Capitalism and Other American Delicacies: A Bataillean Taste of *The Texas Chain Saw Massacre*." *Film-Philosophy* 14, No. 1 (2010). Accessed June 30, 2013, http://www.film-philosophy.com/index.php/f-p/article/view/190.
Micklos, David. "Eugenics Research Methods." Accessed January 22, 2012, http://www.eugenicsarchive.org/html/eugenics/essay3text.html.
"The Monsters Chat with Jeff Lieberman." Accessed October 19, 2012, http://www.monstersatplay.com/features/interviews/jeff-chat.php.
Morris, Gary. "Beyond the Beach: AIP's Beach Party Movies." *Bright Lights Film Journal* 21 (May 1998). Accessed February 13, 2013, http://brightlightsfilm.com/21/21_beach.php.
Mulholland, Garry. *Stranded at the Drive-In: From* The Breakfast Club *to* The Social Network: *The 100 Best Teen Movies*. London: Orion Ebook, 2011.
Murphy, Clare "Chastity Pressed on U.S. Teens." *BBC News Online*, September 18, 2003. Accessed August 30, 2013, http://news.bbc.co.uk/1/hi/world/americas/3117108.stm.
Murray, John B. *The Remarkable Michael Reeves: His Short and Tragic Life*. Baltimore: Luminary Press, 2004.
"Nation: Hippies and Violence." *Time Magazine*. December 12, 1969.
Nemerov, Alexander. *Icons of Grief: Val Lewton's Home Front Pictures*. Berkeley: University of California Press, 2005.
Northmore, Henry. "Interview—Horror Directors Jen and Sylvia Soska." *The List*. January 20, 2013. Accessed February 6, 2013, http://film.list.co.uk/article/48419-interview-horror-directors-jen-and-sylvia-soska/

Odell, Colin, and Michelle Le Blanc. "Sex and Death in the Horror Film." *Kamera*. Accessed August 11, 2012, http://www.kamera.co.uk/article.php/648.

Ognjanovic, Dejan. "Interview: Brian Yuzna." Accessed August 12, 2013, http://www.beyondhollywood.com/interview-brian-yuzna/.

O'Hagen, Sean. "Everyone to the Barricades." *The Observer*. January 20, 2008.

O'Loughlin, Chris. "Michael Reeves and *Witchfinder General*." *We Belong Dead* Issue 9 (Spring 2013): 69–73.

Peary, Danny. "Mark Robson Remembers RKO, Welles, and Val Lewton." *Velvet Light Trap* No. 10 (Fall 1993): 32–37.

Pedri, Nancy. "Portraiture's Unruly Faces." In Leslie Boldt-Irons, Corardo Federici and Ernesto Virgulti, eds., *Beauty and the Abject: Interdisciplinary Perspectives*, 131–149. New York: Peter Lang, 2007.

"The People: A Time of Violence and Tragedy." *Time Magazine*. August 4, 1967.

Pirie, David. *A Heritage of Horror*. London: Gordon Fraser, 1973.

Plantinga, Carl. "The Scene of Empathy and the Human Face on Film." In Carl Plantinga and Greg M. Smith, eds., *Passionate Views: Film, Cognition, and Emotion*, 239–55. Baltimore: Johns Hopkins University Press, 1999.

Potter, Cherry. *Screen Language: From Film Writing to Film-Making*. London: Methuen, 2001.

Powell Cohen, Katherine. *The Haight Ashbury Map and Guide*. San Francisco: Reineck and Reineck, 2010.

"Prurience Proves an Irritant to Democracy." *The Independent*. February 12, 1994, http://www.independent.co.uk/voices/leading-article-prurience-proves-an-irritant-to-democracy-1393544.html.

Pym, John. "The Texas Chain Saw Massacre." *Monthly Film Bulletin* 43 (December 1976): 258.

Reeves, Richard. "Black Monday Is the Day Wall Street Yuppies and Reagan Grew Up." *SunSentinel*. October 25, 1987. Accessed August 3, 2013, http://articles.sun-sentinel.com/1987-10-25/news/8702010935_1_mark-mehl-government-new-yorkers.

Risker, Paul. "The Gospel of American Mary—The Twisted Twins Interview." *Flickering Myth.com*. January 23, 2013. Accessed February 6, 2013, http://www.flickeringmyth.com/2013/01/the-gospel-of-american-mary-review.html.

Roberts, Steven V. "Reagan on Homelessness: Many Chose to Live in the Streets." *New York Times*. December 23, 1988.

Robinson, David. "The Unattainable Narrative: Identity, Consumerism and the Slasher Film in Mary Harron's *American Psycho*." *CineAction* No. 68 (Winter 2006): 26–35.

Rosen, Christine. "The Democratization of Beauty." *The New Atlantis: A Journal of Technology and Society* No. 5 (Spring 2004): 19–21.

Roud, Richard. *Cinema: A Critical Dictionary: The Major Film-Makers*. London: Secker and Warburg, 1980.

Rowlett, Curt. "The Summer of Love Breeds a Season of Hate: The Effects of the Manson Murders on Public Perceptions of the Hippie Lifestyle." Steamshovelpresswww. Accessed June 19, 2013, http://www.steamshovelpress.com/fromeditor48.html.

Russo, John A. *Night of the Living Dead*. New York: Pocket Books, 1974.

Ryan, Carol. "Irish Church's Forgotten Victims Take Case to U.N." *New York Times*. May 25, 2011.

Sammon, Paul M. "David Cronenberg." *Cinefantastique* 10, No. 4 (Spring 1981): 23.

Schulberg, Budd. *Moving Pictures: Memories of a Hollywood Prince*. New York: Stein and Day, 1981.

Seligson, Tom. "George Romero: Revealing the Monsters Within Us." *Rod Serling's The Twilight Zone Magazine*. August 1981, reprinted in Williams, *George A. Romero: Interviews*, 74–87.

Shai, Oren. "The Women in Prison Film: From Reform to Revolution, 1922–1974." *Bright Lights Film Journal* Issue 79 (February 2013). Accessed February 13, 2013, http://brightlightsfilm.com/79/79-women-in-prison-movies-cinema-genre-caged_shai.php.

Shapiro, Walter. "The Birth and—Maybe—Death of Yuppiedom." *Time Magazine*. April 8, 1991. Accessed August 3, 2013, http://www.time.com/time/magazine/article/0,9171,972695-1,00.html.

Sharrett, Christopher. "Apocalypticism in the Contemporary Horror Film: A Typological Survey of a Theme in the Fantastic Cinema, Its Relationship to Cultural Tradition and Current Filmic Expression." New York University, 1983. Ph.D. dissertation (unpublished).

_____. "The Horror Film in Neoconservative Culture." In Barry Keith Grant, ed., *The Dread of Difference*, 253–76. Austin: University of Texas Press, 1996.

_____. "The Idea of Apocalypse in *The Texas Chain Saw Massacre*." In Grant, *Planks of Reason*, 255–276. Metuchen, NJ: Scarecrow, 1984.

Shary, Timothy. *Teen Movies: American Youth On Screen*. London: Wallflower Press, 2005.

Siegel, Joel. *Val Lewton—The Reality of Terror*. New York: Viking Press, 1972.

Sinclair, Iain. *Lights Out for the Territory*. London: Granta Books, 1997.

Skal, David J. *The Monster Show: A Cultural History of Horror*. London: Plexus, 1993.

Skal, David J., and Elias Savada, *Dark Carnival: The*

Secret World of Tod Browning, Hollywood's Master of the Macabre. New York: Anchor Books, 1995.

Smith, Ken. "Mental Hygiene: The Dos and Don'ts of the Doo-Wop Age." *New York Times*. January 2, 2000. Accessed February 13, 2013, http://www.nytimes.com/2000/01/02/movies/film-the-dos-and-don-ts-of-the-doo-wop-age.

Sontag, Susan. "The Imagination of Disaster." In Susan Sontag, *Against Interpretation and Other Essays*, 208–25. New York: Farrar, Straus & Giroux, 1966.

Stein, Elliot. "Tod Browning." In Richard Roud, ed., *Cinema: A Critical Dictionary* (Vol. 1), 156–66. London: Secker & Warburg, 1980.

Stiglitz, Joseph. *Globalization and Its Discontents*. London: Allen Lane, 2002.

Szulkin, David A. *Wes Craven's Last House on the Left: The Making of a Cult Classic*. Guildford: FAB, 1997.

Taylor, John Russell. "James Whale." In Richard Roud, ed., *Cinema: A Critical Dictionary* (Vol. 1), 156–66. London: Secker & Warburg, 1980.

Telotte, J. P. *Dreams of Darkness: Fantasy and the Films of Val Lewton*. Urbana: University of Illinois Press, 1985.

"The Texas Chainsaw Massacre Rated 18 by the BBFC." Accessed June 30, 2013, http://www.bbfc.co.uk/website/Classified.nsf/0/d35ce290a629176b80256737002b7882?OpenDocument&ExpandSection=4.

"Tobe Hooper Interview." Accessed September 9, 2012, http://www.avclub.com/articles/tobe-hooper,13680/.

Totaro, Donato. "Interview with Brian Yuzna and Jillian McWhirter." *Offscreen* 3, No. 2 (1999). Accessed August 12, 2013, http://www.horschamp.qc.ca/9902/offscreen_columns/yuzna2.html.

Totaro, Donato. "Your Mother Ate My Dog! Peter Jackson and Gore-Gag Comedy." *Offscreen* 5, No. 4 (2001). Accessed August 12, 2013, http://www.horschamp.qc.ca/new_offscreen/goregag.html.

Towlson, Jon. "Interview with Kevin Van Hentenryck, Star of *Basket Case*." *Starburst Magazine*. Accessed August 12, 2013, http://www.starburstmagazine.com/features/interviews/3641-interview-kevin-van-hentenryck-star-of-basket-case-.

Tropp, Martin. "Recreating the Monster: Frankenstein and Film." In Barbera Tepa Lupack, ed., *Nineteenth Century Women and The Movies: Adapting Classic Women's Fiction to Film*, 23–77. Bowling Green: Bowling Green State University Popular Press, 1999.

Tudor, Andrew. *Monsters and Mad Scientists: A Cultural History of the Horror Film*. Oxford: Basil Blackwell, 1989.

Turnour, Quentin. "Witchfinder General." *Senses of Cinema* Issue 31 (April 2004), http://sensesofcinema.com/2004/cteq/witchfinder_general/.

"Victory Girls." *Encyclopedia of Children and Childhood in History and Society*. Accessed February 16, 2013, http://www.faqs.org/childhood/Th-W/Victory-Girls.html.

Watson, David. "The American Mary Interview." *FilmJuice*. Accessed February 6, 2013, http://www.filmjuice.com/the-american-mary-interview/.

Weaver, Tom. "Herman Cohen." In Tom Weaver, *Attack of the Monster Movie Makers: Interviews with Twenty Genre Giants*, 53–8. Jefferson, NC: McFarland, 1994.

Wheeler-Dixon, Winston. "Fear and Self-Loathing: Horror and Homophobia in the Films of Herman Cohen." *Senses of Cinema* Issue 49 (February 2009). Accessed February 13, 2013, http://sensesofcinema.com/2009/feature-articles/herman-cohen/#1.

Williams, Tony. *The Cinema of George A. Romero: Knight of the Living Dead*. London: Wallflower Press, 2003.

_____. *Hearths of Darkness: The Family in the American Horror Film*. Madison, NJ: Associated University Presses, 1996.

_____. "Wes Craven: An Interview." *Journal of Popular Culture and Television* 8, No. 3 (1980): 10–14.

Williams, Tony, ed. *George A. Romero: Interviews*. Jackson: University Press of Mississippi, 2011.

Wilson, Colin, and Donald Seaman. *The Encyclopaedia of Modern Murder*. London: Pan Books, 1989.

Wood, Robin. *Hollywood from Vietnam to Reagan*. New York: Columbia University Press, 1986, reprint 2003.

Wood, Robin. "In Memoriam: Michael Reeves." *Movie*, 17 (Winter 1969–70): 5.

Worland, Rick. *The Horror Film: An Introduction*. Oxford: Blackwell, 2007.

Yakir, Dan. "Morning Becomes Romero." *Film Comment* 15, No. 3 (1977). Reprinted in Williams, *George A. Romero: Interviews*, 47–58.

Young, Neil. "John—Portrait of a Film Director: Interview with John McNaughton." Accessed July 30, 2013, http://www.jigsawlounge.co.uk/film/reviews/john-portrait-of-a-film-director-interview-with-john-mcnaughton/

Zedd, Nick. *Cinema of Transgression Manifesto*. Accessed August 12, 2013, http://www.nickzedd.com/

Zinoman, Jason. *Shock Value: How a Few Eccentric Outsiders Gave Us Nightmares, Conquered Hollywood, and Invented Modern Horror*. New York: Penguin, 2011.

INDEX

Numbers in ***bold italic*** indicate pages with photographs

Abbott, Bruce 188
Adams, Eddie 132
Adams, Mary 76
Adams, Maud 191
Adams, Rachel 24, 25, 27
After Hours (1985) 172
Ain't It Cool News (website) 204
Aleiss, Angela 130
Alexander, Toby 222
Alien (1979) 199
All the Little Animals (book) 91
Almendros, Nestor 219
Alonso, Maria Conchito 176
Altamont 11, 83, 131, 134, 217
Altieri, Mitchell *see* The Butcher Brothers
Altman, Robert 3
American International Pictures (AIP) 62, 64–65, 66, 75, 196
American Mary (2012) 4, 192, 196, 197, 198, 204, ***207***, ***209***; and the American Dream 208–209; and body modification 205; dualism in 207–208; as rape-revenge drama 209–210; three act structure of 206
The American Nightmare (1999) 3, 6, 132
"The American Nightmare" (Wood) 3
American Psycho (2000) 163, 164, ***173***, ***174***, ***177***, 206; graphic violence in 175–176; and male identity 173–174; volte face ending of 177–178; as yuppie nightmare movie 172–173
American Psycho (book) 172, 173
Amphibious (2010) 188
Amplas, John 53, 167
Anderson, Arthur 120
Anderson, Brad 7, 220, 221, 222
Anderson, Lindsay 94
Antonioni, Michelangelo 146
Appleman, Haley 200
Appreciating Our Parents (1950) 71

April Fool's Day (2008) 215
Arab-Israeli War 125
Arachnid (2011) 188
Are You Popular? (1947) 71
Are You Ready for Marriage? (1950) 71
Arkoff, Samuel Z. 64, 66
Armstrong, Michael 91
Arnold, Jack 62
Arnold, Tracy ***166***, 168
Aronofsky, Darren 213
Ates, Rosco 25
Atterbury, Malcolm 66
Awaiting Armageddon (book) 10

B, Beth 187
Backus, Richard 118, ***121***, ***122***
Bad Biology (2008) 182, 185, 186, 187
Bad Taste (1987) 182–183
Baffico, Jim 159
Baker, Carlee 218
Baker, Simon 212
Balaban, Bob 190
Bale, Christian 173, ***174***, ***177***, 221
Balme, Timothy 183, ***184***
Band, Charles 187
Bansak, Edmund G. 44, 60
Barr, Patrick 95, 96
Barry, Hilda 102
Basket Case (1982) 180, ***185***, 186, 187
Basket Case 2 (1990) 186
Basket Case 3 (1992) 186
Beach Party film series 66
Beacham, Stephanie 101
Bedlam (1946) 59, 61
Belafonte, Harry 109
Bell, James 54
Ben-Hur (1959) 189
Beneath Still Waters (2005) 188
Benedict XVI, Pope 101
Benson, Perry 222
Berg, Phil 23, 42
Bergen, Candice 131

Bernsen, Corbin 193, ***194***, ***195***
Berserk! (1967) 79
The Better Angels of Our Nature (book) 126
Bettis, Angela 218
Betty Boop 205
Bevan, Stewart 101
Beyond Re-animator (2003) 188
The Birds (1963) 109, 110, 144, 154, 155
Bissell, Whit 71, 76, 78
Black, Cyril 96
The Black Cat (1934) ***12***, 13
The Black Stork (1917) 28
Black Zoo (1963) 63, 79
Blackboard Jungle (1955) 69, 70
Blaine, Jerry ***77***
Blake, Linnie 124, 127, 128, 129, 159, 164, 167, 213
The Blob (1958) 69
Bloch, Robert 146
Blood Feast (1963) 181
Blood of Dracula (1957) 63, 75–76, ***77***
Bloom, Clive 134
Blue Sunshine (1977) 1, 2, 12, 13, 151, ***154***, 155, ***156***, 158–159; as invasion-metamorphosis narrative 157
Blue Velvet (1986) 165, 168, 173
Bly, Robert 217
Blythe, Janus 136
Bodeen, DeWitt 50
The Body Snatcher (1945) 59, 60–61
The Bonus Army 37–38
Booth, Elmer 23
The Boys in Company C (1978) 106
Brain Damage (1988) 180, 185, 186
Braindead see Dead Alive (1992)
Brando, Marlon 66
Brecht, Bertolt 118
Breen, Joseph 41, 43

239

Index

Bride of Frankenstein (1935) *17*, *37*, 38, 42, 186
Bride of Re-animator (1990) 182, 188, 189
Bridgers, Sean 218
Brind, Tess 60
British Board of Film Classification 149
British Broadcasting Corporation (BBC) 109, 126
British Film Institute 108
Brody, Adrien 164
Brooks, Jean 54
Brooks, Ray 94, 97
Brophy, Philip 183
Brown, Norman O. 12, 151
Browning, Tod 5, 6, 7, 9, 13, 14, 21, 41, 42, 44, 54, 85, 186, 198; and degenerate heredity 28; and *Freaks* 22, 24–27, 29–31; personal obsessions of 22–23
Bugliosi, Vincent 148
Bundy, Ted 173
Buñuel, Luis 99, 101, 108, 194
Burns, Marilyn 143, 148, *149*
Bury the Dead (play) 118
Bush, George W. 197, 198, 201, 211, 212
Butcher, Kim 99
The Butcher Brothers 7, 214, 215, 216

The Cabinet of Dr. Caligari (1919) 7, *8*
Cage, Nicolas 173, 176, 177
Caged (1950) 75–76
Cahn, Edward L. 109
Calley, William 117, 131
Canby, Vincent 126
Cardille, Bill 109
Carlin, Lynn 118, *122*
Carlyle, Robert 211
Carné (1991) 147
Carpenter, John 154, 190, 220
Carpineta, Emiliano 188
Carr, Cynthia 137
Carrie (1976) 197, 199
Carroll, Lane 126, *127*, *128*
Carter, Ann 48, *56*, *58*
Cashin, Fergus 99
Cassell, Sandra 132
Cat People (1942) 43, *49*, *51*, 52–54, 57, 71; gender ideology of 47–48; and Jungian psychology 48–50; lesbian subtext of 50–51; shock value in 46–47
Cathey, Reg E. 175
Chambers, Marilyn 199
Channel 11's *Chiller Theatre* 109
Chibnall, Steve 92, 93, 94, 96, 97, 99, 100, 102

Child, Samuel 214
Christensen, Hayden 221
Cigarette Burns (2005) 220
cinéma vérité 108, 145, 166
Clark, Bob 105, 118, 119, 120
Clarke, Mae 34, *35*
Clarke, Mindy *181*, 189
Clinton, Bill 198
Clive, Colin 33, 34
Clover, Carol J. 149
Cloverfield (2008) 211
Clueless (1995) 199
Cohen, Herman 9, 62, 66, 69, 70, 72, 75, 76, 79, 81, 92, 180, 189, 196; association with American International Pictures 64–65; authority figures in the films of 63, 77–78; *see also* American International Pictures
Cohen, Larry 19
Cohn, Harry 42
Colbert, Claudette 47
Cold War 5, 9, 10, 62, 66, 69, 74, 79, 112, 156
The Collector (1965) 86
Collier's Year Book (book) 84
Columbia Pictures 42, 64
Combs, Jeffrey 188
Coming Home (1978) 106
Communism 11, 66, 69, 146
Considine, Paddy 214
Control Your Emotions (1950) 70, 73
Conway, Tom 51, 53
Cool It Carol (1970) 93
Cooper, Ann *154*
Cooper, David 98, 99
Corll, Dean 142
Corman, Roger 64, 216
Covey, Russell D. 36
Crampton, Barbara 188
Crane, Jonathan L. 141
Cranfield, Ingrid 85, 91
Craven, Wes 3, 6, 7, 9, 11, 12, 13, 14, 19, 91, 104, 105, 151, 154, 155, 161; and *Last House on the Left* 131–135, 137–142; rejection of his Christian fundamentalist upbringing 136
Crawford, Joan 79
Craze (1974) 79
The Crazies (1973) 3, 6, 16, 104, 105, 106, 113, 114, 124–125, *127*, *128*, 158, 211, 212; as allegory of the Vietnam war 123; male violence in 126; rugged individualism in 127–129
Creature with the Atom Brain (1955) 109, 187
Creed, Barbara 199
Creepshow (1982) 114, 163

Crime in the Streets (1957) 70
Cronenberg, David 3, 7, 12, 151, 152, 153, 154, 157, 161, 163, 191, 192, 199, 208
Crying Freedom (1995) 188
Cuban Missile Crisis 10, 11, 114
Cupo, Antonio 207
Curnow, Graham 78
The Curse of the Cat People (1944) 43, 46, 47, 48, 50, 54, *55*, *56*, *58*, 59, 61; revised ending of 57–58
Curtis, James 32, 33, 36, 37, 41, 42
Curtiz, Michael 12

Dagon (2011) 187
Daly, Jane 121
Damici, Nick 219
Daniell, Henry 61
Danziger, Allen 143
Dark Dreams (book) 110
Darwin, Major 21
Davies, Rupert 99
Dawn of the Dead (1978) 3, 11, 12, 14, 113, 114, 116, 126, 127, 129, 130, 131, 151, 154, 157, 158, *160*, 162–163, 181, 182, 212; frontier theme in 160–161; political satire in 159–160
The Day the Earth Stood Still (1951) 62
Days of Heaven (1978) 219
Dead Alive (1992) (aka *Braindead*) 180, 182, 183, *184*, 189
Dead Hooker in a Trunk (2009) 205
Dead Man's Shoes (2004) 213
Dead Sushi (2012) 181
The Dead Zone (1983) 154, 163
Dean, Julia 57
Death Wish (1974) 133
Deathdream (1972) 18, 104, 105, 106, *121*, *122*; debunking of patriotism in 120–123; depictions of the American family in 117–119
Dee, Frances 53
degenerate heredity (eugenics) 24
Deliverance 1, 217
Denis, Claire 216
The Dentist (1996) 180, 188, 189, 193, *194*, *195*
The Dentist 2 (1998) 180, 188, 195–196
Deranged (1974) 215
Derry, Charles 110, 155
The Desire to Desire (book) 52
Devenyi, Tony 207
The Devil-Doll (1936) 41
The Devils (1971) *102*
The Devil's Rejects (2005) 215
Dillard, R.H.W. 110

Index

Dix, Richard 59, 96
Dixon, Wheeler Winston 75, 78
Doane, Mary Ann 52
Doherty, Thomas 66
Don't Go in the House (1979) 169
Dracula (1931) 22
Dracula's Daughter (1936) 12, 42
Drew, Ellen 61
Duck and Cover (1952) 10, 73–74
Dwyer, Hilary *87*, 88

Earles, Daisy 28
Earles, Harry 23, *26*
Eastman, Marilyn 114, *115*, 116
Easy Rider (1969) 9
Eck, Johnny 25
Edmond, J. Trevor *181*
Eggshells (1969) 9, 143, 144, 145–146
Eisenhower, Dwight "Ike" 10
El (1953) 194
Ellis, Brett Easton 172, 173, 176, 178
Ellison, James 53
Emge, David 159, *160*
Encyclopedia of Modern Murder (book) 164
Eraserhead (1976) 185
Ercy, Elizabeth 84
Eshley, Norman 101
The Evil Dead (1982) 180, 216
The Exorcist (1973) 102

Fahrenheit 9/11 (2004) 212
Fairfax, Deborah 99
Farrow, Mia 192
Fast Workers (1933) 14, 22, 41
Faust: Love of the Damned (2000) 188
Fedora, Olga 222
Fellini, Frederico 146
Fenton, Harvey 4, 94
Ferdinando, Peter 223
Fessenden, Larry 219
Fight Club (1999) *173*
Fincher, David 173
Firgens, Mackenzie 214
First Blood (book) 120
Fisher, Terence 101
Flores, Phil *see* The Butcher Brothers
Florida Sun Sentinel (newspaper) 178
The Fly (1986) 163, 192
Ford, John 142, 219, 220
Ford, Wallace 25, *29*
Foree, Ken 159, *160*
Forman, Mahlon 145
Forman, Milos 108
Forsythe, Henderson 120
The Fourth Kind (2009) 216

Francis, Freddie 222
Franju, George 147
Frankenhooker (1990) 182, 185, 186
Frankenstein (1931) 6, 10, 12, 16, 18, 21, 31–34, *35*, *38*, *40*, 42, 48, 65, 105, 143, 169; blasphemy in 35; evolutionary regression of the monster in 36–37; the monster as social outcast in 38–39; and the sexual psychopath 39–41
Freaks (1932) 5, 14, 15, 21–23, *26*, 27, 29, *30*, 31, 41, 42, 105, 185, 186, 198; reproduction of the "genetically unfit" as depicted in 28–29; voyeurism in 24–25
Free Jack (1992) 182
Freedman, Estelle B. 39, 164
Freese, Rob 156
Fresnadillo, Juan Carlos 211
Freund, Karl 12, 22
Frightmare (1974) 16, 81, 91, 97, 98–100, 102, 119, 222
Fritzl, Josef 223
From Beyond (1986) 187
Fromm, Erich 80, 83, 84, 85, 86, 88, 89, 96
Frye, Dwight 33
Fuller, Amanda 213

The Gaither Report 10
Gale, David 188
Gans, Christophe 188
Garnett, Tony 209
Gein, Ed 142, 146, 173
Genelli, Tom, and Lyn Davis 49, 58
George, Alice L. 10
George, Susan 85
The Ghost Ship (1943) 59, 60, 61, 96
Ginger Snaps (2000) 196
Globalization and Its Discontents (book) 211
Glover, Edmund 59
Goddard, Mark 157
Good Eating Habits (1951) 67
Goodbye Pork Pie (1981) 182
Gordon, Christine 53
Gordon, Dorothy 95
Gordon, Stuart 163, 187, 188, 189
Gough, Michael 76, 78, 79
Grable, Betty 47
Gracey, James 4, 200
Grand Guignol Theater 181
Grant, Barry Keith 109
Grantham, Lucy 137, *138*, *140*
The Grapes of Wrath (1940) 219, 220
The Grapes of Wrath (book) 27

The Great Depression 4, 5, 6, 7, 9, 12, 14, 21, 22, 23, 25, 27, 31, 32, 33, 37, 38, 39, 47, 64, 99, 165, 219, 220
The Great Train Robbery (1903) 19
Green Hell (1940) 42
Greenspan, Alan 178
The Guyver (1991) 188

Haberman, Steve 54
Haggard, Piers 91
Haight-Ashbury 134–135, 158, 216
Hail the Conquering Hero (1944) 120, 121
Halligan, Benjamin 80, 82, 90, 91
Hallin, Daniel C. 132
Halloween (1978) 154
Halperin, Victor 108
Halsey, Mary *51*
Hamilton, Walker 91
The Hamiltons (2006) 4, 214–215
Hampton, Paul 152
Handgun (1981) 209
Hansen, Gunnar 143, 145, 148
Happiness (1998) 197
Hardman, Karl 113
Harris, Marilyn *40*
Harris, Robert H. 78
Harris, Theresa 52
Harrison, Sandra 75, *77*
Harron, Mary 164, 172, 173, 174, 175, 176, 178, 208
Hart, William S., Jr. 23
Haynes, Todd 197
Hays Code 41; *see also* Production Code Administration
Hearst, Rick 186
Heath, Edward 92, 93
Heavenly Creatures (1994) 184
Hellman, Monte 3
Hells Angels 134, 215
Helter Skelter (book) 148
Hendershot, Cyndy 71, 72
Henenlotter, Frank 4, 163, 180, 181, 182, 184, 185, 186, 187, 197
Henkel, Kim 12, 142, 142, 143, 145, 148, 149
Henley, Elmer Wayne 142, 145
Henry, Victor 85
Henry—Portrait of a Serial Killer (1986) 163, 164, *166*, *167*, *171*, 172, 177, 223, 224; and the sympathetic monster 169–170; and trickle-down economics 165, 167–168
Hensley, John 203
Herbert West—Re-animator (short story) 187
A Heritage of Horror (book) 94

Index

Heroes (1977) 106
Herrmann, Bernard 195
Hess, David A. 135, 139
Hill, Reuben 71
The Hills Have Eyes (1977) 3, 11, 12, 16, 98, 130, 131, 136, 137, 141, 142, 154, 155, 157, 161, 213, 215
Hilton, Violet, and Daisy 25
hippies 1, 112, 131, 143, 146; and violence 134–135
Hitchcock, Alfred 92, 102, 108, 154, 155, 195, 220
Hitler, Adolf 42, 43
Hoffman, Linda 194
Hollar, Lloyd 125
Holliday, Twan 208
Honey, I Shrunk the Kids (1989) 188
Hooper, Tobe 3, 7, 8, 9, 12, 104, 141, 142, *143*, 144, 145, 154
Hoover, Herbert 12, 37
Hopper, Dennis 168, 212
Horowitz, Gad 15, 141
Horror and the Horror Film (book) 52
Horrors of the Black Museum (1959) 63, *78*, 79, 81
Hostel (2003) 7
House of Mortal Sin (1976), aka *The Confessional* and *The Confessional Murders* 81, 91, 98, 100, *101*, 102–103
House of Whipcord (1974) 81, 91, 93, 94, *95*, 96–98, 101, 102
Houston Mass Murders 142, 145
How Do You Know It's Love? (1950) 71
How Much Affection? (1951) 67
How to Be Well Groomed (1949) 67
How to Make a Monster (1958) 63, 75, 78
Howard, Ainsley 222
Howarth, Alan 195
Hoyle, Rebekah 215
Huey Lewis and the News 175, 176
Hunt, Leon 81
Hunter, Kim 54
Hunter, Neith 191
Hutchings, Peter 44, 130
Hyams, Leila 25, *26*, *30*

I Am Legend (book) 109
I Spit on Your Grave (1978) 197, 199
I Walked with a Zombie (1943) 53–54, 98
I Was a Cold War Monster (book) 71
I Was a Teenage Frankenstein (1957) 63, 75, 78
I Was a Teenage Werewolf (1957) 62, 63, 64, *65*, 66, 68, 69, *72*, 76, 77; atomic age fears in 72–75; representation of juvenile delinquency in 69–71
If 94
Iguchi, Noboru 181
In the Name of Sanity (book) 72
The Incredible Shrinking Man (1957) 156
Infested (1993) 188
Initiation (1990) 180, 182, 188, 189, 191–192, 193
Invaders from Mars (1953) 62, 190
Invasion of the Body Snatchers (1956) 62, 116, 152, 190
Invisible Invaders (1959) 109
The Invisible Man (1933) 42
Ionesco, Eugene 110, 221
Iron Man (1931) 22
Irving, Penny 94
Isabelle, Katharine 198, 204, *207*, *209*
Isle of the Dead (1945) 59, 61
It's Alive (1974) 19

Jack's Wife (1972) 126
Jackson, Peter 163, 180, 181, 182–184, 189
Jacobs, W.W. 118
Janowitz, Hans 8
Jarsky, Joris *212*
Jennifer's Body (2009) 196, 197
Jennings, Patrice 190
Jensen, Paul M. 31
Johns, Mervyn 103
Johnson, Gerard 223, 224
Jones, Duane 109, *112*, 113
Jones, Harold Wayne 127, *128*
Jung, Carl 49
Just Before Dawn (1981) 1, 2, 154, 155, 163
juvenile delinquency in the 1950s 65–67

Kahn, Albert E. 74
Kandel, Aben 64, 78
Karloff, Boris 12, *17*, 18, 31, 35, 36, 37, 38, 40, 41, 44, 59, 61, 82, *83*, *86*, 96, 104, 169
Karr, Lee 113
Kawin, Bruce 52
Keeler, Christine 81, 93
Keith, Sheila 94, *95*, 96, 99, 102
Kennedy, John F. 10, 11, 80
Kennedy, Robert 11, 80, 117
Kenny, Enda 97
Kent State shootings 11, 80, 111, 116, 123, 125, 128, 133, 217

Kern, Richard 187
Kerr, Frederick 38
Kesey, Ken 59
Kessler-Harris, Alice 47
Ketchum, Jack 218
The Killing Game (play) 110
Kimber, Shaun 166
King, Martin Luther, Jr. 11, 80, 117
King, Stephen 154
King, Zalman 156, 158
Kissinger, Henry 125, 149
Knaggs, Skelton 59
Knauf, Cory 214, 215, *217*
Knightriders (1981) 8, 14, 163
Konga 79
Krauss, Werner *8*
Kuhn, Annette 46

Lacey, Catherine 82, *83*, *86*
Lacey, Dlady 41
Lachman, Ellie 117
Laemmle, Carl, Jr. 45
Laemmle, Junior 42
Laing, R.D. 98, 99
Land of the Dead (2005) 14, 114, 212
Landon, Michael 65, *72*
Lang, Fritz 39
Lange, Dorothea 219
Last House on the Left (1972) 3, 11, 12, 18, 108, 130, 137, *138*, 139, *140*, 141, 142, 145, 150, 154, 157, 215; censorship of 138; depictions of violent counterculture in 133–136; and Vietnam war news reports 131–132
Last House on the Left (2009) 141
The Last Man on Earth (1963) 109
The Last Picture Show (1971) 213
Lavater, Johann Casper 24
Le Blanc, Michelle 7
Lee, Ang 197
Lee, Anna 61
Leguizamo, John 212, 221
The Leopard Man (1943) 53, 54
Letchworth Village 21
Leto, Jared 176
Lewis, David 36, 39
Lewis, Herschell Gordon 181
Lewis, Louise 70, 75
Lewton, Val 9, 13, 14, 43, 44, 47, 54, 59, 60, 61, 76, 96, 126; and *Cat People* 48–53; childhood experience of 45–46; and *Curse of the Cat People* 54–59
Liberty, Richard 128
Lichtenstein, Mitchell 7, 197, 198; and *Teeth* 199–204
Lieberman, Jeff 1, 4, 9, 10, 12, 13, 151, 154, 155, 156, 157, 158, 159, 163

Index

Life Against Death: The Psychological Meaning of History (book) 151
Lights Out for the Territory (book) 82
Lime, Yvonne 71
Lincoln, Fred 137, **140**
Lindberg, Paula 205, **207**
Liotta, Ray 168
The Listener (magazine) 90
The Living and the Dead (2006) 213, 214
Loach, Ken 108
Lombroso, Cesare 36
Longford, Lord 92–93, 96
Lord of the Flies (1963) 1
Lorinz, James 186
Lorre, Peter 39
Losey, Joseph 86
Lovecraft, H.P. 187, 188
The Lovely Bones (2009) 184
Lovgren, David 207
Lowenstein, Adam 133, 152
Lowry, Lynn 128, 152
LSD 1, 13, 134, 155, 156
Lunch, Lydia 187

M (1931) 39
The Machinist (2004) 220, 221
MacQueen, Scott 40
Mademoiselle Fifi (1944) 55
Magdalene laundries 97
Making the White Man's Indian (book) 130
Malick, Terrence 219
The Man in the Iron Mask (1939) 42
The Man with the Golden Arm (1955) 186
Maniac (1980) 169
Mank, Greg 45, 46, 50, 51, 55, 57
Mann, Anthony 142
Manson "Family" murders 11, 83, 131, 133, 134, 135, 141, 148, 149, 216
Map of the Human Heart (1992) 182
March, Eve 57
Marcuse, Herbert 13, 15, 82
Mark of the Vampire (1935) 41
Markham, Barbara 95
Marley, John 118
"Marriage as a Psychological Relationship" (Jung) 49
Martin (1977) 3, 17, 53, 159, 167, 168
Marx, Karl 170
Matheson, Richard 109
Mathijs, Ernest 151, 154
Mayer, Carl 8
Mayles, Albert 108
Mazes, Michael **121**

McCarty, John 181
McCord, Kent 193
McCoy, Horace 9, 41
McCully, Robert J. 124
McGee, Frank 131
McGillis, Kelly 219
McGillivray, David 81, 93, 94, 96, 97, 99, 100, 101, 102, 103
McGregor, Gail 66
McIntosh, Pollyanna 218
McKee, Lucky 7, 217, 218
McKelheer, Joseph 214
McMillan, W.G. 126, **127**, **128**
McMinn, Terri 147
McNaughton, John 163, 164, 167, 168, 169, 170, 172; blue collar roots of 165–166
McWhirter, Jillian 192, 195
Meadows, Shane 213
Meet the Feebles (1990) 182–183
Mental Hygiene: Classroom Films (book) 67
mental hygiene films 60, 67–68, 69, 70, 71, 73
Merritt, Naomi 147
MGM 22, 23, 42
Michelle, Ann 94, 97
Mickle, Jim 7, 219, 220
Migicovsky, Alan 152
Miles, Dido 222
Miller, Ken 70
Millington, Mary 93
Miner, Steve 188
Minion, Joseph 172, 173
Miracles for Sale (1939) 41
Mitchell, William D. 37
Moore, Michael 212
Morrell, David 120
Morris, Desmond 83
Mother's Day (2010) 216
Ms. 45 (1981) 197, 199
Mulheron, Danny 183
Mullen, Patty 186
Mum and Dad (2008) 4, 15, 98, 222–223
Mumford, Lewis 72
Mumsy, Nanny, Sonny and Girly (1970) 222
Munroe, Kathleen **212**
Murnau, F.W. 176
Murphy, Geoff 182
Murphy, Stephen 96
Music of the Heart (1999) 14
Mutant Girls Squad (2010) 181
My Lai massacre 11, 83, 88, 106, 117, 118, 120, 122, 123, 131, 132
Mystery of the Wax Museum (1933) 13

Naha, Ed 188
The Naked Ape (book) 83

National Festival of Light 92
National Union of Miners 92
Natural Born Killers (1994) 163
"The Nature of Violence" (Fromm) 84, 88
The Navigator (1988) 182
Nazimova, Alla 45
Nazis 12, 30, 42
Neal, Ed 143
Nelson, Ralph 130–131
Nemerov, Alexander 50
The New Atlantis (magazine) 23
New York Times 126
Newman, Kim 81, 83
Newton, Thandi 221
Nicholson, Jack 216
Nicholson, James 64, 65
Night of the Living Dead (1968) 8, 12, 13, 16, 18, 63, 104, 105, **107**, 109, **111**, **112**, **115**, 117, 123, 124, 127, 128, 130, 144, 158, 159, 162, 221; breaking of social taboo in 114–116; cinéma vérité techniques in 108; depictions of racism in 112–113; horror of apocalypse in 110; as political allegory 106–108
A Nightmare on Elm Street (1984) 183
Nilsen, Dennis 223
9/11 4, 5, 6, 197, 198; impact on horror/sci-fi cinema 211–213
Nixon, Richard 11–12, 16, 125, 129, 142–143, 149
Noe, Gaspar 147
Nosferatu (1922) 176

O'Dea, Judith 108
Odell, Colin 7
Office of War Information 44, 47
Ogilvy, Ian 6, 82, **83**, 84, 88, **89**
Ognjanovic, Dejan 189
O'Hagen, Sean 106, 108
The Old Dark House (1932) 42
O'Loughlin, Chris 90
Los Olvidados (1950) 99
On the Beach (1959) 109
One Flew Over the Cuckoo's Nest (book) 59
OPEC Oil Crisis 92, 125, 144
Organic Theatre Company 187
Ormsby, Alan 105, 118, 119, 121
Ormsby, Anya 118
Out of the Past (1947) 94
Outside The Law (1930) 23

Paglia, Camille 199
Pais, Josh 202
Palance, Jack 79
Paolo, Connor 219
Parents (1989) 190

Index

Paris Texas (1984) 214
Partain, Paul 146, *147*, 148
Pasolini, Pier Paolo 218
Pauling, Linus 75
Pearl, Daniel *143*
Pearson, Brian 207
Peeping Tom (1960) 81, 172
Peñalva, Diana 183
Penhaligon, Susan 100
Pennebaker, D.A. 108
Penthouse (magazine) 205
Petrie, Susan 152, *153*
Phillips, Barney 70
Pierce, Jack 36, 38
Pinker, Steven 126
Pirie, David 94
The Plague of the Zombies (1966) 109
Plantinga, Carl 17
Polanski, Roman 109–108, 192, 220
Porter, Edwin S. 19
Potter, Cherry 206
Powell, Michael 81
Prelinger, Rick 165
Price, Vincent 6, *87*, 87, 88, 89, 109
Prince Randian 25
Production Code Administration 32, 40, 43, 63; *see also* Hays Code
Profumo, John 81, 82, 92, 93
Progeny (1999) 182, 188, 189, 192
Prousalis, Christina 216, *217*
Psycho (book) 146
Psycho (1960) 54, 94, 98, 146, 155, 169, 172

Rabe, David 119, 122
Rabid (1977) 157, 192, 197, 199
Racial Integrity Act of 1924 28
Raimi, Sam 163, 180, 181
Rain, Jeramie 135
Randel, Tony 188
Randolph, Jane 48, *51*, *55*
The Raven (1935) 13
Rayner, Tim 93
Re-animator (1985) 180–181, 187–189, 193
Reagan, Ronald 163, 164, 165, 166, 172, 173, 175, 176, 178, 197
Rebel Without a Cause (1955) 63, 69
"Recreating the Monster: Frankenstein and Film" (Tropp) 36
Red, White and Blue (2010) 213–214
Reeves, Michael 11, 12, 13, 63, 79, 80, 84, 85, 86, 92, 132, 170; and generation gap horror 81–82; violence in the films of 83, 87, 90–91

Reeves, Richard 178
Reiniger, Scott H. 159, *160*
Remote Control (1988) 2
Repression: Basic and Surplus Repression in Psychoanalytic Theory: Freud, Reich, and Marcuse (book) 15
Repulsion (1965) 108, 109
Return of the Living Dead (1985) 180, 181
Return of the Living Dead 3 (1993) 180, *181*, 182, 188, *189*, 191, 192–193, 195
Revolt of the Zombies (1936) 108
Rex, Nick 19
Rice-Davies, Mandy 93
Richard, Dawn 71
Ridley, Judith 111, *115*
The Ringer (1972) 155
Risk, Tristan 205
River's Edge (1986) 165
RKO Studios 14, 44, 46, 52, 53, 54, 59, 60, 61, 104
Road to Mandalay (1926) 23
Robbins, Tod 23
Roberts, Bret 215
Robinson, David 174, 175, 178
Robson, Mark 46
Rock Around the Clock (1955) 67, 69
Roman Catholic Church 32, 100, 101, 102, 103, 114, 187, 189
Romero, George A. 3, 7, 8, 9, 10, 11, 12, 13, 14, 16, 17, 53, 130, 151, 154, 155, 181, 211, 212, 219, 221; and *The Crazies* (1973) 123–129; and *Dawn of the Dead* (1978) 158–162; and *Night of the Living Dead* (1968) 104–117
Rooker, Michael 166, *167*, 169, 171, 187
Roosevelt's New Deal 29
Rosemary's Baby (1968) 105, 155, 192
Rosen, Christine 23–24, 26
Rosie the Riveter 44, 47
Ross, Gaylen 159, *160*
Rossitto, Angelo *30*
Rottweiler (2004) 188
Rousseau, Jean-Jacques 170
Rowlett, Curt 134, 135
Rumley, Simon 7, 213, 214
Russell, Elizabeth 50, 57
Russell, Ken 102
Russell, Robert 88
Russo, John 104

St. James, Gaylord 137
St. Thomas, Clay 208
Samul, Ryan 219
Le Sang des bêtes (1949) 147

Santa Sangre (1989) 169
Satan's Little Helper (2004) 2, 163
Sauls, Christa *195*
Savini, Tom 182
"The Scene of Empathy and the Human Face on Film" (Plantinga) 17
Schlitze 21, 25
Schon, Kyra *115*
Scorsese, Martin 44, 166
Scream (1996) 172
Screaming Mad George 188
The Searchers (1956) 142, 220
Seduction of the Innocent (book) 65
Seligson, Tom 123
Selwyn, George 94
Selznick, David O. 47
Senter, Marc 213
The Servant (1963) 86
Session 9 (2001) 220–221
The Seventh Victim (1943) 46, 51, 53, 54, 55
The 7th Voyage of Sinbad (1958) 187
Sevigny, Chloë 177
Sexual Personae (book) 199
Shade, Taylor 216
Shai, Oren 75, 76, 95
Sharp, Anthony 100, *101*, 102
Sharrett, Christopher 7, 131, 132, 133, 134, 136, 141, 145, 150, 154
Shary, Timothy 63, 66, 70
Shaw, Irwin 118
Sheffler, Marc 135
Sheil, Steven 4, 7, 222, 223
Shepis, Tiffany 216
Shivers (1975) 3, 12, 131, 151–152, *153*, 154, 157, 158, 161, 191
Shock Value (book) 136
Sholder, Jack 188
Showboat (1936) 42
Sideshow USA (book) 24
Siedow, Jim 142, 143, 149
Siegel, Don 62, 92
Siegel, Joel 45
Simon, Adam 3
Simon, Simone 48, *49*, 50, *55*, *56*, 57
Since You Went Away (1944) 47
Sinclair, Iain 82, 84, 90
Sinclair, Stephen 183
Siodmak, Curt 44
Skal, David J. 23, 24, 42, 43
Slack, Ben 190
Smith, Ken 67, 68
Smith, Kent 48, *49*, *55*, *58*, 60
Smith, Terri Susan 185
Society (1989) 180, 188, 189, 190–191, 192
Soldier Blue (1970) 130–131, 149, 201

Index

Solondz, Todd 197
Something Wild (1986) 165, 168, 172
Son of Frankenstein (1939) 43
The Sons of Anarchy (television series) 215
Sontag, Susan 14
The Sorcerers (1967) 80, 81–82, **83, 86**, 87, 89, 91, 93, 97; class conflict in 85–86; lustful destructiveness in 84–85; *see also* Fromm, Erich; "The Nature of Violence"
Soska, Jen, and Sylvia 7; and *American Mary* 204–208
Sounds Like (2006) 220–222
Species (1995) 199, 204
Splatstick 163, 179, 180–182, 183, 184, 188, 191, 193, 196, 197, 205
Springer, Ashley 200
"Spurs" (short story) 23, 27, 29
Squirm (1976) 1, 2, 3, 13, 154, 155
Stake Land (2010) 4, **219–220**
Stamp, Terence 86, 218
Stanford Law Review 36
Starburst Magazine 3–4
Steele, Barbara 152, **153**
Steinbeck, John 9, 27, 219–220
Steiner, Russell 108
Stevenson, Robert Louis 57
Stewart, James 195
Sticks and Bones (play) 119, 120, 122, 123
Stiglitz, Joseph 211
Stockstad, Courtney 207
The Strangers (2008) 216
Strauss, Peter 130–131, 201
Sturges, Preston 120
"Summer of Love" 105, 134, 135, 146, 158
Summer of Sam (1999) 164
Survival of the Dead (2009) 14, **212**
Swahn, Nicole 203
Szulkin, David A. 132

Tarantula (1955) 62
Targets (1968) 105
Tarkovsky, Andrei 3
Taxi Driver (1976) 223
Taylor, John Russell 31
Taylor, Noah 213
Tayman, Robert 97
Teen Movies: American Youth on Screen (book) 63
Teeth (2008) 4, 192, 196, 197, **200, 202**; 206; and abstinence-only education 198–199, 200; as genre hybrid 199, 203–204; and the vagina dentata myth 202–203
Telotte, J. P. 48

Temple-Saville, Christine 96
The Ten Commandments (1956) 189
The Terrible Truth (1951) 67
Tet Offensive 117
The Texas Chain Saw Massacre (1974) 3, 9, 11, 12, 16, 18, 98, 108, 130, 131, 134, 14, **143**, 144–147, **149**, 150, 154, 157, 161, 172, 213; and generation gap horror 143; moral schizophrenia in 142; savagery-civilization dichotomy of 148–150
Thalberg, Irving 44–45
Thatcher, Margaret 3, 163, 223
Theorem (1968) 218
There's Always Vanilla (1970) 8–9
They Dare Not Love (1941) 42
They Live (1988) 190–191
They Shoot Horses, Don't They? (book) 41
3rd International Eugenics Congress 21
The Thompsons (2012) 215
Three on a Meathook (1972) 215
Tierney, Lawrence 60
Time (magazine) 106, 111, 134, 178
Tomorrow's Children (1934) 28
Tony: London Serial Killer (2009) 223–224
Totaro, Donato 4, 184, 192
Tourneur, Jacques 45–46, 53, 94
Towles, Tom 168, **171**
Tracey, John Emmet 207
Trevelyan, John 90
The Trip (1967) 64
Trog (1970) 79
Tropp, Martin 37, 38
Trouble Every Day (2001) 216
Tudor, Andrew 13, 157
Turner, Guinevere 173
Turnour, Quentin 88
12th Street Riots, Detroit 11, 80, 105, 106, 111
28 Weeks Later (2007) 211, 212
Twenty-Thousand Homeless Men: A Study of Unemployed Men in Chicago Shelters (social study) 39
Two Thousand Maniacs! (1964) 181

Ulmer, Edgar G. 12
Uncensored War (book) 132
Underground (television play) 109
The Unholy Three (1925) 23
Universal Studios 7, 22, 32, 39, 42, 43, 44, 48, 55, 65, 104, 105, 143
The Unknown (1927) 23
Ut, Nick 132

Vail, William 147
Vampire's Kiss (1988) 172, 173, 176, 177
Van Hentenryck, Kevin 185, 186
Van Sloan, Edward 33
Vanishing on 7th Street (2010) 221–222
Veidt, Conrad **8**
Vernon, Glenn 60
Vertigo (1958) 195
Victor, Henry 25, **30**
Videodrome (1983) 163
VideoScope magazine 4, 156
Vietnam War 3, 5, 6, 9, 10, 11, 16, 42, 80, 88, 104, 105, 116, 118, 119, 120, 121, 122, 123, 124, 129, 131, 133, 134, 136, 137, 138, 142, 144, 145, 149, 150, 188, 213; atrocities in 130, 140, 141; campus shootings during 123; Christmas Day bombing in 16, 125, 149; and civil rights struggles 112; executions of Viet Cong in 128; mass movement against 110–111; televised reportage of 106–108, 132, 139; Tet Offensive in 117; *see also* My Lai massacre
The Violent Kind (2010) 215–216, **217**
Violent London (book) 134
Voight, Jon 1

Wade, Russell 59–60
Wald, Jerry 66
Walker, Pete 7, 13, 79, 80, 81, 91, 94, 95, 96, 97, 99, 100, 102, 103, 104; and the cannibal family horror film 98; collaboration between David McGillivray and 93; and generation gap horror 92, 97; use of the camera by 101
Walsh, Fran 183
Ward, Vincent 182
Warlock (1989) 188
Warlock, Billy 190
Watergate 5, 9, 11, 16, 125, 142, 145, 149, 156
Watts riots 11, 80, 106, 110–111
Wayne, John 90, 106, 118, 220
Wayne, Keith 111
We Belong Dead (magazine) 90
The Weather Underground 83, 134
Weaver, Tom 61, 63
Weekend at Bernie's (1989) 205
Weeks, Stephen 91
Weixler, Jess 197, **200, 202**
Wertham, Dr. Frederick 65
West, Nathanael 9
West of Zanzibar (1928) 23

Whale, James 5, 6, 9, 10, 17, 44, 65, 101, 106, 169, 186; background and sexuality 31–32; and *Frankenstein* 32–42
What About Juvenile Delinquency? (1955) 67–70
What Dreams May Come (1998) 182
What Made Sammy Speed (1957) 67
What Makes a Good Party? (1950) 67
White Zombie (1932) 108
Whitehouse, Mary 92, 93, 96
The Wild Angels (1966) 64, 216
The Wild Bunch (1969) 149
The Wild One (1954) 65, 66
Williams, Tony 112, 113, 114, 117, 119, 121, 125, 126, 133, 134
Wilson, Colin 164, 170
Wilson, Harold 92
Winter Soldier (1972) 117, 133, 134

Winters, Deborah *156*, 157
Witchfinder General (1968) 6, 11, 80, 81, 82, *87*, *89*, 91, 93, 96, 170; ecstatic hate in 88–90; *see also* Fromm, Erich; "The Nature of Violence"
Witherspoon, Reese 175
The Wolf Man (1941) 43, 44
The Woman (2011) 4, 197, 217–218
Wong, Anna May 28
Wood, Robin 3, 11, 13, 14, 16, 18, 34, 38, 43, 91, 98, 100, 113, 118, 119, 153, 161, 204
The World, the Flesh and the Devil (1959) 109
World War I 6, 8, 9, 10, 33, 37
World War II 12, 23, 43, 46, 61, 67, 120, 130
Wounds of Nations (book) 167
The Wrestler (2008) 213
Wrong Turn (2003) 213
Wuornos, Aileen 203–204

Yablonsky, Lewis 134
Young, Karen 209
Young, Ray 157
Young Guns 2 (1990) 182
You're Next (2012) 216
Youth Runs Wild (1944) 14, 55, 59, *60*, 70
Yuzna, Brian 9, 163, 179, 180, 181, 182, 190, 191, 192, 193, 194, 195; bodily transformation in the films of 189–190; collaboration between Stuart Gordon and 187–188

Zabriskie Point (1970) 146
Zedd, Nick 187
Zinoman, Jason 136, 144
Zombie Ass: Toilet of the Dead (2011) 181
Zombieland (2009) 219
Zombies of Mora Tau (1957) 109